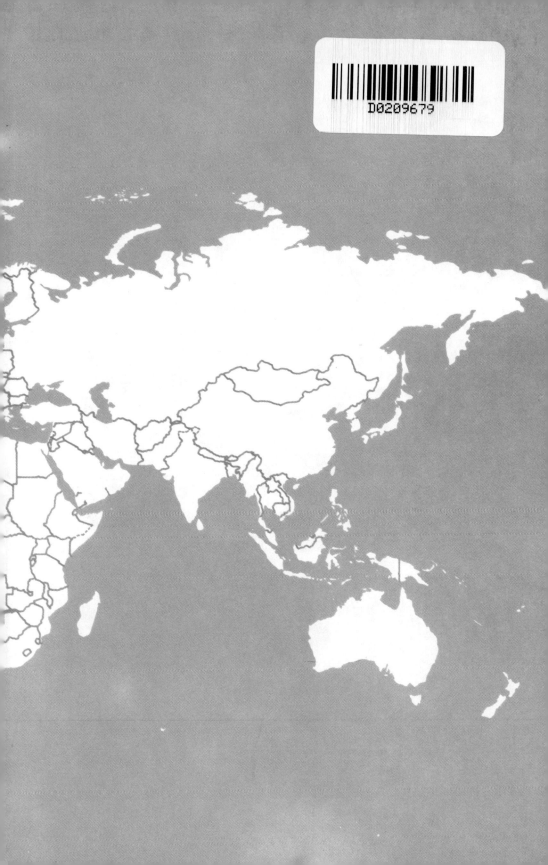

Turkey
a country study

Federal Research Division
Library of Congress
Edited by
Helen Chapin Metz
Research Completed
January 1995

On the cover: Yeni Mosque, Istanbul, one of Turkey's
famous mosques

Fifth Edition, First Printing, 1996.

Library of Congress Cataloging-in-Publication Data

Turkey : a country study / Federal Research Division, Library
   of Congress ; edited by Helen Chapin Metz. — 5th ed.
      p. cm. — (Area handbook series, ISSN 1057–5294)
   (DA Pam ; 550–80)
      "Supersedes the 1988 edition of Turkey : a country
   study, edited by Paul M. Pitman, III."—T.p. verso.
      "Research completed January 1995."
      Includes bibliographical references (pp. 399–423) and
   index.
         ISBN 0–8444–0864–6 (alk. paper)
         —————— Z663.275 .T87 1996
      1. Turkey. I. Metz, Helen Chapin, 1928– . II. Library
   of Congress. Federal Research Division. III. Series. IV.
   Series: DA Pam ; 550–80
DR417.T874 1996   95–49612
956.1—dc20   CIP

Headquarters, Department of the Army
DA Pam 550–80

For sale by the Superintendent of Documents, U.S. Government Printing Office
Washington, D.C. 20402

Foreword

This volume is one in a continuing series of books prepared by the Federal Research Division of the Library of Congress under the Country Studies/Area Handbook Program sponsored by the Department of the Army. The last two pages of this book list the other published studies.

Most books in the series deal with a particular foreign country, describing and analyzing its political, economic, social, and national security systems and institutions, and examining the interrelationships of those systems and the ways they are shaped by cultural factors. Each study is written by a multidisciplinary team of social scientists. The authors seek to provide a basic understanding of the observed society, striving for a dynamic rather than a static portrayal. Particular attention is devoted to the people who make up the society, their origins, dominant beliefs and values, their common interests and the issues on which they are divided, the nature and extent of their involvement with national institutions, and their attitudes toward each other and toward their social system and political order.

The books represent the analysis of the authors and should not be construed as an expression of an official United States government position, policy, or decision. The authors have sought to adhere to accepted standards of scholarly objectivity. Corrections, additions, and suggestions for changes from readers will be welcomed for use in future editions.

Louis R. Mortimer
Chief
Federal Research Division
Library of Congress
Washington, DC 20540–4840

Acknowledgments

The authors wish to acknowledge the contributions of the writers of the 1988 edition of *Turkey: A Country Study*, edited by Paul M. Pitman III. Their work provided general background for the present volume.

The authors are grateful to individuals in various government agencies and private institutions who gave of their time, research materials, and expertise in the production of this book. These individuals include Ralph K. Benesch, who oversees the Country Studies/Area Handbook program for the Department of the Army. The authors also wish to thank members of the Federal Research Division staff who contributed directly to the preparation of the manuscript. These people include Sandra W. Meditz, who reviewed all drafts, served as liaison with the sponsoring agency, and managed book production; Marilyn L. Majeska, who managed editing; Andrea T. Merrill, who edited tables and figures; Lauren Morris, who assisted with bibliographic research; Barbara Edgerton and Izella Watson, who did word processing; David P. Cabitto, Stephen C. Cranton, Janie L. Gilchrist, and Izella Watson, who prepared the camera-ready copy; and Rita M. Byrnes, who assisted with proofreading.

Also involved in preparing the text were Vincent Ercolano, who edited chapters; Catherine Schwartzstein, who performed the prepublication editorial review; and Joan C. Cook, who compiled the index.

Graphics were prepared by David P. Cabitto. David P. Cabitto and the firm of Greenhorne and O'Mara prepared the final maps. Special thanks are owed to Hermine Dreyfuss, whose photographs form the basis for the illustrations prepared by Wayne Horne that appear on the title page of each chapter and the cover art.

Finally, the authors acknowledge the generosity of the Turkish Information Office in Washington and the other government and private bodies and individuals who allowed their photographs to be used in this study.

Contents

List of Figures

Preface

This edition of *Turkey: A Country Study* replaces the previous edition published in 1988. Like its predecessor, the present book attempts to treat in a compact and objective manner the dominant historical, social, economic, political, and national security aspects of contemporary Turkey. Sources of information included scholarly books, journals, and monographs; official reports and documents of governments and international organizations; and foreign and domestic newspapers and periodicals. Relatively up-to-date economic data were available from several sources, but the sources were not always in agreement.

Chapter bibliographies appear at the end of the book; brief comments on some of the more valuable sources for further reading appear at the conclusion of each chapter. Measurements are given in the metric system; a conversion table is provided to assist those who are unfamiliar with the metric system (see table 1, Appendix A). Appendix B is a list of selected political parties and labor organizations, with their acronyms. The Glossary provides brief definitions of terms that may be unfamiliar to the general reader.

The authors have attempted to follow standard Turkish spelling of Turkish words, phrases, and place-names. The principal guide used was *The Concise Oxford Turkish Dictionary* (1971 edition). The place-names used are those established by the United States Board on Geographic Names as of September 1984. A few exceptions were made for well-known geographical features. For example, the study uses Bosporus and Dardanelles instead of Istanbul Bogazı and Çanakkale Bogazı. In addition, although Mustafa Kemal did not become Kemal Atatürk until the Law of Surnames was enacted in 1934, he is referred to throughout as Atatürk. However, the Turkish names appearing in the text of this volume are missing most of the diacritics used by the language. In this case, it is a matter of lagging technology: the typesetting software being used simply cannot produce all of the necessary diacritics in the text (although they appear on the maps). For this the authors apologize and hope that by the time this country study is updated, missing diacritics will no longer be the norm.

The body of the text reflects information available as of January 1995. Certain other portions of the text, however, have been updated. The Introduction discusses significant events that have occurred since the completion of research, and the Country Profile and Appendix B include updated information as available.

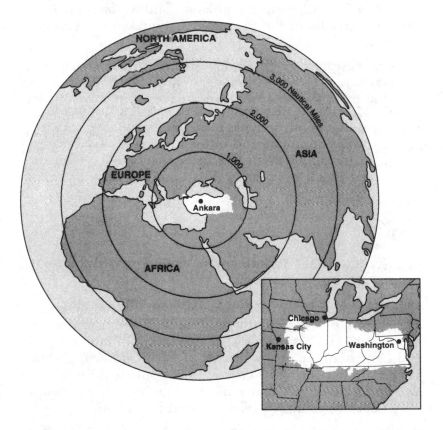

Country

Formal Name: Republic of Turkey.

Short Form: Turkey.

Term for Citizens: Turk(s).

Capital: Ankara.

Geography

Size: About 779,452 square kilometers, somewhat smaller than Texas and Louisiana combined.

Topography: Seven natural regions—Black Sea, Aegean, Mediterranean, Pontus and Taurus mountain ranges, Anatolian Plateau, eastern highlands, and Arabian Platform. Country includes one of the most earthquake-prone areas of the world.

Climate: Periphery of Turkey has Mediterranean climate with cool, rainy winters and hot, moderately dry summers. Interior, shielded from Mediterranean influences by mountains, has continental climate with cold winters and dry, hot summers. Eastern mountainous area has inhospitable climate, with hot, extremely dry summers and bitter winters. Rainfall varies, ranging from annual average of more than 2,500 millimeters on eastern Black Sea coast to less than 250 millimeters in central plateau area.

Society

Population: (1994) Turkish government figure 61.2 million, growing at 2.1 percent a year.

Languages and Ethnic Groups: Turkish, official language, spoken by most citizens; mother tongue of about 82 percent. Kurdish spoken by roughly 17 percent of population. Arabic and Caucasian languages spoken by small minority groups. Turks constitute at least 80 percent of population; Kurds form at least 10 percent. Other minorities include Arabs, people from Caucasus countries, Dönme, Greeks, and Jews.

Religion: About 99 percent nominally Muslim, of whom about 66 percent Sunni Muslims, and about 33 percent Alevi (Shia) Muslims. Constitution proclaims Turkey secular nation.

Education: Steadily increasing enrollments in tuition-free schools, universities, and numerous technical institutes. Attendance compulsory at five-year primary schools and three-year middle schools. Middle and high schools offer academic, technical, and vocational education. Twenty-seven public universities form core of higher education system. In 1990 literacy above 81 percent for people over fifteen years of age.

Health: Inadequate sewer systems in some urban areas and poor water supplies in many villages pose continuing health threats, but major infectious diseases under control. Life expectancy (1992): males, sixty-eight years; females, seventy-two years; infant mortality fifty-five per 1,000 births.

Economy

Gross Domestic Product (GDP): US$312.4 billion in 1993 (US$5,000 per capita). Economy gradually being liberalized and industrialized; real growth averaged 7.3 percent in 1993.

Agriculture: Less than 15 percent of GDP in 1993 but remains crucial sector of the economy, providing more than 50 percent of employment, most raw materials for industry, and 15 percent of exports. Wheat and barley main crops; cotton, sugar beets, hazelnuts, and tobacco major cash crops. Livestock production extensive and growing. Valuable forest areas poorly managed; fisheries underdeveloped.

Industry: Major growth sector contributing more than 30 percent of GDP in 1993, employing 33 percent of labor force. Food processing and textiles major industries; basic metals, chemicals, and petrochemicals well established.

Imports: US$29.4 billion in 1993. Main imports included machinery and equipment, 60 percent; petroleum, 8.5 percent; and foodstuffs, 4 percent.

Exports: US$15.3 billion in 1993, consisting of manufactured goods (mainly textiles and processed leather products), 70 percent; foodstuffs, 20 percent; mineral products, 4 percent.

Major Trading Partners: Industrialized countries, especially members of European Union, United States, Russia, and Saudi Arabia.

Balance of Payments: In 1993–94 Turkey experienced its fourth major balance of payments crisis in last forty years. Domestic fiscal policy and International Monetary Fund (IMF) helped reduce imports in 1994. Trade deficit was US$4.8 billion in 1994. Soaring imports during first seven months of 1995 pushed trade deficit up to US$6 billion.

General Economic Conditions: In 1995 economy grew during first nine months; inflation became more severe. December 1995 elections important for fiscal stability.

Currency and Exchange Rate: 1 Turkish lira (TL) = 100 kurus; (August 31, 1995) US$1.00 = TL47,963.00.

Transportation and Telecommunications

Railroads: 8,430 kilometers (standard gauge—1.435 meters), of which 796 kilometers electrified in 1995.

Roads: (1995) Nearly 59,770 kilometers of all-weather highways of which 27,000 kilometers paved. Highways main means of transport. Government planned large highway expansion by year 2000.

Ports: Five major ports: Istanbul, Mersin, Ismir, Iskenderun, and Kocaeli; ten secondary ports, eighteen minor ports.

Airports: 105 usable airports, sixty-nine with paved runways in 1994.

Telecommunications: Telephone system overloaded in 1995; modernization program promised to make telephones available and eliminate waiting circuits.

Government and Politics

Government: Democratic, secular, and parliamentary, according to provisions of 1982 constitution. Divided into legislative, executive, and judicial establishments, with legislative power vested in unicameral National Assembly consisting of 450 deputies elected every five years. Executive authority greater than under 1961 constitution.

Judicial System: Independent of other state organs; autonomy protected by High Council of Judges and Public Prosecutors. Higher courts include Constitutional Court, Council of State, Court of Jurisdictional Dispute, Court of Cassation, and Military Court of Cassation. For purpose of civil and criminal justice, Court of Cassation serves as supreme court.

Administrative System: In 1995 centralized administrative system of seventy-six provinces, divided into districts, and subdistricts. Provinces headed by governors appointed by executive branch and responsible to central administration.

Politics: True Path (Dogru Yol Partisi—DYP) ruling coalition with Social Democratic Populist Party (Sosyal Demokrat Halkçı Parti—SHP) collapsed in September 1995 after SHP deputies voted to join new Republican People's Party (Cumhuriyet Halk Partisi—CHP). New government of DYP-CHP formed in October 1995 to serve in a caretaker capacity prior to parliamentary elections on December 24. Other parties are Motherland Party (Anavatan Partisi—ANAP), Welfare Party (Refah Partisi—RP), and Democratic Left (Demokratik Sol Partisi—DSP).

International Affairs: Allied with West through North Atlantic Treaty Organization (NATO). Tensions with NATO allies followed 1980 military takeover but reduced after 1983. Continued conflict with Greece over Cyprus and control of Aegean waters.

National Security

Armed Forces (1994–95): Total personnel on active duty 503,800, including 410,200 draftees serving for fifteen months. Reserves total 952,300. Component services: army of 393,000 (345,000 conscripts), air force of 56,800 (28,700 conscripts), and navy of 54,000 (36,500 conscripts plus 3,000 marines).

Major Tactical Military Units (1994–95): Army: one mechanized division, one mechanized division headquarters, one infantry division, fourteen armored brigades, seventeen mechanized brigades, nine infantry brigades, four commando brigades, one infantry regiment, one Presidential Guard regiment, five border defense regiments, and twenty-six border defense battalions. Air Force: fourteen fighter-ground attack squadrons, six fighter squadrons, three training squadrons, and eight surface-to-air missile squadrons. Navy: seventeen submarines, eleven destroyers, sixteen frigates, sixteen fast-attack craft, miscellaneous patrol, coastal, and mine-warfare combatants, and twenty-eight helicopters.

Military Equipment (1995): Heavy dependence on United States and other Western allies for armored fighting vehicles, artillery, aircraft, missiles, and fighting ships. Modernization programs underway stressing improved antitank and air defense capability. New effort to meet needs through domestic manufacture, including F–16 fighter airplanes on coproduction basis, artillery, tank upgrades, communication and navigation equipment, frigates, and submarines.

Military Budget: About TL93,453 billion (US$4.6 billion) plus US$3 billion for the gendarmerie in 1994. Defense expenditures estimated to be 9.4 percent of GNP in 1994. Turkey's defense expenditures per capita lowest among NATO countries.

Foreign Military Treaties: Member of NATO since 1952.

Internal Security Forces: Principal security agencies: National Police, believed to number about 50,000, oriented to urban areas, and gendarmerie, a force of about 70,000 active-duty personnel with 50,000 reserves, oriented primarily to rural and border areas. Gendarmerie under army command in wartime and in areas where martial law prevails; deploys three mobile brigades equipped as light mechanized infantry. Special police units fight drug traffic and terrorism and support gendarmerie and army operations against Kurdish insurgents. National Intelligence Organization primary body concerned with intelligence on subversive activity.

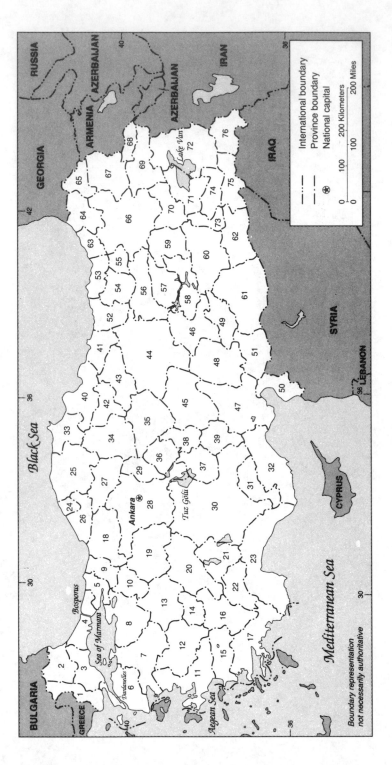

Figure 1. Administrative Divisions of Turkey, 1995

Provinces of Turkey

Adana (47)	Burdur (22)	Isparta (21)	Nevşehir (38)
Adıyaman (49)	Bursa (8)	İstanbul (4)	Niğde (39)
Afyon (20)	Çanakkale (6)	İzmir (11)	Ordu (41)
Ağri (69)	Çankırı (27)	Kahramanmaraş (48)	Rize (63)
Aksaray (37)	Çorum (34)	Karaman (31)	Sakarya (9)
Amasya (42)	Denizli (16)	Kars (67)	Samsun (40)
Ankara (28)	Diyarbakır (60)	Kastamonu (25)	Sanlı Urfa (61)
Antalya (23)	Edirne (1)	Kayseri (45)	Siirt (74)
Ardahan (65)	Elaziğ (58)	Kırıkkale (29)	Sinop (33)
Artvin (64)	Erzincan (56)	Kırklareli (2)	Şirnak (75)
Aydin (15)	Erzurum (66)	Kirşehir (36)	Sivas (44)
Balıkesir (7)	Eskişehir (19)	Kocaeli (5)	Tekirdağ (3)
Bartın (24)	Gaziantep (51)	Konya (30)	Tokat (43)
Batman (73)	Giresun (52)	Kütahya (13)	Trabzon (53)
Bayburt (55)	Gümüşhane (54)	Malatya (46)	Tunceli (57)
Bilecik (10)	Hakkâri (76)	Manisa (12)	Uşak (14)
Bingöl (59)	Hatay (50)	Mardin (62)	Van (72)
Bitlis (71)	İçel (32)	Muğla (17)	Yozgat (35)
Bolu (18)	Iğdir (68)	Muş (70)	Zonguldak (26)

Introduction

THE REPUBLIC OF TURKEY (Türkiye Cumhuriyeti) was
established on October 29, 1923, under the firm control and
leadership of Mustafa Kemal, better known as Kemal Atatürk.
The new state was at once the successor to and victor over the
Ottoman Empire, long a major power in the European states
system. The creation of the modern Turkish polity reflected
not only a successful struggle against external enemies but also
a triumph over deeply rooted domestic traditions. The republic deliberately rejected important elements of Turkey's Ottoman past, especially the Ottoman dynasty's claim to spiritual
leadership of Muslims worldwide. However, the official disestablishment of Islam as the state religion in 1924 did not
result in the creation of a fully secular society as Atatürk and his
colleagues had hoped.

Although a commitment to secularism has continued to be
almost a prerequisite for membership in the country's political
elite, Turkey has experienced several popular movements of
Islamic political activism. The most recent movement, which
began in the mid-1980s and is continuing, has threatened secularism in ways the republic's founders could not have imagined
in the 1920s and 1930s.

Although the republic emerged through the work and effort
of many people, it bore the indelible imprint of Atatürk. During World War I, the Ottoman Empire had been an ally of Germany, and in the chaos that accompanied the empire's defeat
by the Allied powers, Atatürk, as the victor over Australian and
British forces at Gallipoli, emerged as one of the few national
heroes. His military reputation was enhanced further during
the four-year War of Independence, when he led the forces
that expelled the Greek invading army from the country. Of
even greater long-term importance, Atatürk was a pragmatic
political leader with a penchant for social reform. In keeping
with long-standing Ottoman concepts of government, however,
he was also an elitist; his reforms did not change significantly
the relationship of the privileged governing stratum with the
masses, although they did alter to some extent the nature of
the elite. By the mid-1990s, the continuing impact of Atatürk
and his precepts in shaping the form and nature of Turkish

society were being challenged by Turkey's diverse ethnic, religious, and social groups.

Atatürk's avowed goal was to create from the Anatolian remnant of the Ottoman Empire a new society patterned directly on the societies of Western Europe. In pursuit of this goal, he tolerated only token opposition. Turkey's president from 1923 until his death in 1938, he apparently was persuaded that the masses needed a period of tutelage. Although the presidency technically possessed relatively few constitutional powers, Atatürk ruled for fifteen years as charismatic governor and teacher—training, cajoling, and forcing the government, his political party, the bureaucracy, the military, and the masses to behave in the manner he thought appropriate. Atatürk's "Six Arrows"—secularism, republicanism, etatism (see Glossary), populism, nationalism, and reformism—were incorporated into the constitutions of 1924, 1961, and 1982. In a general sense, Atatürkism (also known as Kemalism) has been accepted by the Turkish political elite but has been contested by various organized groups.

There is general agreement among scholars that secularism was and remains the most significant, and by far the most controversial, aspect of Atatürkism. The Turks, whose origins go back to Central Asia, had converted to Islam by the time they began establishing their political sovereignty in parts of Anatolia during the tenth century. Throughout the next nine centuries, Islam was the primary guiding as well as delimiting force in societal development. From administrative institutions to social customs, from ideals of governance to the concepts of being a subject or a citizen, from birth to death, most aspects of life were influenced and regulated by Islamic tenets, precepts, and laws. Various forms of popular or folk Islam gained an important hold on the Turkish imagination, and Sufi brotherhoods became vital socioreligious institutions.

Atatürk and his associates rejected the historical legacy of Islam and were determined to create a secular republic. Following the disestablishment of Islam and continuing into the mid-1940s, the government suppressed public manifestations and observances of religion that the secularist minority deemed inimical to the development of a modern, European-style state. The regime closed the religious schools, shut down the Sufi brotherhoods, and banned their rituals and meetings. The reformers replaced Islamic law, the *seriat*, with codes borrowed from European countries; dropped the Islamic calendar in favor of the Gregorian; and abolished the pervasive legal and religious functions of the religious scholars and lawyers. Atatürk imposed outward signs of secularization by discouraging or outlawing articles of clothing closely identified with Islamic traditions such as the veil for women and the fez for men. Finally, the use of Arabic script for writing in Turkish was declared illegal, despite its sacerdotal association as the language of the Kuran (Quran) and hence the language of God.

Although Atatürk believed that the secularist campaign made a period of authoritarian government necessary, his successors wanted to establish a democratic government. Thus, Ismet Inönü, who had become president after Atatürk's death in 1938, permitted the creation of a multiparty political system following World War II. In the first contested election in 1946, the ruling Republican People's Party (Cumhuriyet Halk Partisi—CHP) retained its majority in the Turkish Grand National Assembly, although opposition candidates accused the CHP of electoral irregularities. When the Democrat Party (Demokrat Parti—DP) subsequently won a majority in the 1950 election, Inönü voluntarily relinquished power, despite offers from elements of the armed forces to stage a coup. Thus began Turkey's experiment in democracy: the military-bureaucratic elite that had established the republican order gradually turned over its power to an elected parliament, which reflected the interests and desires of broader sectors of society.

Although the Kemalists have made compromises with traditional forces in Turkish society, they never have abandoned the main tenets of the secularist program. By the end of the 1950s, the armed forces had assumed a role as guardians, not only of national security, but also of Atatürk's legacy. On three occasions, in 1960, 1971, and 1980, the senior military intervened to safeguard Turkey's political development from forces that the military believed threatened the integrity of the state. In each case, civilian leaders had proved unable or unwilling to deliver policies acceptable to the military. In both 1960 and 1980, a military junta took over the government, and rule by martial law included widespread suppression of civil rights and purges of the political class. On both occasions, after a period of direct military rule the military restored civilian government, but only after implementing constitutional changes, social reforms, and economic policies designed to put Turkey back on the path of achieving Atatürk's goal: a modern, secular republic.

Before the 1980 military coup, Turkish society had experienced what was perhaps its most serious crisis since the War of Independence. The framework instituted by the relatively liberal constitution of 1961, along with the fragmented party system, had contributed to political disorder: unstable coalitions rapidly succeeded one another while failing to address the country's pressing social, economic, and political problems. Underlying the political crisis were rapid and profound social changes. Massive population shifts from villages to towns and cities, expanded access to primary and secondary education, the availability of mass media, and the experiences of many Turkish workers in Western Europe exposed a nation of primarily peasants to new and generally disruptive influences. The extension of the Westernization process from the educated elite to the Anatolian masses both challenged and reinforced the latter's adherence to Islamic and Turkish traditions. During the second half of the 1970s, the economy, which had undergone rapid growth in the postwar decades, entered a severe depression. Turkey's economic difficulties resulted from the inherent limitations of import-substitution industrialization and were exacerbated by the deterioration of world economic conditions that followed the 1973 oil crisis. By the late 1970s, at least one-quarter of the work force was unemployed, the annual inflation rate exceeded 100 percent, and shortages of foreign exchange reduced imports of essential commodities, causing widespread reductions in industrial production.

One result of these interrelated crises was the mobilization of opposing social and cultural forces, which found political expression in radical parties and organizations. These included leftists active in the Turkish Communist Party (TCP) and the Confederation of Revolutionary Trade Unions of Turkey (Türkiye Devrimçi Isçi Sendikaları Konfederasyonu—DISK), Islamicly motivated political elements behind Necmettin Erbakan's National Salvation Party (Milli Selamet Partisi—MSP), and extreme nationalist groups linked to Alparslan Türkes's Nationalist Action Party (Milliyetçi Hareket Partisi—MHP). As political life became increasingly tense, offshoots of these political groups fought each other and carried out terrorist attacks against representatives of the established order; an estimated 5,000 persons were killed in politically related civil strife between 1971 and 1980. The coalition governments of the 1970s lacked sufficient political support to effect the kinds of social reforms that would alleviate the main causes of popular discontent, and the country consequently descended into conditions resembling civil war.

Following the September 1980 coup, the military made the restoration of political stability its main priority. The commanders of the armed forces formed the National Security Council (NSC—see Glossary), which ruled the country until November 1983. The NSC ordered the arrest and imprisonment of thousands of militants, political leaders, and trade unionists; it also imposed widespread censorship and purged the armed forces, the bureaucracy, and the universities. These and other measures effectively suppressed both violence and normal political life. The NSC's objective was to eliminate leftist, nationalist, Islamic, and ethnic organizations that contested Atatürk's political legacy. The NSC retained Turgut Özal, an economist who had served in Süleyman Demirel's civilian cabinet ousted by the coup and who enjoyed the confidence of the international financial community, and gave him responsibility for economic policy. Although Özal's austerity package brought immediate hardship for many Turks, it ended the balance of payments crisis and contributed to an economic recovery.

After restoring public order and overcoming the most pressing economic problems, the NSC supervised the drafting of a new constitution and electoral laws designed to rectify the perceived defects of the 1961 constitution by limiting the role of smaller parties and strengthening the powers of the president, the prime minister, and the party that won a majority in parliamentary elections. However, the new constitution also curtailed political rights, thus arousing sharp criticism both in Turkey and abroad. Particularly controversial was a ten-year ban on the political activities of about 200 leading politicians, including former prime ministers Bülent Ecevit and Demirel. The NSC sought to maintain its role by means of a clause under which the NSC chairman, General Kenan Evren, was named president for a six-year term.

Having established a new political framework, the NSC gradually relaxed restrictions on political life and arranged a return to civilian government after a parliamentary election held in November 1983. The NSC strictly supervised this election; it allowed only three parties to present candidates, and President Evren blatantly intervened on behalf of the NSC's favorite, the Nationalist Democracy Party (Milliyetçi Demokrasi Partisi—MDP). Nevertheless, Özal's Motherland Party (Anavatan Partisi—ANAP), the only independently established party that had been tolerated by the NSC, achieved a strong majority, an outcome that was widely interpreted as a sign of the electorate's disapproval of military rule.

Özal, whose primary goal was economic liberalization, claimed that his triumph represented a mandate for sweeping changes in the economy. In power from November 1983 to November 1989, he sought to limit state intervention in the economy. Rejecting protectionism and import substitution, he opened the economy to international markets, arguing that economic growth and technical modernization would do more than traditional social policies to ease the country's problems. His package of economic reforms aimed to make Turkey economically similar to the countries of the European Union (EU—see Glossary), a body that Özal hoped Turkey could join. The package of reforms included reduction of government price-setting, positive real interest rates, devaluation and floating of the Turkish lira (TL; for value of the lira—see Glossary), liberalization of import regulations, and export subsidies.

Turkey's economic performance after 1983 was impressive. Real gross domestic product (GDP—see Glossary) averaged an annual 5.5 percent growth rate. GDP actually reached 8 percent in 1986, higher than that of any other member of the Organisation for Economic Co-operation and Development (OECD—see Glossary). Inflation, estimated at more than 30 percent during the 1983–85 period, fell in the 1986–89 period. Unemployment, however, remained a serious problem, rising every year during the 1980s except for 1986, a year when growth was sufficient to allow employment to increase faster than the increase in the working population.

The restoration of civilian rule and the general improvement in the overall economy failed to resolve outstanding social issues, which have continued to bedevil Turkey's leadership. Although the government tends to play down the diversity of the population, the country's inhabitants in fact form a mosaic of diverse religious and ethnic groups. Most of the country's citizens continue to accept as true Turks only Sunni (see Glossary) Muslims whose native language is Turkish—effectively excluding other religious and ethnic groups such as the Alevi Muslims and Kurds, who together comprise at least 20 percent of the population. Conflicts between the country's Turkish-speaking, Sunni majority and its various ethnic and religious minorities have intensified since the mid-1980s, threatening to disrupt public order and projecting an illiberal spirit at odds with the dominant political culture of the EU that Turkey aspires to join. In effect, the question of Turkey's national identity remains a focal point for political controversy and social conflict.

The government's troubled relations with its Kurdish minority reveal the limits of social integration. Beginning in 1984, the Kurdistan Workers' Party (Partiya Karkere Kurdistan—PKK) launched guerrilla attacks on government personnel and installations in the predominantly Kurdish-populated provinces of southeastern Turkey. The PKK's announced objective was the establishment of a separate state of Kurdistan. PKK guerrillas have evoked some sympathy among Kurds in the southeast, a region characterized by endemic poverty, lack of jobs, inadequate schools and health care facilities, and severe underdevelopment of basic infrastructure such as electricity, piped water, and sewerage systems. The Özal government sought to counter the appeal of the PKK by making government aid to the long-neglected southeast a priority, and it invested large sums to extend electricity, telephones, and roads to the region. Özal envisioned the major southeastern Anatolia irrigation and power project as a program to provide the basis for real economic development that eventually would assuage local resentments of the central government. In the short run, however, the government has continued to depend on police actions to suppress the activities of Kurdish insurgents. Nevertheless, the armed forces have been unable to maintain order in the region, despite the deployment of large military and paramilitary forces, and the southeastern provinces remain under de facto martial law.

Turkey also has experienced a revival of religiously motivated political activity since the early 1980s. Veteran Islamist activist Necmettin Erbakan organized the new Welfare Party (Refah Partisi—RP; also seen as Prosperity Party) in 1983, but the military prohibited it from participating in the parliamentary elections held in the fall of that year. Subsequently, the new civilian government under Özal relaxed restrictions on avowedly religious parties, thus enabling the Welfare Party to organize freely and compete in local and national elections. With the notable exception of Erbakan, the Welfare Party's leaders represent a new generation that has grown up and been educated in a secular Turkey but professes a commitment to Islamic values. The Welfare Party rejects the use of political violence and seeks to propagate its political message through example. Working at the grassroots level in Turkey's cities and towns, the party's strongest appeal has been in lower-middle-class neighborhoods. However, the Welfare Party also has attracted support among some upper-middle-class professionals and ethnic Kurds. Although the Welfare Party calls for the application of Islamic principles in relations between government agencies and the people, its primary appeal seems to derive from its advocacy of economic reform policies designed to control inflation and limit the amount of interest banks may charge on loans.

The Welfare Party's popularity has grown gradually but steadily. In the 1991 parliamentary elections, it obtained more than 10 percent of the vote, thus surpassing the minimum threshold for winning seats in the National Assembly. Its electoral performance in the 1994 municipal elections was even better: the party won 19 percent of the total vote and control of the government of several large cities, including both Ankara and Istanbul. In the December 1995 National Assembly elections, the Welfare Party won 21 percent of the vote and the largest number of seats of any party—158.

The return to civilian rule in 1983 also affected Turkey's foreign policy. The three years of military government had harmed the country's reputation among its allies in the North Atlantic Treaty Organization (NATO) and the OECD, all of which had democratic governments. Turkey's leaders had been committed to becoming an equal partner of the countries of Western Europe since the late 1940s. For example, Turkey became a member of the Council of Europe in 1949, dispatched its troops to participate in the United States-led United Nations military force in Korea in 1950, and became a full member of the NATO military alliance in 1952. Thus, West European criticisms of Turkey's undemocratic government and human rights abuses were very painful. In addition, Turkey's image suffered from the continuing tension with neighboring Greece—also a member of NATO—over Cyprus and the control of the Aegean Sea. Özal therefore wanted to repair Turkey's international reputation as quickly as possible. He envisioned EU membership as an important means to demonstrate that Turkey is an essential part of Western Europe. In addition, he believed that EU membership would provide Turkey with vital economic benefits.

Although a substantial portion of the political and economic elite supported Özal's objective of EU membership, it was not a goal shared by all Turks. For example, the Welfare Party opposed any further integration with Europe, arguing instead that Turkey should search for new export markets in its natural and historical hinterland, the Middle East. The Özal government did not dismiss the idea of expanding political and economic ties with other Islamic countries, and actually did cultivate relations with Iran and Iraq. These two neighbors were at war with each other from 1980 to 1988, and Turkey was able to reap economic dividends by remaining strictly neutral with respect to that conflict. Nevertheless, the government continued to believe that Turkey's national interests would be served best by strengthening ties to Western Europe. Thus, Özal undertook a series of economic and political reform measures that he believed would provide credibility for Turkey's formal application to join the EU. The application finally was submitted in April 1987. To demonstrate that Turkey was committed to democracy, and thus worthy of membership in the EU, all martial law decrees were repealed in March, although a state of emergency remained in force in the southeastern provinces. New parliamentary elections also were announced for the fall, a full year before they were required.

The November 1987 parliamentary elections were a turning point in the democratization process in Turkey inasmuch as these were the first genuinely free elections since the 1980 coup. All political parties were permitted to take part. In addition, the ban on political activities of 200 senior political leaders had been lifted as a result of a popular referendum held earlier in September 1987. Consequently, former prime ministers Süleyman Demirel and Bülent Ecevit campaigned actively, the former as head of the True Path Party (Dogru Yol Partisi—DYP) and the latter as head of the Democratic Left Party (Demokratik Sol Partisi—DSP). Although Özal's Motherland Party retained its parliamentary majority (292 of 450 seats), the True Path Party obtained fifty-nine seats, thus gaining for Demirel an important national political platform. During the next four years, Demirel used his organizing and persuasive skills to rebuild the True Path Party with the objective of attracting enough Motherland voters to propel his party to the leading position. Within eighteen months, Demirel's persistent criticisms of Özal administration policies brought initial political dividends for the True Path Party. As a result of the March 1989 municipal council elections, the Motherland Party suffered a major setback; it received only 26 percent of the total vote nationwide and ranked third behind the Social Democratic Populist Party (Sosyal Demokrat Halkçı Parti—SHP) and the True Path Party.

Neither Demirel nor other True Path leaders considered the opportunity to share responsibility for local government to be equivalent to the control of the national government, which remained in the hands of Özal's Motherland Party. However, they appreciated the significance of their increased share of the popular vote and the fact that they had party cadres in positions to dispense some city and town patronage. Capitalizing on the momentum of the victories, the True Path Party intensified its organizing efforts in anticipation of the next parliamentary elections. These elections, which were held in October 1991, proved to be both sweet and sour for Demirel. The True Path Party defeated its rival, the Motherland Party, by edging it out in the popular vote, 27 to 24 percent. Although Demirel could draw satisfaction from the True Path's emergence from the elections as the largest party in parliament with 178 seats, he simultaneously was disappointed that it had not won the absolute majority—226 seats—required to form a government. After weeks of negotiations, Demirel and SHP leader Erdal Inönü—the son of Ismet Inönü—reached agreement on the formation of a True Path-SHP coalition government. Thus, Demirel, whom the military had overthrown in 1980, once again became prime minister of Turkey.

Demirel's victory was not at the expense of Özal. Two years earlier, Özal had been elected president to replace General Evren, whose constitutionally mandated seven-year term had concluded at the end of 1989. The 1982 constitution provides for the president to be elected by the parliament. Because the Motherland Party still held a majority of parliamentary seats in 1989, Özal's election seemed assured once he announced his candidacy. Nevertheless, Demirel and other politicians refused to support Özal's bid for the presidency, and their tactics prevented his confirmation until the third ballot. Demirel's own opposition to Özal seemed to be more personal than ideological. Prior to the 1980 coup, Özal had been a member of Demirel's Justice Party (Adalet Partisi—AP) and had held a junior ministerial post in the Demirel cabinet. Demirel apparently never forgave Özal for joining the military government following the coup. Thus, when Demirel became prime minister, Turkish politicians had reservations as to whether he and President Özal would be able to cooperate. Indeed, as leader of an opposition party in parliament during 1990 and 1991, Demirel had expressed frequent criticism of Özal's role in foreign policy, especially the latter's decisions to align Turkey on the side of the United States-led coalition against Iraq during the Kuwait crisis and Persian Gulf War of 1990–91. Nevertheless, once Demirel became prime minister, he and Özal did cooperate.

Demirel had served as prime minister for less than eighteen months when the unexpected death of Özal in April 1993 provided the opportunity for him to succeed to the presidency. During his tenure as head of government, Demirel had been preoccupied with both domestic and international challenges. Within Turkey, the PKK had intensified its attacks on Turkish security and civilian personnel in southeastern Anatolia. The PKK's insurgency had received an unexpected boost from the 1991 collapse of central government authority in northern Iraq's Kurdish region, which borders southeastern Turkey. Since the mid-1980s, the PKK had established in this territory clandestine bases from which it carried out some of its operations. By the end of 1991, the absence of any security on the Iraqi side of the border had enabled the PKK both to expand its network of bases and to use them as sanctuaries. One of Demirel's most important policy decisions was to approve in October 1992 a plan by the Turkish military to attack PKK bases in northern Iraq. This plan was particularly controversial because three of Turkey's NATO allies—Britain, France, and the United States—were enforcing a ban on any Iraqi military presence in northern Iraq in order to protect Iraqi Kurds from being attacked by their own government.

Demirel's government also had to deal with the unanticipated collapse of the Soviet Union and Yugoslavia. The Soviet Union had been a powerful and generally feared neighbor ever since the establishment of the Turkish Republic. Its sudden disappearance necessitated the formulation of new diplomatic, economic, and political strategies to deal with the multifaceted consequences. Demirel and his colleagues had a special interest in Central Asia, and they hoped that Turkey could serve as a role model for the new Turkic-speaking states of Azerbaijan, Kazakhstan, Kyrgyzstan, Turkmenistan, and Uzbekistan. However, from a geographic perspective, these new countries were closer to Iran than to Turkey, and officials frequently expressed concern about suspected Iranian intentions in Central Asia. Throughout 1992 the Demirel administration perceived Turkey to be engaged in a competitive race with Iran for regional influence. However, by the time Demirel became president in May 1993, most officials had come to realize that neither their country nor Iran had sufficient resources for such a competition.

Demirel had to give up his leadership of the True Path Party when the National Assembly elected him president. The DYP deputies in the assembly subsequently chose Tansu Çiller as their leader—the first woman to head a political party—and in June 1993 she became Turkey's first woman prime minister. Under Çiller's administration, the status of Turkey's Kurdish minority continued to be the country's most serious domestic problem, one that had multiple international repercussions. Although the PKK had renounced its goal of a separate Kurdish state in 1993, reaching a political compromise proved difficult because the Turkish military insisted on a military solution. Because both Çiller and Demirel were sensitive about past military interventions in domestic politics, neither was prepared to risk a civilian-military confrontation by challenging the military's assumption of almost a free hand in dealing with the security situation in southeastern Turkey. By 1995 more than 220,000 soldiers, in addition to 50,000 gendarmerie and other security forces, were stationed in the southeast. Nevertheless, the progressive intensification of the military offensive against the PKK failed to repress the PKK's ability to mount deadly assaults.

The military campaign provoked criticism from Kurdish and Turkish politicians, and in response the military resurrected the Prevention of Terrorism Law, which criminalized any activity—including speech—that threatened the integrity of the state. This law was used in 1994 and 1995 to arrest journalists and elected members of the National Assembly, who were tried in special state security courts that are under the jurisdiction of the military.

The Kurdish problem has had significant reverberations on Turkey's foreign policy. The arrest of seven members of the National Assembly, all of whom were Kurdish deputies charged with endangering state security through their discussions of the Kurdish issue with fellow parliamentarians in Europe and North America, was especially troublesome for EU countries. Member governments of the EU condemned the arrests, the stripping of the Kurdish deputies' parliamentary immunity, and the subsequent December 1994 sentencing of the deputies to long prison terms. Much to the embarrassment of the Turkish government, imprisoned Deputy Leyla Zane, who was one of the first women elected to the National Assembly, was among the several human rights activists whom the Norwegian parliament nominated for the 1995 Nobel Peace Prize. Several EU countries cited the trial of the elected Kurdish deputies and similar prosecutions of journalists as well as of Turkey's most famous novelist, Yashar Kamal, as evidence that authoritarianism was stronger than democratic practices in Turkey and that, therefore, the country's outstanding application for EU membership should not be considered.

Because joining the EU was as important an economic goal for the Çiller administration as it had been for her predecessors, Çiller sought to dampen European criticisms in January 1995 by proposing to repeal those clauses of the Prevention of Terrorism Law that criminalized speech and publications. Her objective was to obtain enough support to win EU approval of an agreement that accepted Turkey into a customs union with the EU. The EU voted in March 1995 to accept Turkey into a customs union on condition that the Council of Europe (the European parliament) certify that the country had made progress in the institutionalization of democratic practices.

Immediately following the EU vote, a new crisis in Turkish-EU relations erupted when more than 35,000 Turkish troops invaded northern Iraq in yet another attempt to destroy suspected PKK bases. The military offensive in northern Iraq lasted for more than three months and reignited European criticisms of Turkish policies. Attention inevitably focused on the government of Turkey's relations with its Kurdish minority. Criticism of Turkey's human rights practices at an April 1995 meeting of the Council of Europe was so intense that the Turkish delegates walked out, partly in protest and partly to avoid the humiliation of being present for a vote against Turkey. To dilute European criticisms, Çiller proposed that the National Assembly adopt amendments to the 1982 constitution that would strengthen democratic procedures. For example, the amendments would end the ban on political activities by associations such as labor unions and professional groups, permit civil servants and university students to organize, and make it difficult for courts to strip parliamentary deputies of their immunity from prosecution. The National Assembly's adoption of the amendments in July 1995, coupled with the withdrawal of the last Turkish military units from Iraq, helped to ease some of the tension between Turkey and its erstwhile European friends.

The democratization process is not without controversy within Turkey. An influential minority of the political elite believe that the country's laws and institutions provide adequate protection of civil liberties and that EU pressures constitute unacceptable interference in Turkey's internal affairs. This view is particularly strong among some military officers, and their opposition to Çiller's proposal to repeal Article 8 of the Prevention of Terrorism Law was sufficient to persuade a majority of deputies in the National Assembly to vote against the bill.

The failure to win approval for repealing the controversial Article 8 of the Prevention of Terrorism Law had serious implications for the Çiller government. During the summer of 1995, the DYP coalition partner, the SHP, effectively dissolved itself by incorporating with the more liberal Republican People's Party (CHP), which, since its revival in 1992, had adopted a strong position in favor of abolishing Article 8. The merger necessitated party elections for a new leader, elections that resulted in Deniz Baykal's selection as head of the expanded CHP in September 1995. Baykal not only was opposed to Article 8, but also advocated civil rights legislation that would include punishment for security officials who abuse the rights of political detainees. Given his views, Baykal was not expected to keep the CHP in the coalition government, and, only ten days after his victory, he withdrew, causing the government's collapse. Çiller tried to form a minority government in October, but within ten days was forced to resign for the second time in less than one month when her DYP government failed to win a vote of confidence from the National Assembly. Baykal then agreed to join a new coalition government on two conditions: that the Article 8 amendments be resubmitted to the National Assembly and that new parliamentary elections be scheduled. Çiller imposed strict party discipline for the second vote, thus ensuring a majority favoring passage of the amendments to Article 8 of the Prevention of Terrorism Law, and she reluctantly called for new elections, to be held in December 1995.

The December 1995 elections represented a major setback for Çiller and her party, which came in third with 19 percent of the vote. The Welfare Party emerged in first place with 21 percent of the vote, followed by the Motherland Party with 19.6

percent. The failure of any party to win a majority of seats in the National Assembly mandated the formation of a coalition government. However, this task proved to be politically difficult because none of the secular parties was willing to participate in a Welfare-dominated government, and neither the DYP nor the Motherland Party was keen on cooperation. Finally, after more than ten weeks of sometimes tense political wrangling, Çiller and Motherland Party leader Mesut Yilmaz agreed to put aside their bitter rivalry and form a minority government with Yilmaz as prime minister for the first year and Çiller replacing him in 1997. This Motherland-DYP coalition won a vote of confidence in March 1996 because Ecevit's DSP, which had seventy-five National Assembly seats, agreed to abstain on confidence votes.

The performance of Turkey's economy was mixed during 1995. The monetary policies of the Çiller government included strict controls over public-sector expenditures, which contributed to an easing of the financial crisis that had developed in early 1994. Although exports rose steadily during the first two quarters of the year, imports increased at a faster rate, and this surge in imports added to the country's severe balance of payments deficit. In addition, inflation continued to be a major economic problem, totalling 78.9 percent for all of 1995. Several years of high inflation rates and low wage increases had aggravated employer-employee relations. The strain was reflected in the large number of strikes during 1995, including a crippling two-month-long strike by more than 350,000 public-sector workers in the autumn. Moreover, the privatization of state-owned enterprises—the principal feature of the Çiller administration's structural adjustment program—made little progress in 1995. Within the National Assembly, a majority of deputies opposed the sale of major public factories for ideological (the relevant industries were strategic) or political (fear that sales would lead to increased unemployment) reasons.

March 18, 1996   Paul M. Pitman, III, and
                                                         Eric Hooglund

Chapter 1. Historical Setting

Isak Pasa Palace, in Dogubayazit, east central Turkey, built in 1685

TURKEY IS A NEW COUNTRY in an old land. The modern Turkish state—beginning with the creation of the Republic of Turkey in the years immediately after World War I—drew on a national consciousness that had developed only in the late nineteenth century. But the history of nomadic Turkish tribes can be traced with certainty to the sixth century A.D., when they wandered the steppes of central Asia. Asia Minor, which the Turks invaded in the eleventh century, has a recorded history that dates back to the Hittites, who flourished there in the second millennium B.C. Archaeological evidence of far older cultures has been found in the region, however.

The term *Turkey*, although sometimes used to signify the Ottoman Empire, was not assigned to a specific political entity or geographic area until the republic was founded in 1923. The conquering Turks called Asia Minor, the large peninsular territory they had wrested from the Byzantine Empire, by its Greek name, Anatolé (sunrise; figuratively, the East), or Anatolia. The term *Anatolia* is also used when events described affected both that region and Turkish Thrace ("Turkey-in-Europe") because of the two areas' closely linked political, social, and cultural development.

Anatolia is a bridge connecting the Middle East and Europe, and it shares in the history of both those parts of the world. Despite the diversity of its peoples and their cultures, and the constantly shifting borders of its ethnic map, Anatolia has a history characterized by remarkable continuity. Wave after wave of conquerors and settlers have imposed their language and other unique features of their culture on it, but they also have invariably assimilated the customs of the peoples who preceded them.

The history of Turkey encompasses, first, the history of Anatolia before the coming of the Turks and of the civilizations—Hittite, Thracian, Hellenistic, and Byzantine—of which the Turkish nation is the heir by assimilation or example. Second, it includes the history of the Turkish peoples, including the Seljuks, who brought Islam and the Turkish language to Anatolia. Third, it is the history of the Ottoman Empire, a vast, cosmopolitan, pan-Islamic state that developed from a small Turkish amirate in Anatolia and that for centuries was a world power.

Finally, Turkey's history is that of the republic established in 1923 under the leadership of Mustafa Kemal (1881–1938), called Atatürk—the "Father Turk." The creation of the new republic in the heartland of the old Islamic empire was achieved in the face of internal traditionalist opposition and foreign intervention. Atatürk's goal was to build on the ruins of Ottoman Turkey a new country and society patterned directly on Western Europe. He equated Westernization with the introduction of technology, the modernization of administration, and the evolution of democratic institutions.

The Turkish horsemen who stormed into Anatolia in the eleventh century were called *gazis* (warriors of the faith), but they followed their tribal leaders to win booty and to take land as well as to spread Islam. The Ottoman Empire, built on the conquests of the *gazis*, was Islamic but not specifically Turkish. Engendered in reaction to this Ottoman universalism, early Turkish nationalism was often pan-Turanian, envisioning a common destiny for all Turkic-speaking peoples. By contrast, Atatürk narrowed the focus of his nationalism to the Turks of Turkey. Under his influence, twentieth-century Turkish historiography bypassed the Islamic Ottoman period to link the Turkish nation with ancient Anatolia in such a way that the Hittites, for instance, were recognized as proto-Turks from whom modern Turks can trace descent. Although contemporary Turkey is relatively homogeneous linguistically, it is estimated that perhaps 75 percent of the country's genetic pool is non-Turkish in origin.

Atatürk's ideological legacy—known as Kemalism—consists of the "Six Arrows": republicanism, nationalism, populism, reformism, etatism (see Glossary), and secularism. These principles have been embodied in successive constitutions, and appeals for both reforms and retrenchment have been made in their name.

In the late 1940s, Atatürk's long-time lieutenant and successor, Ismet Inönü (earlier known as Ismet Pasha), introduced democratic elections and opened the political system to multiparty activity. In 1950 the Republican People's Party (Cumhuriyet Halk Partisi—CHP)—Atatürk's party—was badly defeated at the polls by the new Democrat Party, headed by Adnan Menderes. The Menderes government attempted to redirect the economy, allowing for greater private initiative, and was more tolerant of traditional religious and social attitudes in the countryside. In their role as guardians of Kemalism, military leaders became convinced in 1960 that the Menderes government had departed dangerously from the principles of the republic's founder, and overthrew it in a military coup. After a brief interval of military rule, a new, liberal constitution was adopted for the so-called Second Republic, and the government returned to civilian hands.

The 1960s witnessed coalition governments led, until 1965, by the CHP under Inönü. A new grouping—the right-wing Justice Party organized under Süleyman Demirel and recognized as the successor to the outlawed Democrat Party—came to power in that year. In opposition, the new leader of the CHP, Bülent Ecevit, introduced a platform that shifted Atatürk's party leftward. Political factionalism became so extreme as to prejudice public order and the smooth functioning of the government and economy.

In 1971 the leaders of the armed forces demanded appointment of a government "above parties" charged with restoring law and order. A succession of nonparty governments came to power, but, unable to gain adequate parliamentary support, each quickly fell during a period of political instability that lasted until 1974. Demirel and Ecevit alternated in office as head of government during the remainder of the 1970s, a period marked by the rise of political extremism and religious revivalism, terrorist activities, and rapid economic changes accompanied by high inflation and severe unemployment. The apparent inability of parliamentary government to deal with the situation prompted another military coup in 1980, led by Chief of Staff General Kenan Evren. The new regime's National Security Council acted to restore order and stabilize the economy. It also moved deliberately toward reinstating civilian rule. A constitution for the Third Republic, promulgated in 1982, increased the executive authority of the president and provided for Evren's appointment to a seven-year term in that office. General elections to the new National Assembly held the following year enabled Turgut Özal to form a one-party majority government that promised to bring stability to the political process.

In two subsequent parliamentary elections, in 1987 and 1991, Turkey demonstrated a commitment to pluralist politics and a peaceful transfer of power. The 1991 election ended the eight-year rule of Özal's Motherland Party and brought to power the True Path Party, headed by Süleyman Demirel. Upon the death of Özal in 1993, Demirel ascended to the presidency, and Tansu Çiller became Turkey's first woman prime minister.

Ancient Anatolia

There is abundant archaeological evidence of a thriving neolithic culture in Anatolia at least as early as the seventh millennium B.C. What may have been the world's first urban settlement (dated ca. 6500 B.C.) has been uncovered at Çatalhüyük in the Konya Ovası (Konya Basin). Introduced early in the third millennium B.C., metallurgy made possible a flourishing "copper age" (ca. 2500–2000 B.C.) during which cultural patterns throughout the region were remarkably uniform. The use of bronze weapons and implements was widespread by 2000 B.C. Colonies of Assyrian merchants, who settled in Anatolia during the copper age, provided metal for the military empires of Mesopotamia, and their accounts and business correspondence are the earliest written records found in Anatolia. From about 1500 B.C., southern Anatolia, which had plentiful sources of ore and numerous furnace sites, developed as a center of iron production. Two of the area's most celebrated archaeological excavations are the sites at Troy and Hattusas (Bogazköy) (see fig. 2).

The cape projecting into the Aegean between the Dardanelles and the Gulf of Edremit was known in antiquity as Troas. There, a thirty-meter-high mound called Hisarlik was identified as the site of ancient Troy in diggings begun by German archaeologist Heinrich Schliemann in the 1870s. The first five levels of the nine discovered at Hisarlik contained remains of cities from the third millennium B.C. that controlled access to the shortest crossing of the Dardanelles and that probably derived their prosperity from tolls. Artifacts give evidence of 1,000 years of cultural continuity in the cities built on these levels. A sharp break with the past occurred on the sixth level, settled about 1900 B.C. by newcomers believed to have been related to the early Greeks. Built after an earthquake devastated the previous city about 1300 B.C., the seventh level was clearly the victim of sacking and burning about 1150 B.C., and it is recognized as having been the Troy of Homer's *Iliad*. Hisarlik subsequently was the site of a Greek city, Ilion, and a Roman one, Ilium.

Hittites

Late in the third millennium B.C., waves of invaders speaking Indo-European languages crossed the Caucasus Mountains into Anatolia. Among them were the bronze-working, chariot-borne warriors who conquered and settled the central plain. Building on older cultures, these invaders borrowed even their name, the Hittites, from the indigenous Hatti whom they had subjugated. They adopted the native Hattic deities and adapted to their written language the cuneiform alphabet and literary conventions of the Semitic cultures of Mesopotamia. The Hittites imposed their political and social organization on their dominions in the Anatolian interior and northern Syria, where the indigenous peasantry supported the Hittite warrior caste with rents, services, and taxes. In time the Hittites won reputations as merchants and statesmen who schooled the ancient Middle East in both commerce and diplomacy. The Hittite Empire achieved the zenith of its political power and cultural accomplishment in the fourteenth and thirteenth centuries B.C., but the state collapsed after 1200 B.C. when the Phrygians, clients of the Hittites, rebelled and burned Hattusas.

Phrygians and Lydians

The twelfth to ninth centuries B.C. were a time of turmoil throughout Anatolia and the Aegean world. The destruction of Troy, Hattusas, and numerous other cities in the region was a collective disaster that coincided with the rise of the aggressive Assyrian Empire in Mesopotamia, the Dorian invasion of Greece, and the appearance of the "sea peoples" who ravaged the Aegean and eastern Mediterranean.

The first light to penetrate the dark age in Anatolia was lit by the very Phrygians who had destroyed Hattusas. Architects, builders, and skilled workers of iron, they had assimilated the Hittites' syncretic culture and adopted many of their political institutions. Phrygian kings apparently ruled most of western and central Anatolia in the ninth century B.C. from their capital at Gordium (a site sixty kilometers southwest of modern Ankara). Phrygian strength soon waned, however, and the kingdom was overthrown in the seventh century B.C. by the Cimmerians, a nomadic people who had been pursued over the Caucasus into Anatolia by the Scythians.

Order was restored in Anatolia by the Lydians, a Thracian warrior caste who dominated the indigenous peasantry and derived their great wealth from alluvial gold found in the tributaries of the Hermus River (Gediz Nehri). From their court at

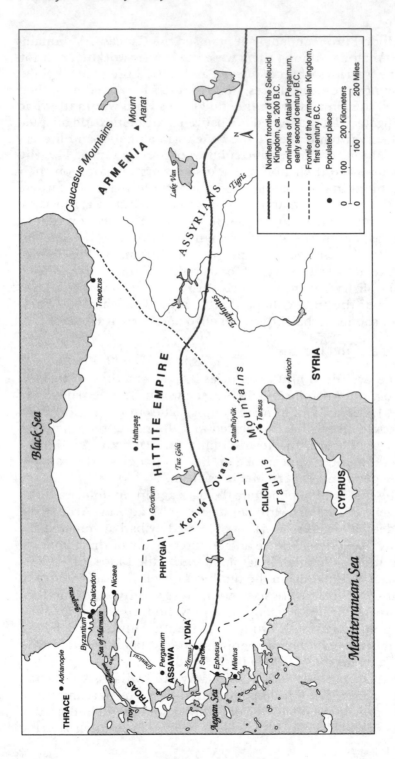

Figure 2. Anatolia in Antiquity, First Century B.C.

Sardis, such Lydian kings as Croesus controlled western Anatolia until their kingdom fell to the Persians in 546 B.C.

Armenians and Kurds

The Armenians took refuge in the Lake Van region in the seventh century B.C., apparently in reaction to Cimmerian raids. Their country was described by Xenophon around 400 B.C. as a tributary of Persia. By the first century B.C., a united Armenian kingdom that stretched from the Black Sea to the Caspian Sea had been established as a client of the Roman Empire to buffer the frontier with Persia.

Xenophon also recorded the presence of the Kurds. Contemporary linguistic evidence has challenged the previously held view that the Kurds are descendants of the Medes, although many Kurds still accept this explanation of their origin. Kurdish people migrated from the Eurasian steppes in the second millennium B.C. and joined indigenous inhabitants living in the region.

Greeks

The Aegean coast of Anatolia was an integral part of a Minoan-Mycenean civilization (ca. 2600–1200 B.C.) that drew its cultural impulses from Crete. During the Aegean region's so-called Dark Age (ca. 1050–800 B.C.), Ionian Greek refugees fled across the sea to Anatolia, then under Lydian rule, to escape the onslaught of the Dorians. Many more cities were founded along the Anatolian coast during the great period of Greek expansion after the eighth century B.C. One among them was Byzantium, a distant colony established on the Bosporus by the city-state of Megara. Despite endemic political unrest, the cities founded by the Ionians and subsequent Greek settlers prospered from commerce with Phrygia and Lydia, grew in size and number, and generated a renaissance that put Ionia in the cultural vanguard of the Hellenic world.

At first the Greeks welcomed the Persians, grateful to be freed from Lydian control. But when the Persians began to impose unpopular tyrants on the city-states, the Greeks rebelled and called on their kinsmen in Greece for aid. In 334 B.C., Alexander the Great crossed the Hellespont, defeated the Persians at the Granicus River (Biga Çayi), and during four years of campaigning liberated the Ionian city-states, incorporating them into an empire that at his death in 323 B.C. stretched from the Nile to the Indus.

After Alexander died, control of Anatolia was contested by several of the Macedonian generals among whom his empire was divided. By 280 B.C. one of them, Seleucus Nicator, had made good his claim to an extensive kingdom that included southern and western Anatolia and Thrace as well as Syria, Mesopotamia, and, for a time, Persia. Under the Seleucid Dynasty, which survived until 64 B.C., colonists were brought from Greece, and the process of hellenization was extended among the non-Greek elites.

The Seleucids were plagued by rebellions, and their domains in Anatolia were steadily eaten away by secession and attacks by rival Hellenistic regimes. Pergamum became independent in 262 B.C., during the Attalid Dynasty, and won fame as the paragon of Hellenistic states. Noted for the cleanliness of its streets and the splendor of its art, Pergamum, in west-central Anatolia, derived its extraordinary wealth from trade in pitch, parchment, and perfume, while slave labor produced a food surplus on scientifically managed state farms. It was also a center of learning that boasted a medical school and a library second in renown only to that of Alexandria. But Pergamum was both despised and envied by the other Greek states because of its alliance with Rome.

Rome and the Byzantine Empire

The last of the Attalid kings bequeathed Pergamum to his Roman allies upon his death in 138 B.C. Rome organized this extensive territory under a proconsul as the province of Asia. All of Anatolia except Armenia, which was a Roman client-state, was integrated into the imperial system by A.D. 43. After the accession of the Roman emperor Augustus (r. 27 B.C.–A.D. 14), and for generations thereafter, the Anatolian provinces enjoyed prosperity and security. The cities were administered by local councils and sent delegates to provincial assemblies that advised the Roman governors. Their inhabitants were citizens of a cosmopolitan world state, subject to a common legal system and sharing a common Roman identity. Roman in allegiance and Greek in culture, the region nonetheless retained its ethnic complexity.

In A.D. 285, the emperor Diocletian undertook the reorganization of the Roman Empire, dividing jurisdiction between its Latin-speaking and Greek-speaking halves. In 330 Diocletian's successor, Constantine, established his capital at the Greek city of Byzantium, a "New Rome" strategically situated on the European side of the Bosporus at its entrance to the Sea of Marmara. For nearly twelve centuries the city, embellished and renamed Constantinople, remained the capital of the Roman Empire—better known in its continuous development in the East as the Byzantine Empire.

Christianity was introduced to Anatolia through the missionary activity of Saint Paul, a Greek-speaking Jew from Tarsus in Cilicia, and his companions. Christians possibly even constituted a majority of the population in most of Anatolia by the time Christianity was granted official toleration under the Edict of Milan in A.D. 313. Before the end of the fourth century, a patriarchate was established in Constantinople with ecclesiastical jurisdiction over much of the Greek East. The basilica of Hagia Sophia (Holy Wisdom), whose construction in Constantinople was ordered by Emperor Justinian in 532, became the spiritual focus of Greek Christendom.

Although Greek in language and culture, the Byzantine Empire was thoroughly Roman in its laws and administration. The emperor's Greek-speaking subjects, conscious of their imperial vocation, called themselves *romaioi*—Romans. Almost until the end of its long history, the Byzantine Empire was seen as ecumenical—intended to encompass all Christian peoples—rather than as a specifically Greek state.

In the early seventh century, the emperor in Constantinople presided over a realm that included not only Greece and Anatolia but Syria, Egypt, Sicily, most of Italy, and the Balkans, with outposts across North Africa as far as Morocco. Anatolia was the most productive part of this extensive empire and was also the principal reservoir of manpower for its defense. With the loss of Syria to Muslim conquest in the seventh century, Anatolia became the frontier as well as the heartland of the empire. The military demands imposed on the Byzantine state to police its provinces and defend its frontiers were enormous, but despite the gradual contraction of the empire and frequent political unrest, Byzantine forces generally remained strong until the eleventh century.

Turkish Origins

The first historical references to the Turks appear in Chinese records dating around 200 B.C. These records refer to tribes called the Hsiung-nu (an early form of the Western term *Hun*), who lived in an area bounded by the Altai Mountains, Lake Baykal, and the northern edge of the Gobi Desert, and

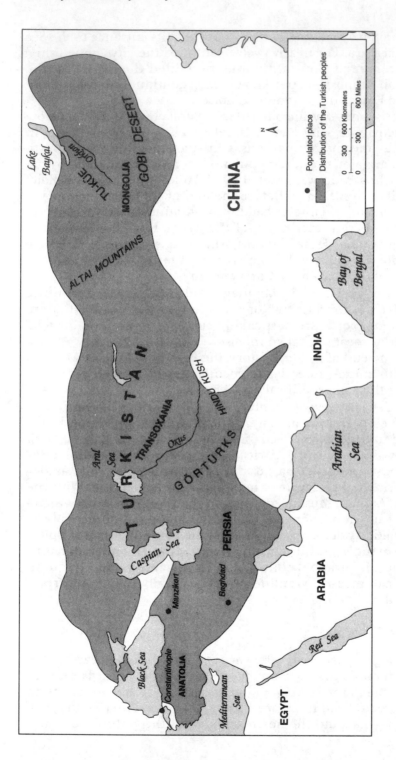

Figure 3. Distribution of the Turkish Peoples: Migrations and Conquests, Seventh Through Eleventh Centuries

who are believed to have been the ancestors of the Turks (see fig. 3). Specific references in Chinese sources in the sixth century A.D. identify the tribal kingdom called Tu-Küe located on the Orkhon River south of Lake Baykal. The khans (chiefs) of this tribe accepted the nominal suzerainty of the Tang Dynasty. The earliest known example of writing in a Turkic language was found in that area and has been dated around A.D. 730.

Other Turkish nomads from the Altai region founded the Görtürk Empire, a confederation of tribes under a dynasty of khans whose influence extended during the sixth through eighth centuries from the Aral Sea to the Hindu Kush in the land bridge known as Transoxania (i.e., across the Oxus River). The Görtürks are known to have been enlisted by a Byzantine emperor in the seventh century as allies against the Sassanians. In the eighth century, separate Turkish tribes, among them the Oguz, moved south of the Oxus River, while others migrated west to the northern shore of the Black Sea.

Great Seljuks

The Turkish migrations after the sixth century were part of a general movement of peoples out of central Asia during the first millennium A.D. that was influenced by a number of inter-related factors—climatic changes, the strain of growing populations on a fragile pastoral economy, and pressure from stronger neighbors also on the move. Among those who migrated were the Oguz Turks, who had embraced Islam in the tenth century. They established themselves around Bukhara in Transoxania under their khan, Seljuk. Split by dissension among the tribes, one branch of the Oguz, led by descendants of Seljuk, moved west and entered service with the Abbasid caliphs of Baghdad.

The Turkish horsemen, known as *gazis*, were organized into tribal bands to defend the frontiers of the caliphate, often against their own kinsmen. However, in 1055 a Seljuk khan, Tugrul Bey, occupied Baghdad at the head of an army composed of *gazis* and mamluks (slave-soldiers, a number of whom became military leaders and rulers). Tugrul forced the caliph (the spiritual leader of Islam) to recognize him as sultan, or temporal leader, in Persia and Mesopotamia. While they engaged in state building, the Seljuks also emerged as the champions of Sunni (see Glossary) Islam against the religion's Shia (see Glossary) sect. Tugrul's successor, Mehmet ibn Daud (r. 1063–72)—better known as Alp Arslan, the "Lion Hero"—

prepared for a campaign against the Shia Fatimid caliphate in Egypt but was forced to divert his attention to Anatolia by the *gazis*, on whose endurance and mobility the Seljuks depended. The Seljuk elite could not persuade these *gazis* to live within the framework of a bureaucratic Persian state, content with collecting taxes and patrolling trade routes. Each year the *gazis* cut deeper into Byzantine territory, raiding and taking booty according to their tradition. Some served as mercenaries in the private wars of Byzantine nobles and occasionally settled on land they had taken. The Seljuks followed the *gazis* into Anatolia in order to retain control over them. In 1071 Alp Arslan routed the Byzantine army at Manzikert near Lake Van, opening all of Anatolia to conquest by the Turks.

Armenia had been annexed by the Byzantine Empire in 1045, but religious animosity between the Armenians and the Greeks prevented these two Christian peoples from cooperating against the Turks on the frontier. Although Christianity had been adopted as the official religion of the state by King Titidates III around A.D. 300, nearly 100 years before similar action was taken in the Roman Empire, Armenians were converted to a form of Christianity at variance with the Orthodox tradition of the Greek church, and they had their own patriarchate independent of Constantinople. After their conquest by the Sassanians around 400, their religion bound them together as a nation and provided the inspiration for a flowering of Armenian culture in the fifth century. When their homeland fell to the Seljuks in the late eleventh century, large numbers of Armenians were dispersed throughout the Byzantine Empire, many of them settling in Constantinople, where in its centuries of decline they became generals and statesmen as well as craftsmen, builders, and traders.

Sultanate of Rum

Within ten years of the Battle of Manzikert, the Seljuks had won control of most of Anatolia. Although successful in the west, the Seljuk sultanate in Baghdad reeled under attacks from the Mongols in the east and was unable—indeed unwilling—to exert its authority directly in Anatolia. The *gazis* carved out a number of states there, under the nominal suzerainty of Baghdad, states that were continually reinforced by further Turkish immigration. The strongest of these states to emerge was the Seljuk sultanate of Rum ("Rome," i.e., Byzantine Empire), which had its capital at Konya (Iconium). During the twelfth and thirteenth centuries, Rum became dominant over the other Turkish states (see fig. 4).

The society and economy of the Anatolian countryside were unchanged by the Seljuks, who had simply replaced Byzantine officials with a new elite that was Turkish and Muslim. Conversion to Islam and the imposition of the language, mores, and customs of the Turks progressed steadily in the countryside, facilitated by intermarriage. The cleavage widened, however, between the unruly *gazi* warriors and the state-building bureaucracy in Konya.

The Crusades

The success of the Seljuk Turks stimulated a response from Latin Europe in the form of the First Crusade. A counteroffensive launched in 1097 by the Byzantine emperor with the aid of the crusaders dealt the Seljuks a decisive defeat. Konya fell to the crusaders, and after a few years of campaigning Byzantine rule was restored in the western third of Anatolia.

Although a Turkish revival in the 1140s nullified many of the Christian gains, greater damage was done to Byzantine security by dynastic strife in Constantinople in which the largely French contingents of the Fourth Crusade and their Venetian allies intervened. In 1204 these crusaders installed Count Baldwin of Flanders in the Byzantine capital as emperor of the so-called Latin Empire of Constantinople, dismembering the old realm into tributary states where West European feudal institutions were transplanted intact. Independent Greek kingdoms were established at Nicaea and Trebizond (present-day Trabzon) and in Epirus from remnant Byzantine provinces. Turks allied with Greeks in Anatolia against the Latins, and Greeks with Turks against the Mongols. In 1261 Michael Palaeologus of Nicaea drove the Latins from Constantinople and restored the Byzantine Empire, but as an essentially Balkan state reduced in size to Thrace and northwestern Anatolia.

Seljuk Rum survived in the late thirteenth century as a vassal state of the Mongols, who had already subjugated the Great Seljuk sultanate at Baghdad. Mongol influence in the region had disappeared by the 1330s, leaving behind *gazi* amirates competing for supremacy. From the chaotic conditions that prevailed throughout the Middle East, however, a new power emerged in Anatolia—the Ottoman Turks.

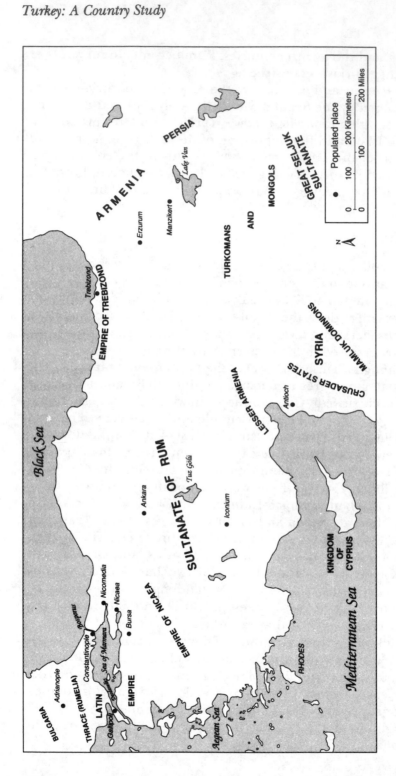

Figure 4. Anatolia in the Thirteenth Century

The Ottoman Empire

Documentation of the early history of the Ottomans is scarce. According to semilegendary accounts, Ertugrul, khan of the Kayı tribe of the Oguz Turks, took service with the sultan of Rum at the head of a *gazi* force numbering "400 tents." He was granted territory—if he could seize and hold it—in Bithynia, facing the Byzantine strongholds at Bursa, Nicomedia (Izmit), and Nicaea. Leadership subsequently passed to Ertugrul's son, Osman I (r. ca. 1284–1324), founder of the Osmanli Dynasty—better known in the West as the Ottomans. This dynasty was to endure for six centuries through the reigns of thirty-six sultans (see table 2, Appendix A).

Osman I's small amirate attracted *gazis* from other amirates, who required plunder from new conquests to maintain their way of life. Such growth gave the Ottoman state a military stature that was out of proportion to its size. Acquiring the title of sultan, Osman I organized a politically centralized administration that subordinated the activities of the *gazis* to its needs and facilitated rapid territorial expansion. Bursa fell in the final year of his reign. His successor, Orhan (r. 1324–60), crossed the Dardanelles in force and established a permanent European base at Gallipoli in 1354. Murad I (r. 1360–89) annexed most of Thrace (called Rumelia, or "Roman land," by the Turks), encircling Constantinople, and moved the seat of Ottoman government to Adrianople (Edirne) in Europe. In 1389 the Ottoman *gazis* defeated the Serbs at the Battle of Kosovo, although at the cost of Murad's life. The steady stream of Ottoman victories in the Balkans continued under Bayezid I (r. 1389–1402). Bulgaria was subdued in 1393, and in 1396 a French-led force of crusaders that had crossed the Danube from Hungary was annihilated at Nicopolis (see fig. 5).

In Anatolia, where Ottoman policy had been directed toward consolidating the sultan's hold over the *gazi* amirates by means of conquest, usurpation, and purchase, the Ottomans were confronted by the forces of the Mongol leader Timur (Tamerlane), to whom many of the Turkish *gazis* had defected. Timur crushed Ottoman forces near Ankara in 1402 and captured Bayezid I. The unfortunate sultan died in captivity the next year, leaving four heirs, who for a decade competed for control of what remained of Ottoman Anatolia. By the 1420s, however, Ottoman power had revived to the extent that fresh campaigns were undertaken in Greece.

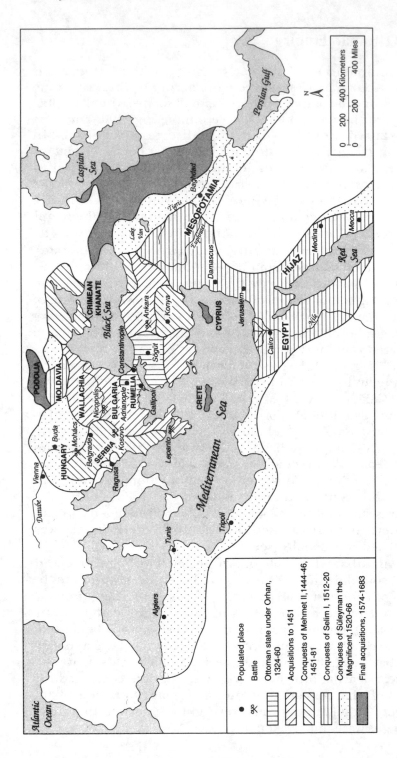

Figure 5. Expansion of the Ottoman Empire, 1324–1683

Aside from scattered outposts in Greece, all that remained of the Byzantine Empire was its capital, Constantinople. Cut off by land since 1365, the city, despite long periods of truce with the Turks, was supplied and reinforced by Venetian traders who controlled its commerce by sea. On becoming sultan in 1444, Mehmet II (r. 1444–46, 1451–81) immediately set out to conquer the city. The military campaigning season of 1453 commenced with the fifty-day siege of Constantinople, during which Mehmet II brought warships overland on greased runners into the Bosporus inlet known as the Golden Horn to bypass the chain barrage and fortresses that had blocked the entrance to Constantinople's harbor. On May 29, the Turks fought their way through the gates of the city and brought the siege to a successful conclusion.

As an isolated military action, the taking of Constantinople did not have a critical effect on European security, but to the Ottoman Dynasty the capture of the imperial capital was of supreme symbolic importance. Mehmet II regarded himself as the direct successor to the Byzantine emperors. He made Constantinople the imperial capital, as it had been under the Byzantine emperors, and set about rebuilding the city. The cathedral of Hagia Sophia was converted to a mosque, and Constantinople—which the Turks called Istanbul (from the Greek phrase *eis tin polin*, "to the city")—replaced Baghdad as the center of Sunni Islam. The city also remained the ecclesiastical center of the Greek Orthodox Church, of which Mehmet II proclaimed himself the protector and for which he appointed a new patriarch after the custom of the Byzantine emperors.

Ottoman Institutions

At the apex of the hierarchical Ottoman system was the sultan, who acted in political, military, judicial, social, and religious capacities, under a variety of titles. He was theoretically responsible only to God and God's law—the Islamic *seriat* (in Arabic, *sharia*), of which he was the chief executor. All offices were filled by his authority, and every law was issued by him in the form of a *firman* (decree). He was supreme military commander and had official title to all land. During the early sixteenth-century Ottoman expansion in Arabia, Selim I also adopted the title of caliph, thus indicating that he was the universal Muslim ruler. Although theocratic and absolute in theory and in principle, the sultan's powers were in practice limited. The attitudes of important members of the dynasty, the bureaucratic and military establishments, and religious leaders had to be considered.

Three characteristics were necessary for acceptance into the ruling class: Islamic faith, loyalty to the sultan, and compliance with the standards of behavior of the Ottoman court. The last qualification effectively excluded the majority of common Turks, whose language and manners were very different from those of the Ottomans. The language of the court and government was Ottoman Turkish, a highly formalized hybrid language that included Persian and Arabic loanwords. In time Greeks, Armenians, and Jews were also employed in state service, usually in diplomatic, technical, or commercial capacities.

The day-to-day conduct of government and the formulation of policy were in the hands of the divan, a relatively small council of ministers directed by the chief minister, the grand vizier. The entranceway to the public buildings in which the divan met—and which in the seventeenth century became the residence of the grand vizier—was called the Bab-ı Ali (High Gate, or Sublime Porte). In diplomatic correspondence, the term *Porte* was synonymous with the Ottoman government, a usage that acknowledged the power wielded by the grand vizier.

The Ottoman Empire had Turkish origins and Islamic foundations, but from the start it was a heterogeneous mixture of ethnic groups and religious creeds. Ethnicity was determined solely by religious affiliation. Non-Muslim peoples, including Greeks, Armenians, and Jews, were recognized as *millets* (see Glossary) and were granted communal autonomy. Such groups were allowed to operate schools, religious establishments, and courts based on their own customary law.

Selim I and Süleyman the Magnificent

Selim I (r. 1512–20) extended Ottoman sovereignty southward, conquering Syria, Palestine, and Egypt. He also gained recognition as guardian of the holy cities of Mecca and Medina.

Selim I's son, Süleyman I (r. 1520–66), was called the "lawgiver" (*kanuni*) by his Muslim subjects because of a new codification of *seriat* undertaken during his reign. In Europe, however, he was known as Süleyman the Magnificent, a recognition of his prowess by those who had most to fear from it. Belgrade fell to Süleyman in 1521, and in 1522 he compelled the Knights of Saint John to abandon Rhodes. In 1526 the Ottoman victory at the Battle of Mohács led to the taking of Buda on the Danube. Vienna was besieged unsuccessfully during the campaign season of 1529. North Africa up to the Moroccan frontier was brought under Ottoman suzerainty in the 1520s and 1530s, and governors named by the sultan were installed in Algiers, Tunis, and Tripoli. In 1534 Kurdistan and Mesopotamia were taken from Persia. The latter conquest gave the Ottomans an outlet to the Persian Gulf, where they were soon engaged in a naval war with the Portuguese.

When Süleyman died in 1566, the Ottoman Empire was a world power. Most of the great cities of Islam—Mecca, Medina, Jerusalem, Damascus, Cairo, Tunis, and Baghdad—were under the sultan's crescent flag. The Porte exercised direct control over Anatolia, the sub-Danubian Balkan provinces, Syria, Palestine, and Mesopotamia. Egypt, Mecca, and the North African provinces were governed under special regulations, as were satellite domains in Arabia and the Caucasus, and among the Crimean Tartars. In addition, the native rulers of Wallachia, Moldavia, Transylvania, and Ragusa (Dubrovnik) were vassals of the sultan.

The Ottomans had always dealt with the European states from a position of strength. Treaties with them took the form of truces approved by the sultan as a favor to lesser princes, provided that payment of tribute accompanied the settlement. The Ottomans were slow to recognize the shift in the military balance to Europe and the reasons for it. They also increasingly permitted European commerce to penetrate the barriers built to protect imperial autarky. Some native craft industries were destroyed by the influx of European goods, and, in general, the balance of trade shifted to the disadvantage of the empire, making it in time an indebted client of European producers.

European political intervention followed economic penetration. In 1536 the Ottoman Empire, then at the height of its power, had voluntarily granted concessions to France, but the system of capitulations introduced at that time was later used to impose important limitations on Ottoman sovereignty. Commercial privileges were greatly extended, and residents who came under the protection of a treaty country were thereby made subject to the jurisdiction of that country's law rather than Ottoman law, an arrangement that led to flagrant abuses of justice. The last thirty years of the sixteenth century saw the rapid onset of a decline in Ottoman power symbolized by the defeat of the Turkish fleet by the Spanish and Portuguese at the Battle of Lepanto in 1571 and by the unbridled bloody succession struggles within the imperial palace, the Seraglio of Constantinople.

Köprülü Era

Ottoman imperial decadence was finally halted by a notable family of imperial bureaucrats, the Köprülü family, which for more than forty years (1656–1703) provided the empire with grand viziers, combining ambition and ruthlessness with genuine talent. Mehmet, followed by his son Ahmet, overhauled the bureaucracy and instituted military reforms. Crete and Lemnos were taken from Venice, and large provinces in Ukraine were wrested temporarily from Poland and Russia. The Köprülü family also resumed the offensive against Austria, pushing the Ottoman frontier to within 120 kilometers of Vienna. An attempt in 1664 to capture the Habsburg capital was beaten back, but Ahmet Köprülü extorted a huge tribute as the price of a nineteen-year truce. When it expired in 1683, the Ottoman army again invaded Austria, laying siege to Vienna for two months, only to be routed ultimately by a relief force led by the king of Poland, Jan Sobieski.

The siege of Vienna was the high-water mark of Ottoman expansion in Europe, and its failure opened Hungary to reconquest by the European powers. In a ruinous sixteen-year war, Russia and the Holy League—composed of Austria, Poland, and Venice, and organized under the aegis of the pope—finally drove the Ottomans south of the Danube and east of the Carpathians. Under the terms of the Treaty of Karlowitz in 1699, the first in which the Ottomans acknowledged defeat, Hungary, Transylvania, and Croatia were formally relinquished to Austria. Poland recovered Podolia, and Dalmatia and the Morea were ceded to Venice. In a separate peace the next year, Russia received the Azov region (see fig. 6).

The last of the Köprülü rulers fell from power when Mustafa II (r. 1695–1703) was forced by rebellious janissaries to abdicate. Under Ahmet III (r. 1703–30), effective control of the government passed to the military leaders. Ahmet III's reign is referred to as the "tulip period" because of the popularity of tulip cultivation in Istanbul during those years. At this time, Peter the Great of Russia moved to eliminate the Ottoman presence on the north shore of the Black Sea. Russia's main objective in the region subsequently was to win access to warm-water ports on the Black Sea and then to obtain an opening to the Mediterranean through the Ottoman-controlled Bosporus and Dardanelles straits. Despite territorial gains at Ottoman expense, however, Russia was unable to achieve these goals, and the Black Sea remained for the time an "Ottoman lake" on which Russian warships were prohibited.

External Threats and Internal Transformations

During the eighteenth century, the Ottoman Empire was almost continuously at war with one or more of its enemies—Persia, Poland, Austria, and Russia. Under the humiliating terms of the Treaty of Kuchuk-Kaynarja that ended the Russo-Ottoman War of 1768–74, the Porte abandoned the Tartar khanate in the Crimea, granted autonomy to the Trans-Danubian provinces, allowed Russian ships free access to Ottoman waters, and agreed to pay a large war indemnity.

The implications of the decline of Ottoman power, the vulnerability and attractiveness of the empire's vast holdings, the stirrings of nationalism among its subject peoples, and the periodic crises resulting from these and other factors became collectively known to European diplomats in the nineteenth century as "the Eastern Question." In 1853 Tsar Nicholas I of Russia described the Ottoman Empire as "the sick man of Europe." The problem from the viewpoint of European diplomacy was how to dispose of the empire in such a manner that no one power would gain an advantage at the expense of the others and upset the political balance of Europe.

The first nineteenth-century crisis to bring about European intervention was the Greek War of Independence (1821–32). In 1827 an Anglo-French fleet destroyed the Ottoman and Egyptian fleets at the Battle of Navarino, while the Russian army advanced as far as Edirne before a cease-fire was called in 1829. The European powers forced the Porte to recognize Greek independence under the London Convention of 1832.

Muhammad Ali, an Ottoman officer who had been designated pasha of Egypt by the sultan in 1805, had given substantial aid to the Ottoman cause in the Greek war. When he was not rewarded as promised for his assistance, he invaded Syria in 1831 and pursued the retreating Ottoman army deep into Anatolia. In desperation, the Porte appealed to Russia for support. Britain then intervened, constraining Muhammad Ali to withdraw from Anatolia to Syria. The price the sultan paid Russia for its assistance was the Treaty of Hünkar Iskelesi of 1833.

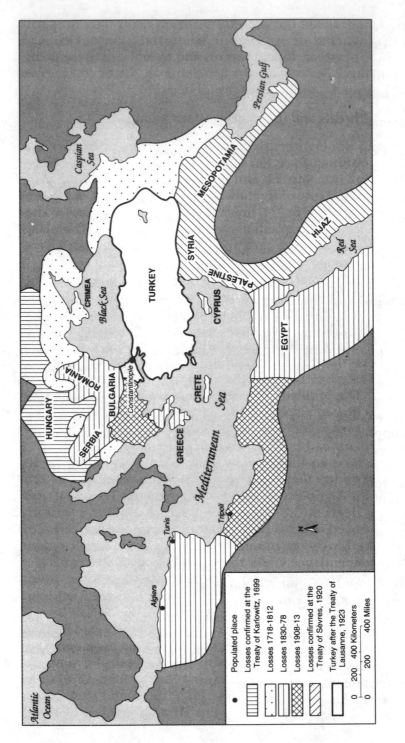

Figure 6. Decline of the Ottoman Empire from the Treaty of Karlowitz, 1699, to the Treaty of Lausanne, 1923

Under this treaty, the Bosporus and Dardanelles straits were to be closed on Russian demand to naval vessels of other powers.

War with Muhammad Ali resumed in 1839, and Ottoman forces were again defeated. Russia waived its rights under the 1833 treaty and aligned itself with British efforts to support the Ottoman Empire militarily and diplomatically. Under the London Convention of 1840, Muhammad Ali was forced to abandon his claim to Syria, but he was recognized as hereditary ruler of Egypt under nominal Ottoman suzerainty. Under an additional protocol, in 1841 the Porte undertook to close the straits to warships of all powers.

The Ottoman Empire fought two more wars with Russia in the nineteenth century. The Crimean War (1854–56) pitted France, Britain, and the Ottoman Empire against Russia. Under the Treaty of Paris, which ended the war, Russia abandoned its claim to protect Orthodox Christians in the Ottoman Empire and renounced the right to intervene in the Balkans. War resumed between Russia and the Ottoman Empire in 1877. Russia opened hostilities in response to Ottoman suppression of uprisings in Bulgaria and to the threat posed to Serbia by Ottoman forces. The Russian army had driven through Bulgaria and reached as far as Edirne when the Porte acceded to the terms imposed by a new agreement, the Treaty of San Stefano. The treaty reduced Ottoman holdings in Europe to eastern Thrace and created a large, independent Bulgarian state under Russian protection.

Refusing to accept the dominant position of Russia in the Balkans, the other European powers called the Congress of Berlin in 1878. At this conclave, the Europeans agreed to a much smaller autonomous Bulgarian state under nominal Ottoman suzerainty. Serbia and Romania were recognized as fully independent states, and the Ottoman provinces of Bosnia and Herzegovina were placed under Austrian administration. Cyprus, although remaining technically part of the Ottoman Empire, became a British protectorate. For all its wartime exertions, Russia received only minor territorial concessions in Bessarabia and the Caucasus. In the course of the nineteenth century, France seized Algeria and Tunisia, while Britain began its occupation of Egypt in 1882. In all these cases, the occupied territories formerly had belonged to the Ottoman Empire.

The Ottoman Empire had a dual economy in the nineteenth century consisting of a large subsistence sector and a small colonial-style commercial sector linked to European markets and controlled by foreign interests. The empire's first railroads, for example, were built by foreign investors to bring the cash crops of Anatolia's coastal valleys—tobacco, grapes, and other fruit—to Smyrna (Izmir) for processing and export. The cost of maintaining a modern army without a thorough reform of economic institutions caused expenditures to be made in excess of tax revenues. Heavy borrowing from foreign banks in the 1870s to reinforce the treasury and the undertaking of new loans to pay the interest on older ones created a financial crisis that in 1881 obliged the Porte to surrender administration of the Ottoman debt to a commission representing foreign investors. The debt commission collected public revenues and transferred the receipts directly to creditors in Europe.

The 1860s and early 1870s saw the emergence of the Young Ottoman movement among Western-oriented intellectuals who wanted to see the empire accepted as an equal by the European powers. They sought to adopt Western political institutions, including an efficient centralized government, an elected parliament, and a written constitution. The "Ottomanism" they advocated also called for an integrated dynastic state that would subordinate Islam to secular interests and allow non-Muslim subjects to participate in representative parliamentary institutions.

In 1876 the hapless sultan was deposed by a *fetva* (legal opinion) obtained by Midhat Pasha, a reformist minister sympathetic to the aims of the Young Ottomans. His successor, Abdül Hamid II (r. 1876–1909), came to the throne with the approval of Midhat and other reformers. In December of that year, on the eve of the war with Russia, the new sultan promulgated a constitution, based on European models, that had been drafted by senior political, military, and religious officials under Midhat's direction. Embodying the substance of the Young Ottoman program, this document created a representative parliament, guaranteed religious liberty, and provided for enlarged freedom of expression. Abdül Hamid II's acceptance of constitutionalism was a temporary tactical expedient to gain the throne, however. Midhat was dismissed in February 1877 and was later murdered. The sultan called the empire's first parliament but dissolved it within a year.

Unrest in Eastern Rumelia led the European powers to insist on the union of that province with Bulgaria in 1885. Meanwhile, Greek and Bulgarian partisans were carrying on a running battle with Ottoman forces in Macedonia. In addition, the repression of revolutionary activities in Armenia during 1894–96 cost about 300,000 lives and aroused European public opinion against the Ottoman regime. Outside support for a rebellion on Crete also caused the Porte to declare war on Greece in 1897. Although the Ottoman army defeated the Greeks decisively in Thrace, the European powers forced a compromise peace that kept Crete under Ottoman suzerainty while installing the son of the Greek king as its governor.

More isolated from Europe than it had been for half a century, the Ottoman regime could count on support only from Germany, whose friendship offered Abdül Hamid II a congenial alternative to British and French intervention. In 1902 Germany was granted a ninety-nine-year concession to build and operate a Berlin-to-Baghdad rail connection. Germany continued to invest in the Ottoman economy, and German officers held training and command posts in the Ottoman army.

Opposition to the sultan's regime continued to assert itself among Westernized intellectuals and liberal members of the ruling class. Some continued to advocate "Ottomanism," whereas others argued for pan-Turanism, the union of Turkic-speaking peoples inside and outside the Ottoman Empire. The Turkish nationalist ideologist of the period was the writer Ziya Gökalp, who defined Turkish nationalism within the context of the Ottoman Empire. Gökalp went much farther than his contemporaries, however, by calling for the adoption of the vernacular in place of Ottoman Turkish. Gökalp's advocacy of a national Turkish state in which folk culture and Western values would play equally important revitalizing roles foreshadowed events a quarter-century in the future.

The Young Turks

The repressive policies of Abdül Hamid II fostered disaffection, especially among those educated in Europe or in Westernized schools. Young officers and students who conspired against the sultan's regime coalesced into small groups, largely outside Istanbul. One young officer, Mustafa Kemal (later known as Atatürk), organized a secret society among fellow officers in Damascus and, later, in Thessaloniki (Salonika) in present-day Greece. Atatürk's group merged with other nationalist reform organizations in 1907 to form the Committee of Union and Progress (CUP). Also known as the Young Turks, this group sought to restore the 1876 constitution and unify the diverse elements of the empire into a homogeneous nation through greater government centralization under a parliamentary regime.

In July 1908, army units in Macedonia revolted and demanded a return to constitutional government. Appearing to yield, Abdül Hamid II approved parliamentary elections in November in which the CUP won all but one of the Turkish seats under a system that allowed proportional representation of all *millets*. The Young Turk government was weakened by splits between nationalist and liberal reformers, however, and was threatened by traditionalist Muslims and by demands from non-Turkish communities for greater autonomy. Abdül Hamid II was forced to abdicate and was succeeded by his brother, Mehmet V, in 1909. Foreign powers took advantage of the political instability in Istanbul to seize portions of the empire. Austria annexed Bosnia and Herzegovina immediately after the 1908 revolution, and Bulgaria proclaimed its complete independence. Italy declared war in 1911 and seized Libya. Having earlier formed a secret alliance, Greece, Serbia, Montenegro, and Bulgaria invaded Ottoman-held Macedonia and Thrace in October 1912. Ottoman forces were defeated, and the empire lost all of its European holdings except part of eastern Thrace.

The disasters befalling the empire led to internal political change. The liberal government in power since July 1912 was overthrown in January 1913 in a coup engineered by Enver Pasha, and the most authoritarian elements of the Young Turk movement gained full control. A second Balkan war broke out in June 1913, when the Balkan allies began fighting among themselves over the division of the spoils from the first war. Taking advantage of the situation, Ottoman forces turned on Bulgaria, regaining Edirne and establishing the western boundary of the empire at the Maritsa River.

After a brief period of constitutional rule, the leadership of the CUP emerged as a military dictatorship with power concentrated in the hands of a triumvirate consisting of Mehmet Talat Pasha, Ahmet Cemal Pasha, and Enver, who, as minister of war, was its acknowledged leader in the war.

World War I

As the two European alliance systems drew closer to war in 1914, Enver's pronounced pro-German sympathies, shared by many in the military and bureaucracy, prevailed over the pragmatic neutrality proposed by Talat and Cemal. Germany had

Ruins of ancient Troy
Courtesy Hermine Dreyfuss

been pro-Ottoman during the Balkan wars, but the Porte had no outstanding differences with either Britain or France in the summer of 1914. In guiding his government toward alignment with Germany, Enver was able to play on fear of the traditional Ottoman enemy, Russia, the ally of Britain and France in the war.

On August 2, 1914, Enver concluded a secret treaty of alliance with Germany. General mobilization was ordered the next day, and in the following weeks concessions granted to foreign powers under the capitulations were canceled. It remained for Germany, however, to provide the casus belli. Two German military vessels—the battleship *Göben* and the heavy cruiser *Breslau*—that had been caught in a neutral Ottoman port when war broke out in Europe were turned over to the Ottoman navy. In October they put to sea with German officers and crews and shelled Odessa and other Russian ports while flying the Ottoman flag. Russia declared war on the Ottoman Empire on November 5, followed the next day by Britain and France. Within six months, the Ottoman army of about 800,000 men was engaged in a four-front war that became part of the greater conflict of World War I.

Enver launched an ill-prepared offensive in the winter of 1914–15 against the Russians in the Caucasus, vainly hoping that an impressive demonstration of Ottoman strength there would incite an insurrection among the tsar's Turkish-speaking subjects. Instead, a Russian counteroffensive inflicted staggering losses on Ottoman forces, driving them back to Lake Van. During the campaign in eastern Anatolia, assistance was given to the Russians by some Armenians, who saw them as liberators rather than invaders. Armenian units were also part of the Russian army. Enver claimed that an Armenian conspiracy existed and that a generalized revolt by the Armenians was imminent. During the winter months of 1915, as the shattered Ottoman army retreated toward Lake Van, a massive deportation of as many as 2 million Armenians was undertaken in the war zone. It shortly degenerated into a massacre, as ethnic Turks and Kurds descended on Armenian villages or slaughtered refugees along the road. The most conservative estimates put the number of dead at 600,000, but other sources cite figures of more than 1 million. The situation of those Armenians who survived the march out of Anatolia was scarcely improved under the military government in Syria. Others managed to escape behind Russian lines. The episode occasioned a revulsion in Western Europe that had its effect in the harsh terms meted out by the Allies in the postwar settlement.

In the spring of 1915, the Allies undertook naval and land operations in the Dardanelles that were intended to knock the Ottoman Empire out of the war with one blow and to open the straits for the passage of supplies to Russia. Amphibious landings were carried out at Gallipoli, but British forces, vigorously opposed by forces commanded by Atatürk, were unable to expand their beachheads. The last units of the expeditionary force were evacuated by February 1916.

In Mesopotamia the Ottoman army defeated a British expeditionary force that had marched on Baghdad from a base established at Basra in 1915. The British mounted a new offensive in 1917, taking Baghdad and driving Ottoman forces out of Mesopotamia. In eastern Anatolia, Russian armies won a series of battles that carried their control west to Erzincan by July

1916, although Atatürk, who was then given command of the eastern front, led a counteroffensive that checked the Russian advance. Russia left the war after the Bolshevik Revolution in 1917. The new Russian government concluded the Treaty of Brest-Litovsk with the Central Powers in March 1918, under which the Ottoman Empire regained its eastern provinces.

Sharif Husayn ibn Ali, the sultan's regent in Mecca and the Hijaz region of western Arabia, launched the Arab Revolt in 1916. The British provided advisers, of whom T.E. Lawrence was to become the best known, as well as supplies. In October 1917, British forces in Egypt opened an offensive into Palestine; they took Jerusalem by December. After hard fighting, British and Arab forces entered Damascus in October 1918. Late in the campaign, Atatürk succeeded to command of Turkish forces in Syria and withdrew many units intact into Anatolia.

Ottoman resistance was exhausted. Early in October, the war government resigned, and the Young Turk triumvirate—Enver, Talat, and Cemal—fled to exile in Germany. Mehmet VI (r. 1918–22), who had succeeded to the rule upon his brother's death in July, sued for peace through a government headed by liberal ministers that signed an armistice at Mudros on October 30, 1918, that had been dictated by the Allies. Allied warships steamed through the Dardanelles and anchored off Istanbul on November 12, the day after the end of the war in Europe. In four years of war, the Ottoman Empire had mobilized about 2.8 million men, of whom about 325,000 were killed in battle. In addition, more than 2 million civilians, including both Turks and Armenians, are believed to have died of war-related causes. Talat and Cemal, who were held responsible for the deportation of Armenians and the mistreatment of refugees, were assassinated by Armenian nationalists in 1921. The following year, Enver was killed while fighting the Bolsheviks in Central Asia.

Atatürk and the Turkish Nation

Atatürk returned to Istanbul at the end of the war, his military reputation untarnished by the defeat of the empire that he had served. Revered by his troops as well as the Turkish masses, Atatürk soon emerged as the standard-bearer of the Turkish nationalist movement.

Born in Thessaloniki in 1881, Atatürk was the son of a minor government official in a city where Turks outnumbered

Greeks. His ardent Turkish nationalism dated from his early days as a cadet in the military school at Monastir (in the present-day Former Yugoslav Republic of Macedonia) during a time of constant conflict between Ottoman troops and Macedonian guerrillas, who attacked the Turkish population in the region. Following graduation from the military academy in Istanbul, Atatürk held various staff positions and served in garrisons at Damascus and Thessaloniki, where he became involved in nationalist activities. He took part in the coup that forced Abdül Hamid II's abdication in 1909. Atatürk organized irregular forces in Libya during the war with Italy in 1911 and subsequently held field commands in the two Balkan wars (1912–13). Assigned to a post in the Ministry of War after the armistice, Atatürk quickly recognized the extent of Allied intentions toward the Ottoman Empire.

Plans for Partitioning Turkey

Allied troops—British, French, and Italian, as well as a contingent of Greeks—occupied Istanbul and were permitted under the conditions of the armistice to intervene in areas where they considered their interests to be imperiled. During the war, the Allies had negotiated a series of agreements that outlined not only the definitive dismantling of the Ottoman Empire but also the partitioning among them of what Turkish nationalists had come to regard as the Turkish homeland. According to these agreements, Russia was at last to be rewarded with possession of Istanbul and the straits, as well as eastern Anatolia as far south as Bitlis below Lake Van. France and Italy were conceded portions of Anatolia, and Britain had promised Izmir to Greece—although it had also been promised to Italy—to encourage Greek entry into the war in 1917.

The Bolshevik government had renounced tsarist claims when it made its separate peace at Brest-Litovsk, but Britain, France, Italy, and Greece all pressed their respective claims at the Paris peace talks in 1919. All agreed with the provisions of President Woodrow Wilson's Fourteen Points calling for an independent Armenia and an autonomous Kurdistan. How the Allies would implement the clause providing that the Turkish-speaking nation "should be assured of a secure sovereignty" was not clear.

The terms of a peace treaty with the Ottoman Empire were presented by the Allies in April 1920 at San Remo, Italy, and were embodied in the Treaty of Sèvres, which was concluded the following August. The treaty was shaped by the wartime agreements made by the Allies. In addition, France received a mandate over Lebanon and Syria (including what is now Hatay Province in Turkey), and Britain's mandate covered Iraq, Jordan, and Palestine. Eastern Thrace up to a line from the Black Sea to the Sea of Marmara as well as Izmir and its hinterland were to be occupied by Greece, with the final disposition of the territory to be decided in a plebiscite. The Treaty of Sèvres was never enforced as such, as events in Turkey soon rendered it irrelevant.

Nationalist Movement

The sultan was kept in the custody of the Allies to ensure the cooperation of an Ottoman administration, which had effective jurisdiction only in Istanbul and part of northern Anatolia, while they disposed of the rest of his empire. At the same time, a Turkish nationalist movement was organized under Atatürk's leadership to resist the dismemberment of Turkish-speaking areas. Atatürk had been sent to eastern Anatolia as inspector general, ostensibly to supervise the demobilization of Ottoman forces and the disposition of supplies, but more particularly to remove him from the capital after he had expressed opposition to the Allied occupation there. Upon his arrival at Samsun in May 1919, Atatürk proceeded to rally support for the nationalist cause and to recruit a nationalist army. Guerrilla warfare against the government gradually grew to full-fledged campaigns against the Greek army that threatened to involve the other Allied occupation forces.

In July 1919, a nationalist congress met at Erzurum with Atatürk presiding to endorse a protocol calling for an independent Turkish state. In September the congress reconvened at Sivas. Although the delegates voiced their loyalty to the sultan-caliph, they also pledged to maintain the integrity of the Turkish nation. The congress adopted the National Pact, which defined objectives of the nationalist movement that were not open to compromise. Among its provisions were the renunciation of claims to the Arab provinces, the principle of the absolute integrity of all remaining Ottoman territory inhabited by a Turkish Muslim majority, a guarantee of minority rights, the retention of Istanbul and the straits, and rejection of any restriction on the political, judicial, and financial rights of the nation.

Negotiations continued between the nationalist congress and the Ottoman government, but to no avail. Atatürk resigned from the army when relieved of his duties. The naming of a chief minister in Istanbul considered sympathetic to the nationalist cause brought a brief improvement in relations, however, and the Ottoman parliament, which met in January 1920, approved the National Pact. In reaction to these developments, Allied occupation forces seized public buildings and reinforced their positions in the capital, arrested and deported numerous nationalist leaders, and had parliament dismissed.

Allied actions brought a quick response from the nationalists. In April they convened the Grand National Assembly in Ankara, in defiance of the Ottoman regime, and elected Atatürk its president. The Law of Fundamental Organization (also known as the Organic Law) was adopted in January 1921. With this legislation, the nationalists proclaimed that sovereignty belonged to the nation and was exercised on its behalf by the Grand National Assembly.

War of Independence

During the summer and fall of 1919, with authorization from the Supreme Allied War Council, the Greeks occupied Edirne, Bursa, and Izmir. A landing was effected at the latter port under the protection of an Allied flotilla that included United States warships. The Greeks soon moved as far as Usak, 175 kilometers inland from Izmir. Military action between Turks and Greeks in Anatolia in 1920 was inconclusive, but the nationalist cause was strengthened the next year by a series of important victories. In January and again in April, Ismet Pasha defeated the Greek army at Inönü, blocking its advance into the interior of Anatolia. In July, in the face of a third offensive, the Turkish forces fell back in good order to the Sakarya River, eighty kilometers from Ankara, where Atatürk took personal command and decisively defeated the Greeks in a twenty-day battle.

An improvement in Turkey's diplomatic situation accompanied its military success. Impressed by the viability of the nationalist forces, both France and Italy withdrew from Anatolia by October 1921. Treaties were signed that year with Soviet Russia, the first European power to recognize the nationalists, establishing the boundary between the two countries. As early as 1919, the Turkish nationalists had cooperated with the Bolshevik government in attacking the newly proclaimed Armenian republic. Armenian resistance was broken by the summer of 1921, and the Kars region was occupied by the Turks. In 1922 the nationalists recognized the Soviet absorption of what remained of the Armenian state.

The final drive against the Greeks began in August 1922. In September the Turks moved into Izmir, where thousands were killed during the ensuing fighting and in the disorder that followed the city's capture. Greek soldiers and refugees, who had crowded into Izmir, were rescued by Allied ships.

The nationalist army then concentrated on driving remaining Greek forces out of eastern Thrace, but the new campaign threatened to put the Turks in direct confrontation with Allied contingents defending access to the straits and holding Istanbul, where they were protecting the Ottoman government. A crisis was averted when Atatürk accepted a British-proposed truce that brought an end to the fighting and also signaled that the Allies were unwilling to intervene on behalf of the Greeks. In compliance with the Armistice of Mundanya, concluded in October, Greek troops withdrew beyond the Maritsa River, allowing the Turkish nationalists to occupy territory up to that boundary. The agreement entailed acceptance of a continued Allied presence in the straits and in Istanbul until a comprehensive settlement could be reached.

At the end of October 1922, the Allies invited the nationalist and Ottoman governments to a conference at Lausanne, Switzerland, but Atatürk was determined that the nationalist government should be Turkey's sole representative. In November 1922, the Grand National Assembly separated the offices of sultan and caliph and abolished the former. The assembly further stated that the Ottoman regime had ceased to be the government of Turkey when the Allies seized the capital in 1920, in effect abolishing the Ottoman Empire. Mehmet VI went into exile on Malta, and his cousin, Abdülmecid, was named caliph.

Turkey was the only power defeated in World War I to negotiate with the Allies as an equal and to influence the provisions of the resultant treaty. Ismet Pasha was the chief Turkish negotiator at the Lausanne Conference, which opened in November 1922. The National Pact of 1919 was the basis of the Turkish negotiating position, and its provisions were incorporated in the Treaty of Lausanne, concluded in July 1923. With this treaty, the Allies recognized the present-day territory of Turkey and denied Turkey's claim to the Mosul area in the east (in present-day Iraq) and Hatay, which included the Mediterranean port of Alexandretta (Iskenderun). The boundary with the newly created state of Iraq was settled by a League of Nations initiative in 1926, and Iskenderun was ceded in 1939 by France during its rule as mandatory power for Syria.

Detailed provisions of the treaty regulated use of the straits. General supervisory powers were given to a straits commission under the League of Nations, and the straits area was to be demilitarized after completion of the Allied withdrawal. Turkey was to hold the presidency of the commission, which included the Soviet Union among its members. The capitulations and foreign administration of the Ottoman public debt, which infringed on the sovereignty of Turkey, were abolished. Turkey, however, assumed 40 percent of the Ottoman debt, the remainder being apportioned among other former Ottoman territories. Turkey was also required to maintain low tariffs on imports from signatory powers until 1929. The Treaty of Lausanne reaffirmed the equality of Muslim and non-Muslim Turkish nationals. Turkey and Greece arranged a mandatory exchange of their respective ethnic Greek and Turkish minorities, with the exception of some Greeks in Istanbul and Turks in western Thrace and the Dodecanese Islands.

On October 29, 1923, the Grand National Assembly proclaimed the Republic of Turkey. Atatürk was named its president and Ankara its capital, and the modern state of Turkey was born.

Atatürk's Reforms

On assuming office, Atatürk initiated a series of radical reforms of the country's political, social, and economic life that were aimed at rapidly transforming Turkey into a modern state (see table A). A secular legal code, modeled along European lines, was introduced that completely altered laws affecting women, marriage, and family relations.

Atatürk also urged his fellow citizens to look and act like Europeans. Turks were encouraged to wear European-style clothing. Surnames were adopted: Mustafa Kemal, for example, became Kemal Atatürk, and Ismet Pasha took Inönü as his surname to commemorate his victories there. Likewise, Atatürk insisted on cutting links with the past that he considered anachronistic. Titles of honor were abolished. The wearing of the fez, which had been introduced a century earlier as a modernizing reform to replace the turban, was outlawed because it

Table A. Chronology of Major Kemalist Reforms

Year	Reform
1922	Sultanate abolished (November 1).
1923	Treaty of Lausanne secured (July 24).
	Republic of Turkey with capital at Ankara proclaimed (October 29).
1924	Caliphate abolished (March 3).
	Traditional religious schools closed, *seriat* abolished. Constitution adopted (April 20).
1925	Dervish brotherhoods abolished.
	Fez outlawed by the Hat Law (November 25). Veiling of women discouraged; Western clothing for men and women encouraged.
	Western (Gregorian) calendar adopted.
1926	New civil, commercial, and penal codes based on European models adopted. New civil code ended Islamic polygamy and divorce by renunciation and introduced civil marriage.
	Millet system ended.
1927	First systematic census.
1928	New Turkish alphabet (modified Latin form) adopted. State declared secular (April 10); constitutional provision establishing Islam as official religion deleted.
1933	Islamic call to worship and public readings of the Kuran (Quran) required to be in Turkish rather than Arabic.
1934	Women given the vote and the right to hold office.
	Law of Surnames adopted—Mustafa Kemal given the name Kemal Atatürk (Father Turk) by the Grand National Assembly; Ismet Pasha took surname of Inönü.
1935	Sunday adopted as legal weekly holiday.
	State role in managing economy written into the constitution.

had become for the nationalists a symbol of the reactionary Ottoman regime.

The ideological foundation of Atatürk's reform program became known as Kemalism. Its main points were enumerated in the "Six Arrows" of Kemalism: republicanism, nationalism, populism, reformism, etatism (statism), and secularism. These were regarded as "fundamental and unchanging principles" guiding the republic, and were written into its constitution. The principle of republicanism was contained in the constitutional declaration that "sovereignty is vested in the nation" and not in a single ruler. Displaying considerable ingenuity, Atatürk set about reinventing the Turkish language and recasting Turkish history in a nationalist mold. The president himself went out into the park in Ankara on Sunday, the newly established day of rest, to teach the Latin alphabet adapted to Turkish as part of the language reform. Populism encompassed not only the notion that all Turkish citizens were equal but that all of them were Turks. What remained of the *millet* system that had provided communal autonomy to other ethnic groups was abolished. Reformism legitimized the radical means by which changes in Turkish political and social life were implemented. Etatism emphasized the central role reserved to the state in directing the nation's economic activities. This concept was cited particularly to justify state planning of Turkey's mixed economy and large-scale investment in state-owned enterprises. An important aim of Atatürk's economic policies was to prevent foreign interests from exercising undue influence on the Turkish economy.

Of all the Kemalist reforms, the exclusion of Islam from an official role in the life of the nation shocked Atatürk's contemporaries most profoundly. The abolition of the caliphate ended any connection between the state and religion. The Islamic religious orders were suppressed, religious schools were closed, public education was secularized, and the *seriat* was revoked. These changes required readjustment of the entire social framework of the Turkish people. Despite subsequent protests, Atatürk conceded nothing to the traditionalists.

In 1924 the Grand National Assembly adopted a new constitution to replace the 1876 document that had continued to serve as the legal framework of the republican government. The 1924 constitution vested sovereign power in the Grand National Assembly as representative of the people, to whom it also guaranteed basic civil rights. Under the new document, the assembly would be a unicameral body elected to a four-year term by universal suffrage. Its legislative authority would include responsibility for approving the budget, ratifying treaties, and declaring war. The president of the republic would be elected to a four-year term by the assembly, and he in turn would appoint the prime minister, who was expected to enjoy the confidence of the assembly (see table 3, Appendix A).

Throughout his presidency, repeatedly extended by the assembly, Atatürk governed Turkey essentially by personal rule in a one-party state. He founded the Republican People's Party (Cumhuriyet Halk Partisi—CHP) in 1923 to represent the nationalist movement in elections and to serve as a vanguard party in support of the Kemalist reform program. Atatürk's Six Arrows were an integral part of the CHP's political platform. By controlling the CHP, Atatürk also controlled the assembly and assured support there for the government he had appointed. Atatürk regarded a stage of personal authoritarian rule as necessary to secure his reforms before he entrusted the government of the country to the democratic process.

Foreign Policy

Atatürk's foreign policy, which had as its main object the preservation of the independence and integrity of the new republic, was careful, conservative, and successful. The president enunciated the principle of "peace at home and peace abroad." This guideline, whose observance was necessary to the task of internal nation building, became the cornerstone of Turkey's foreign relations.

By the end of 1925, friendship treaties had been negotiated with fifteen states. These included a twenty-year treaty of friendship and neutrality signed that year with the Soviet Union that remained in effect until unilaterally abrogated by the Soviet Union in 1945. Turkey subsequently joined Greece, Romania, and Yugoslavia in the Balkan Pact to counter the increasingly aggressive foreign policy of fascist Italy and the effect of a potential Bulgarian alignment with Nazi Germany. Turkey also entered into a nonaggression treaty with Afghanistan, Iraq, and Iran in 1937.

Atatürk attained his greatest diplomatic success in 1936, when Turkey persuaded the signatory powers of the Treaty of Lausanne to allow Turkish control and remilitarization of the straits as part of the Montreux Convention. Under its terms, merchant vessels were to continue to have freedom of navigation of the straits, but Turkey took over the functions of the international commission for registry, sanitary inspection, and the levying of tolls. Turkey was permitted to refortify the straits area and, if at war or under imminent threat of war, to close them to warships.

Turkey after Atatürk

Atatürk's death in Istanbul on November 10, 1938, caused an outpouring of grief throughout the Turkish nation. With much ceremony, the president's body was transported to Ankara and placed in a temporary tomb from which it was transferred in 1953 to a newly completed mausoleum on a hill overlooking Ankara. The building has since become a national shrine.

The stability of the new republic was made evident by the smoothness of the presidential succession. The day after Atatürk's death, the Grand National Assembly elected his chief lieutenant, Inönü, president. Celal Bayar, who had succeeded Inönü as prime minister in 1937, continued in that office.

World War II

As tensions in Europe heightened, Inönü determined to keep Turkey neutral in the event of war, unless the country's vital interests were clearly at stake. The Nazi-Soviet nonaggression pact of August 1939 prompted Turkey to sign a treaty of mutual assistance with Britain and France in October. Hedging its bets, the government concluded a nonaggression treaty with Nazi Germany on June 18, 1941, just four days before the Axis invasion of the Soviet Union. The early military successes of the Axis forces contributed to increased pro-German sentiment, even in some official circles. However, Inönü seems never to have wavered from his position that the Axis powers could not win the war. Despite German pressure, Turkey at no time permitted the passage of Axis troops, ships, or aircraft through or over Turkey and its waters, and the Montreux Convention was scrupulously enforced in the straits. Turkey broke diplomatic relations with Adolf Hitler's government in August 1944, and, in February 1945, declared war on Germany, a necessary precondition for participation in the Conference on International Organization, held in San Francisco in April 1945, from which the United Nations (UN) emerged. Turkey thereby became one of the fifty-one original members of the world organization.

Multiparty Politics, 1946–60

The UN charter was approved by the Grand National Assembly in August 1945, but the debate on the measure during the summer brought about Turkey's first major postwar domestic political conflict. A proposal was entered by former Prime Minister Bayar, Adnan Menderes, and two additional CHP deputies calling for changes in Turkish law to assure the domestic application of the liberties and rights to which the government had ostensibly subscribed by accepting the principles of the UN Charter. When the proposal was disallowed, its four proponents left the CHP and resigned their seats in the assembly.

Despite the rejection of Menderes's proposal, the government relaxed many wartime controls and agreed to the further democratization of the political process. In January 1946, the Democrat Party (DP), headed by Bayar and Menderes, was registered; it subsequently became the main focus of opposition to

Ancient Roman aqueduct
in Istanbul
Courtesy Hermine Dreyfuss

the CHP. The general elections in July 1946 gave the DP sixty-two seats out of 465 in the assembly, demonstrating the appeal of the new party. Although the DP represented the interests of private business and industry, it also received strong support in rural areas.

In the May 1950 general election, about 88 percent of an electorate totaling about 8.5 million went to the polls, returning a huge DP majority. In the assembly, 408 seats went to the DP and only sixty-nine to the CHP, whose unbroken dominance since the founding of the republic was thus ended. Bayar was elected president by the new assembly, replacing Inönü, and named Menderes prime minister. As expected, the Menderes government's economic policy reduced reliance on state direction while encouraging private enterprise and foreign investment in industrial development.

In the May 1954 election, the DP increased its parliamentary majority. Taking its election victory as a mandate to make sweeping changes, including reform of the civil service and state-run enterprises, the Menderes government obtained the passage of a legislative package by means that the opposition characterized as "undemocratic and authoritarian." The CHP concentrated its attacks on a government-sponsored law that limited freedom of the press. Tension increased when the press law was tightened further and restrictions were imposed on public assembly several months before the scheduled October 1957 election. The government argued that the legislation was necessary to prevent "irresponsible journalists" from inciting disorder. The inability of the two main political parties to cooperate in the assembly brought the parliamentary process to a standstill as months passed. When a tour of central Anatolia by CHP leader Inönü in early 1960 became the occasion for outbreaks of violence along his route, the Menderes government reacted by suspending all political activity and imposing martial law. On April 28, 1960, students in Istanbul who were demonstrating against government policies in defiance of martial law were fired on by police; several were killed. The following week, cadets from the military academy staged a protest march in solidarity with the student movement, thereby bringing an element of the armed forces into confrontation with civilian authorities.

The Armed Forces Coup and Interim Rule, 1960–61

Atatürk had always insisted that the military forces, as a national institution above partisanship and factionalism, should stay out of politics. The military leadership traditionally had subscribed to this viewpoint, with the proviso that a major role of the armed forces was to act as guardian of the constitution and Kemalism. By 1960, with the military already deeply involved in political affairs because of the government's use of martial law to enforce its policies, the senior command concluded that the government had departed from Kemalist principles and that the republic was in imminent danger of disintegration. On May 27, 1960, Turkish army units, under the direction of the chief of General Staff, Cemal Gürsel, seized the principal government buildings and communications centers and arrested President Bayar, Prime Minister Menderes, and most of the DP representatives in the Grand National Assembly, as well as a large number of other public officials. Those arrested were charged with abrogating the constitution and instituting a dictatorship.

The coup was accomplished with little violence and was accepted quickly throughout the country. The government was replaced by the Committee of National Unity (CNU), composed of the thirty-eight officers who had organized the coup. The committee acted as supreme authority, appointing a cabinet, initially consisting of five officers and thirteen civilians, to carry out executive functions. The number of civilians in the cabinet, however, was later reduced to three. General Gürsel, who had fought at Gallipoli under Atatürk, temporarily assumed the positions of president, prime minister, and defense minister. At the outset, Gürsel announced that the committee's rule would be of an interim nature and that government would be returned to civilian hands at an early date.

The most pressing problems the CNU faced in the first months after the coup were economic. The ousted regime had been responsible for inflation and heavy debt, and emergency austerity measures had to be taken to stabilize the economy. An economic planning agency, the State Planning Organization, was established to study social and economic conditions and to draw up the country's five-year development plans.

In January 1961, a constituent assembly was formed in which the CNU participated. This interim legislature produced a new constitution, which, after much debate, it ratified in May and submitted to a popular referendum in July. This constitution, which created Turkey's so-called Second Republic, contained a number of substantial departures from the 1924 constitution but continued to embody the principles of Kemalism. The new constitution was approved by 60 percent of the electorate. The large opposition vote was a disappointment to the CNU and showed that sympathy for the DP persisted, particularly in socially conservative small towns and rural constituencies.

Meanwhile, the trial of some 600 former government officials and DP functionaries had begun in October 1960 on the island of Yassıada in the Bosporus. All but about 100 of those tried were found guilty, and fifteen death sentences were pronounced. Partly in response to public appeals for leniency, the death sentences of former President Bayar and eleven others were commuted to life imprisonment, but Menderes and two former cabinet ministers were hanged.

Fourteen political parties offered candidates in the October 1961 election, but only four won seats in the bicameral Grand National Assembly created under the new constitution. The results gave the CHP 173 seats in the lower house—the 450-member National Assembly—and only thirty-six in the 150-member Senate. The Justice Party (Adalet Partisi—AP), generally recognized as the heir of the DP, obtained 158 seats in the lower house and seventy in the upper. The remaining seats were divided between the New Turkey Party and the Republican Peasants' Nation Party, subsequently renamed the Nationalist Action Party (Milliyetçi Haraket Partisi—MHP). The New

Turkey Party was led by onetime DP dissidents who had broken with Menderes in the mid-1950s; the MHP attracted militant rightists. Because neither of the two larger parties commanded a majority, formation of a broad coalition either between the two larger parties or between one of them and the two smaller parties would be necessary.

Politics and Foreign Relations in the 1960s

The new bicameral legislature elected General Gürsel president of the republic. On taking office, he asked seventy-eight-year-old former President İnönü to form a government. İnönü, who had first been named prime minister by Atatürk in 1923, attempted to reach an agreement with the AP for a coalition in which that party would share an equal number of cabinet posts with the CHP, but party leaders failed to resolve their differences concerning amnesty for those convicted in the Yassıada trials. President Gürsel and General Cevdet Sunay, chief of the General Staff, warned that the irresponsibility of some legislators could provoke renewed military intervention in politics. In February 1962, a group of army officers staged a revolt in Ankara in protest of the role of the AP in government-proposed amnesty plans. The uprising was quickly suppressed, and suspected sympathizers in the officer corps were purged. İnönü subsequently introduced legislation granting amnesty to the officers involved in the revolt. In October 283 of those who had been convicted at Yassıada were given executive clemency on the recommendation of the assembly and freed. Another two years elapsed before former President Bayar and the remaining prisoners were released.

The AP made such significant gains in the 1964 local elections that İnönü stepped down as prime minister. After unsuccessful attempts by the AP and the CHP to form a government, an interim administration was appointed to serve until the October 1965 general election. Voters in that election gave the AP a clear majority in the Grand National Assembly. The vote allowed the new prime minister, forty-four-year-old Süleyman Demirel, to form a single-party government and claim a popular mandate for his legislative program. An engineer and former head of the National Water Authority, Demirel was a onetime protégé of Menderes. Although Demirel cultivated a pragmatic and technocratic image for the young party, the AP inherited the DP's identification with right-wing populism and catered to the same broadly based constituency. The party

attracted support from the business community and from artisans and shopkeepers, but its real strength lay in the peasantry
and in the large number of workers who had recently arrived
in the cities from the countryside. Although it never disavowed
the principle of secularism enshrined in Kemalism, the AP promoted tolerance of the open expression of the traditional
Islam that appealed to many in these latter groups. While
accepting a large role for state enterprises in a mixed economy,
the AP also encouraged the development of a stronger private
sector than had been allowed previously and was receptive to
foreign investment in Turkey.

Although Demirel increased defense spending and took a
hard line on law-and-order issues, military leaders remained
suspicious of his party because of its roots in the DP. Demirel
seemed to improve his standing among them by supporting the
successful presidential candidacy of General Sunay when Gürsel died in office in 1966, but objections by the military subsequently forced the prime minister to withdraw legislation that
would have restored full political rights to surviving former DP
leaders. Enactment of other legislation was also hampered by
growing factional splits in the AP. Representing the party's busi-
ness-oriented liberal wing, Demirel urged greater reliance on a
market economy. He was opposed on some issues and prodded
on others by a traditionalist wing that was socially conservative,
more agrarian in its orientation, and had ties to the Islamic
movement.

Following the CHP's defeat in the 1965 general election, that
party engaged in an internal debate to determine its position
in the left-right continuum. When forty-year-old Bülent Ecevit
succeeded Inönü as party leader the following year, he sought
to identify the CHP with the social democratic parties of Western Europe. The party platform favored state-directed investment over private investment and recommended limits on
foreign participation in the Turkish economy. It also called for
rapid expansion of public services financed by taxation that
would restrict the growth of private incomes. Ecevit emphasized the CHP's dedication to maintaining political secularism
in contrast to the AP's leniency in the face of a revival of religious influence. While promising to adhere to Turkey's defense
commitments, he insisted on a more self-reliant foreign policy
that included efforts to improve bilateral relations with the
Soviet Union.

As party leader, Ecevit attempted to transform the CHP from an elitist party seeking to guide the nation from above into a mass movement involving a broadly based constituency in the political process. Ecevit's socialist rhetoric was compatible with the Kemalist principles of state direction of the economy, but the shift to the left he inaugurated caused dissension in the party. In 1967 forty-five CHP deputies broke away to form a centrist party that won nearly 7 percent of the vote in the October 1969 general election. Both major parties lost votes, but right-of-center parties, led by the AP, outpolled the CHP and the small left-wing parties by nearly two to one, and the AP was able to increase its Grand National Assembly majority by sixteen seats. To some observers, the election results indicated a polarization of Turkish politics that would pull the AP and CHP in opposite directions and aggravate political extremism.

The extreme left was represented in the Grand National Assembly during the 1960s by the Turkish Workers' Party (TWP). Its platform called for the redistribution of land, nationalization of industry and financial institutions, and the exclusion of foreign capital, and urged closer cooperation with the Soviet Union. The party attracted the support of only a small number of trade unionists and leftist intellectuals. Although it had won fifteen seats in the 1961 election, its share of the vote in 1965 and 1969 averaged less than 3 percent. Of greater consequence in the 1960s—and for the future—was the party of the extreme right led by Alparslan Türkes, one of the architects of the 1960 coup. Türkes had been among those officers ousted from the CNU for opposing the restoration of democratic institutions. He subsequently resigned from the army and in 1965 took control of the Republican Peasants' Nation Party, later the MHP. Türkes came to personify the ultranationalistic and authoritarian nature of his party. Labeled by some as fascist, the MHP demanded strong state action to maintain order and manage the economy. Although sympathetic to private ownership, the party was hostile toward capitalism and foreign investment. Essentially secularist, the MHP nonetheless regarded Islam as one of the pillars of the Turkish state, and Türkes incorporated references to religion into his nationalist platform.

Türkes's party had won 14 percent of the vote and fifty-four seats in the 1961 election, but electoral support plummeted to under 3 percent in 1965, when many marginal rightist voters switched to the AP. In 1969 the MHP was reduced to a single

*St. Sophia in Istanbul, an Orthodox cathedral that became
a mosque after the Ottoman conquest
Courtesy Hermine Dreyfuss*

seat in the Grand National Assembly; however, Türkes's inflammatory rhetoric and confrontational tactics gave the party a higher profile than its strength at the polls alone would have justified. He organized the party on military lines and indoctrinated party activists, imposing strict discipline on them. The party's youth movement included a paramilitary arm, the "Gray Wolves," whose members disrupted left-wing student activities, initiated physical attacks on political opponents, and retaliated for assaults on MHP members. MHP-incited violence escalated in the late 1960s and set the tone for the volatile political atmosphere of the 1970s.

Turkey's links to the United States grew rapidly in the aftermath of World War II. Turkey took a resolutely pro-Western stance as the Cold War developed in the late 1940s and, in 1950, sent an infantry brigade to the Korean Peninsula to serve under UN command there. The pattern of close bilateral ties with the United States that characterized postwar Turkish foreign relations began to take shape with an agreement signed in Ankara in September 1947 implementing a policy formulated by President Harry S Truman the previous March. Known as

47

the Truman Doctrine, the president's policy declaration spelled out United States intentions to guarantee the security of Turkey and Greece. Truman won approval from the United States Congress for an initial appropriation of US$400 million to aid both countries. Congress also authorized United States civilian and military personnel to assist in economic reconstruction and development and to provide military training. Turkey subsequently participated in the United States-sponsored European Recovery Program (Marshall Plan). Turkey also was admitted to membership in the Council of Europe and in 1959 applied for association with the European Community (EC), later called the European Union (EU—see Glossary). Set aside after the 1960 coup, Turkey's application finally was approved in 1964.

Turkey was admitted to the North Atlantic Treaty Organization (NATO—see Glossary) in 1952, and in 1955 joined with Britain, Iran, Iraq, and Pakistan in the Baghdad Pact, a multilateral defense agreement that became the Central Treaty Organization (CENTO) after the overthrow of the Iraqi monarchy in 1958. Turkey played a vital diplomatic and strategic role as the bridge between the NATO and CENTO alliance systems. The headquarters of NATO's Allied Land Forces Southeastern Europe (LANDSOUTHEAST) was established at Izmir. In addition, operational bases near Adana were developed for NATO purposes. A 1954 military facilities agreement with the United States permitted the opening of other NATO installations and the stationing of United States forces in Turkey. Headquarters for CENTO were moved to Ankara when Iraq withdrew from the alliance.

Turkish participation in NATO was complicated by a regional dispute between Turkey and Greece involving the status of the island of Cyprus, until 1960 a British crown colony. The Greek-speaking Cypriots sought an end to British rule and many favored enosis (union) with Greece. Fearing discrimination and the loss of identity, the Turkish-speaking minority countered with proposals for partition of the island between the two ethnic communities. Conflict between the two communities led to major crises in 1964 and again in 1967, during which Turkey and Greece—both members of NATO—reached the verge of war.

Crisis in Turkish Democracy

The Demirel government's majority in the Grand National

Assembly gradually dissipated after the 1969 general election as factions within the circle of its initial supporters regrouped in new political constellations. In 1970 three small rightist parties that had usually cooperated with the government merged as the National Salvation Party (Milli Selamet Partisi—MSP), an explicitly Islamic-oriented party that imposed politically compromising demands on Demirel as the price of their continued support. Some former AP members deserted the AP in 1971 to form the more right-wing Democratic Party. Other, more liberal AP members, dissatisfied with Demirel's concessions to the right, defected from the party and sat as independents. As a result of these shifts, the Demirel government lost its parliamentary majority and, in the eyes of critics, forfeited its right to govern the country. Acts of politically motivated violence and terrorism escalated in frequency and intensity. Unrest was fueled in part by economic distress, perceptions of social inequities, and the slowness of reform, but protest was increasingly directed at Turkey's military and economic ties to the West.

Politics and Elections in the 1970s

On March 12, 1971, the armed forces chiefs, headed by army commander General Faruk Gürler, presented a memorandum to President Sunay demanding the installation of a "strong and credible government." The military leaders warned civilian officials that the armed forces would be compelled to take over the administration of the state once again unless a government were found that could curb the violence and implement the economic and social reforms, including land reform, stipulated in the 1961 constitution. Demirel resigned the same day. The incident was referred to as the "coup by memorandum."

After consultation with Gürler and the other armed forces chiefs, Sunay asked Nihat Erim, a university professor and CHP centrist, to form a "national unity, above-party government" that would enlist the support of the major parties. Erim led the first of a series of weak caretaker cabinets that governed Turkey until the October 1973 elections.

A joint session of the Grand National Assembly was convened in March 1973 to elect a successor to President Sunay. Many observers had assumed that General Gürler, whose candidacy had the open backing of the armed forces, would be elected without serious opposition, but Demirel was determined to resist what he considered dictation by the military. The AP nominated Tekin Ariburun, chairman of the Senate, to

oppose Gürler. After seven ballots, Gürler and Ariburun withdrew. When Sunay's term expired on March 28, Ariburun, in
his capacity as Senate chairman, became acting president
under the constitution. On April 6, deputies and senators in
the Grand National Assembly elected Fahri Korutürk president
on the fifteenth ballot. Significantly, the new president, a sev-
enty-year-old retired admiral who had served as an independent member of the Senate since 1968, had a direct tie to
Atatürk, who reportedly had conferred on him the name
Korutürk, meaning "Protect the Turks."

In the 1973 election, Ecevit's CHP increased its support by
more than 1 million votes by calling for redistribution of wealth
through taxation and social services, rural development, land
reform, continued state direction of economic activity, and a
general amnesty for political prisoners detained under martial
law. However, holding only 185 seats, the party failed to gain an
overall majority in the Grand National Assembly. The AP,
which saw its share of the vote decline to 30 percent, retained
only 149 seats. A large segment of its right-wing support was
siphoned off by the MSP and the Democratic Party, which won
forty-eight seats and forty-five seats, respectively. The Republican Reliance Party (RRP), formed by the merger of centrist
groups that had seceded earlier from the CHP, won thirteen
seats. The MHP took three seats.

The most significant consequence of the 1973 election was
that the Democratic Party and the MSP held the balance of
power in parliament, and it was unlikely that any coalition government could be formed without the participation of one or
both of them. The politicians in the Democratic Party strongly
resented the warnings periodically handed down to elected
officials by military leaders, but also disapproved of Demirel on
personal as well as political grounds. The MSP was led by Necmettin Erbakan, who had been leader of the proscribed New
Order Party. The MSP was regarded as a revival of that party
under a new name. The principal plank in the MSP's platform
was the restoration of Islamic law and practice in Turkey. The
party sought improved relations with other Muslim countries
and less reliance on the West, yet was also ardently anticommu-
nist. Advocating direct election of the president and the
strengthening of executive authority, the MSP, while upholding
the right to private property, opposed the liberal economic policies favored by the AP.

In January 1974, Ecevit, leader of the party founded by Atatürk, reached a short-lived agreement with Erbakan, the head of an Islamic revivalist party, to join in a coalition government in which Erbakan would be Ecevit's deputy prime minister. In September the MSP pulled out of the coalition. Ecevit remained prime minister at the head of another caretaker government while Korutürk vainly tried to interest Demirel in joining with the CHP in a government of national unity. In November, Korutürk persuaded Sadi Irmak, an elderly senator and an independent, to preside over a nonparty government and prepare the country for an early general election. Irmak's failure to obtain a parliamentary vote of confidence created a parliamentary crisis that left Turkey without a stable, majority-based government for more than a year, during which time economic conditions continued to deteriorate, fanning unrest around the country. Late in 1974, four of the five right-of-center parties in the Grand National Assembly—the AP, MSP, MHP, and RRP—formed an opposition bloc, called the National Front. In March 1975, the National Front parties joined in a minority coalition government under Demirel's premiership. Despite its ineffectiveness, the National Front coalition managed to struggle along for two years, maintaining a slim parliamentary majority dependent on support from independents.

Trading on Ecevit's enormous popularity, in the 1977 election the CHP increased its share of the vote to more than 40 percent and remained the largest party in the Grand National Assembly. However, the 213 seats that it won were still insufficient to form a single-party government. The AP had also improved its standing by taking back some of the votes lost to other right-wing parties in 1973; it returned 189 deputies. MSP representation was cut in half, to twenty-four seats, and the Democratic Party was reduced to one seat. The MHP, however, nearly doubled its vote and elected sixteen deputies. Despite its electoral success, the CHP failed to form a governing coalition.

At length Demirel put together another right-of-center government, linking the AP with the MSP and the MHP in a coalition that depended on a four-seat majority. But the inducements that he offered to assure cooperation caused concern within the liberal wing of his own party. Under the arrangement, responsibility for key areas of concern—public order, the economy, and social reform—was divided among the three party leaders. Demirel was assigned internal security,

Erbakan the economy, and Türkes social affairs, including education. Each leader expected to exercise exclusive authority in his particular area, but the arrangement soon proved unworkable. Meanwhile, groups identified with one of the coalition partners, the MHP, were among the principal instigators of the mounting political violence.

Anger and frustration at the government's ineffectiveness in dealing with the economy and restoring public order led to an erosion of support from liberal AP deputies. On the last day of 1977, the Demirel government was defeated on a vote of confidence in which a dozen AP deputies sided with the CHP opposition. The party leaders having ruled out a "grand coalition," President Korutürk turned to Ecevit to lead a new government, which was backed by a four-seat parliamentary majority.

The Ecevit administration was crisis-ridden from the start. The prime minister's attempt to combine regard for civil liberties with tougher law-and-order measures satisfied no one, least of all the military and the police. In December 1978, the government was forced to proclaim martial law in thirteen provinces in reaction to a serious outbreak of sectarian violence. The calm imposed by martial law was only temporary, and in April 1979, the government extended legal restrictions.

Ecevit resigned in October 1979, after the CHP lost ground to the AP in by-elections, and advised President Korutürk to summon Demirel to replace him. Demirel rejected Ecevit's subsequent proposal for a "grand coalition" and chose instead to put together a technocratic government whose members were selected for their competence rather than their political affiliation. Subsidies to state enterprises were reduced as part of a plan for restructuring, but attempts to rationalize the workforce and control labor costs were challenged by the trade unions in a series of strikes. Demirel countered by extending martial law still further, imposing severe curbs on union activity, and restricting public assembly. Meanwhile, military leaders made no secret of their uneasiness at the growing influence that religious sectarianism was having on politics in obvious defiance of the constitution.

President Korutürk's seven-year term in office expired in April 1980. After 100 ballots, the joint session of the Grand National Assembly failed to agree on a successor. Korutürk retired on schedule, and the chairman of the Senate, Ihsan Sabri Çaglayangil, was installed as acting president of the republic. Çaglayangil could do little more than provide the signature necessary for the enactment of legislation.

Conflict and Diplomacy: Cyprus and Beyond

The historical distrust between Turkey and Greece was compounded during the 1970s by the unfolding Cyprus dispute and conflicting claims in the Aegean Sea. Problems arising from the relationship between Turkish- and Greek-speaking Cypriots on the island had produced a pattern of confrontation between the two countries during the previous decade.

In July 1974, the president of Cyprus, Archbishop Makarios III, demanded withdrawal of Greek army officers assigned to the National Guard on the well-founded charge that they were using their position to subvert his government. In reaction, Athens engineered an anti-Makarios coup, which was carried out successfully by conspirators planning union with Greece. In Ankara, Prime Minister Ecevit condemned the coup as constituting a direct threat to Cyprus's Turkish minority. At the UN, the Turkish representative stated that his government had determined that Greece's direct involvement in the coup was aimed at the annexation of Cyprus in violation of the 1960 independence agreement guaranteed by Turkey, Greece, and Britain. He stressed that Turkey had a clear responsibility under the agreement to protect the rights of the Turkish Cypriot community.

Between July 20 and 22, 1974, some 30,000 Turkish troops, supported by air and naval units, were dropped or landed on Cyprus in the Kyrenia area and advanced toward Nicosia, the Cypriot capital. By the time a UN-sponsored cease-fire went into effect on July 22, Turkish troops controlled the twenty-kilometer-long Nicosia-Kyrenia road and occupied territory on both sides of it, in some places thirty kilometers deep, in an area that had a large Turkish Cypriot population.

The discredited Greek government fell within days as a result of the Cyprus imbroglio. Meeting in Geneva on July 30, the foreign ministers of the three guaranteeing powers—Turan Günes of Turkey, James Callaghan of Britain, and Georgios Mavros representing the new provisional Greek government—accepted the establishment of a buffer zone between the two sides on Cyprus, patrolled by UN forces. They agreed to meet again at Geneva in a week's time to work out terms for a constitutional government that would be representative of both communities on the island.

Despite the cease-fire and a UN Security Council resolution calling for the phased reduction of hostile forces on Cyprus, the Turks continued to land reinforcements. In the week between the cease-fire and the first Geneva foreign ministers' conference, they pushed Greek Cypriot forces to the western extremity of the Kyrenia Range and consolidated their positions around Nicosia. Glafcos Clerides, acting president of Cyprus, and Rauf Denktas, leader of the Turkish-Cypriot community, attended the second session of the Geneva talks, held August 8–14. Denktas rejected the notion of communal autonomy within a federal system favored by Greece and the Greek Cypriot authorities, proposing instead the creation of a single autonomous Turkish region in the northern third of the island, a suggestion Clerides refused to consider. Although Turkey backed the Turkish Cypriot demand for regional autonomy, Günes, speaking for his government, offered an alternative plan that would have allowed the Turkish Cypriots the same amount of land by halving their holdings in the north and creating several autonomous Turkish enclaves elsewhere on the island. The Günes plan would have sharply reduced the number of refugees from both communities. Talks broke down, however, when Günes abruptly rejected a request from Mavros and Clerides for a three-day adjournment to enable them to communicate the Turkish proposal to their respective governments.

Two hours after the collapse of the Geneva talks, Turkish forces on Cyprus moved out of the Kyrenia bridgehead to cut off the northeastern third of the island. After three days of fighting, Clerides accepted a Turkish cease-fire offer that left the Turks in control of all territory north of a line that ran from Lefka in the west to Famagusta in the east. Ecevit held that this division should form the basis for two autonomous regions within a federal state. In February 1975, the Turkish Federated State of Cyprus was established in the northern region with Denktas as president. In 1983 this entity was constituted as the Turkish Republic of Northern Cyprus (TRNC). To date, only Turkey has granted official recognition to the TRNC.

The partition of Cyprus created about 200,000 refugees out of a population of about 600,000. About 10,000 Turkish Cypriot refugees from enclaves in the south were flown to northern Cyprus from British bases by way of Turkey. Greek Cypriot authorities protested this action and charged that at the same time the Turks were sending in settlers from Anatolia to colonize areas where Greek Cypriots had been dispossessed.

Relations between Turkey and Greece had already been tense before the Cyprus crisis as a consequence of the continuing dispute over competing rights in the Aegean region. Tensions heightened after March 1974, when Greek drillers struck oil off the island of Thasos. Given the dependence of both countries on oil imports, this development brought into focus a range of outstanding regional disputes: the demarcation of the continental shelf for the purpose of establishing seabed mineral rights, extension of territorial waters and airspace, and the militarization of Greek islands off the Turkish coast. A few months earlier, in late 1973, Turkey had granted oil concessions in several Aegean seabed areas, some of which were on part of the continental shelf claimed by Greece.

In January 1975, Greece submitted a claim to the International Court of Justice in The Hague for sole rights to the continental shelf. Greece claimed seabed rights off each of the several hundred Greek islands in the Aegean, some of them no more than a few nautical miles from the Turkish coast. Greece also unilaterally attempted to extend its territorial waters from six nautical miles to the twelve nautical miles accepted elsewhere in the world and prohibited Turkish overflights in those areas. Prime Minister Irmak responded that it was "unthinkable" that Turkey would accept the Aegean as a "Greek lake" and charged that Greek claims and alleged Greek militarization of the Aegean were in contravention of the 1923 Treaty of Lausanne. However, Greece maintained that it had primary responsibility for the defense of the Aegean as part of its NATO commitments.

During the summer of 1976, Turkish naval escorts confronted Greek warships when the latter challenged a Turkish vessel engaged in seismic research on the seabed in disputed waters between the Turkish islands of Gökçeada (Imroz) and Bozca Ada (Tenedos). For a brief period, war between the two NATO allies seemed imminent. Although Turkey and Greece subsequently agreed to settle outstanding disputes through negotiation, troop alerts and naval demonstrations were repeated the following year. Ecevit and Greek prime minister Konstantinos Karamanlis met in Switzerland in March 1978 to find a mutually acceptable framework for resolving their differences. Two months later, they met again in Washington to discuss issues of bilateral interest. At these meetings, the two leaders affirmed their mutual wish to find peaceful solutions to their unresolved disputes, but relations between the two countries remained strained.

In February 1975, the United States Congress imposed an arms embargo on Turkey on the grounds that United States-supplied military equipment had been used illegally during the Cyprus operation. In June Turkey confirmed that twenty United States installations in Turkey would be subject to a "new situation" unless negotiations were opened on their future status. President Gerald Ford urged Congress to reconsider the arms embargo, citing the damage it would do to vital United States interests in the eastern Mediterranean. Angered by the defeat in Congress the following month of a measure to lift the embargo, the Turkish government announced the abrogation of the 1969 defense cooperation treaty with the United States and placed United States installations, mainly communications and monitoring stations, under Turkish control. This action, however, did not affect the only United States combat unit in Turkey, an aircraft squadron based in Incirlik under NATO command.

President Ford signed legislation in October that partially lifted the embargo, allowing the release of arms already purchased by Turkey. In 1978 the administration of President Jimmy Carter succeeded in persuading Congress to end the embargo, although an amendment to the Security Aid Act required periodic review of conditions as a prerequisite to continued military assistance. Shortly thereafter, Turkey allowed United States installations to reopen under Turkish supervision while a completely new defense cooperation pact was negotiated.

In 1980 United States military assistance to Turkey amounted to US$250 million, and economic aid to about US$200 million. The United States also joined other countries of the Organisation for Economic Co-operation and Development (OECD) in pledging emergency credits in a bid to halt Turkey's slide into bankruptcy during the financial crisis of the late 1970s.

The Economy: An Unresolved Issue

The Turkish economy was severely hurt by the increase in oil prices after 1973. Conditions deteriorated over the next several years, reaching the crisis level by 1977. Inflation reached a rate exceeding 50 percent that year, while unemployment was unof-

Christian church carved into the rock in Göreme in central Anatolia
Courtesy Hermine Dreyfuss

ficially estimated at as high as 30 percent of the available workforce. Domestic industries also lost ground in export markets because of increases in the cost of raw materials and energy. Turkey's trade deficit reached US$4 billion in 1977, contributing to a balance of payments deficit nearly five times the 1974 level. Becoming skeptical of Turkey's ability to repay existing debts, a number of foreign creditors refused to extend further loans. As a result, the country virtually ran out of foreign exchange to meet its immediate commitments and was faced with national bankruptcy, which was averted only when the Central Bank intervened by suspending payments for many imports and, in effect, forced credit from foreign exporters.

Under pressure from the International Monetary Fund (IMF—see Glossary), the Demirel government belatedly announced such measures as a 10 percent devaluation of the currency and substantial increases of some government-subsidized prices. By the end of 1977, Turkey had accumulated a total external debt of more than US$11 billion. The Ecevit government came to power in January 1978 with a stabilization program that essentially had had to be approved by the IMF and the OECD. The plan included incentives for foreign investment and further price adjustments to restrain domestic demand. An international consortium of six banks collaborated in restructuring the Turkish debt and arranged for a US$500 million loan to the Central Bank for economic development. Subsidies to state-directed enterprises were cut, but Ecevit insisted on increased public spending for employment and regional development, which he argued were required to maintain "domestic peace."

Despite the stabilization program, another major devaluation of the Turkish lira (for value of the Turkish lira—see Glossary), and rescheduling of the foreign debt, there were no clear signs in 1978 that economic recovery was under way. In fact, austerities imposed under the program had the opposite effect to what was intended. Because of energy conservation efforts and restrictions imposed on imports of raw materials, industrial production fell. Consequently, exports lagged and unemployment continued to increase. State enterprises registered losses of about US$2 billion for the year. Because of a lack of confidence in the government, the stabilization program failed to attract new investment from abroad.

On returning to office in November 1979, Demirel proposed a new economic stabilization program that for the first time emphasized private-sector initiatives. The program, drawn up in consultation with a consortium of international banks, was approved by parliament, and Turgut Özal, an economist, was placed in charge of implementing it. Some progress was recorded, but the government's attention was diverted by intensified political violence, which by mid-1980 was claiming twenty or more lives a day.

Challenges to Public Order

Turkey faced recurrent political violence throughout the 1970s. Political parties, particularly those of the extreme right, organized strong-arm auxiliaries for street fighting. Kurdish nationalism and sectarian divisions were also factors. From time to time, specifically from 1971 to 1973 and again in December 1978, the frequency of such violence and the involvement of increasing numbers of persons led to the imposition of martial law in parts of the country.

Most of the violence-prone groups of the right were apparently attached, directly or indirectly, to Türkes and the MHP. The best organized of these, the Gray Wolves, were armed and regularly resorted to terrorist tactics. Other groups—particularly those on the left—used violence in the hope that the reaction of the state would lead to revolution. Their members assaulted politicians and public officials, the police, journalists, and members of rival groups. United States military personnel stationed in Turkey were also targets of attack. Some groups involved in the violence were identified with the Kurdish nationalist movement.

The Ecevit government initially tried to play down the significance of Kurdish separatism and to avoid actions that might alienate the many Kurds who supported the CHP and lead them to join extremist groups that they might otherwise ignore. Opposition members in the Grand National Assembly, who tended to identify any sign of restiveness in the Kurdish regions with Kurdish separatism, insisted on stronger measures from the government. In April 1979, the martial law that had been proclaimed in some parts of the country the previous December was extended to provinces with Kurdish-speaking majorities.

Estimates vary, but some sources claim that as many as 2,000 persons died in political violence in the two-year period 1978–79. The single most serious incident erupted in the town of Kahramanmaras in December 1978, when more than 100 persons were killed in sectarian conflict between Sunni and Alevi (see Glossary) Muslims. The incident led to the imposition of martial law in the Kahramanmaras Province that same month.

The military became increasingly uneasy over continued criticism of the armed forces in the Grand National Assembly. The apparent inability of successive governments to deal with problems of the economy and public order led many in the military to conclude that the 1961 constitution was defective. Their frustration with the political process was confirmed in September 1980, when the assembly was unable to fulfill its constitutional responsibility to elect a new president.

Military Intervention and the Return to Civilian Rule

Military Interlude

The summer of 1980 was a chaotic time in Turkey. Political violence and sectarian unrest mounted in the cities and spread through the countryside. The work of parliament had come almost to a standstill, and the country was left without an elected president. On September 5, Ecevit aligned the CHP with Erbakan and his NSP to force the resignation of Demirel's foreign minister, Hayrettin Erkman, whose strongly pro-Western views had won him the approval of General Staff officers. The next day, the NSP sponsored a massive rally at Konya, where Islamists (also seen as fundamentalists) demonstrated to demand the reinstatement of Islamic law in Turkey, reportedly showing disrespect for the flag and the national anthem. These acts were regarded as an open renunciation of Kemalism and a direct challenge to the military. On September 7, General Evren met secretly with armed forces and police commanders to set in motion plans for another coup.

In the early morning hours of September 12, 1980, the armed forces seized control of the country. There was no organized resistance to the coup; indeed, many Turks welcomed it as the only alternative to anarchy. Whereas the 1960 and 1971 military coups had institutional reform as their objective, the 1980 action was undertaken to shore up the order created by the earlier interventions. A five-member executive body, the National Security Council (NSC—see Glossary), was appointed. Composed of the service chiefs and the gendarmerie commander, it was headed by General Evren, who was recognized as head of state. On September 21, the NSC installed a predominantly civilian cabinet and named Bülent Ulusu, a recently retired admiral, prime minister. A 160-member Consultative Assembly subsequently was appointed to draft a constitution for what would become Turkey's Third Republic.

The first order of business for the military regime was to reestablish law and order in the strife-torn country. Martial law was extended to all the provinces. Suspected militants of all political persuasions as well as trade union and student activists were arrested, and party leaders were taken into custody along with a large number of deputies. Demirel and Ecevit were soon released but told to keep a low profile. When Ecevit began to publish political articles, he was rearrested and jailed for several months. The Grand National Assembly was dissolved and its members barred from politics for periods of up to ten years. Political parties were abolished and their assets liquidated by the state. The trade unions were purged and strikes banned. Workers who were striking at the time of the coup were given substantial pay raises and ordered back to their jobs.

Altogether, some 30,000 people were reported arrested in the first few weeks after the coup. Figures are uncertain, but a year later about 25,000 were still being held, and, after two years, an estimated 10,000 remained in custody, some without having been formally charged. Türkeş and nearly 600 of his followers from the MHP were tried on charges of committing or abetting terrorist acts. A number of those found guilty of terrorism were hanged. Erbakan and Türkeş were subsequently convicted of election tampering and given two-year prison terms. Turkey's international reputation suffered as a result of charges of political repression, arbitrary arrest, imprisonment without trial, torture, and other human rights violations. West European governments appealed to the military regime to restore parliamentary rule, and a portion of the OECD's relief package for Turkey was withheld. The European Community also suspended financial assistance, and Turkish delegates were denied their seats in the assembly of the Council of Europe.

The performance of the Turkish economy improved significantly in the first two years after the military intervention. The new regime saw to it that the economic stabilization program introduced by Demirel was implemented under the direction of Özal, one of the few members of the former government retained after the coup. Austerity measures were strictly enforced, bringing the inflation rate down to 30 percent in 1982. Disagreement developed within the government, however, over the strict monetarist policies promoted by Özal, which were seen in some quarters as running counter to Kemalist principles. Özal was forced to resign as minister of state in July 1982, when the country's largest money broker, the Kastelli Bank, collapsed.

Politics and the Return to Civilian Rule

The draft of a new constitution was presented by the Consultative Assembly to the nation on July 17, 1982. In providing for a strong presidency, it took partial inspiration from the 1958 constitution that established France's Fifth Republic. The constitution was put to a national referendum on November 7, 1982, and received approval from 91.4 percent of the electorate. The only parts of the country to register significant "no" votes were those with large Kurdish populations. Included in the vote was approval of Evren as president for a seven-year term. He took office on November 9, 1982.

A new law on political parties was issued in March 1983, which included a ten-year ban on all politicians active in the pre-September 1980 period. Parties were invited to form so as to contest parliamentary elections later in the year but were required to receive approval from the military rulers. Of fifteen parties requesting certification, only three received approval: the Motherland Party (Anavatan Partisi—ANAP), the Populist Party (Halkçı Partisi—HP), and the Nationalist Democracy Party (Milliyetçi Demokrasi Partisi—MDP), the latter being the clear favorite of the military.

The Motherland Party was led by Turgut Özal, who had helped formulate the economic stabilization plan under the 1979 Demirel government and then implemented the program under the military government. Özal was able to draw on support from a broad coalition of forces from the political landscape of the 1970s. The Motherland Party drew to its ranks adherents of the old Justice Party, the Islamist National Salvation Party, and the extreme right-wing Nationalist Action Party. The Populist Party, which came closest to expressing the traditional Kemalist values of the CHP, was led by Necdet Calp. The Nationalist Democracy Party was seen by the electorate as the party of the generals, who openly supported it. Its leader, Turgut Sunalp, was a retired general. The Motherland Party came to be viewed by the electorate as the most distant from the military, and its success in the first postcoup election may be largely attributed to this perception.

In parliamentary elections held on November 6, 1983, the Motherland Party won 45.2 percent of the vote and an absolute majority of seats in the new unicameral National Assembly. The Populist Party won 30.5 percent of the vote, and the Nationalist Democracy Party obtained only 23.3 percent of the vote. The results were widely viewed as a rebuke to the military.

Municipal elections followed the parliamentary elections early the following year. Prior to the March 25, 1984, election date, the assembly voted to allow some of the banned parties to participate. Among the new parties were the Social Democratic Party (Sosyal Demokrat Parti—Sodep), led by university professor Erdal Inönü, son of Turkey's second president, and the True Path Party (Dogru Yol Partisi—DYP), led unofficially by Süleyman Demirel. The Motherland Party continued as Turkey's leading party, claiming 41.5 percent of the vote nationwide; the Social Democratic Party drew 23.5 percent, and the True Path Party 13.5 percent. Another new party with a religious orientation, the Welfare Party (Refah Partisi—RP; also seen as Prosperity Party), garnered 4.5 percent.

The two parties that had competed with the Motherland Party in the previous general elections now appeared even weaker, receiving some 7 percent of the vote each. The 1984 municipal elections would be the last in which each would compete. In November 1985, the Populist Party merged with the Social Democratic Party, and in May 1986 the leadership of the Nationalist Democracy Party voted to dissolve the organization. Most of the party faithful found a new home in the broad spectrum that made up the Motherland Party; others joined the True Path Party. At this time, Ecevit also emerged with a rival left-of-center party, the Democratic Left Party (Demokratik Sol Partisi—DSP), officially led by his wife, Rahsan.

In national elections for local government officials held on September 28, 1986, Özal's party saw its popularity decline, although it still garnered a plurality of votes. The Motherland Party received 32 percent of votes cast, compared with 23.7 percent for the True Path Party, which emerged as the second largest party at a time when Demirel, its de facto leader, was still officially banned from politics. The product of a merger, the new Social Democratic Populist Party (Sosyal Demokrat Halkçı Parti—SHP) took 22.7 percent of the vote; the DSP drew 8.5 percent. Following this election, Özal found himself under increasing pressure to restore the political rights of the banned politicians. The assembly repealed the provisional article of the constitution that would have banned them from political activity until 1991.

Following the constitutional amendments, which also enlarged the National Assembly to 450 seats, the prime minister announced that assembly elections would be held early, on November 29. Özal also amended the election laws to increase the advantage to large parties, which under existing laws already stood to gain from minimum-threshold provisions and the manner in which extra seats were allocated. The Motherland Party saw its electoral percentage drop to 36.3 percent, nearly 10 percentage points below its 1983 total, but given the late amendments to the electoral law, the party retained an absolute majority in the assembly with 292 seats, or 65 percent of the total. The SHP won 24.8 percent of the vote and received 22 percent of the seats; Demirel's party won 19.2 percent of the vote but only 13 percent of the seats. The leader of the True Path Party denounced the late changes to the election law and dubbed the new government the "election-law government." None of the other parties competing reached the required 10 percent threshold; Ecevit's DSP received 8.5 percent of the vote, while Erbakan's Welfare Party received less than 7 percent.

In 1989, as Evren's term as president drew to an end, Özal announced that he would seek to succeed him. This decision was made despite the steadily declining popularity of Özal and the Motherland Party. In municipal elections on March 26, the Motherland Party polled only 21.9 percent of the vote, third behind the SHP's 28.2 percent and the True Path Party's 25.6 percent. On October 30, 1989, parliament elected Özal Turkey's eighth president. He was sworn in on November 9, after Bayar the second civilian in modern Turkish history to hold the position.

Özal's popularity declined steadily, largely because of problems in the economy. Of particular concern was the recurrence of high inflation, which had returned to precoup levels and was rapidly eroding the purchasing power of most Turks. Coupled with economic difficulties were widespread perceptions of government corruption and nepotism, which forced the resignation of several members of Özal's government.

In the summer of 1990, the crisis in the Persian Gulf resulting from Iraq's invasion of Kuwait gave Özal the opportunity to regain the political initiative. The Turkish government moved quickly to support UN sanctions against Iraq, on August 7 stop-

*Old-style house of Ottoman
times in Istanbul
Courtesy Hermine Dreyfuss*

ping the flow of oil through the pipeline from Iraq to Turkey's
Mediterranean coast. In September the assembly voted to allow
foreign troops onto Turkish soil and to authorize Turkish
troops to serve in the Persian Gulf. Opposition parties found
little to offer in the way of other options. Özal no doubt hoped
that Turkey's willing participation in the United States-led coalition would strengthen the country's image abroad as a crucial
ally, a particular concern in the post-Cold War world. Some
have speculated that he hoped Turkish involvement would lead
to EC admission, much as Turkey's participation in the Korean
War had provided the opportunity to join NATO. The government authorized the use of the air base at Incirlik by Allied aircraft in the bombing campaign against Iraq. In addition,
Turkish troops were deployed along the Turkish-Iraqi border,
although Ankara insisted that it did not intend to open a second front against Iraq and that it remained committed to Iraq's
territorial integrity.

In the aftermath of the Persian Gulf War, Iraqi Kurds
attempted to throw off the rule of Saddam Husayn in northern
Iraq, following encouragement by United States officials. The
uprising, which failed to receive support from the allied coalition, was quickly crushed, leading a massive number of Iraqi
Kurdish civilians to seek safety in Iran and Turkey. The Turkish
government was unable or unwilling to permit several hundred

thousand refugees to enter the country. The coalition allies, together with Turkey, proposed the creation of a "security zone" in northern Iraq. By mid-May 1991, some 200,000 Kurdish refugees had been persuaded to return to Iraq.

The collapse of the Soviet Union and its East European bloc had significant implications for Turkey's foreign policy. In the trans-Caucasian region of the former Soviet Union, the armed conflict between the newly independent republics of Armenia and Azerbaijan over the Nagorno-Karabakh region found the Turkish government trying to remain above the fray, despite popular sympathy for the Azerbaijani claims. Turkey sought close ties with the new republics of Central Asia, arguing that Turkey's experience as a secular republic could serve as a useful model for these states.

Relations with Bulgaria, which were strained by the faltering communist regime's persecution of ethnic Turkish Bulgarians in the late 1980s, improved following that regime's collapse. The new government abandoned the campaign of ethnic harassment. Elsewhere in the Balkans, Turkey maintained close relations with Albania and established contact with the Former Yugoslav Republic of Macedonia.

Relations with Greece continued to be complicated by longstanding differences over Cyprus and naval and air rights in the Aegean Sea. In 1986 Özal paid an official visit to the self-proclaimed Turkish Republic of Northern Cyprus, which to date remains without diplomatic recognition from any state other than Turkey. In March 1987, Greece and Turkey nearly came to blows over oil-drilling rights in the Aegean Sea. Nevertheless, both countries' governments displayed a willingness to emphasize diplomacy over force. In June 1989, Özal became the first Turkish prime minister to visit Athens in thirty-six years. Talks on the future of Cyprus, held under UN auspices, have remained inconclusive, and the island remains under a de facto partition after more than twenty years.

Turkey's 1991 parliamentary elections may have been the most significant since the restoration of civilian rule. Political power passed peacefully from the Motherland Party to its major rival, the True Path Party. In the vote held on October 21, Demirel's party won about 27 percent and captured the largest block of seats, 178. The Motherland Party, widely predicted as destined for oblivion, surprised its critics by polling some 24 percent of the vote and winning 115 seats. The SHP, which had expected to do better, won 20.8 percent of the vote, or eighty-eight seats. Left-of-center votes were split between the SHP and the DSP; the latter gained about 10.8 percent of the vote and seven seats. The Welfare Party appeared to do very well, with 16.9 percent and sixty-two seats, but this result reflected a strategic decision to join forces with another religiously oriented party in order to surpass the 10 percent threshold. Following the elections, the alliance was dissolved in the assembly. Although the Motherland and True Path parties were not too far apart ideologically, the personal discord between Özal and Demirel precluded any coalition arrangement. Instead, Demirel made common cause with Erdal Inönü's SHP, an alliance with the left that he had resisted throughout the 1970s. The coalition controlled 266 seats in parliament and reflected the support of almost 48 percent of the electorate.

Defining the place of the Kurdish ethnic minority in Turkey remained a difficult challenge throughout this period; indeed, it may have ranked as the primary challenge to domestic political stability. Given the founding principles of the Turkish republic, conceiving the country as the homeland of the Turks, any proposed recognition of Kurdish linguistic or cultural rights has been questioned on the grounds that such recognition would threaten the unity of the Turkish nation.

President Özal went farther than any Turkish official in extending recognition of Kurdish identity when, in January 1991, he proposed rescinding a law prohibiting the playing of Kurdish music or the use of Kurdish speech. Law 2932, passed in 1983 (declaring the mother tongue of Turkish citizens to be Turkish), was repealed in April 1991, thereby legalizing Kurdish speech, song, and music. Proposals were also floated for a relaxation of the ban on Kurdish in the print and broadcast media and in education, but such liberalization did not occur.

Since the restoration of civilian rule, Turkish governments have been faced with the armed insurrection of the Kurdistan Workers' Party (Partiya Karkeran Kurdistan—PKK). The PKK, one of several armed Kurdish guerrilla organizations, was founded by Abdullah Öcalan in 1978. Öcalan fled to Syria after the 1980 coup. The PKK, which was officially banned by the Turkish government, began a sustained guerrilla campaign in March 1984, timed to coincide with the beginning of the Kurdish new year. The conflict, which between 1984 and 1994 claimed about 12,000 lives, showed no signs of abating by the early 1990s. The Turkish army was unable to defeat the PKK with military force alone, while the PKK was no closer to its goal of an independent Kurdish state in southeastern Turkey (see Political Parties, ch. 4; Kurdish Separatists, ch. 5).

Economic Stabilization and Prospects for the 1990s

In 1980 the rate of inflation was more than 100 percent at one point and stayed at 70 percent for most of the year. The economic stabilization program, begun before the coup, now proceeded unhindered by political resistance. The program aimed to improve Turkey's balance of payments, bring inflation under control, and create an export-oriented free-market economy. To achieve these goals, the plan sought devaluation of the lira on a continuing basis, increases in interest rates to reduce inflation and overconsumption, a freeze on wages, and a reduction in state subsidies. Exports were to be encouraged through subsidies for exporters, reductions in bureaucratic regulations, and the abolition of customs duties on imports needed for export-oriented industries. Foreign investment was actively encouraged by laws providing for easy repatriation of capital and export of profits,and the establishment of four free-trade zones.

The results of the ambitious programs of the 1980s were mixed. On the negative side, purchasing power declined 40 to 60 percent in the decade from 1979 to 1989. Inflation, which had been brought down to annual rates of 30 to 40 percent in the early 1980s, was back up to nearly 70 percent by 1988. The steady decline in Özal's popularity with the electorate can be attributed in large part to these disappointing results. The government continued to run a high deficit, partly because of its unwillingness or inability to end support of large state-owned industries. On the positive side, exports grew by an average of 22 percent each year between 1980 and 1987. Exports in 1979 amounted to US$2.3 billion; in 1988 the value of exports had increased to US$11.7 billion. Moreover, industrial exports rose in this period from less than 45 percent of all exports to more than 72 percent.

The government also undertook to modernize the country's infrastructure, emphasizing improvements in roads and telecommunications. In July 1988, a second bridge across the Bosporus was opened, paralleling the first bridge opened in 1973. Together with a bypass road around Istanbul, the bridges were intended to facilitate commercial traffic moving to and from Europe and the Middle East. Of perhaps the most long-term significance was the ongoing commitment to the Southeast Anatolia Project (Güneydogu Anadolu Projesi—GAP), a series of dams along the Tigris and Euphrates rivers that when completed would include hydroelectric plants as well as extensive irrigation works. The latter were projected to allow for the irrigation of 1.6 million hectares of land, or twice the area previously under cultivation. In addition, the plentiful hydroelectricity would supply energy for Turkish industry. Because of Turkey's inability to come to agreement with its downstream neighbors, Iraq and Syria, no international funds were made available for GAP. The project, consequently, was self-financed. In 1992 a milestone was reached with the opening of the Atatürk Dam on the Euphrates, northwest of Urfa.

On April 17, 1993, President Özal died suddenly of a heart attack. On its third ballot, on May 16, the assembly elected Süleyman Demirel as Turkey's ninth president. Demirel was succeeded by former economics minister Tansu Çiller, who became Turkey's first woman prime minister. She received nearly 90 percent of the votes cast in a special election for the leadership of the True Path Party. The smooth succession of power may be seen as evidence that civilian rule was firmly in place. Moreover, the accession of Çiller to the prime minister's office, the second highest position in the nation, showed the extent to which Atatürk's legacy, and in particular the political rights of women, was becoming ingrained in the Turkish body politic.

*   *   *

A useful introduction to Turkish history from antiquity to the 1980s is *Turkey: A Short History*, by Roderic H. Davison, updated to 1988. The most thorough scholarly survey of Turkish history to 1975 available in English is the two-volume *History of the Ottoman Empire and Modern Turkey*, by Stanford J. Shaw and Ezel Kural Shaw. For the modern period, Bernard Lewis's *The Emergence of Modern Turkey* remains useful. It may be supplemented by two recent works, Feroz Ahmad's *The Making of Modern Turkey* and Erik J. Zürcher's *Turkey: A Modern History*. Also useful for the period up to 1975 is *Modern Turkey*, by Geoffrey Lewis. Patrick Balfour Kinross has written the standard English biography of Atatürk, offering a sympathetic evaluation of Turkey's founding father. For contemporary Turkish history, see George S. Harris's *Turkey: Coping with Crisis*, Feroz Ahmad's *The*

Turkish Experiment in Democracy, 1950–1975, and Frank Tachau's *Turkey: The Politics of Authority, Democracy, and Development.* (For further information and complete citations, see Bibliography.)

Chapter 2. The Society and Its Environment

Christianity and Islam have long coexisted, as reflected in this scene in Kars in eastern Turkey.

THE OFFICIAL IMAGE OF TURKISH society promoted by the ruling elite since the 1920s is one of relative homogeneity. This image has been enshrined in successive constitutions of the republic, including the 1982 document, in which it is stated that "the Turkish state, with its territory and nation, is an indivisible entity. Its language is Turkish." In reality, however, Turkish society is a mosaic of diverse and at times contending ethnic and linguistic groups. The question, "Who is a Turk?," continued to provoke controversy in the mid-1990s.

Sociologists and other scholars, both Turkish and foreign, have noted that a majority of the population—estimated at the end of 1994 at 61.2 million—accepts as true Turks only those individuals whose native tongue is Turkish and who adhere to Sunni (see Glossary) Islam. This definition excludes a sizable minority of Turkish citizens from consideration as true Turks. The largest group within this minority is the Kurds, the overwhelming majority of whom speak Kurdish, an Indo-European language related to Persian, as their native tongue. In 1994 estimates of the size of the Kurdish minority in Turkey ranged from 10 to 20 percent of the country's total population. Since 1990 demands by Kurdish political leaders that the Kurdish minority be permitted to read, write, and speak Kurdish have created a major political issue in Turkey (see Political Interest Groups, ch. 4).

Although most adult Kurds are Sunni Muslims, perhaps as much as one-third of the total Kurdish population in Turkey belongs to a Shia Muslim sect known as Alevi (see Glossary). In addition to the Kurdish Alevi, many of the nation's estimated 700,000 to 1 million Arabs are Alevi. The Alevi Arabs—most of whom live in or near Hatay Province—also are known as Nusayri and maintain discreet ties with the Alawi (also seen as Alawites) of neighboring Syria. A significant number of Alevi are ethnic Turks.

The continued presence of linguistic and religious minorities conflicts with the elite's conception of a modern society that is Turkish-speaking and secular. This notion was an integral part of the social revolution begun after World War I by Mustafa Kemal (later known as Atatürk). Linguistic reform was essential to Atatürk's vision of the new Turkey, and the reconstituted Turkish language has been both a central symbol and a powerful mechanism for the establishment of a new national identity. Atatürk institutionalized the secularization of the country through measures that included abolishing the caliphate, disestablishing Islam as the state religion, suppressing the unorthodox but highly influential dervish—or mystical— orders, closing the religious courts, and ending locally based religious education (see Atatürk's Reforms, ch. 1; Secularist Reforms, this ch.). Under Atatürk's leadership, the ideologically secularist and modernist urban elite ended state support and patronage of Islamic institutions and attempted to make religion a matter solely of private conscience.

The result of Atatürk's reforms was the creation of two cultures: a secularized and Westernized elite culture and a mass culture based on traditional religious values. Prior to 1950, the elite's attitude toward traditional culture tended to be contemptuous in general and specifically hostile toward religious expression. Since 1950, however, the elite generally has become more tolerant of religion, or at least of orthodox Sunni Islam, and various political parties have attempted to conciliate religious interests, albeit within the framework of Atatürk's institutional secularism. Nevertheless, in the mid-1990s the single most significant distinction in Turkish society remained the gap separating the secular elite from traditional culture.

Since the early nineteenth century, Western-oriented secular education has been a major factor distinguishing the elite and traditional cultures. By 1908 a substantial portion of the governing stratum, particularly the military officers and higher-ranking members of the bureaucracy, had received a secular education in their youth. Their values, knowledge, and viewpoints separated them sharply from the illiterate, religiously observant, and socially traditional masses. The cultural difference between the educated and the uneducated, the urban and the rural, the modernist and the traditionalist, has continued to affect Turkish society in multiple, intertwined ways. The views of Atatürk, who articulated the values of the secular elite in the 1920s and 1930s, remain central in Turkey more than fifty years after his death. Atatürk identified "civilization" with the culture of Europe, contrasting it with what he said was the backwardness, ignorance, and obscurantism of the common people of Turkey. He actively promoted a "modern" Turkey that embraced the civilization of Europe as its inspiration and model. Since Atatürk's time, mediation between Turkey's two cultures has been and remains politically problematic. The emergence in the late 1980s and early 1990s of a relatively popular political party appealing to what it defined as Islamic values has tended to increase the polarization of the elite and nonelite cultures. In the mid-1990s, the Turkish government was attempting to reconcile this heretofore divisive trend.

In the early republican period of the 1920s and 1930s, civil and military officials occupied the unchallenged pinnacle of the social structure. Since that time, however, competing elements, especially businesspeople, industrialists, professionals, and employees of private organizations, have challenged the supremacy of the officials. As a result, the social complexion of the political elite has been in transition since the early 1980s, not just in Ankara and Istanbul but in other cities as well. In rural areas, however, and for the vast majority of the population, traditional forms and values, such as the centrality of family life and adherence to an ethical blueprint of behavior perceived in religious terms, have survived, although in altered form. Consequently, the balance between traditional and "modern" values remains uneasy.

Geography

Turkey is a large, roughly rectangular peninsula situated bridge-like between southeastern Europe and Asia. Indeed, the country has functioned as a bridge for human movement throughout history. Turkey extends more than 1,600 kilometers from west to east but generally less than 800 kilometers from north to south. Total land area is about 779,452 square kilometers, of which 755,688 square kilometers are in Asia and 23,764 square kilometers in Europe.

The European portion of Turkey, known as Thrace (Trakya), encompasses 3 percent of the total area but is home to more than 10 percent of the total population. Thrace is separated from the Asian portion of Turkey by the Bosporus Strait (Istanbul Bogazı or Karadeniz Bogazı), the Sea of Marmara (Marmara Denizi), and the Dardanelles Strait (Çanakkale Bogazı). The Asian part of the country is known by a variety of names— Asia Minor, Asiatic Turkey, the Anatolian Plateau, and Anatolia (Anadolu). The term *Anatolia* is most frequently used in specific reference to the large, semiarid central plateau, which is rimmed by hills and mountains that in many places limit access to the fertile, densely settled coastal regions. Astride the straits separating the two continents, Istanbul is the country's primary industrial, commercial, and intellectual center. However, the Anatolian city of Ankara, which Atatürk and his associates picked as the capital of the new republic, is the political center of the country and has emerged as an important industrial and cultural center in its own right (see fig. 1).

External Boundaries

Turkey is bounded by eight countries and six bodies of water. Surrounded by water on three sides and protected by high mountains along its eastern border, the country generally has well-defined natural borders. Its demarcated land frontiers were settled by treaty early in the twentieth century and have since remained stable. The boundary with Greece—206 kilometers—was confirmed by the Treaty of Lausanne in 1923, which resolved persistent boundary and territorial claims involving areas in Thrace and provided for a population exchange (see War of Independence, ch. 1). Under the agreement, most members of the sizable Greek-speaking community of western Turkey were forced to resettle in Greece, and the majority of the Turkish-speaking residents of Greek Thrace were removed to Turkey. The 1923 treaty also confirmed Turkey's 240-kilometer boundary with Bulgaria.

Since 1991 the more than 500-kilometer boundary with the former Soviet Union, which was defined in the 1921 treaties of Moscow and Kars, has formed Turkey's borders with the independent countries of Armenia (268 kilometers), Azerbaijan (nine kilometers), and Georgia (252 kilometers). The 499-kilometer boundary with Iran was confirmed by treaty in 1937. Turkey's two southern neighbors, Iraq and Syria, had been part of the Ottoman Empire up to 1918. According to the terms of the Treaty of Lausanne, Turkey ceded all its claims to these two countries, which had been organized as League of Nations mandates under the governing responsibility of Britain and France, respectively. Turkey and Britain agreed on the 331-kilometer boundary between Turkish and Iraqi territory in the 1926 Treaty of Angora (Ankara). Turkey's boundary with Syria—822 kilometers long—has not been accepted by Syria. As a result of the Treaty of Lausanne, the former Ottoman Sanjak (province) of Alexandretta (present-day Hatay Province) was ceded to Syria. However, France agreed in June 1939 to transfer Hatay Province to Turkish sovereignty, despite the strong objections of Syria's political leaders. Since achieving independence in 1946, Syria has harbored a lingering resentment over the loss of the province and its principal towns of Antakya and Iskenderun (formerly Antioch and Alexandretta). This issue has continued to be an irritant in Syrian-Turkish relations.

Geology

Turkey's varied landscapes are the product of complex earth movements that have shaped Anatolia over thousands of years and still manifest themselves in fairly frequent earthquakes and occasional volcanic eruptions. Except for a relatively small portion of its territory along the Syrian border that is a continuation of the Arabian Platform, Turkey geologically is part of the great Alpine belt that extends from the Atlantic Ocean to the Himalaya Mountains. This belt was formed during the Tertiary Period (about 65 million to 1.6 million B.C.), as the Arabian, African, and Indian continental plates began to collide with the Eurasian plate, and the sedimentary layers laid down by the prehistoric Tethyan Sea buckled, folded, and contorted. The intensive folding and uplifting of this mountain belt was accompanied by strong volcanic activity and intrusions of igneous rock material, followed by extensive faulting during the Quaternary Period, which began about 1.6. million B.C. This folding and faulting process is still at work, as the Turkish and Aegean plates, moving south and southwest, respectively, continue to collide. As a result, Turkey is one of the world's more active earthquake and volcano regions.

Earthquakes range from barely perceptible tremors to major movements measuring five or higher on the open-ended Richter scale. Earthquakes measuring more than six can cause massive damage to buildings and, especially if they occur on winter nights, numerous deaths and injuries. Turkey's most severe earthquake in the twentieth century occurred in Erzincan on the night of December 28–29, 1939; it devastated most of the city and caused an estimated 160,000 deaths. Earthquakes of moderate intensity often continue with sporadic aftershocks over periods of several days or even weeks. The most earthquake-prone part of Turkey is an arc-shaped region stretching from the general vicinity of Kocaeli to the area north of Lake Van on the border with Armenia and Georgia (see fig. 7).

Turkey's terrain is structurally complex. A central massif composed of uplifted blocks and downfolded troughs, covered by recent deposits and giving the appearance of a plateau with rough terrain, is wedged between two folded mountain ranges that converge in the east. True lowland is confined to the Ergene Plain in Thrace, extending along rivers that discharge into the Aegean Sea or the Sea of Marmara, and to a few narrow coastal strips along the Black Sea and Mediterranean Sea coasts. Nearly 85 percent of the land is at an elevation of at least 450 meters; the median altitude of the country is 1,128 meters. In Asiatic Turkey, flat or gently sloping land is rare and largely confined to the deltas of the Kızılırmak River, the coastal plains of Antalya and Adana, and the valley floors of the Gediz River and the Büyükmenderes River, and some interior high plains in Anatolia, mainly around Tuz Gölü (Salt Lake) and Konya Ovası (Konya Basin). Moderately sloping terrain is limited almost entirely outside Thrace to the hills of the Arabian Platform along the border with Syria.

More than 80 percent of the land surface is rough, broken, and mountainous, and therefore is of limited agricultural value (see Agriculture, ch. 3). The terrain's ruggedness is accentuated in the eastern part of the country, where the two mountain ranges converge into a lofty region with a median elevation of more than 1,500 meters, which reaches its highest point along the borders with Armenia, Azerbaijan, and Iran. Turkey's highest peak, Mount Ararat (Agrı Dagı)—about 5,166 meters high—is situated near the point where the boundaries of the four countries meet.

Landform Regions

Distinct contrasts between the interior and periphery of Turkey are manifested in its landform regions, climate, soils, and vegetation. The periphery is divided into the Black Sea region, the Aegean region, and the Mediterranean region. The interior is also divided into three regions: the Pontus and Taurus mountain ranges, the Anatolian Plateau, and the eastern highlands. The seventh region of the country is the Arabian Platform in the southeast, adjacent to the Syrian border.

Black Sea Region

The Black Sea region has a steep, rocky coast with rivers that cascade through the gorges of the coastal ranges. A few larger rivers, those cutting back through the Pontus Mountains (Dogukaradeniz Dagları), have tributaries that flow in broad, elevated basins. Access inland from the coast is limited to a few narrow valleys because mountain ridges, with elevations of

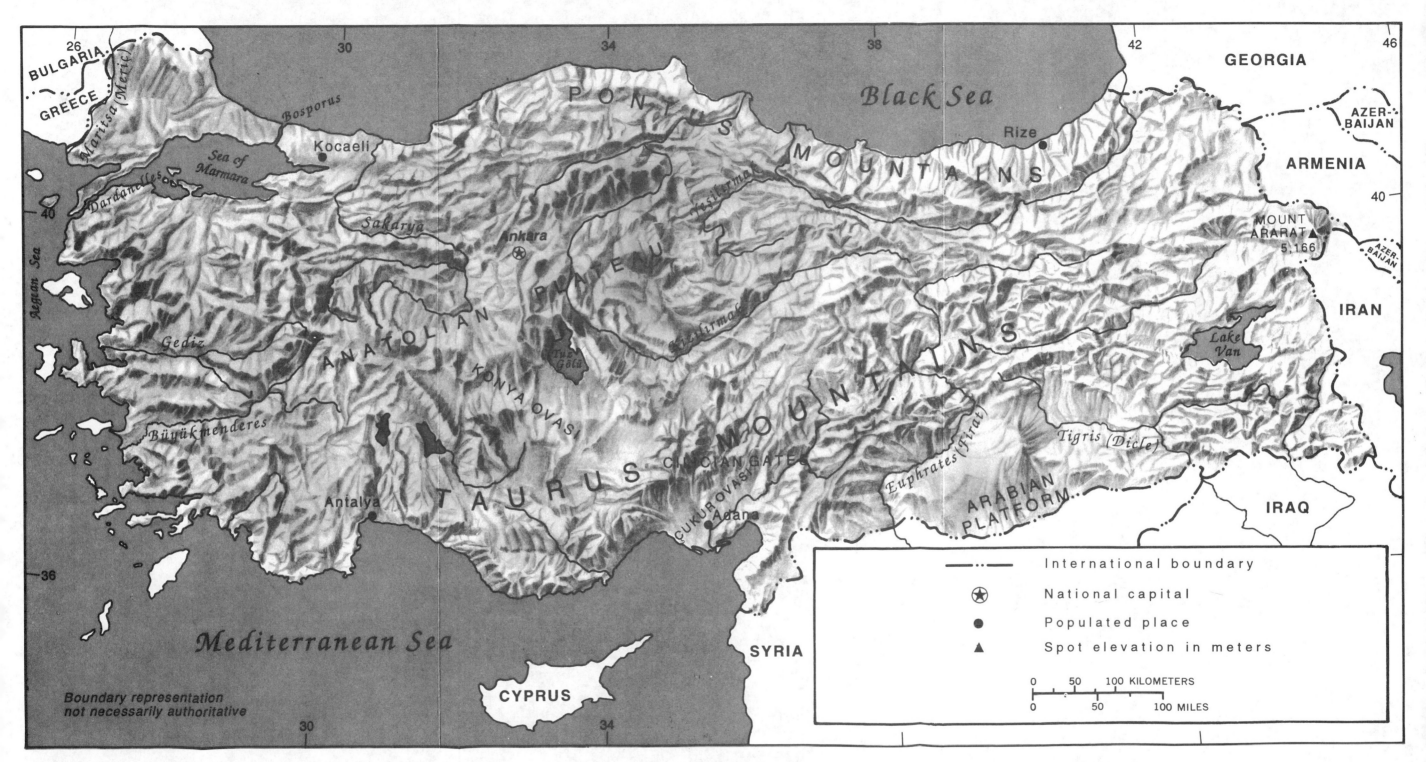

Figure 7. Topography and Drainage

80

1,525 to 1,800 meters in the west and 3,000 to 4,000 meters in the east, form an almost unbroken wall separating the coast from the interior. The higher slopes facing northwest tend to be densely forested. Because of these natural conditions, the Black Sea coast historically has been isolated from Anatolia.

Running from Zonguldak in the west to Rize in the east, the narrow coastal strip widens at several places into fertile, intensely cultivated deltas. The Samsun area, close to the midpoint, is a major tobacco-growing region; east of it are numerous citrus groves. East of Samsun, the area around Trabzon is world-renowned for the production of hazelnuts, and farther east the Rize region has numerous tea plantations. All cultivable areas, including mountain slopes wherever they are not too steep, are sown or used as pasture. The mild, damp climate of the Black Sea coast makes commercial farming profitable. The western part of the Black Sea region, especially the Zonguldak area, is a center of coal mining and heavy industry.

Aegean Region

The European portion of the Aegean region consists mainly of rolling plateau country well suited to agriculture. It receives about 520 millimeters of rainfall annually. Densely populated, this area includes the cities of Istanbul and Edirne. The Bosporus, which links the Sea of Marmara and the Black Sea, is about twenty-five kilometers long and averages 1.5 kilometers in width but narrows in places to less than 500 meters. Both its Asian and European banks rise steeply from the water and form a succession of cliffs, coves, and nearly landlocked bays. Most of the shores are densely wooded and are marked by numerous small towns and villages. The Dardanelles Strait, which links the Sea of Marmara and the Aegean Sea, is approximately forty kilometers long and increases in width toward the south. Unlike the Bosporus, the Dardanelles has few settlements along its shores.

On its Asian side, the Aegean region has fertile soils and a typically Mediterranean climate with mild, wet winters and hot, dry summers. The broad, cultivated valley lowlands contain about half of the country's richest farmland. Major crops are olives, citrus, nuts (especially almonds), and tobacco. The most important valleys are the Kocaeli Valley, the Bursa Ovası (Bursa Basin), and the Plains of Troy. The valley lowlands are densely populated, particularly around Bursa and Izmir, the country's third largest city and a major manufacturing center.

Mediterranean Region

The narrow coastal plains of the Mediterranean region, separated from Anatolia by the Taurus Mountains, which reach elevations of 2,000 to 2,750 meters, are cultivated intensively. Fertile soils and a warm climate make the Mediterranean coast ideal for growing citrus fruits, grapes, figs, bananas, various vegetables, barley, wheat, and, in irrigated areas, rice and cotton. The Cukur Ova in the east is a plain that is the most developed agricultural area of the Mediterranean region. It is a significant cotton-growing center and also supports a major cotton-based textile industry. In general, summers are hot and dry in the Mediterranean region. The weather in combination with the region's numerous sandy beaches has encouraged the development of a tourist industry.

Toward the east, the extensive plains around Adana, Turkey's fourth largest city, consist largely of reclaimed flood lands. In general, rivers have not cut valleys to the sea in the western part of the region. Historically, movement inland from the western Mediterranean coast was difficult. East of Adana, much of the coastal plain has limestone features such as collapsed caverns and sinkholes. Between Adana and Antalya, the Taurus Mountains rise sharply from the coast to high elevations. Other than Adana, Antalya, and Mersin, the Mediterranean coast has few major cities, although it has numerous farming villages.

Pontus and Taurus Mountains

The Pontus Mountains (also called the North Anatolian Mountains) in the north are an interrupted chain of folded highlands that generally parallel the Black Sea coast. In the west, the mountains tend to be low, with elevations rarely exceeding 1,500 meters, but they rise in an easterly direction to heights greater than 3,000 meters south of Rize. Lengthy, troughlike valleys and basins characterize the mountains. Rivers flow from the mountains toward the Black Sea. The southern slopes—facing the Anatolian Plateau—are mostly unwooded, but the northern slopes contain dense growths of both deciduous and evergreen trees.

Paralleling the Mediterranean coast, the Taurus (Toros Dagları) is Turkey's second chain of folded mountains. The range rises just inland from the coast and trends generally in an easterly direction until it reaches the Arabian Platform, where it arcs around the northern side of the platform. The Taurus Mountains are more rugged and less dissected by rivers than the Pontus Mountains and historically have served as a barrier to human movement inland from the Mediterranean coast except where there are mountain passes such as the Cilician Gates (Gülek Bogazı), northwest of Adana.

Frequently interspersed throughout the folded mountains, and also situated on the Anatolian Plateau, are well-defined basins, which the Turks call *ova*. Some are no more than a widening of a stream valley; others, such as the Konya Ovası, are large basins of inland drainage or are the result of limestone erosion. Most of the basins take their names from cities or towns located at their rims. Where a lake has formed within the basin, the water body is usually saline as a result of the internal drainage—the water has no outlet to the sea.

Anatolian Plateau

Stretching inland from the Aegean coastal plain, the Anatolian Plateau occupies the area between the two zones of the folded mountains, extending east to the point where the two ranges converge. The plateau-like, semiarid highlands of Anatolia are considered the heartland of the country. The region varies in elevation from 600 to 1,200 meters from west to east. The two largest basins on the plateau are the Konya Ovası and the basin occupied by the large salt lake, Tuz Gölü. Both basins are characterized by inland drainage. Wooded areas are confined to the northwest and northeast of the plateau. Rain-fed cultivation is widespread, with wheat being the principal crop. Irrigated agriculture is restricted to the areas surrounding rivers and wherever sufficient underground water is available. Important irrigated crops include barley, corn, cotton, various fruits, grapes, opium poppies, sugar beets, roses, and tobacco. There also is extensive grazing throughout the plateau.

The Anatolian Plateau receives little annual rainfall. For instance, the semiarid center of the plateau receives an average yearly precipitation of only 300 millimeters. However, actual rainfall from year to year is irregular and occasionally may be less than 200 millimeters, leading to severe reductions in crop yields for both rain-fed and irrigated agriculture. In years of low rainfall, stock losses also can be high. Overgrazing has contributed to soil erosion on the plateau. During the summers, frequent dust storms blow a fine yellow powder across the plateau. Locusts occasionally ravage the eastern area in April and May. In general, the plateau experiences extreme heat, with almost no rainfall in summer and cold weather with heavy snow in winter.

Eastern Highlands

Eastern Anatolia, where the Pontus and Taurus mountain ranges converge, is rugged country with higher elevations, a more severe climate, and greater precipitation than are found on the Anatolian Plateau. The region is known as the Anti-Taurus, and the average elevation of its peaks exceeds 3,000 meters. Mount Ararat, at 5,166 meters the highest point in Turkey, is located in the Anti-Taurus. Many of the Anti-Taurus peaks apparently are recently extinct volcanoes, to judge from extensive lava flows. Turkey's largest lake, Lake Van, is situated in the mountains at an elevation of 1,546 meters. The headwaters of three major rivers arise in the Anti-Taurus: the east-flowing Aras, which empties into the Caspian Sea; the south-flowing Euphrates; and the south-flowing Tigris, which eventually joins the Euphrates in Iraq before emptying into the Persian Gulf. Several small streams that empty into the Black Sea or landlocked Lake Van also originate in these mountains.

Most of eastern Anatolia comprises the area known historically as Kurdistan. In addition to its rugged mountains, the area is known for severe winters with heavy snowfalls. The few valleys and plains in these mountains tend to be fertile and to support diverse agriculture. The main basin is the Mus Valley, west of Lake Van. Narrow valleys also lie at the foot of the lofty peaks along river corridors.

Arabian Platform

The Arabian Platform is in southeast Anatolia south of the Anti-Taurus Mountains. It is a region of rolling hills and a broad plateau surface that extends into Syria. Elevations decrease gradually, from about 800 meters in the north to about 500 meters in the south. Traditionally, wheat and barley were the main crops of the region, but the inauguration of major new irrigation projects in the 1980s has led to greater agricultural diversity and development.

Climate

Turkey's diverse regions have different climates, with the weather system on the coasts contrasting with that prevailing in the interior. The Aegean and Mediterranean coasts have cool, rainy winters and hot, moderately dry summers. Annual precip-

Land formations once used for dwellings in central Anatolia
Farmer in eastern Turkey
Courtesy Hermine Dreyfuss

itation in those areas varies from 580 to 1,300 millimeters, depending on location. Generally, rainfall is less to the east. The Black Sea coast receives the greatest amount of rainfall. The eastern part of that coast averages 1,400 millimeters annually and is the only region of Turkey that receives rainfall throughout the year.

Mountains close to the coast prevent Mediterranean influences from extending inland, giving the interior of Turkey a continental climate with distinct seasons. The Anatolian Plateau is much more subject to extremes than are the coastal areas. Winters on the plateau are especially severe. Temperatures of –30°C to –40°C can occur in the mountainous areas in the east, and snow may lie on the ground 120 days of the year. In the west, winter temperatures average below 1°C. Summers are hot and dry, with temperatures above 30°C. Annual precipitation averages about 400 millimeters, with actual amounts determined by elevation. The driest regions are the Konya Ovası and the Malatya Ovası, where annual rainfall frequently is less than 300 millimeters. May is generally the wettest month and July and August the driest.

The climate of the Anti-Taurus Mountain region of eastern Turkey can be inhospitable. Summers tend to be hot and extremely dry. Winters are bitterly cold with frequent, heavy snowfall. Villages can be isolated for several days during winter storms. Spring and autumn are generally mild, but during both seasons sudden hot and cold spells frequently occur.

Population

Turkey's population at the end of 1994 was estimated at 61.2 million. This number represented an 8.4 percent increase over the 56.5 million enumerated in the twelfth quinquennial census, conducted in October 1990. The State Institute of Statistics (SIS) has estimated that since 1990 the country's population has been growing at an average annual rate of 2.1 percent, a decrease from the 2.5 percent average annual rate recorded during the 1980s. Turkey's population in 1985 was about 50.7 million, and in 1980 about 44.7 million. In the fourteen years from 1980 to 1994, the population increased nearly 37 percent.

Turkey's first census of the republican era was taken in 1927 and counted a total population of about 13.6 million. Less than seventy years later, the country's population had more than quadrupled. Between 1927 and 1945, growth was slow; in certain years during the 1930s, the population actually declined.

Significant growth occurred between 1945 and 1980, when the population increased almost 2.5 times. Although the rate of growth has been slowing gradually since 1980, Turkey's average annual population increase is relatively high in comparison to that of European countries. In fact, member states of the European Union (EU—see Glossary) have cited this high population growth rate as justification for delaying a decision on Turkey's long-pending application to join the EU.

The 1990 census is the most recent one for which detailed statistical data are available. That census revealed the relative youth of the population, with 20 percent being ten years of age or under (see table 4, Appendix A). About 50.5 percent of the population was male, and 49.5 percent female. The average life expectancy for females of seventy-two years was greater than the corresponding figure for men of sixty-eight years. The birth rate was twenty-eight per 1,000 population; the death rate was six per 1,000.

Population Density, Distribution, and Settlement

Population density has increased along with the relatively rapid growth rate. For example, although Turkey had an average of only twenty-seven inhabitants per square kilometer in 1950, this figure had nearly tripled, to 72.5 persons people per square kilometer, by 1990. Population density was estimated at 78.5 people per square kilometer at the end of 1994. According to the 1990 census, the most densely populated provinces included Istanbul, with 1,330 persons per square kilometer; Kocaeli, with 260; and Izmir, with 220. The most lightly populated provinces included Tunceli and Karaman, with seventeen and twenty-four persons, respectively, per square kilometer. Turkey's overall population density was less than one-half the densities in major EU countries such as Britain, Germany, and Italy.

Although overall population density is low, some regions of Turkey, especially Thrace and the Aegean and Black Sea coasts, are densely populated. The uneven population distribution is most obvious in the coastal area stretching from Zonguldak westward to Istanbul, then around the Sea of Marmara and south along the Aegean coast to Izmir. Although this area includes less than 25 percent of Turkey's total land, more than 45 percent of the total population lived there in 1990. In contrast, the Anatolian Plateau and mountainous east account for 62 percent of the total land, but only 40 percent of the population resided there in 1990. The remaining 15 percent of the population lived along the southern Mediterranean coast, which makes up 13 percent of Turkey's territory.

In 1990 about 50 percent of the population was classified as rural. This figure represented a decline of more than 30 percent since 1950, when the rural population accounted for 82 percent of the country's total. The rural population lived in more than 36,000 villages in 1990, most of which had fewer than 1,000 inhabitants (see Village Life, this ch.). For administrative purposes, a village can be a small settlement or a number of scattered rural households, jointly administered by a village headman (*muhtar*).

By 1995 more than 65 percent of Turkey's population lived in cities, defined as built-up areas with 10,000 or more inhabitants. The urban population has been growing at a rapid rate since 1950, when it accounted for only 18 percent of Turkey's total. The main factor in the growth of the cities has been the steady migration of villagers to urban areas, a process that was continuing in the 1990s. The trend toward urbanization was revealed in the 1990 census, which enumerated more than 17.6 million people—more than 30 percent of the total population—as living in nineteen cities with populations then of more than 200,000. The largest was Istanbul, with a population then of about 6.6 million, approximately 12 percent of Turkey's overall population. Two other cities also had populations in excess of 1 million: Ankara, the capital (about 2.6 million), and Izmir, a major port and industrial center on the Aegean Sea (about 1.8 million). Turkey's fourth and fifth largest cities, Adana (about 916,000 in 1990) and Bursa (about 835,000), have been growing at rates in excess of 3 percent per year, and each is expected to have more than 1 million inhabitants before 2000. Gaziantep in the southeast and Konya on the Anatolian Plateau were the only other cities with populations in excess of 500,000 in 1990. The ten largest cities also included Mersin (about 422,000), Kayseri (about 421,000), and Eskisehir (about 413,000).

Migration

During the decade 1915 to 1925, the country experienced large population transfers—a substantial movement outward of minority groups and an influx of refugees and immigrants. The first major population shift began in 1915, when the Ottoman government, for a variety of complex and in some instances contradictory reasons, decided to deport an estimated 2 million Armenians from their historical homeland in eastern Anatolia (see Armenians, this ch.; World War I, ch. 1). The movement of Greeks out of Turkey, which began during the 1912–13 Balkan Wars, climaxed in the 1920s with an internationally sanctioned exchange of population between Turkey and the Balkan states, primarily. In accordance with the 1923 Treaty of Lausanne, Turkey accepted approximately 500,000 Muslims, who were forced to leave their homes in the Balkans, in exchange for nearly 2 million Greeks, who were forced to leave Anatolia. By special arrangement, Greeks living in Istanbul and Turks living in the Greek part of Thrace were exempted from the compulsory exchanges.

After 1925 Turkey continued to accept Muslims speaking Turkic languages as immigrants and did not discourage the emigration of members of non-Turkic minorities. More than 90 percent of all immigrants arrived from the Balkan countries. Between 1935 and 1940, for example, approximately 124,000 Bulgarians and Romanians of Turkish origin immigrated to Turkey, and between 1954 and 1956 about 35,000 Muslim Slavs immigrated from Yugoslavia. In the fifty-five-year period ending in 1980, Turkey admitted approximately 1.3 million immigrants; 36 percent came from Bulgaria, 30 percent from Greece, 22.1 percent from Yugoslavia, and 8.9 percent from Romania. These Balkan immigrants, as well as smaller numbers of Turkic immigrants from Cyprus and the Soviet Union, were granted full citizenship upon their arrival in Turkey. The immigrants were settled primarily in the Marmara and Aegean regions (78 percent) and in central Anatolia (11.7 percent).

The most recent immigration influx was that of Bulgarian Turks and Bosnian Muslims. In 1989 an estimated 320,000 Bulgarian Turks fled to Turkey to escape a campaign of forced assimilation. Following the collapse of Bulgaria's communist government that same year, the number of Bulgarian Turks seeking refuge in Turkey declined to under 1,000 per month. In fact, the number of Bulgarian Turks who voluntarily repatriated—125,000—exceeded new arrivals. By March 1994, a total of 245,000 Bulgarian Turks had been granted Turkish citizenship. However, Turkey no longer regards Bulgarian Turks as refugees. Beginning in 1994, new entrants to Turkey have been detained and deported. As of December 31, 1994, an estimated 20,000 Bosnians were living in Turkey, mostly in the Istanbul area. About 2,600 were living in camps; the rest were dispersed in private residences.

In 1994 the government claimed that as many as 2 million Iranians were living in Turkey, a figure that most international organizations consider to be grossly exaggerated. Turkey is one of the few countries that Iranians may enter without first obtaining a visa; authorities believe that the relative ease of travel from Iran to Turkey encourages many Iranians to visit Turkey as tourists, or to use Turkey as a way station to obtain visas for the countries of Europe and North America. Consequently, as many as 2 million Iranians actually may transit Turkey—including multiple reentries for many individuals—in a given year. Specialized agencies of the European Union and the United Nations that deal with issues of migrants and refugees believe a more realistic figure of the number of Iranians who live in Turkey, and do not have a residence in Iran or elsewhere, is closer to 50,000.

In the 1960s, working-age Turks, primarily men, began migrating to Western Europe to find employment as guest workers. Many of these Turkish workers eventually brought their families to Europe. An estimated 2 million Turkish workers and their dependents resided in Western Europe in the early 1980s, before the onset of an economic recession that led to severe job losses. The Federal Republic of Germany (West Germany) initiated the program of accepting Turkish guest workers. In the 1990s, however, Germany adopted a policy of economic incentives to encourage the voluntary repatriation of Turkish workers. At the end of 1994, an estimated 1.1 million Turks continued to reside in Western Europe as semipermanent aliens. About two-thirds of these Turkish migrants lived in Germany, and another 10 percent in France. Other European countries with sizable Turkish communities included Austria, Belgium, the Netherlands, Sweden, and Switzerland. In addition, at least 150,000 Turks were working in Saudi Arabia and other Arab oil-exporting countries of the Persian Gulf.

Government Population Policies

For almost forty years after the establishment of the republic in 1923, the government of Turkey encouraged population growth. Use of contraceptives and distribution of information about them were prohibited by law, and the state provided financial incentives to encourage large families. During the 1950s, however, members of the political elite gradually became concerned that the country's relatively high population growth rate of nearly 3 percent was hurting economic development. Following the military coup of May 1960, population planning became a major government objective. A 1965 family planning law provided for the establishment of the Family Planning Division within the Ministry of Health and Social Assistance to extend birth control information and services to as many couples as possible. A 1967 law decriminalized abortion and authorized use of this procedure for a broad range of medical causes. Access to abortion was liberalized further by legislation in 1983 stipulating that a pregnancy could be terminated lawfully upon request in a public hospital up to ten weeks after conception. A married woman seeking an abortion was required to obtain her husband's permission or submit a formal statement of assumption of all responsibility prior to the procedure.

Family planning services have expanded considerably since the mid-1960s. A primary focus has been on educating couples about the material and health benefits of both limiting and spacing births. The Ministry of Health adopted the 1978 International Congress on Primary Health Care recommendations that family planning be combined with maternal and child health services and undertaken in cooperation with state hospitals, maternity hospitals, health centers, and clinics in both urban and rural areas. In addition to its support of public education about family planning, the ministry has solicited the cooperation of volunteer associations and international organizations to promote its programs. But despite concerted government efforts to encourage smaller families, Turkey's birth rate between 1965 and 1994 declined at a relatively slow pace, falling only from thirty-three to twenty-eight births per 1,000 population.

Concern about the continuing high birth rate prompted the Ministry of Health in 1986 to launch a new population control campaign that concentrated on rural areas, where the fertility rate was highest. The campaign included the construction of new health clinics, the expansion of centers training medical professionals in family planning counseling, and the enlistment of private-sector cooperation in the distribution of birth control information and materials in factories. Private businesses established the Turkish Family Health and Planning Foundation, which has supplemented the state's population control efforts since 1986 through its financial support for special training programs and nationwide television advertisements.

Religion has not been an impediment to birth control. Turkey's Sunni Muslim religious leaders, who have addressed the subject of birth control in religious publications, have stated that Islam does not prohibit married couples from trying to space births or limit the size of their families. The use of specific birth control devices generally has not been addressed in religious literature. However, during the early 1990s there appeared to be a consensus among religious leaders that the resort to sterilization or abortion as a means of birth control was not permissible under Islam.

Language Reform: From Ottoman to Turkish

Within the Ottoman Empire, the Turks had constituted merely one of many linguistic and ethnic groups. In fact, for the ruling elite, the word *Türk* connoted crudeness and boorishness. Members of the civil, military, and religious elites conversed and conducted their business in Ottoman Turkish, which was a mixture of Arabic, Persian, and Turkish. Arabic remained the primary language of religion and religious law (see Religious Life, this ch.). Persian was the language of art, refined literature, and diplomacy. At an official level, Ottoman Turkish usually was used only for matters pertaining to the administration of the empire. Ottoman Turkish not only borrowed vocabulary from Arabic and Persian but also lifted entire expressions and syntactic structures out of these languages and incorporated them into the Ottoman idiom.

The multiple linguistic influences on Ottoman Turkish caused difficulties in spelling and writing. The constituent parts—Turkish, Persian, and Arabic—belong to three different language families—Ural-Altaic, Indo-European, and Semitic, respectively—and the writing system fits only Semitic. Phonological, grammatical, and etymological principles are quite different among the three families. For these reasons, modernist intellectuals during the nineteenth century began to call for a reform of the language. They advocated a language that would be easier to read and write and contain more purely Turkish words. The principle of Turkish language reform thus was tied intimately to the reforms of the 1839–78 period (see External Threats and Internal Transformations, ch. 1). Later in the nineteenth century, language reform became a political issue. Turkish nationalists sought a language that would unite rather than divide the people. In the writings of Ziya Gökalp (d. 1924), Turkish nationalism was presented as the force uniting all those who were Turks by language and ethnic background.

With the establishment of the republic, Atatürk made language reform an important part of the nationalist program. The goal was to produce a language that was more Turkish and less Arabic, Persian, and Islamic; one that was more modern, practical, and precise, and less difficult to learn. The republican language reform called for a drastic alteration of both the spoken and the written language. This process was to be accomplished through two basic strategies—adoption of a new alphabet and purification of the vocabulary.

The language revolution (*dil devrimi*) officially began in May 1928, when numbers written in Arabic were replaced with their Western equivalents. In November the Grand National Assembly approved a new Latin alphabet that had been devised by a committee of scholars. Many members of the assembly favored gradually introducing the new letters over a period lasting up to five years. Atatürk, however, insisted that the transition last only a few months, and his opinion prevailed. With chalk and a portable blackboard, he traveled throughout the country giving writing lessons in the new Latin alphabet in schools, village squares, and other public places to a people whose illiteracy rate was suddenly 100 percent. On January 1, 1929, it became unlawful to use the Arabic alphabet to write Turkish.

The new Latin alphabet represented the Turkish vowels and consonants more clearly than had the Arabic alphabet. One symbol was used for each sound of standard Turkish, which was identified as the educated speech of Istanbul. By replacing the Arabic with the Latin alphabet, Turkey turned consciously toward the West and effectively severed a major link with a part of its Islamic heritage. By providing the new generation no need or opportunity to learn Arabic letters, the alphabet reform cut it off from Turkey's Ottoman past, culture, and value system, as well as from religion (see Atatürk's Reforms, ch. 1).

Atatürk and his language reformers viewed non-Turkish words as symbols of the past. They encouraged a national campaign, supported by government policies, to purify the language. Lexicographers began to drop Arabic and Persian words from dictionaries, substituting for them resurrected archaic terms or words from Turkish dialects or new words coined from old stems and roots. The Turkish Language Society (Türk Dil Kurumu), founded in 1932, supervised the collection and dissemination of Turkish folk vocabulary and folk phrases to be used in place of foreign words. The citizenry at large was invited to suggest alternatives to words and expressions of non-Turkish origin, and many responded. In 1934 lists of new Turkish words began to be published, and in 1935 they began to appear in newspapers.

Enthusiasm for language reform reached its height in the mid-1930s. Some of the suggested reforms were so extreme as to endanger the comprehension of the language. Although purists and zealots favored the complete banishment of all words of non-Turkish origin, many officials realized that some of the suggested reforms verged on the ridiculous. Atatürk resolved the problem with an ingenious political invention that, although embarrassing to language experts, appealed to the nationalists. He suggested the historically inaccurate but politically efficacious Sun-Language Theory, which asserted that Turkish was the "mother of all languages," and that therefore all foreign words originally were Turkish. Thus, if a suitable Turkish equivalent for a foreign word could not be found, the loanword could be retained without violating the "purity" of the Turkish language.

By the late 1940s, considerable opposition to the purification movement had emerged. Teachers, writers, poets, journalists, editors, and others began to complain publicly about the instability and arbitrariness of the officially sanctioned vocabulary. In 1950 the Turkish Language Society lost its semi-official status. Eventually, some Arabic and Persian loanwords began to reappear in government publications.

The language reform's long-term effects have been mixed. The phonetically designed alphabet based on the Latin script facilitated the quick acquisition of literacy. In addition, the developers of modern Turkish consciously incorporated scientific and technological terms. By making possible a uniform mass language that soon acquired its own literature, the reform also helped to lessen the linguistic gap between the classes, a legacy of Ottoman society. Although the newly created works lacked some of the rich connotations of the older lexicon, modern Turkish developed as a fertile literary language as prose writers and poets created powerful works in this new idiom, especially after 1950. The cost of language reform, however, has been a drastic and permanent estrangement from the literary and linguistic heritage of the Ottomans. Although some prerepublican writings have been transliterated into the new alphabet, the vocabulary and syntax are barely understandable to a speaker of modern Turkish.

Language and language reform continue to be political issues in Turkey. Each decade since Atatürk's death has been characterized by its own particular stance vis-à-vis language reform: whether to support a more traditional lexicon or a modern, Turkified one abounding in Western loanwords and indigenous coinages. Language reform and modern usage have pushed forward during periods of liberal governments and been deemphasized under conservative governments such as those of the 1980s. Meanwhile, religious publications have not been as affected by language reforms as secular literature. Religious publications have continued to use an idiom that is heavily Arabic or Persian in vocabulary and Persian in syntax. The emergence of a popular religious-oriented political movement in the 1990s has resulted in the reintroduction of many Islamic terms into spoken Turkish.

Linguistic and Ethnic Groups

Since the founding of the Republic of Turkey, the government has sought to diminish the significance of ethnic, linguistic, and religious distinctions. For instance, the 1965 census was the last one to list linguistic minorities. The country's largest minority, the Kurds, has posed the most serious and most persistent challenge to the official image of a homogeneous society. During the 1930s and 1940s, the government had disguised the presence of the Kurds statistically by categorizing them as "Mountain Turks." With official encouragement, some scholars even suggested that Kurdish, an Indo-European language closely related to Persian, was a dialect of Turkish. By the 1980s, the Mountain Turks' label had been dropped in favor of a new euphemism for Kurds: "Eastern Turks" (*dogulu*). Officials of the SIS were prosecuted after preparing guidelines for the 1985 census that instructed enumerators to list Kurdish, when appropriate, as a language spoken in addition to Turkish. The same official and popular confusion exists in the application of the term *Laz*, which sometimes is used erroneously to refer to the inhabitants of the eastern end of Turkey's Black Sea coastal region. In actuality, the Laz constitute a small ethnic group (26,007 according to the 1965 census), speaking Lazi, a Caucasian language that is neither Indo-European nor Altaic.

The 1982 constitution includes a seemingly contradictory policy on the use of non-Turkish languages. Whereas one article prohibits discrimination on the basis of language, other articles ban the public use of languages "prohibited by law." Although legislation forbidding the use of specific languages has never been enacted, many Kurdish citizens were arrested prior to 1991 on charges relating to the public use of Kurdish. Although speaking or reading Kurdish no longer is cause for arrest, at an official level there remains an entrenched bias against the use of Kurdish. At the end of 1994, for example, imprisoned Kurds still were required to communicate with their lawyers and visiting family members in Turkish, even if they did not speak or understand that language.

In a holdover from the Ottoman system of *millets* (see Glossary), Turks traditionally have tended to consider all Sunni Muslims as Turks and to regard non-Sunni speakers of Turkish as non-Turks. The revival of popular interest in religion since the early 1980s has reinvigorated popular prejudices against religious minorities, especially the adherents of the Shia Muslim sect, the Alevi, most of whom are ethnic Kurds or Arabs. Also, since 1984 the extensive migration of Kurds from the predominantly Kurdish and rural provinces of the southeast to the cities of western Turkey has resulted at the popular level in the emergence of a relatively strong, urban-based Kurdish ethnic consciousness and popular resentment of the Kurds' presence among ethnic Turks.

Turks

People identified as ethnic Turks comprise 80 to 88 percent of Turkey's population. The Turks include a number of regional groups who differ from one another in dialect, dress, customs, and outlook. In most cases, these differences reflect variations in historical and environmental circumstances. In general, regional differences are beginning to decrease while differences arising from urbanization and social class stratification are assuming greater importance. The three most important Turkish groups are the Anatolian Turks, the Rumelian Turks (primarily immigrants from former Ottoman territories in the Balkans and their descendants), and the Central Asian Turks (Turkic-speaking immigrants from the Caucasus region, southern Russia, and Central Asia and their descendants).

The Anatolian Turks historically lived on the central Anatolian Plateau in isolated villages and small towns. Following the implementation of the Ottoman Land Code in the late 1860s, rural Anatolian Turks were likely to own their own land, cultivating wheat and other cereal grains in addition to herding sheep and goats. During the early republican period, the Anatolian Turks' reputation for physical toughness and obstinate patience was applied to all Turks, and the Anatolians' culture, albeit as interpreted by the urban elite, became part of the foundation of Turkish nationalism. The Turks who lived in the coastal stretches along the Black, Aegean, and Mediterranean seas also were considered Anatolian Turks, although the more diverse and agreeable climate of the coastal areas encouraged the evolution of cultural patterns different from those predominating on the interior plateau. However, extensive industrialization, urbanization, and village-to-city migration since 1960 have tended to minimize regional differences, creating instead new class and occupational distinctions. Despite the social and economic changes, transhumance has remained an efficient means of raising livestock on the Anatolian Plateau, and as many as 1 million Turks were seminomadic herders of sheep and goats in the early 1990s. Included in this population were an estimated 600,000 Yürüks, Turks of Asiatic origin, whom the government has not officially recognized as a separate group.

The Rumelian Turks are descended from Turks who settled in the Balkans when, from the fifteenth to the nineteenth centuries, that region of southern Europe was part of the Ottoman Empire. They were stranded when imperial territories began acquiring national independence in the nineteenth century (see Migration, this ch.). Most of the Rumelian Turks resettled in Turkey between 1878 and 1924. In rural areas, Rumelian Turks tended to become farmers or artisans in the coastal villages evacuated by Greeks during the 1920s population exchanges. Rumelian Turks also settled in urban centers, especially Edirne, Tekirdag, Kirklareli, Nigde, Bilecik, and Bursa.

The Central Asian Turks include Crimean Tartars and Turkomans. They live in scattered communities in various parts of the country; for example, there are several Crimean Tartar villages in the vicinity of Eskisehir. In 1945 an estimated 10,000 people spoke Tartar as their first language; since then several thousand additional Crimean Tartars have resettled in Turkey. The Turkomans, who speak a Turkic dialect distinct from Anatolian Turkish, have lived in eastern Turkey for several centuries. Historically, Turkomans were organized by tribe; tribal affiliations still retained importance for some Turkomans in

1995. Since the establishment of the republic, no reliable estimate of the number of Turkomans has been published. Traditionally, Turkomans have been Shia Muslims; scholars believe that most still adhere to Shia Islam.

Kurds

Turkey's largest non-Turkish ethnic group, the Kurds, are concentrated in eleven provinces of the southeast, the same area that their ancestors inhabited when Xenophon mentioned the Kurds in the fifth century B.C. There also are isolated Kurdish villages in other parts of Turkey. Kurds have been migrating to Istanbul for centuries, and since 1960 they have migrated to almost all other urban centers as well. There are Kurdish neighborhoods, for example, in many of the *gecekondus* (see Glossary) or shantytowns, which have grown up around large cities in western Turkey. About half of all Kurds worldwide live in Turkey. Most of the rest live in adjacent regions of Iran, Iraq, and Syria. Turkey's censuses do not list Kurds as a separate ethnic group. Consequently, there are no reliable data on their total numbers. In 1995 estimates of the number of Kurds in Turkey ranged from 6 million to 12 million.

Because of the size of the Kurdish population, the Kurds are perceived as the only minority that could pose a threat to Turkish national unity. Indeed, there has been an active Kurdish separatist movement in southeastern Turkey since 1984 (see Political Parties, ch. 4). The government's main strategy for assimilating the Kurds has been language suppression. Yet, despite official attempts over several decades to spread Turkish among them, most Kurds have retained their native language. In Turkey two major Kurdish dialects are spoken: Kermanji, which is used by the majority of Kurds, as well as by some of the Kurds in Iran and Iraq; and Zaza, spoken mainly in a triangular region in southeastern Turkey between Diyarbakır, Ezurum, and Sivas, as well as in parts of Iran. Literate Kurds in Turkey have used Kermanji as the written form of Kurdish since the seventeenth century. However, almost all literary development of the language since 1924 has occurred outside Turkey. In 1932 Kurds in exile developed a Latin script for Kermanji, and this alphabet continued to be used in the mid-1990s.

Prior to the 1980 military coup, government authorities considered Kurdish one of the unnamed languages banned by law. Use of Kurdish was strictly prohibited in all government institutions, including the courts and schools. Nevertheless, during

Kurdish village on Mount Ararat (Ağrı Dağı)
Kurdish village in the mountains near Lake Van, eastern Turkey
Courtesy Hermine Dreyfuss

the 1960s and again in the mid-1970s, Kurdish intellectuals attempted to start Kurdish-language journals and newspapers. None of these publications survived for more than a few issues because state prosecutors inevitably found legal pretexts for closing them down. Between 1980 and 1983, the military government passed several laws expressly banning the use of Kurdish and the possession of written or audio materials in Kurdish.

The initiation of armed insurrection by the Kurdistan Workers' Party (Partiya Karkere Kurdistan—PKK) in 1984, along with the increasing international media interest in the Kurds of Iraq beginning in the mid-1980s, compelled some members of Turkey's political elite to question government policy toward the country's Kurdish population. Turgut Özal, who became prime minister in 1983 and president in 1989, broke the official taboo on using the term *Kurd* by referring publicly to the people of eastern Anatolia as Kurds. Subsequently, independent Turkish newspapers began using the term and discussing the political and economic problems in the eleven predominantly Kurdish provinces. In 1991 Özal supported a bill that revoked the ban on the use of Kurdish and possession of materials in Kurdish. However, as of 1995, the use of Kurdish in government institutions such as the courts and schools still was prohibited.

Although the Kurds comprise a distinct ethnic group, they are divided by class, regional, and sectarian differences similar to those affecting ethnic Turks. Religious divisions often have been a source of conflict among the Kurds. Although the government of Turkey does not compile official data on religious affiliation, scholars estimate that at least two-thirds of the Kurds in Turkey nominally are Sunni Muslims, and that as many as one-third are Shia Muslims of the Alevi sect. Unlike the Sunni Turks, who follow the Hanafi school of Islamic law, the Sunni Kurds follow the Shafii school. Like their Turkish counterparts, adult male Kurds with religious inclinations tend to join Sufi brotherhoods. The Naksibendi and Kadiri orders, both of which predate the republic, have large Kurdish followings in Turkey although their greatest strength is among the Kurds of Iran. The Nurcular, a brotherhood that came to prominence during the early republican years, also has many Kurdish adherents in Turkey.

Whereas the number of Kurds belonging to the Alevi sect of Shia Islam is uncertain, the majority of Alevi are either Arabs or Turks. Historically, the Alevi lived in isolated mountain communities in southeastern Turkey and western Syria. The Kurdish Alevi have been migrating from their villages to the cities of central Anatolia since the 1950s. Whereas Kurdish and Turkish Alevi generally have good relations, the competition between Alevi and Sunni Turks for urban jobs led to a revival of traditional sectarian tensions by the mid-1970s. These intertwined economic and religious tensions culminated in a series of violent sectarian clashes in Kahramanmaras, Corum, and other cities in 1978–79 in which hundreds of Alevi died.

A small but unknown number of Kurds also adhere to the secretive Yazidi sect, which historically has been persecuted by both Sunni and Shia Muslims. Small communities of Yazidi live in Mardin, Siirt, and Sanli Urfa provinces. Yazidi are also found among Kurds in Armenia, Iran, and Iraq. In Turkey the Yazidi believe that the government does not protect them from religious persecution. Consequently, as many as 50 percent of all Yazidi have immigrated to Germany, where they feel free to practice their heterodox form of Islam.

Class differences also divide the Kurds. Wealthy landowners in rural areas and entrepreneurs in urban areas tend to cooperate with the government and espouse assimilation. Many of these Kurds are bilingual or even speak Turkish more comfortably than Kurdish, which they disparage as the language of the uneducated. The economic changes that began in the 1960s have exacerbated the differences between the minority of assimilated Kurds and the majority who have retained a Kurdish identity. Militant Kurdish political groups such as the PKK have exploited these class differences since 1984.

Arabs

In 1995 Turkey's ethnic Arab population was estimated at 800,000 to 1 million. The Arabs are heavily concentrated along the Syrian border, especially in Hatay Province, which France, having at that time had mandatory power in Syria, ceded to Turkey in 1939. Arabs then constituted about two-thirds of the population of Hatay (known to the Arabs as Alexandretta), and the province has remained predominantly Arab. Almost all of the Arabs in Turkey are Alevi Muslims, and most have family ties with the Alevi (also seen as Alawi or Alawite) living in Syria. As Alevi, the Arabs of Turkey believe they are subjected to state-condoned discrimination. Fear of persecution actually prompted several thousand Arab Alevi to seek refuge in Syria following Hatay's incorporation into Turkey. The kinship relations established as a result of the 1939–40 emigration have been continually reinforced by marriages and the practice of sending Arab youths from Hatay to colleges in Syria. Since the mid-1960s, the Syrian government has tended to encourage educated Alevi to resettle in Syria, especially if they seem likely to join the ruling Baath Party.

Peoples from the Caucasus

Three small but distinct ethnic groups (aside from the more numerous Armenians) have their origins in the Caucasus Mountains: the Circassians, the Georgians (including the Abkhaz), and the Laz. Approximately 70,000 Circassian Muslim immigrants, most originally from Russia, gradually settled, beginning in the late eighteenth century, in the Adana region, where they and their descendants continue to live as farmers and farm laborers.

The Muslim Georgians and Laz are concentrated in the northeastern provinces. The Laz, who are primarily Black Sea fisherfolk, live in villages near the coastal city of Rize. The term *Georgian* actually refers to several different peoples who speak similar but mutually unintelligible languages. One distinct group of Georgians are the Abkhaz, who are primarily cultivators and herders. Most Georgians live in Artvin Province, particularly east of the Coruh River and along the border with Georgia.

Dönme

The Dönme are descendants of the Jewish followers of a self-proclaimed messiah, Sabbatai Sebi (or Zevi, 1626–76), who was forced by the sultan to convert to Islam in 1666. Their doctrine includes Jewish and Islamic elements. They consider themselves Muslims and officially are recognized as such. Their name is the Turkish word for *convert*, but it carries overtones of *turncoat* as well.

The Dönme have been successful in business and in the professions, but historically they have not been part of the social elite because neither Jews nor Muslims fully accept them. Experience with prejudice inclines some Dönme to hide their identity to avoid discrimination and also has encouraged the Dönme to become a tightly knit, generally endogamous group. Since the early 1980s, however, overt discrimination has lessened, and intermarriage between Dönme and other Muslims has grown common.

Men drinking tea, eastern Turkey
Courtesy Hermine Dreyfuss

Greeks

In 1995 fewer than 20,000 Greeks still lived in Turkey. Most of them are Eastern or Greek Orthodox Christians and live in Istanbul or on the two islands of Gökçeada (Imroz) and Bozca Ada (Tenedos), off the western entrance to the Dardanelles. They are the remnants of the estimated 200,000 Greeks who were permitted under the provisions of the Treaty of Lausanne to remain in Turkey following the 1924 population exchange, which involved the forcible resettlement of approximately 2 million Greeks from Anatolia. Since 1924 the status of the Greek minority in Turkey has been ambiguous. Most Turks do not accept the country's Greek citizens as their equals. Beginning in the 1930s, the government encouraged the Greeks to emigrate, and thousands, in particular the educated youth, did so, reducing the Greek population to about 48,000 by 1965. Although the size of the Greek minority has continued to decline, the Greek citizens of Turkey generally constitute one of the country's wealthiest communities.

Armenians

The tiny Armenian minority, estimated at 40,000 in 1995, also is a remnant of a once-larger community. Before World War I, some 1.5 million Armenians lived in eastern Anatolia.

103

Starting in the late nineteenth century, intergroup tensions prompted the emigration of possibly as many as 100,000 Armenians in the 1890s. In 1915 the Ottoman government ordered all Armenians deported from eastern Anatolia; at least 600,000 of the Armenians, who numbered up to 2 million, died during a forced march southward during the winter of 1915–16. Armenians believe—and Turks deny—that the catastrophe that befell their community was the result of atrocities committed by Turkish soldiers following government directives. Armenians outside Turkey refer to the deaths of 1915–16 as an instance of genocide, and over the years various Armenian political groups have sought to avenge the tragedy by carrying out terrorist attacks against Turkish diplomats and officials abroad (see Armenian Terrorism, ch. 5).

Most Armenians living in Turkey are concentrated in and around Istanbul. Like the Greeks, they are bankers and merchants with extensive international contacts. The Armenians support their own newspapers and schools. They are intensely attached to their Christian faith and their identity as Armenians rather than Turks. In addition, they have relatives in the Armenian diaspora throughout the world. The establishment of an independent Armenia on Turkey's eastern border following the dissolution of the Soviet Union in 1991 was a source of ethnic pride for the Armenians of Turkey. However, Armenia's conflict with Turkic Azerbaijan, combined with the jingoistic support of Azerbaijan in the Turkish media, has raised apprehensions among the Armenian minority about their future status in Turkey.

Jews

In 1995 an estimated 18,000 to 20,000 Jews lived in Turkey. During the first half of the twentieth century, the Jewish population remained relatively stable at around 90,000. Following the establishment of Israel in 1948, an estimated 30,000 Jews immigrated to the new state. An average of 1,000 Jews annually left for Israel during the 1950s and early 1960s. By 1965 the Jewish minority had been reduced to an estimated 44,000, most of whom lived in Istanbul, where many Jewish men operated shops and other small businesses.

Unlike the Armenians and Greeks, the Jewish minority is neither ethnically nor linguistically homogeneous. Most of its members are Sephardic Jews whose ancestors were expelled from Spain by the Roman Catholic Inquisition in 1492. They speak Ladino, a variant of fifteenth-century Spanish with borrowings from several other languages. The Ashkenazic minority—Jews from central and northern Europe—speak Yiddish, a German-derived language. Both languages are written in the Hebrew script. Most Jews also speak Turkish. The Karaites—viewed by most other Jews as herctics—speak Greek as their native language. In general, the different Jewish communities have tended not to intermarry and thus have retained their identities.

Religious Life

The institutional secularization of Turkey was the most prominent and most controversial feature of Atatürk's reforms. Under his leadership, the caliphate—office of the successors to Muhammad, the supreme politico-religious office of Islam, and symbol of the sultan's claim to world leadership of all Muslims—was abolished. The secular power of the religious authorities and functionaries was reduced and eventually eliminated. The religious foundations (*evkaf;* sing., *vakıf*) were nationalized, and religious education was restricted and for a time prohibited. The influential and popular mystical orders of the dervish brotherhoods also were suppressed.

Although Turkey was secularized at the official level, religion remained a strong force at the popular level. After 1950 some political leaders tried to benefit from popular attachment to religion by espousing support for programs and policies that appealed to the religiously inclined. Such efforts were opposed by most of the political elite, who believed that secularism was an essential principle of Kemalism. This disinclination to appreciate religious values and beliefs gradually led to a polarization of society. The polarization became especially evident in the 1980s as a new generation of educated but religiously motivated local leaders emerged to challenge the dominance of the secularized political elite. These new leaders have been assertively proud of Turkey's Islamic heritage and generally have been successful at adapting familiar religious idioms to describe dissatisfaction with various government policies. By their own example of piety, prayer, and political activism, they have helped to spark a revival of Islamic observance in Turkey. By 1994 slogans promising that a return to Islam would cure economic ills and solve the problems of bureaucratic inefficiencies had enough general appeal to enable avowed religious candidates to win mayoral elections in Istanbul and Ankara, the country's two most secularized cities.

Islam

Islam is a monotheistic religion. A believer is a Muslim, literally, "one who submits to God." Muslims believe that Allah (Arabic for God) gave revelations through the angel Gabriel to the Prophet Muhammad (A.D. 570–632), a native of the Arabian Peninsula city of Mecca. Muhammad's efforts to convert people to monotheism disturbed the merchant elite, who feared that his preaching would adversely affect the pilgrims who regularly visited Mecca, which in the early seventh century had shrines to several gods and goddesses. Mecca's principal destination for pilgrims was the Kaaba, a shrine housing a venerated black rock which over the years had been surrounded by various idols. The lack of acceptance by Meccans of Muhammad's preaching caused him and his followers in A.D. 622 to migrate to Medina in response to an invitation by that city's leaders. Muhammad's migration to Medina enabled him to organize the politico-religious community—the *umma*—that marked the beginning of Islam as a political movement as well as a religious faith. Thus, the date of the migration, or *hicret* (from the Arabic *hijra*), was adopted by the Muslim community as the beginning of the Islamic era. The Islamic calendar is based on a lunar year, which averages eleven days less than a solar year. The Islamic calendar is used in Turkey for religious purposes.

By the time of the Prophet's death ten years after his migration to Medina, most of the Arabian Peninsula, including the city of Mecca, had converted to Islam. During the last two years of his life, Muhammad led fellow Muslims on pilgrimages to Mecca, where the Kaaba was relieved of its idols and dedicated to the worship of Allah. Since then, praying at the Kaaba has been the ultimate goal of the pilgrimage, or hajj, which every able-bodied adult Muslim is expected to make at least once in his or her lifetime.

Tenets of Islam

Muslims believe that all of Allah's revelations to the Prophet are contained in the Kuran (in Arabic, Quran), which is composed in rhymed prose. The Kuran consists of 114 chapters, called *suras*, the first of which is a short "opening" chapter. The remaining 113 segments are arranged roughly in order of decreasing length. The short *suras* at the end of the book are early revelations, each consisting of material revealed on the same occasion. The longer *suras* toward the beginning of the book are compilations of verses revealed at different times in Muhammad's life.

The central beliefs of Islam are monotheism and Muhammad's status as the "seal of the Prophets," that is, the final prophet to whom God revealed messages for the spiritual guidance of humanity. Jesus Christ and the prophets of the Old Testament are also accepted as Islamic prophets. Muslims who profess belief in God and Muhammad's prophethood, pray regularly, and live by Islamic ethical and moral principles are assured that their souls will find eternal salvation in heaven. The profession of belief in one God and the prophethood of Muhammad is known as the *sahadet* (in Arabic, *shahada*), and is one of the five basic obligations or "pillars" of Islam. The profession of faith—"There is no God but God and Muhammad is his Prophet"—always is recited in Arabic. It is repeated during prayer and on many other ritual occasions.

The four other pillars of Islam are prayer (*namaz; salat* in Arabic), giving alms to the needy (*zekat; zakah* in Arabic), fasting (*oruç; sawm* in Arabic) during the month of Ramazan (from the Arabic, *Ramadan*), and the pilgrimage (*hac,* from the Arabic *hajj*) to Mecca. The prescribed prayers are recited in Arabic and are accompanied by a series of ritual body movements meant to demonstrate submission to God: standing, bowing, kneeling, and full prostration. Muslims say the prayers at five prescribed times a day, always while facing in the direction of Mecca. Prayers are preceded by a ritual ablution, and, unless the prayer is said in a mosque, a ritual purification of the ground is achieved by the unrolling of a clean prayer rug. Although it is permissible to pray almost anywhere, men pray in congregation at mosques whenever possible, especially on Fridays. Women are not required to pray in public but may attend worship at mosques, which maintain separate sections for women. Despite more than sixty years of secularist government policies, a majority of Turkey's Muslims continue to recite prayers at least occasionally. In fact, mosque attendance in the urban areas, which formerly was significantly less than in rural areas, increased considerably during the 1980s. During the early 1990s, most city mosques were filled to capacity on Fridays and religious holidays.

The third pillar of Islam, almsgiving, is required of all Muslims. The faithful are expected to give in proportion to their wealth. In various historical periods, *zekat* assumed the status of a tithe that mosques collected and distributed for charitable purposes. In addition to *zekat*, Muslims are encouraged to make free-will gifts (*sadaka*, from the Arabic *sadaqa*).

Abstinence from dawn to dusk from all food and beverages during the Islamic month of Ramazan is the fourth pillar of the faith required of Muslims. Persons who are ill; women who are pregnant, nursing, or menstruating; soldiers on duty; travelers on necessary journeys; and young children are exempted from the fast. However, adults who are unable to fast during Ramazan are expected to observe a fast later. Ramazan is a period of spiritual renewal, and the daytime fasting is meant to help concentrate a Muslim's thoughts on religious matters. Many mosques, especially in urban areas, sponsor special prayer meetings and study groups during the month. The evening meal that breaks the fast has special religious significance and also is an occasion for sharing among families and friends. Muslims who can afford to do so often host one or more fast-breaking meals for indigents during Ramazan. The month of fasting is followed by a three-day celebration, Seker Bayramı (in Arabic, Id al Fitr), which is observed in Turkey as a national holiday.

The fifth pillar of Islam is the *hac*. Each Muslim who is financially and physically able is expected at least once in his or her lifetime to make the pilgrimage to Mecca and participate in prescribed religious rites performed at various specific sites in the holy city and its environs during the twelfth month of the lunar calendar. In one of their most important rites, pilgrims pray while circumambulating the Kaaba, the sanctuary Muslims believe Ibrahim (Abraham) and his son Ismail (Ishmael) built to honor the one God. During the *hac*, pilgrims sacrifice domesticated animals such as sheep and distribute the meat among the needy. Known as the Feast of Sacrifice, Kurban Bayramı (in Arabic, Id al Adha), this occasion is celebrated not only by the pilgrims but by all Muslims, and is observed in Turkey as a national holiday. The returning pilgrim is entitled to use the honorific *haci* (in Arabic, *hajji*) before his or her name, a title that indicates successful completion of the pilgrimage.

A pious Muslim strives to follow a code of ethical conduct that encourages generosity, fairness, chastity, honesty, and respect. Certain acts, including murder, cruelty, adultery, gambling, and usury, are considered contrary to Islamic practice. Muslims also are enjoined not to consume carrion, blood, pork, or alcohol. Many of the precepts for appropriate behavior are specified in the Kuran. Other spiritual and ethical guidelines are found in the *hadis* (in Arabic, *hadith*), an authenticated record of the sayings and actions of Muhammad and his earliest companions. Devout Muslims regard their words, acts, and decisions—called collectively the *sunna*—as models to be emulated by later generations. Because of its normative character, the *sunna* is revered along with the Kuran as a primary source of *seriat* (in Arabic, *sharia*), or Islamic law.

Islamic law evolved between the eighth and tenth centuries. Islamic scholars reputed for their knowledge of the Kuran, *hadis*, and *sunna* were accepted as authoritative interpreters of *seriat*. Several of them compiled texts of case law that formed the basis of legal schools. Eventually, Sunni Muslims came to accept four schools of law as equally valid. Two schools of *seriat* exist in contemporary Turkey: the Hanafi, founded by Iraqi theologian Abu Hanifa (ca. 700–67), and the Shafii, founded by the Meccan jurist Muhammad ash Shafii (767–820). Most Muslim Turks follow the Hanafi school, whereas most Sunni Kurds follow the Shafii school.

Early Development

Following the death of the Prophet in 632, the Muslim community failed to reach consensus on who should succeed him as the caliph. A majority of Muhammad's close followers supported the idea of an elected caliph, but a minority believed that leadership, or the imamate, should remain within the Prophet's family, passing first to Muhammad's cousin, son-in-law, and principal deputy, Ali ibn Abu Talib, and subsequently to Ali's sons and their male descendants. The majority, who believed they were following the *sunna* of the Prophet, became known as Sunni Muslims. To them, the caliph was the symbolic religious head of the community; however, caliphs would also rule as the secular leaders of a major empire for six centuries. The first four caliphs—Abu Bakr, Omar, Osman, and Ali—were chosen by a consensus of Muslim leaders. Subsequently, however, the caliphate was converted by its holders into a hereditary office, the first two dynasties being the Umayyad, which ruled from Damascus, and the second being the Abbasid, which ruled from Baghdad. After the Mongols captured Baghdad and executed the Abbasid caliph in 1258, a period of more than 250 years followed when no one was recognized as caliph by all Sunni Muslims. During the sixteenth century, the Ottoman Dynasty resurrected the title, and gradually even Muslims outside the Ottoman Empire came to accept the Ottoman sultan as the symbolic leader—caliph—of Sunni Islam.

The partisans of Ali—the Shiat Ali—evolved into a separate Islamic denomination that became known as the Shia. By the ninth century, however, the Shia Muslims split into numerous sects as a result of disagreements over which of several brothers was the legitimate leader, or *imam,* of the community. The major divisions occurred over the question of succession to the fourth, sixth, and twelfth imams. Consequently, the origins of almost all Shia sects can be traced to the followers of the fifth, seventh, or twelfth imam. By the fifteenth century, the sect known as the Twelve Imam Shia—a group that recognized Ali and eleven of his direct descendants as the legitimate successors to the Prophet—had emerged as the predominant Shia sect.

In addition to the orthodox Twelve Imam Shia, several sects that revered the twelve imams but otherwise subscribed to heterodox beliefs and practices emerged between the ninth and twelfth centuries. One of these heterodox sects, the Nusayri, originated in the mid-ninth century among the followers of the religious teacher Muhammad ibn Nusayr an Namiri. The Nusayri became established in what is now northern Syria and southern Turkey during the tenth century when a Shia dynasty based in Aleppo ruled the region. Because of the special devotion of the Nusayri to Ali, Sunni Muslims historically and pejoratively referred to them as Alevi (see The Alevi, this ch.).

Development of Islam in Turkey

By the end of the seventh century, conversion to Islam had begun among the Turkish-speaking tribes, who were migrating westward from Central Asia. The initial wave of Turkish migrants converted to Sunni Islam and became champions of Islamic orthodoxy. As warriors of the Islamic faith, or *gazis,* they colonized and settled Anatolia in the name of Islam, especially following the defeat of the Byzantines at the Battle of Manzikert (1071). Beginning in the twelfth century, new waves of Turkic migrants became attracted to militant Sufi orders, which gradually incorporated heterodox Shia beliefs. One Sufi order that appealed to Turks in Anatolia after 1300 was the Safavi, based in northwest Iran. During the fourteenth and fifteenth centuries, the Safavi and similar orders such as the Bektasi became rivals of the Ottomans—who were orthodox Sunni Muslims—for political control of eastern Anatolia. Concern about the growing influence of the Safavi probably was one of the factors that prompted the Ottomans to permit unorthodox Bektasi Sufism to become the official order of the janissary soldiers (see The Ottoman Empire, ch. 1). Although the Bektasi became accepted as a sect of orthodox Sunni Muslims, they did not abandon their heterodox Shia beliefs. In contrast, the Safavi eventually conquered Iran, shed their heterodox religious beliefs, and became proponents of orthodox Twelve Imam Shia Islam.

The conquest of the Byzantine capital of Constantinople—which the Turks called Istanbul (from the Greek phrase *eis tin polin,* "to the city")—in 1453 enabled the Ottomans to consolidate their empire in Anatolia and Thrace. The Ottomans revived the title of caliph, based their legitimacy on Islam, and integrated religion into the government and administration. Despite the absence of a formal institutional structure, Sunni religious functionaries played an important political role. Justice was dispensed by religious courts; in theory, the codified system of *seriat* regulated all aspects of life, at least for the Muslim subjects of the empire. The head of the judiciary ranked directly below the sultan and was second in power only to the grand vizier. Early in the Ottoman period, the office of grand mufti of Istanbul evolved into that of *seyhülislam* (shaykh, or leader of Islam), which had ultimate jurisdiction over all the courts in the empire and consequently exercised authority over the interpretation and application of *seriat.* Legal opinions pronounced by the *seyhülislam* were considered definitive interpretations.

Sufism and Folk Islam

From the earliest days of Islam, some Muslims have been attracted to mystical interpretations of their religion. In Turkey, at least since the thirteenth century, Islamic mysticism has been expressed through participation in Sufi brotherhoods that serve as centers of spiritual and social life. The term *Sufi* derives from the Arabic *suf,* which means wool. Early Muslims used the term *Sufi* to refer to fellow believers who wore simple woolen garments to demonstrate their rejection of materialism and worldly temptations and their devotion to a life of asceticism and prayer. Eventually, some Sufis who had acquired repu-

View of Istanbul and the Blue Mosque
Courtesy Hermine Dreyfuss

tations for their learning and piety attracted disciples who aspired to learn from and emulate these Sufi masters. Initially, Sufi followers were like students whose bonds to a Sufi teacher were based on personal loyalty. Since the twelfth century, however, most Sufis have organized themselves into orders or brotherhoods (*tarikat*; pl., *tarikatlar*—see Glossary) that follow the teachings of a particular Sufi master.

Many Sufi *tarikatlar* established institutional bases, called *tekke* or *dergah* (lodges), that lasted for several generations and, in some instances, even for centuries. For example, two of contemporary Turkey's largest *tarikatlar*, the Naksibendi and the Kadiri, date back at least to the fourteenth century. Some *tarikatlar* carry the name of the founding Sufi master, the *seyh* (in Arabic, *shaykh*). One example is the Mevlevi brotherhood. Its members popularly are called whirling dervishes because of the rhythmic whirling they engage in as a spiritual exercise and a means to achieve ecstatic proximity to God. The brotherhood is named after its founder, Mevlana (Jalal ad Din Rumi, d. 1273). Ordinarily, a designated successor to the *seyh* inherited his position of leadership as well as the mantle of his spiritual power. Induction into a particular *tarikat* became regulated and usually depended on the performance of prescribed initiation procedures. Initiates were placed at different levels, depending on the instruction they had mastered. Some of the larger Sufi *tarikatlar* established branches and through *evkaf* accumulated land and buildings, which functioned as *tekkes*, Kuran schools, residential monasteries, orphanages, and hospices.

The early *tarikatlar* were strongly influenced by Shia doctrines. Consequently, the political conflicts between the Sunni Ottoman and Shia Safavi dynasties affected the Sufi orders in Turkey. Sunni *tarikatlar* eventually deemphasized such practices as the veneration of Ali ibn Abu Talib and received official patronage from some·Ottoman sultans. However, at least one Shia *tarikat*, the Bektasi, supported the Ottomans and actually exercised significant political influence without changing their heterodox beliefs. The Bektasi and the Sunni *tarikatlar* also served an important social function by providing educational and social welfare services, constituting a means of social mobility, and offering spiritual guidance to the people, especially in rural areas.

Folk Islam in Turkey has derived many of its popular practices from Sufism. Particular Sufi *seyhs*—and occasionally other individuals reputed to be pious—were regarded after death as saints having special powers to mediate between believers and God. Veneration of saints (both male and female) and pilgrimages to their shrines and graves represent an important aspect of popular Islam in both the city and the country. Folk Islam has continued to embrace such practices although the veneration of saints officially has been discouraged since the 1930s. Plaques posted in various sanctuaries forbid the lighting of candles, the offering of votive objects, and related devotional activities in these places.

The Alevi

A significant Shia minority lives in Turkey. As in the Ottoman period, a census of the Shia population has never been taken in the republican period. Thus, there is no accurate information on the size of the Shia community, which has been estimated to constitute as little as 7 percent and as much as 30 percent of Turkey's total population. Sunni in Turkey tend to refer to all Shia as Alevi. In actuality, Alevi constitute but one of four Shia sects in the country. But Alevi are by far the largest Shia sect in Turkey, accounting for at least 70 percent of the country's Shia. Twelve Imam Shia and followers of the heterodox Ahl-ı Haq and Bektasi have resided in Turkey for centuries. Twelve Imam Shia comprise a majority of all Shia worldwide, although their numbers in Turkey are estimated at only 20 to 25 percent of all Shia in the country. Scholars believe that the unorthodox Ahl-ı Haq, whose adherents are almost exclusively Kurds, and the equally unorthodox Bektasi, whose followers primarily are ethnic Turks, are even fewer in number than the Twelve Imam Shia.

Even though scholars of the contemporary Middle East tend to associate Alevi with Syria, where they have played an influential political role since the 1960s, a majority of all Alevi actually live in Turkey. Alevi include almost all of Turkey's Arab minority, from 10 to 30 percent of the country's Kurds, and many ethnic Turks. In fact, a majority of Alevi may be Turks. Historically, Alevi resided predominantly in southeastern Turkey, but the mass rural-to-urban migration that has been relatively continuous since 1960 has resulted in thousands of Alevi moving to cities in central and western Anatolia. Consequently, Alevi communities of varying size were located in most of the country's major cities by the mid-1990s.

Because of centuries of persecution by Sunni Muslims, Alevi became highly secretive about the tenets of their faith and their religious practices. Consequently, almost no reliable information about Alevi Islam is available. Unsympathetic published sources reported that Alevi worshiped Ali ibn Abu Talib, observed various Christian rituals, and venerated both Christian and Muslim saints. Prior to the twentieth century, information on the sect was so sparse and distorted that even Twelve Imam Shia regarded Alevi as heretics. However, the tendency among most contemporary Twelve Imam clergy is to recognize the Alevi as a distinct legal school within the Twelve Imam tradition. In addition, major Twelve Imam Shia theological colleges in Iran and Iraq have accepted Alevi students since the 1940s.

Secularist Policies

In 1922 the new nationalist regime abolished the Ottoman sultanate, and in 1924 it abolished the caliphate, the religious office that Ottoman sultans had held for four centuries. Thus, for the first time in Islamic history, no ruler claimed spiritual leadership of Islam. The withdrawal of Turkey, heir to the Ottoman Empire, as the presumptive leader of the world Muslim community was symbolic of the change in the government's relationship to Islam. Indeed, secularism or laicism (*laiklik*) became one of the "Six Arrows" of Atatürk's program for remaking Turkey. Whereas Islam had formed the identity of Muslims within the Ottoman Empire, secularism was seen as molding the new Turkish nation and its citizens.

Atatürk and his associates not only abolished certain religious practices and institutions but also questioned the value of religion, preferring to place their trust in science. They regarded organized religion as an anachronism and contrasted it unfavorably with "civilization," which to them meant a rationalist, secular culture. Establishment of secularism in Turkey was not, as it had been in the West, a gradual process of separation of church and state. In the Ottoman Empire, all spheres of life, at least theoretically, had been subject to religious law, and Sunni religious organizations had been part of the state structure. When the reformers of the early 1920s opted for a secular state, they removed religion from the sphere of public policy and restricted it exclusively to that of personal morals, behavior, and faith. Although private observance of religious rituals could continue, religion and religious organization were excluded from public life.

The policies directly affecting religion were numerous and sweeping. In addition to the abolition of the caliphate, new laws mandated abolition of the office of *seyhülislam*; abolition of the religious hierarchy; the closing and confiscation of Sufi lodges, meeting places, and monasteries and the outlawing of their rituals and meetings; establishment of government control over the *evkaf*, which had been inalienable under *seriat*; replacement of *seriat* with adapted European legal codes; the closing of religious schools; abandonment of the Islamic calendar in favor of the Gregorian calendar used in the West; restrictions on public attire that had religious associations, with the fez outlawed for men and the veil discouraged for women; and the outlawing of the traditional garb of local religious leaders.

Atatürk and his colleagues also attempted to Turkify Islam through official encouragement of such practices as using Turkish rather than Arabic at devotions, substituting the Turkish word *Tanrı* for the Arabic word *Allah*, and introducing Turkish for the daily calls to prayer. These changes in devotional practices deeply disturbed faithful Muslims and caused widespread resentment, which led in 1933 to a return to the Arabic version of the call to prayer. Of longer-lasting effect were the regime's measures prohibiting religious education, restricting the building of new mosques, and transferring existing mosques to secular purposes. Most notably, the Hagia Sophia (Justinian's sixth-century Christian basilica, which had been converted into a mosque by Mehmet II) was made a museum in 1935. The effect of these changes was to make religion, or more correctly Sunni Islam, subject to the control of a hostile state. Muftis and imams (prayer leaders) were appointed by the government, and religious instruction was taken over by the Ministry of National Education.

Retreat from Secularism

The expectation of the secular ruling elite that the policies of the 1920s and 1930s would diminish the role of religion in public life did not materialize. As early as 1925, religious grievances were one of the principal causes of the Seyh Sait rebellion, an uprising in southeastern Turkey that may have claimed as many as 30,000 lives before being suppressed. Following the relaxation of authoritarian political controls in 1946, large numbers of people began to call openly for a return to traditional religious practice. During the 1950s, even certain political leaders found it expedient to join religious leaders in advocating more state respect for religion (see Multiparty Politics, 1946–60, ch. 1).

A more direct manifestation of the growing reaction against secularism was the revival of the Sufi brotherhoods. Not only did suppressed *tarikatlar* such as the Kadiri, Mevlevi, and Naksibendi reemerge, but new orders were formed, including the Nurcular, Süleymançı, and Ticani. The Ticani became especially militant in confronting the state. For example, Ticani damaged monuments to Atatürk to symbolize their opposition to his policy of secularization. Throughout the 1950s, there were numerous trials of Ticani and other Sufi leaders for anti-state activities. Simultaneously, however, some *tarikatlar*, notably the Süleymançı and Nurcular, cooperated with those politicians perceived as supportive of pro-Islamic policies. The Nurcular eventually advocated support for Turkey's multiparty political system, and one of its offshoots, the Isikçilar, has openly supported the Motherland Party since the mid-1980s.

The demand for restoration of religious education in public schools began in the late 1940s. The government initially responded by authorizing religious instruction in state schools for those students whose parents requested it. Under Democrat Party rule during the 1950s, religious education was made compulsory in secondary schools unless parents made a specific request to have their children excused. Religious education was made compulsory for all primary and secondary school children in 1982.

Inevitably, the reintroduction of religion into the school curriculum raised the question of religious higher education. The secular elites, who tended to distrust traditional religious leaders, believed that Islam could be "reformed" if future leaders were trained in state-controlled seminaries. To further this goal, the government in 1949 established a faculty of divinity at Ankara University to train teachers of Islam and imams. In 1951 the Democrat Party government set up special secondary schools (*imam hatip okulları*) for the training of imams and preachers. Initially, the *imam hatip* schools grew very slowly, but their numbers expanded rapidly to more than 250 during the 1970s, when the pro-Islam National Salvation Party participated in coalition governments. Following the 1980 coup, the military, although secular in orientation, viewed religion as an effective means to counter socialist ideas and thus authorized the construction of ninety more *imam hatip* high schools.

During the 1970s and 1980s, Islam experienced a kind of political rehabilitation because right-of-center secular leaders perceived religion as a potential bulwark in their ideological struggle with left-of-center secular leaders. A small advocacy group that became extremely influential was the Hearth of Intellectuals, an organization that maintains that true Turkish culture is a synthesis of the Turks' pre-Islamic traditions and Islam. According to the Hearth, Islam not only constitutes an essential aspect of Turkish culture but is a force that can be regulated by the state to help socialize the people to be obedient citizens acquiescent to the overall secular order. After the 1980 military coup, many of the Hearth's proposals for restructuring schools, colleges, and state broadcasting were adopted. The result was a purge from these state institutions of more than 2,000 intellectuals perceived as espousing leftist ideas incompatible with the Hearth's vision of Turkey's national culture.

The state's more tolerant attitude toward Islam encouraged the proliferation of private religious activities, including the construction of new mosques and Kuran schools in the cities, the establishment of Islamic centers for research on and conferences about Islam and its role in Turkey, and the establishment of religiously oriented professional and women's journals. The printing of newspapers, the publication of religious books, and the growth of innumerable religious projects ranging from health centers, child-care facilities, and youth hostels to financial institutions and consumer cooperatives flourished. When the government legalized private broadcasting after 1990, several Islamic radio stations were organized. In the summer of 1994, the first Islamic television station, Channel 7, began broadcasting, first in Istanbul and subsequently in Ankara.

Although the *tarikatlar* have played a seminal role in Turkey's religious revival and in the mid-1990s still published several of the country's most widely circulated religious journals and newspapers, a new phenomenon, *Islamçi aydin* (the Islamist intellectual) unaffiliated with the traditional Sufi orders, emerged during the 1980s. Prolific and popular writers such as Ali Bulaç, Rasim Özdenoren, and Ismet Özel have drawn upon their knowledge of Western philosophy, Marxist sociology, and radical Islamist political theory to advocate a modern Islamic perspective that does not hesitate to criticize genuine societal ills while simultaneously remaining faithful to the ethical values and spiritual dimensions of religion. Islamist intellectuals are harshly critical of Turkey's secular intellectuals, whom they fault for trying to do in Turkey what Western intellectuals did in Europe: substitute worldly materialism, in its capitalist or socialist version, for religious values.

Although intellectual debates on the role of Islam attracted widespread interest, they did not provoke the kind of controversy that erupted over the issue of appropriate attire for Muslim women. During the early 1980s, female college students who were determined to demonstrate their commitment to Islam began to cover their heads and necks with large scarves and wear long, shape-concealing overcoats. The appearance of these women in the citadels of Turkish secularism shocked those men and women who tended to perceive such attire as a symbol of the Islamic traditionalism they rejected. Militant secularists persuaded the Higher Education Council to issue a regulation in 1987 forbidding female university students to cover their heads in class. Protests by thousands of religious students and some university professors forced several universities to waive enforcement of the dress code. The issue continued to be seriously divisive in the mid-1990s. Throughout the first half of the 1990s, highly educated, articulate, but religiously pious women have appeared in public dressed in Islamic attire that conceals all but their faces and hands. Other women, especially in Ankara, Istanbul, and Izmir, have demonstrated against such attire by wearing revealing fashions and Atatürk badges. The issue is discussed and debated in almost every type of forum—artistic, commercial, cultural, economic, political, and religious. For many citizens of Turkey, women's dress has become the issue—at least for the 1990s—that defines whether a Muslim is secularist or religious.

Non-Muslim Minorities

Because of the absence since 1965 of census data on the ethnic background and religious affiliation of Turkish citizens, the size of non-Muslim communities in Turkey in 1995 was difficult to estimate. The 1965 census enumerated about 207,000 Christians, about 169,000 of whom resided in urban areas and about 38,000 in the countryside. The Christians included Armenian, Greek, and Syrian Orthodox; Armenian and Syrian Catholics; and members of various Protestant denominations. The Jewish population in 1965 numbered about 44,000, all but a tiny frac-

*Muslim woman with prayer
beads, Ortahisar, central
Anatolia
Courtesy Hermine Dreyfuss*

*People praying on Ulu Dag
Mountain, near Bursa, in
northwestern Turkey
Courtesy Hermine Dreyfuss*

tion of whom were urban residents. By 1995 it was estimated
that the size of these populations had decreased substantially,
the Christians to just under 140,000 and the Jews to about
20,000. The members of these religious minorities are found
primarily in the coastal cities and towns, but some live in the
mountainous regions of eastern Anatolia near the borders with
Armenia and Georgia.

In 1995 members of religious minorities continued to
occupy an anomalous position in Turkish society. Non-Muslims
remain to some extent second-class citizens, although they generally are not subject to overt discrimination. A disproportion-
ately large segment of the minority population is represented
among the wealthy business and professional groups. Prosely-
tizing by non-Muslim religions is strongly discouraged by the
government. Under the law, a Muslim man or woman may
marry a non-Muslim spouse, but such marriages are infrequent
and usually do not entail conversion.

The Syrian Orthodox, or Jacobite, community, which numbered about 50,000 in 1995, ranks as the largest Christian denomination in Turkey. An Arabic-speaking community that uses ancient Aramaic in its liturgy, the Syrian Orthodox historically have lived in villages in the vicinity of Mardin and Midyat in southeastern Turkey. Since the late 1980s, intense fighting in this region between government forces and the PKK has threatened many villages and prompted a migration to local cities and even to Istanbul, where a community of Syrian Orthodox, initially established during the Ottoman era, was estimated to number 10,000 in 1995. The Syrian Orthodox Church has its own head, referred to as a metropolitan. The metropolitan (Timotheos Samuel Aktash in 1995) resides in an ancient mountain monastery near Midyat. Also, an estimated 2,000 Syrian Catholics, whose ancestors converted from the Syrian Orthodox rite, are scattered in small communities in the southeast. Syrian Catholics retain the distinct Syrian Orthodox rite but recognize the spiritual authority of the Roman Catholic pope.

The Armenian Orthodox (or Gregorian) community, with some 35,000 members in 1995, ranks as the second largest Christian denomination in Turkey. In addition, an estimated 7,000 other Armenians belong to an autonomous Orthodox church, to an Armenian Catholic church in union with Rome, or to various Protestant denominations. In 1995 the Armenian Orthodox Church's patriarch, Karekin Bedros Kazandjian, resided in Istanbul. In 1995 the Armenian Orthodox Church maintained more than thirty churches and chapels; seventy-five elementary and middle schools, and two orphanages. Armenian Catholics maintained ten churches in Istanbul, as well as six elementary and middle schools.

The Greek Orthodox Church, the largest Christian church in Turkey as recently as 1960, had fewer than 20,000 members in 1995. The Ecumenical Patriarchate of Constantinople, located in the Fener quarter of Istanbul, is the central church authority for Greek Orthodox Christians in most of Europe and beyond. Because the patriarch's authority extends to all Orthodox believers outside Greece and the Middle East, he is considered the honorary head of the church for communities of Orthodox Christians living in the United States, Canada, Central and South America, Australia, and New Zealand. From these communities, the patriarchate in Istanbul receives moral and financial support. The ecumenical patriarch's status has been affected by the continual tension in Turkish-Greek relations. During the 1950s and 1960s, thousands of members of the Greek Orthodox community left Turkey on account of the discrimination or overt hostility they experienced following Greco-Turkish conflicts over the status of Cyprus. The diminution of the community has weakened the patriarchate and undermined its status in its dealings with the Turkish government. Nevertheless, the patriarchate's importance has remained considerable because of its ecumenical and international connections.

Other Christian communities present in Turkey include several small groups affiliated with the Roman Catholic Church. Melchites (Greek Catholics) and Maronites live among the Arabs in southeast Hatay Province. Although accepted by the Vatican as part of the Roman Catholic Church, Melchites and Maronite Catholics retain their own separate liturgies. Chaldean-rite Catholics live in the Diyarbakır region, while Bulgarian, Greek, and Latin-rite Catholics live in Istanbul and Izmir. The total number of Catholics of various persuasions in early 1995 has been estimated at 25,000.

Since 1948 the Jewish population has decreased steadily. In 1995 the Jewish community, estimated at 18,000 to 20,000, consisted primarily of Sephardic Jews. At least 90 percent of Turkey's Jews live in Istanbul, where a chief rabbi presides. In 1995 the Jewish community maintained one high school and four elementary schools offering limited courses in Hebrew.

Structure of Society

Contemporary Turkish society has evolved both as a consequence of and a response to the major socioeconomic changes initiated by the republican government since the early 1920s. A predominantly agrarian society with little industry and high illiteracy rates when the Ottoman Empire collapsed at the end of World War I, Turkey by the 1990s had become a predominantly urban and industrialized society in which mass public education and the ability to vote for government leaders in competitive elections are regarded as basic rights. Accompanying the changes has been the growth of new classes and interest groups, especially in the large cities, where the demands of entrepreneurs and industrial workers are championed by various political parties. A notable characteristic of many government programs aimed at inducing specific socioeconomic changes, however, has been the penchant of ruling civilian and military elites for implementing policies without consulting those who might be affected and for using force whenever popular resistance is encountered. One consequence of this approach has been the gradual creation of two distinct cultures in Turkey: a secular, elitist culture that defines what is progressive and modern; and a mass culture that continues to be influenced by Islam, whether in its traditional, mystical, modern, or radical interpretations.

The Changing National Elite

Turkey's national political elite is a self-perpetuating group; membership is based on a demonstrated commitment to secularism and the other principles of Atatürk. During the initial years of the republic, the elite was recruited from the Ottoman bureaucracy and military. Its members thus shared a sense that they knew best how to carry out policies that served the interests of the state and country. In addition, most of the early republican elite had been involved with or sympathetic to the pre-World War I Ottoman political parties that had espoused major political and economic reforms. Atatürk himself, for example, had been a member of the Unionist Party while serving as an Ottoman army officer in Macedonia (see The Young Turks, ch. 1). During the 1920s and 1930s, the ruling elite accepted the need for significant, even revolutionary, reforms and generally embraced Atatürk's programs enthusiastically. In effect, service to the country and higher education, rather than wealth per se, became primary qualifications for acceptance into the political elite as early as 1930.

The national political elite essentially ruled Turkey unchallenged for more than thirty years. Beginning in the 1950s, however, the socioeconomic changes resulting from government policies provided numerous and varied opportunities for the accumulation of private capital in finance, commerce, trade, and industry. The emergence of a wealthy business class inevitably led to the development of class-specific political interests and ambitions. Because of this new business elite's experience in entrepreneurial activities rather than the bureaucracy, its members' views differed sharply from those of the established ruling elite, which generally supported state intervention in the economy. Increasing competition between the two elites over appropriate state policies was one of the reasons for the polarization that characterized Turkey's national politics during the 1970s.

A nongovernment professional elite also gradually emerged after 1950, including architects, engineers, lawyers, managers, physicians, and university professors, who were not necessarily unified in their political views. Nevertheless, as a group they tended to resent what they perceived as the patronizing, even authoritarian, political attitudes of the ruling elite. This group's frustration with the political system, emerging at the same time as dissatisfaction within the business elite, highlighted the need for genuine political reform. During the 1970s, some members of the ruling elite recognized this need, but they were unable to enact remedial legislation.

The 1980 military coup symbolized the deep divisions that had emerged within the ruling elite over strategies for dealing with the political demands of diverse and competitive interest groups. The officers and their civilian supporters, who included some factions of the business elite, wanted the state to impose social order through the type of authoritarian methods they believed had worked successfully under Atatürk. They were sufficiently angry with dissenting members of the ruling elite to arrest the most prominent politicians, including two former prime ministers. The coup in effect split the ruling elite into two ideological factions that continue to coexist uneasily in the mid-1990s. One elite group believes in the efficacy of a strong government to maintain social and political stability; the other elite faction believes in accommodating interest group demands that do not threaten the national cohesion of the country and generally supports broadening political pluralism.

Urban Life

By 1995 approximately two-thirds of Turkey's population lived in urban areas, which continued to grow rapidly (see Population Density, Distribution, and Settlement, this ch.). Urbanization and industrialization have helped to create social-class structures that are similar in all large cities (population of more than 100,000) and most smaller ones (population 20,000 to 100,000). Government officials, wealthy businesspeople, and professionals together constitute the urban upper class. The business elite in most cities is very diverse and generally includes industrialists, financiers, large-scale retailers and wholesalers, real estate developers, construction firm owners, transportation company operators, and, in Ankara and Istanbul, owners of commercial publishing and broadcasting companies. The business elite, which constitutes the largest component of the upper class, has been expanding since the early 1980s as a result of government incentives for private investors and entrepreneurs. However, because statistics on personal income in Turkey are neither complete nor reliable, there is no accurate means of determining the composition of the upper class. Political power and education/continue to be significant, albeit much less so than before the 1980 coup, as qualifications for upper-class status. The upper class makes up about 10 percent of the total population of all cities.

The urban middle class is larger and more diverse than the upper class. It includes various types of administrators; middle-level bureaucrats and public employees; engineers lacking advanced college degrees; journalists and other writers; managers of industrial enterprises, commercial offices, and social-service centers; owners of small-scale retail establishments and restaurants; technicians; self-employed artisans; professionals; and tradespeople. Education, particularly a college degree, has been key to joining the middle class. Although the middle class was continuing to expand during the early 1980s, most of its members felt threatened by persistently high inflation rates that had eroded their savings and impeded their upward social mobility. In 1995 the middle class was estimated to constitute 20 to 25 percent of the total urban population. It was larger in prosperous cities but smaller in economically depressed areas.

The phenomenal growth of cities since the 1950s has been the result of large-scale migration of lower-class people from the villages; in 1995 more than 60 percent of Turkey's urban population belonged to the lower class. Most villagers who came to the cities in search of work were unable to find affordable housing. Thus, they built temporary shelters on undeveloped land on the outskirts of Ankara and Istanbul and other large cities. These squatter settlements, or *gecekondus*, soon became permanent neighborhoods, albeit ones that lacked urban amenities such as piped water, electricity, and paved streets. Eventually, some *gecekondus* were incorporated into the cities and provided with electricity. By 1980 up to 60 percent of the residents of Ankara, Adana, Bursa, Istanbul, and Izmir lived in new *gecekondus* or in city neighborhoods that had originated as *gecekondus*. During the 1970s, researchers affiliated with government-funded institutes tried to depict the expanding *gecekondus* as settlements that facilitated the adaptation of rural migrants to the urban environment. In actuality, all such neighborhoods were urban slums where poverty and its associated social ills remained pervasive in the mid-1990s.

Obtaining work in private manufacturing or state industries is a typical goal of lower-class men because of the steady employment and wages offered. Among industrial workers, there has been a long tradition of group identification and solidarity. By 1975, when more than 79 percent of all industrial workers had been unionized, labor leaders were able to exercise political influence on behalf of legislation protecting workers' rights. This situation changed dramatically following the 1980 coup. The military government forcibly dissolved existing labor unions, arrested prominent labor leaders, and banned strikes. Subsequently, to ensure that unions remained under supervision, the civilian government of Turgut Özal encouraged the formation of tradespeople-artisan guilds. By 1995 these guilds, however, represented only 10 percent of the entire labor force and lacked the political influence of their predecessors (see Human Resources and Trade Unions, ch. 3).

In the prevailing climate of economic and political uncertainty following the coup, several factories ceased production, a situation that meant immediate job and income loss for thousands of workers. Even after the restoration of civilian rule, economic conditions for the lower class did not improve. Up to 25 percent of adult males in the *gecekondus* were unemployed in the mid-1980s; throughout the first half of the 1990s, the level of industrial unemployment remained at the 10 to 11 percent level. An excess labor supply relative to available industrial jobs has tended to keep wages depressed.

There are more nonindustrial than industrial jobs in the cities, and as many as two-thirds of all lower-class urban families depend on nonindustrial, unskilled work for their livelihood. Such work includes crafts; automotive repair; brick masonry; butchering; carpentry; deliveries; bus and taxi driving; entertainment; equipment operation in bakeries; laundry, machine shop, and dockyard work; home painting and repairs; maintenance of grounds and buildings; personal services in public bathhouses, barbershops, beauty salons, and private homes; operation of small retail shops; service jobs in hotels, institutions, offices, restaurants, and retail establishments; street cleaning and maintenance; street vending of products and services; textile piecework in the home; and various transport and haulage jobs.

Towns

In addition to large and small cities, Turkey has scores of semiurban places that officially are classified as towns. A town (*kasaba*) is defined as an incorporated settlement with a population between 2,000 and 20,000. Towns generally provide basic economic and political services to the regions in which they are located. The social structure of larger towns is similar to that of the cities. There is an elite composed of government officials, military officers, and a few wealthy landowning, mercantile, and professional families; a middle class made up of administrators, merchants, shopkeepers, soldiers, and teachers; and a lower class consisting of artisans and various categories of workers. Some of these diverse occupational groups may be absent in the smaller towns.

Traditionally, elite status in towns derived from both wealth and family descent. Political and economic influence was exercised for several generations by local landowning families that had intermarried with Ottoman officials sent by the government to administer the towns. The policies introduced by Atatürk during the 1920s and 1930s changed the composition of most town elites, however. Families unable or unwilling to adapt lost influence and power, whereas those families who embraced the new values continued to wield local influence. Since the 1960s, the educated descendants of some members of the traditional landed elite have become governors, mayors, doctors, lawyers, judges, and merchants, as well as large landowners employing modern farm technology and business practices. These individuals also have assumed leadership of the local hierarchies of the political parties.

Village Life

Until the early 1950s, more than 80 percent of the inhabitants of Turkey lived in villages, which numbered more than 36,000. As defined by the government, a village (*koy*) is any settlement with a population of less than 2,000. Although Turkey's rural population has continued to grow, the percentage of the total population living in villages has declined as a result of rural-to-urban migration. In 1970 about 67 percent of the population lived in villages; five years later, this proportion had shrunk to 59 percent. In 1980 more than 54 percent still lived in villages, but by 1985 most people lived in urban areas. In 1995 less than 35 percent of the population lived in villages.

Since the 1950s, agriculture has become increasingly mechanized, and this gradual change has affected land tenure patterns and village society (see Land Tenure, ch. 3). Small landowners and landless families generally have not benefited from this change, and consequently they have been the rural residents most likely to migrate to the cities. In contrast, larger landowners have profited from the new agricultural methods by increasing their holdings and investing their increased wealth in industry. By the early 1980s, the personal and share-cropping relationships between landowners and agricultural laborers and tenants had been replaced by new and impersonal wage relations. This development prompted agricultural wage earners with grievances against landowners to seek advice and relief from labor unions or labor-oriented groups in the towns.

In the 1990s, the extended family network remains the most important social unit in village society, even though most households tend to be composed of nuclear families. The extended family serves a crucial economic function in villages by fostering cooperation among related households by way of informal arrangements concerning shared machinery, shared labor, and even shared cash income. The extended family also is expected to provide support if one of its constituent nuclear households faces an economic, political, or social crisis. An extended family may be composed of a father, his married adult sons, and their children and wives, but usually it is a broader concept embracing several generations headed by one or more senior males who can trace common descent from a male ancestor. In this sense, an extended family is a patrilineage. Although such kin groups lack status as corporate entities in custom or law, they have an important role in defining family members' rights and obligations.

There are important similarities among villages within a given region, as well as differences from one region to the next. In this sense, it is possible to distinguish among villages in three distinct geographic regions: Anatolia, the coastal area, and southern and eastern Turkey.

Anatolian Villages

The family (*aile*) is the basic structure of Anatolian village life. The word lacks a single specific meaning in peasant usage, referring instead to the conceptual group of coresidents, whether in a household, lineage, village, or nomadic band. The unit functions as the primary element in any concerted group action. The two most frequent referents of the concept are household and village community; every sedentary (i.e., non-nomadic) villager in the Anatolian countryside belongs to at least these two groups. Consequently, household and village are what the Anatolian Turk means by *aile.*

The household provides the framework for the most intimate and emotionally important social relations, as well as for most economic activities. The activities of the household, then, form the nucleus of village economic and social life. Household members are expected to work the household's fields cooperatively and reap the harvests that sustain its life. Because household members share an identity in the eyes of the village at large, every member is responsible for the actions of any other member. Wider kinship ties of the extended patrilineal family are also important.

Because of the pervasiveness and significance of kinship groups and relationships defined on the basis of kinship, nonkinship groups in Anatolian villages tend to be few in number and vague in their criteria for membership. Generally, three kinds of voluntary associations can be found in Anatolian villages: religious associations and brotherhoods headed by dervishes, local units of the main political parties, and gossip groups that meet in the guest rooms (*misafir odası*) of well-to-do villagers.

Prior to the 1950s, most Anatolian villagers owned the land they farmed, and within individual villages there were relatively small differences in wealth. Three criteria influenced social rank: ascribed characteristics such as age, sex, and the position of a person in his or her own household, lineage, and kinship network; economic status as indicated by landholding, occupation, and income; and moral stature as demonstrated by piety, religious learning, and moral respectability. However, by 1995 absentee landlordism and large landholdings had become common, and wealth alone tended to be the determining factor in ascribing social status. Thus, resident large landowners often dominated the political, economic, and social life of the villages.

The relationship of wealth to influence and social rank is illustrated by the institution of the guest room. It is estimated that only 10 percent of homes in Anatolian villages have guest rooms because they are very expensive to maintain. Village men gather most evenings in guest rooms and spend much of their time there during the winter months. Regular attendance at a particular guest room implies political and social support of its owner because, by accepting his hospitality, a villager places himself in the owner's debt and acknowledges his superior status.

Every village in Anatolia, as well as elsewhere in Turkey, has an official representative of the central government, the headman (*muhtar*), who is responsible to Ankara and the provincial administrators. The headman is elected every two years by villagers (see Provincial and Local Government, ch. 4). The position generally is not considered a prestigious one because most villagers distrust the government. Thus, in Anatolia, it is not unusual to find relatively young men serving as village headmen.

Coastal Villages

Unlike the traditionally isolated villages of Anatolia, villages in European Turkey and along the Black Sea and Aegean Sea, and to a lesser degree along the Mediterranean Sea, have been exposed to urban influences for several generations. Agriculture tends to be specialized and is generally undertaken in association with fishing and lumber production. Economic links with market towns historically have been very important. Although the extended family plays a significant role throughout a villager's life, economic considerations rather than kinship tend to shape social relations. The commercial nature of these villages has resulted in the substitution of nonkinship roles—such as employer and employee, buyer and seller, and landlord and tenant—for most interactions outside the home.

In coastal villages, the elite is primarily a landed group. Large landowners, by providing employment and—to a lesser degree—land to their laborers and tenants, and by serving as an economic link between the village and urban markets, acquire influence and power. Their personal contact with the laborers and tenants on their lands, however, has lessened since the 1950s. By the 1990s, urban businesspeople with both the resources and the inclination to serve as middlemen between village production and city markets generally wielded as much influence as local large landowners. Businesspeople's influence continues to expand as a result of increasing crop specialization and market dependency.

Villages in the South and East

The villages of southeastern Turkey are predominantly Arab

and Kurdish. Tribal organization—the grouping of several patrilineages claiming a common historical ancestor—remains important in some Kurdish villages. However, the political autonomy once enjoyed by tribal leaders was usurped by the central government during the 1920s and 1930s. Tribal leaders who retain local influence do so because they are large landowners. Large landholdings are typical of the region. In most villages, one or two families own most of the arable land and pasturage; the remainder is divided into small plots owned by several families. Most of the small landowners have holdings fit only for subsistence agriculture. From 10 to 50 percent of all families may be landless. Villagers who do not own land work as agricultural laborers or herders for the large landlords. The poverty of most villagers compels them to enter into dependent economic, political, and social relations with the wealthier landlords.

The fighting between the PKK and the government in southeastern Turkey since 1984 has disrupted life in many villages. About 850 Kurdish villages have been uprooted by the government and their inhabitants forcibly removed to western Anatolia. Thousands of other villagers have migrated to cities to escape the incessant fighting. The migrants have included all types of villagers: the landless, small landowners, and large landlords. The long-term effects of these changes were difficult to assess in the mid-1990s.

The Individual, the Family, and Gender Relations

Prior to the establishment of the republic, matters of personal status, including marriage, divorce, and inheritance, were regulated by Islamic law and influenced by cultural customs that had evolved during several centuries of Ottoman rule. Atatürk and his associates regarded both religious rules and traditional cultural practices as hindrances to the creation of their shared vision of a modern society. In fact, their societal ideal for Turkey was the pattern of personal and family relations that prevailed among the educated upper classes of Europe during the 1920s and 1930s. Consequently, many policies enacted during the early republican period were designed explicitly to remold Turkish society according to an urban European model. One of the most significant measures on behalf of this goal was the abolition of Islamic law. In 1926 a new civil code derived from Swiss civil laws replaced the religious legal system. The disestablishment of Islam as the state

*A dervish whirling to induce
a trance for prayer
Courtesy Hermine Dreyfuss*

religion and other measures aimed at religion reduced the influence of Islam in life-cycle rituals.

The social changes induced by state policies after 1923 failed to create a new Turkish culture. Instead, at least two distinct cultures had emerged in Turkey by the 1950s. One was an elite culture characterized by secular values and patterns of family and gender relationships similar to those found in much of urban, middle-class Europe. The majority popular culture, in contrast, was influenced by a mélange of secular ideas learned in the compulsory state education system (through middle school), religious values learned within the family and from community organizations such as the mosques, and traditional views about the appropriate public role of the sexes.

Marriage

As part of their rejection of the symbols of Islam, Atatürk and his associates outlawed traditional marriage practices. The 1926 civil code mandated that all marriages be registered with civil authorities. Marriages contracted before a member of the religious establishment henceforth were not recognized as lawful unions, and the children of such unions were considered illegitimate. The male prerogative to have up to four wives simultaneously, enshrined in Islamic law, was prohibited. Marriage between a Muslim woman and a non-Muslim man, a practice forbidden under Islamic law, became legal.

Traditionally, marriage has been—and frequently continues to be—a contract negotiated and executed by the families of the betrothed and blessed by a member of the religious establishment. Representatives of the bride and groom negotiate the contract, which stipulates such terms as the size and nature of the bride-price paid by the family of the groom to the family of the bride and whatever conditions of conjugal life are mutually agreeable. After a series of meetings between the two families, an exchange of gifts, and the display of the trousseau, the marriage is formalized at a ceremony presided over by a religious official. The civil code requires only that the bride and groom, as individuals, swear vows before two witnesses and a representative of the state who registers the union. Despite the legal necessity for civil marriage, traditional courtship and marriage practices persist. Many couples, especially among the lower classes in cities and in rural areas, hold two ceremonies, a religious one to satisfy their families and a civil one to entitle them to government social benefits, as well as to confer legitimacy on future children.

Despite government attempts to outlaw the bride-price, during the 1990s this traditional prenuptial practice has continued in both urban and rural areas. The payment of the bride-price involves considerable expenditures and often requires financial cooperation from a number of kinfolk. The exact amount and the terms of payment form a part of the premarital negotiations. For example, the families sometimes agree to postpone payment of the full bride-price until after the wedding, stipulating that the full amount must be paid in the event of divorce, a practice that provides some protection for the bride if the match subsequently proves incompatible. Ordinarily the amount of the bride-price is directly related to the status of the families involved. However, the amount tends to be less if the two families have a close blood relationship. For these reasons, among others, most rural and urban families continue to prefer that their children marry closely related kin—first or second cousins.

Divorce also is affected by the civil code. Under Islamic law, a man can initiate divorce easily and is not required to cite any reasons; the grounds on which a woman can seek divorce, however, are tightly restricted, and she is obligated to prove fault on her husband's part. Under the civil code, divorce, like marriage, is not recognized as legitimate unless registered with civil authorities. The code permits either partner to initiate divorce proceedings, but the state, which claims an interest in maintaining marriage unions, especially in cases involving children, decides whether to grant a request for divorce.

The Extended Family

Although a majority of households in Turkey are nuclear family units, the larger extended family continues to play an important social role in the lives of most individuals. The extended family always includes all relatives by blood or marriage through an individual's paternal grandfather, or sometimes, great-grandfather. In addition, many individuals, especially those of middle-class and elite social status, consider the parents and siblings of their own mother to be part of the extended family. In general, the extended family functions as an emotional support network during life-cycle events such as birth, marriage, and death, or during major family crises. It often functions as an economic support network by providing loans for exceptional personal expenses, finding employment for new graduates, and caring for indigent members who are elderly or disabled. In urban areas, the extended family—especially fathers and sons or two or more brothers—can serve as a means for the formation of business partnerships. In rural areas, members of an extended family may work together to farm large acreages or raise large herds of sheep.

By expressing approval or disapproval of its members' social behavior, the extended family also functions as an effective mechanism of social control. Every individual is expected to comport himself or herself in ways that do not bring dishonor to the family. There are many types of behavior that might bring shame to a family, but sexual promiscuity, especially among women, is considered the most serious offense. Regardless of class, women are expected to avoid any activity that might raise suspicions about their sexual conduct. Thus, unmarried females are expected to abstain from all sexual activity before marriage, and married women are expected to remain faithful to their husbands. Female adultery carries heavy social sanctions; among the lower classes in cities and in villages, it still is socially—albeit not legally—acceptable for a betrayed husband to redeem his family's honor by killing his adulterous wife.

The unequal burden placed upon women to uphold family honor highlights the ambiguous role of women in society. Official state ideology extols the equality of men and women. Intellectually, men tend to accept women as equals, and elite women have been able to achieve high positions in professional careers since the 1960s. Since the mid-1980s, women also have been active in politics; one, Tansu Çiller, became prime minister in 1993. Nevertheless, men traditionally view women as emotionally and physically inferior and thus in need of male protection, which in practice means male control. Both men and women traditionally have judged a woman's social status not on the basis of her personal accomplishments but by the number of sons she has borne. Thus, women—like their husbands—customarily have prized boys over girls. Mothers have tended to socialize their sons and daughters differently, rearing boys to be assertive and girls to be obedient and passive. The relationship between a mother and a son tends to be warm and intimate throughout life.

The traditional status of women continues to be established during the early years of marriage for most lower-middle-class and lower-class women. Within the extended family, a new bride tends to be under the critical surveillance of her husband's relatives, especially his mother. Whether the new couple lives in a separate household—this often is a requirement of the bride-price—or resides temporarily in the home of the groom's parents, the bride is isolated from her own family and friends and is expected to learn from her mother-in-law how to care for her husband. Her situation is recognized in the language: the expression *gelinlik etmek*, used to refer to the status of a new bride, means to be "on call." Although a bride may establish a close personal relationship with her mother-in-law, especially if the latter is also her aunt, friction and tension are more common. In such cases, the mother-in-law expects her son to side with her against his wife. A new bride only gains status and security within a traditional extended family after she has produced a son.

The status of a wife changes as she matures because within all extended families, whether traditional or modern, considerable respect is accorded to age. Younger family members are expected to show respect toward their elders regardless of their gender. Respect has many dimensions, but usually it means not speaking in the presence of one's elders unless requested, and refraining in their presence from arguing, smoking, or behaving in a casual way. Thus, a woman whose children are nearly grown is accorded respect and does not expect to be harassed by her mother-in-law. The authority of a mature wife and her opinions in family matters are important. If she also has employment outside the home, her influence increases. The migration of husbands to cities or foreign countries in search of work also changes the role of married women within families. Left at home to rear the children on remittances sent by her spouse, the wife often is forced to assume many of the daily decision-making roles previously filled by her husband. In addition, since the late 1960s, thousands of migrant workers have sent for their wives and children to join them in the foreign countries where they are employed. These prolonged residences abroad have tended to alter traditional extended-family relationships.

Gender Relations

Male-female relations remain an area of some tension in Turkish society. The conflict between traditional and modern values and between patterns of socialization within the family and at school affect the social relationships that both men and women establish. Even among modernized urban dwellers, family loyalty, family obligations, and family honor remain strong considerations. Thus, even though Turks professing to have modern values may define the "ideal" family as one in which equality exists between spouses, wives who actually attempt to establish themselves as equal partners usually meet with resistance from their husbands. Among more traditional families, both men and women generally expect husbands to be dominant, especially with respect to matters involving household interactions with the public; wives are expected to be obedient. Even in traditional families, however, wives may not accept passive roles, and their efforts to assert themselves can come up against strong disapproval.

The conflicting tensions of traditional and modern values also influence social relations outside the family. The mass media and modern education popularize ideas such as social equality, openness between spouses, romantic love, and platonic friendships between the sexes, concepts that men and women with traditional values find objectionable but that their adolescent children may find appealing. Furthermore, whereas some young women have been readopting headscarves and modest dress to demonstrate their commitment to Islam, others have been attracted to the latest Western fashions in clothes and cosmetics, which traditionalists perceive as evidence of a general decline in female morality.

Men and women generally constitute largely separate subsocieties, each with its own values, attitudes, and perceptions of the other. Even among modernized urbanites, gender roles constrain social relations. For example, friendships between men and women who are unrelated generally are not acceptable. Among elite youth, men and women do meet socially and dating is fashionable, but parents try to monitor such relationships and discourage their daughters from becoming involved with any man unless marriage is contemplated. Among more traditional families, dating would ruin the reputation of a young woman and dishonor her family.

The Status of Women

Traditional views of gender roles and relations have persisted in tandem with changes in the status of women both within and outside the family. These changes began during the latter years of the Ottoman Empire, when women were given opportunities to work as teachers, clerks, and industrial workers. Change accelerated during the early republican era. The 1926 civil code granted women unprecedented legal rights, and in 1934 they received the right to vote and to stand for election. Since the 1950s, their participation in the labor force, the professions, and in politics has increased steadily but unevenly. By 1991 women made up 18 percent of the total urban labor force. But not all changes have resulted in improved conditions. In some instances, especially among rural and newly urbanized women, changes have disturbed a traditional order that has provided meaningful, guaranteed roles for women without introducing new ones.

During the 1950s, rural women who migrated to the urban *gecekondus* generally found work as maids in private homes. Since the 1960s, employment opportunities for women in industry, especially light manufacturing, have been expanding. By 1991, the most recent year for which detailed statistics are available, almost 20 percent of employees in manufacturing were women. Nevertheless, a majority of women in the *gecekondus* do not work outside the home. Most urban working-class women are single and hold jobs for less than five years; they tend to leave paid employment when they get married. While working and contributing to family income, women enjoy enhanced status and respect.

Urban middle-class and upper-middle-class women tend to have more education than working-class women and generally are employed in teaching, health care, and clerical work. Since 1980 more than one-third of all bank clerks have been women. Upper-class women tend to work in the prestigious professions, such as law, medicine, and university teaching. On average about 18 percent of all professionals in Turkey were women in 1991; they were concentrated in Ankara, Istanbul, Izmir, and a few other large urban centers.

In 1995 the status of women in Turkey remained a multifaceted, complex issue. Although the government guarantees women equal work and pay opportunities, the traditional value system elevates gender segregation in the workplace and other public spaces as a social ideal. Even urban, educated, professional women may encounter the persistence of traditional, religiously colored values about gender roles among their putatively modern, secular husbands.

Education

The contemporary Turkish education system was established in 1924 after Atatürk closed the religious schools, set up new secular schools, and made elementary school attendance compulsory. It was many years before the country had the educational infrastructure to provide universal primary education, but since the early 1980s almost all children between the ages of six and ten have been enrolled in school. The most recent data on literacy (1990) put Turkey's overall adult literacy rate around 81 percent. This statistic broke down as 90 percent literacy among males aged fifteen and over, and 71 percent among females in that age-group.

The public education system provides for five stages of education: preschool, primary school, middle school, high school, and university. Noncompulsory preschool programs established in 1953 offer education to children between the ages of four and six. The demand for preschool education has been limited, apparently because of parents' unwillingness to entrust the education of small children to institutions outside the family. Preschool programs are most common in large cities, where, since the 1980s, they have been increasing in popularity and in numbers. Primary education is coeducational as well as compulsory, and encompasses a five-year program for ages six to eleven. Attendance at the country's estimated 46,000 primary schools was reckoned at 97 percent for the 1994–95 school year. Education officials believe school attendance is lower in villages than in urban areas because it is easier for parents to keep older children, especially girls, at home.

The two-year middle-school program, for ages twelve to fourteen, also is coeducational and has been compulsory since 1972. However, authorities generally do not enforce middle-school attendance, especially in rural areas, where middle schools are few in number and most students must travel long distances to attend. The Ministry of National Education does not publish data on middle-school attendance, but overall it probably does not exceed 60 percent of the relevant age-group. To encourage higher levels of attendance, a 1983 law prohibited the employment of youths younger than fourteen. Middle-school graduation is a prerequisite to access to general, vocational, and technical high schools, and is deemed advantageous for admission to many vocational training programs.

Secondary school education is not compulsory but is free at all of the country's estimated 1,300 public high schools. The Ministry of National Education supervises the high schools, which are divided into lycée (general) and vocational schools. The lycées are coeducational and offer three-year college preparatory programs. A select number of lycées in the largest cities are bilingual, teaching classes in Turkish and either English, French, or German. Twelve lycées are open to students from the three legally recognized minorities—Armenians, Greeks, and Jews—and teach classes on some subjects in Armenian or Greek. In contrast, many of the vocational high schools offer four-year programs. Vocational high schools include technical training schools for men; domestic science schools for women; teacher-training schools; auxiliary health care, commercial, and agricultural schools; Muslim teacher-training schools; and other specialized institutions. The Muslim teacher-training schools, called *imam hatip okullan,* have expanded dramatically since the late 1970s. During the early 1990s, they numbered about 350 and enrolled 10 percent of all high school students. Except for the emphasis on religious subjects, the curriculum of the *imam hatip okullan* resembles that of the lycées rather than the vocational schools.

Higher education is available at several hundred institutions, including professional schools and academies, institutes, and conservatories, but primarily at the twenty-seven public univer-

sities, which enrolled more than 450,000 students in 1993–94. In the mid-1980s, when Özal was prime minister, his government authorized Turkey's first private university, Bilkent, in Ankara. The university law of 1946 granted academic autonomy to Turkey's universities. However, government policies since the 1980 coup, especially a 1981 law on higher education, have institutionalized extensive government interference in university affairs. The military leaders believed that the universities had been the center of political ideas they disliked and perceived as harmful to Turkey's stability. They thus sought through the 1981 higher education law and applicable provisions of the 1982 constitution to introduce both structural and curricular changes at the universities. For example, the constitution stipulates that the president of the republic may appoint university rectors, establishes the government's right to found new universities, and assigns duties to the Council of Higher

Education (Yuksek Ögretim Kurumu—YÖK). The higher education law prohibits all teachers and matriculated students from belonging to or working for a political party and requires curricular standardization at all universities.

The YÖK consists of twenty-five members, of whom eight are appointed directly by the president, eight by the Interuniversity Council, six by the Council of Ministers, two by the Ministry of National Education, and one by the General Staff of the armed forces. The chair of the YÖK is appointed by the president of the republic. The YÖK's powers include recommending or appointing rectors, deans, and professors; selecting and assigning students; and planning new universities. The YÖK also has authority to transfer faculty members from one university to another. The YÖK effectively has reduced the faculty senates, which prior to 1980 had authority to enact academic regulations, to mere advisory bodies.

Education has continued to serve as an important means of upward social mobility. Annually since at least 1975, the number of students applying for university admission has exceeded the number of available spaces. To qualify for admission, every applicant must pass the nationwide university entrance exam, which is designed, administered, and evaluated by the Center for Selection and Placement of Students. During the early 1990s, more than 100,000 applicants sat for the entrance exam each year. Scoring is based on a complicated system that assures that the number who pass does not exceed the number of available spaces. Even if an applicant qualifies for admission, the individual's actual score determines whether he or she may study a chosen discipline or must take up a less preferred one.

In addition to the five levels of education described above, the system provides special education for some children with disabilities, as well as a wide range of adult education and vocational programs. Labor specialists consistently have cited inadequate skills as a key factor in Turkey's high level of unemployment, which during the early 1990s averaged 10 percent annually. In 1995 half of the urban unemployed had only a primary education, and an estimated 40 percent of pupils dropped out of school upon completing this level of education. Since 1980 the Ministry of National Education has conducted major literacy campaigns aimed at the population between ages fourteen and forty-four, with emphasis on women, residents of the urban *gecekondus*, and agricultural workers. The ministry also has provided primary, middle school, and secondary equivalency program courses to upgrade education levels. In addition, through its Directorate of Apprenticeship and Nonformal Education, the ministry provides nonformal vocational training to people lacking required skills, such as school dropouts, seasonal agricultural workers, and people in the urban informal sector.

The World Bank (see Glossary), which has provided funds for industrial training programs since the early 1970s, has been a major source of support for nonformal vocational training programs. These programs are intended to provide skilled personnel above and beyond the supply from the formal vocational education system, which was projected to meet 86 percent of the estimated industrial demand for skilled and semiskilled workers through 1995. Government plans have provided for a major expansion of the nonformal vocational training system; 650,000 additional people are expected to receive training in employment-related trades, including 150,000 to be trained in industrial skills during 1994 and 1995. Although the government program was expected to improve the quality and availability of skill education in less-developed regions such as eastern Turkey, the intense fighting there since 1991 has disrupted training.

Health and Welfare

Health care and related social welfare activities in the 1990s remain the responsibility of the Ministry of Health. Legislation has directed and authorized the ministry to provide medical care and preventive health services, train health personnel, make preservice and in-service training available, establish and operate hospitals and other health care centers, supervise private health facilities, regulate the price of medical drugs, and control drug production and all pharmacies. In addition, the ministry supervises all medical and health care personnel in the public sector.

Availability of health care in the mid-1990s is significantly better than it was twenty years earlier, but its quality remains uneven. Medical facilities are concentrated in the cities and larger towns, leaving most rural areas without adequate access to medical care. This situation is especially acute in eastern Anatolia, where medical care is generally available only in the provincial capitals. The salaries paid to state-employed physicians are low compared with what doctors in private practice earn. Consequently, most Turkish physicians prefer to work in the more highly developed urban centers or even to emigrate.

The overall ratio of inhabitants to physicians has continued to improve significantly. Whereas there was one physician for every 2,860 individuals in 1965, that ratio improved to one to 1,755 in 1976, one to 1,391 in 1985, and an estimated one to 1,200 in 1995. From 1977 to 1995, the number of all health care facilities—hospitals, health centers, clinics, and dispensaries—rose from 7,944 to 12,500. Simultaneously, the number of available hospital beds increased even more rapidly than the rate of population growth; the ratio was one bed per 400 citizens in 1995.

Turkey has achieved progress in controlling various debilitating and crippling diseases and in treating major infectious diseases. The incidence of measles, pertussis, typhoid fever, and diphtheria all declined dramatically between 1969 and 1994. The greater availability of potable water in both urban and rural areas has contributed to a general fall in the former prevalence of water-borne illnesses, especially of diarrhea among children and infants. Infant mortality, which at 120 per 1,000 live births in 1980 was among the highest rates worldwide, had declined to fifty-five per 1,000 live births by 1992. Nevertheless, this rate was still very high by European standards, being six times the rate of neighboring Greece, which had an infant mortality rate of nine per 1,000 live births.

Turkey had reported sixteen cases of acquired immune deficiency syndrome (AIDS) to the World Health Organization in the first nine months of 1994. The rate of AIDS cases per 100,000 population was 0.1 for both 1992 and 1993, with twenty-nine cases reported in 1992 and thirty in 1993.

In the early 1990s, the most important underwriters of social security plans were the Government Employees' Retirement Fund, the Social Insurance Institution, and the Social Insurance Institution for the Self-Employed. In 1995 at least 15 percent of the working population participated in the social welfare system. If the agricultural sector is excluded, this percentage rises to 40 percent. Less than 1 percent of agricultural workers were part of the social security system in 1995, but the government has made efforts for at least a decade to increase their participation. Employers pay insurance premiums to cover work-related injuries, occupational diseases, and maternity leave. Both employers and employees contribute specified proportions to cover premiums for illness, disability, retirement, and death benefits. Thus, in these and other instances, Turkey is moving toward a more Westernized approach to socioeconomic, educational, and health matters, and is seeking to lay a firmer basis for participation in the EU.

*   *   *

Feroz Ahmad's *The Making of Modern Turkey* includes a detailed analysis of Atatürk's secularist and linguistic reforms, as well as an excellent overview of the impact of social changes from the 1930s to the end of the 1980s. With the exception of the Kurds, studies on the experience of Turkey's ethnic and religious minorities have not been published for more than two decades. Martin van Bruinessen has written extensively about the social and economic conditions of Turkey's Kurds. His book *Agha, Shaikh, and State* analyzes how state policies have induced changes in the social organization of Kurdistan during the nineteenth and twentieth centuries. Numerous articles about contemporary Islam in Turkey have appeared since the mid-1980s. An excellent collection that examines social and educational issues is a volume edited by Richard Tapper, *Islam in Modern Turkey*. Insight into the effect of the post-1980 economic reforms on labor relations and class structure can be obtained from articles in *The Political and Socioeconomic Transformation of Turkey*, edited by Atila Eralp, Muharrem Tünay, and Birol Yesilada. Nermin Abadan-Unat has published books and articles about the changing status of women in Turkey; see especially her *Women in the Developing World: Evidence from Turkey*, which contains a wealth of statistical data. Jenny B. White's *Money Makes Us Relatives* is a detailed study of the intertwined cultural, social, and economic aspects of the lives of women who undertake at-home contract labor in Istanbul's lower-class neighborhoods. (For further information and complete citations, see Bibliography.)

Chapter 3. The Economy

Ferry on the Bosporus with Istanbul and the Galata Tower in the background

THE TURKISH ECONOMY is being transformed in the 1990s from a state-led to a market-oriented economy. As in most economies undergoing market reforms, the process of change has caused severe internal dislocations. External economic "shocks" such as the Persian Gulf War of 1991 and the resulting United Nations (UN) embargo on Iraq have complicated the transition.

The Turkish economy's ongoing and turbulent reorientation has left the economy a study in contrasts. Modern industries coexist with pockets of subsistence agriculture. The major cities of western Anatolia are cosmopolitan centers of industry, finance, and trade, whereas the eastern part of the country is relatively underdeveloped. Several decades of state planning followed by economic liberalization have made industry Turkey's leading economic sector, even as most Turks continue to work on farms. Industry has undergone a fairly rapid transformation as a consequence of the far-reaching market reforms implemented in the 1980s and early 1990s. Despite the reforms, however, public enterprises continue to dominate raw-materials processing and the manufacture of heavy industrial and military goods. The smaller firms that dominate the private sector produce intermediate and consumer goods for domestic and foreign markets. The services sector is perhaps the most diverse, embracing large export-oriented marketing groups and world-scale banks as well as small shops and individual domestic workers.

To a large extent, the last 200 years in Turkey have been marked by its rulers' attempts to transform it into a modern European industrial nation. The Ottoman Empire encountered serious economic problems beginning in the eighteenth century with the imposition of unequal treaties, the capitulations (see Glossary), which affected trade and taxation. The *tanzimat* (reorganization) reforms of 1839–78, an important component of which was the reorientation of the economy toward development of an indigenous industrial base, led to deepening indebtedness to Western imperial powers by the end of the nineteenth century. This dependence on the West, which was seen as one of the main causes of Turkey's "backwardness," created the context for the economic policy of the new republic formed in 1923. The other important influence on the new leaders of the republic was the example of state planning in the Soviet Union. Given these influences, state planning was the route Turkey's new leaders took to modernize the country.

From the 1930s until 1980, the state pursued import-substitution industrialization by means of public enterprises and development planning. This policy created a mixed economy in which industrial development was rapid. However, during the post-World War II period the drawbacks of excessive state intervention became ever more apparent to policy makers and the public. State enterprises, which came to account for about 40 percent of manufacturing by 1980, were often overstaffed and inefficient; their losses were a significant drain on the government budget. State planning targets were often excessively ambitious, yet they neglected such essential sectors as agriculture. Concentration on import substitution deemphasized exports, resulting in chronic trade deficits and a pattern in which periods of rapid growth, financed in part by foreign borrowing, led to balance of payments crises that necessitated austerity programs.

The rapid transition from an agricultural to an industrial society also produced distortions in the country's labor markets and led to unequal income distribution. As was the case in most developing countries, there was a high birth rate, which contributed to unemployment in the postwar period by causing the labor force to grow rapidly. In addition, the modernization of agriculture tended to make small farms economically nonviable. As a result, many rural people migrated to urban areas. Those who left farming, however, often lacked skills needed in modern industry and could find employment only in the informal sector of the urban economy. Meanwhile, industrial enterprises became more capital intensive, which increased productivity but reduced the demand for unskilled labor. At the same time, firms had trouble recruiting skilled employees.

In January 1980, the Turkish government undertook a major reform program to open the Turkish economy to international markets. Leading the reform was Turgut Özal, then deputy prime minister and minister for economic affairs. Özal became prime minister in 1983, following a three-year military regime, and served as president from 1989 until his death in 1993. Özal's reform program included a reduced state role in the economy, a realistic exchange rate and realistic monetary policies, cutbacks on subsidies and price controls, and encouragement of exports and foreign direct investment. During its early years, the liberalization program achieved considerable success in reducing external deficits and restoring economic growth. Despite significant foreign direct investment during the 1980s and early 1990s, however, Turkey's balance of payments remained burdened by an external debt of more than US$65 billion at the end of 1993. A balance of payments crisis occurred in 1994 in the aftermath of a domestic political crisis in the wake of deep divisions within the administration over economic policy and a sharp decrease in exports to Turkey's beleaguered neighbors, Iraq and Iran. This situation led to a steep fall in the Turkish lira (TL; for value of the lira—see Glossary).

The success of the Özal program was predicated on developing satisfactory relationships with the country's economic partners and continued access to export markets. Rapid development required large capital imports because domestic savings were insufficient for needed investments. Foreign investors, attracted by Turkey's great economic potential and increasingly liberal economic policies, made major commitments to infrastructure projects during the mid-1980s. However, continued high inflation, as well as memories of the political instability of the late 1970s, caused investors to hesitate. These insecurities were heightened after the Iraqi invasion of Kuwait in 1990, the rise of strong Islamist (sometimes seen as fundamentalist) parties in the early 1990s, and persistent macroeconomic problems.

Whatever short-term difficulties Turkey faces, most observers believe the country's long-term economic prospects are good. Mining and agriculture provide raw materials for industry, and the growing and resourceful population provides abundant labor. Turkey is one of the few countries that is self-sufficient in food; indeed it can export food to European and Middle Eastern markets. Economic reforms have led to increases in exports of processed foods, textiles, motor vehicles, and consumer durables. Considerable investments in tourism, the revitalization of banking, and upgraded transportation facilities should allow Turkey to compete in the international services market in the 1990s.

Turkey has made great strides toward building close economic ties with Europe, and Turkey's leaders have promoted the country as a vital link between the industrial economies of Europe and the underdeveloped economies of the Middle East and Central Asia. On several fronts, however, Turkey suffered a number of setbacks in the early 1990s. A critical one was the embargo on Iraq. Because of it, Turkey lost a huge export market as well as fees for allowing Iraqi oil to pass through a pipeline on Turkish territory. In addition, Iran, a major trading partner in the 1980s, reoriented its trade directly with Europe and Asia in the late 1980s and early 1990s. Early expectations for commerce with the Central Asian countries have gone unfulfilled because of the economic and social dislocations they have suffered in breaking away from the Soviet Union. Worst of all, Turkey's political relations with Europe have deteriorated, mainly because of human rights abuses of its Kurdish population and increasing intolerance in Europe of Turkish immigrants. As a result, Turkey's accession to the European Union (EU—see Glossary) appeared increasingly unlikely to happen as targeted in 1995, despite its having been an associate member since 1963 of the EU's predecessor body, the European Community (EC—see Glossary), and having applied for full membership in 1987.

Growth and Structure of the Economy

At the time of the collapse of the Ottoman Empire during World War I, the Turkish economy was underdeveloped: agriculture depended on outmoded techniques and poor-quality livestock, and the few factories producing basic products such as sugar and flour were under foreign control. Between 1923 and 1985, the economy grew at an average annual rate of 6 percent. In large part as a result of government policies, a backward economy developed into a complex economic system producing a wide range of agricultural, industrial, and service products for both domestic and export markets.

Economic Development

At the birth of the republic, Turkey's industrial base was weak because Ottoman industries had been undermined by the capitulations. World War I and the War of Independence (1919–22) also had extensively disrupted the Turkish economy. The loss of Ottoman territories, for example, cut off Anatolia from traditional markets. Agricultural output—the source of income for most of the population—had dropped sharply as peasants went to war. Even the production of wheat, Turkey's main crop, was insufficient to meet domestic demand. In addition, massacres and the emigration of Greeks, Armenians, and Jews, who had dominated urban economic life, caused a shortage of skilled laborers and entrepreneurs.

Turkey's economy recovered remarkably once hostilities ceased. From 1923 to 1926, agricultural output rose by 87 percent, as agricultural production returned to prewar levels. Industry and services grew at more than 9 percent per year from 1923 to 1929; however, their share of the economy remained quite low at the end of the decade. By 1930, as a result of the world depression, external markets for Turkish agricultural exports had collapsed, causing a sharp decline in national income. The government stepped in during the early 1930s to promote economic recovery, following a doctrine known as etatism (see Glossary). Growth slowed during the worst years of the depression but between 1935 and 1939 reached 6 percent per year. During the 1940s, the economy stagnated, in large part because maintaining armed neutrality during World War II increased the country's military expenditures while almost entirely curtailing foreign trade.

After 1950 the country suffered economic disruptions about once a decade; the most serious crisis occurred in the late 1970s. In each case, an industry-led period of rapid expansion, marked by a sharp increase in exports, resulted in a balance of payments crisis. Devaluations of the Turkish lira and austerity programs designed to dampen domestic demand for foreign goods were implemented in accordance with International Monetary Fund (IMF—see Glossary) guidelines. These measures usually led to sufficient improvement in the country's external accounts to make possible the resumption of loans to Turkey by foreign creditors. Although the military interventions of 1960 and 1971 were prompted in part by economic difficulties, after each intervention Turkish politicians boosted government spending, causing the economy to overheat. In the absence of serious structural reforms, Turkey ran chronic current account deficits usually financed by external borrowing that made the country's external debt rise from decade to decade, reaching by 1980 about US$16.2 billion, or more than one-quarter of annual gross domestic product (GDP—see Glossary). Debt-servicing costs in that year equaled 33 percent of exports of goods and services.

By the late 1970s, Turkey's economy had perhaps reached its worst crisis since the fall of the Ottoman Empire. Turkish authorities had failed to take sufficient measures to adjust to the effects of the sharp increase in world oil prices in 1973–74 and had financed the resulting deficits with short-term loans from foreign lenders. By 1979 inflation had reached triple-digit levels, unemployment had risen to about 15 percent, industry was using only half its capacity, and the government was unable to pay even the interest on foreign loans. It seemed that Turkey would be able to sustain crisis-free development only if major changes were made in the government's import-substitution approach to development. Many observers doubted the ability of Turkish politicians to carry out the needed reforms.

Reforms under Özal

In January 1980, the government of Prime Minister Süleyman Demirel (who had served as prime minister 1965–71, 1975–78, and 1979–80) began implementing a far-reaching reform program designed by then Deputy Prime Minister Turgut Özal to shift Turkey's economy toward export-led growth.

The Özal strategy called for import-substitution policies to be replaced with policies designed to encourage exports that could finance imports, giving Turkey a chance to break out of the postwar pattern of alternating periods of rapid growth and deflation. With this strategy, planners hoped Turkey could experience export-led growth over the long run. The government pursued these goals by means of a comprehensive package: devaluation of the Turkish lira and institution of flexible exchange rates, maintenance of positive real interest rates and tight control of the money supply and credit, elimination of most subsidies and the freeing of prices charged by state enterprises, reform of the tax system, and encouragement of foreign investment. In July 1982, when Özal left office, many of his reforms were placed on hold. Starting in November 1983, however, when he again became prime minister, he was able to extend the liberalization program.

The liberalization program overcame the balance of payments crisis, reestablished Turkey's ability to borrow in international capital markets, and led to renewed economic growth. Merchandise exports grew from US$2.3 billion in 1979 to US$8.3 billion in 1985. Merchandise import growth in the same period—from US$4.8 billion to US$11.2 billion—did not keep pace with export growth and proportionately narrowed the trade deficit, although the deficit level stabilized at around US$2.5 billion. Özal's policies had a particularly positive impact on the services account of the current account. Despite a jump

Atatürk Dam, major part of Southeast Anatolian Project (GAP)
Courtesy Turkish Information Office

in interest payments, from US$200 million in 1979 to US$1.4 billion in 1985, the services account accumulated a growing surplus during this period. Expanding tourist receipts and pipeline fees from Iraq were the main reasons for this improvement. Stabilizing the current account helped restore creditworthiness on international capital markets. Foreign investment, which had been negligible in the 1970s, now started to grow, although it remained modest in the mid-1980s. Also, Turkey was able to borrow on the international market, whereas in the late 1970s it could only seek assistance from the IMF and other official creditors.

The reduction in public expenditures, which was at the heart of the stabilization program, slowed the economy sharply in the late 1970s and early 1980s. Real gross national product (GNP—see Glossary) declined 1.5 percent in 1979 and 1.3 percent in 1980. The manufacturing and services sectors felt much of the impact of this drop in income, with the manufacturing sector operating at close to 50 percent of total capacity. As the external-payments constraint eased, the economy bounced back sharply. Between 1981 and 1985, real GNP grew 3 percent per year, led by growth in the manufacturing sector. With tight controls on workers' earnings and activities, the industrial sector began drawing on unused industrial capacity and raised output by an average rate of 9.1 percent per year between 1981 and 1985. The devaluation of the lira also helped make Turkey more economically competitive. As a result, exports of manufactures increased by an average rate of 45 percent per annum during this period.

The rapid resurgence of growth and the improvement in the balance of payments were insufficient to overcome unemployment and inflation, which remained serious problems. The official jobless rate fell from 15 percent in 1979 to 11 percent in 1980, but, partly because of the rapid growth of the labor force, unemployment rose again, to 13 percent in 1985. Inflation fell to about 25 percent in the 1981–82 period, but it climbed again, to more than 30 percent in 1983 and more than 40 percent in 1984. Although inflation eased somewhat in 1985 and 1986, it remained one of the primary problems facing economic policy makers.

Economic Performance in the Early 1990s

Turkey benefited economically from the Iran-Iraq War (1980–88). Both Iran and Iraq became major trading partners, and Turkish business supplied both combatants, encouraged by government export credits. With limited access to the Persian Gulf, Iraq also came to depend heavily on Turkey for export routes for its crude oil. Iraq had financed two pipelines located next to one another from its northern Kirkuk oilfields to the Turkish Mediterranean port of Çeyhan, slightly northwest of Iskenderun. The capacity of the pipelines totaled around 1.1 million barrels per day (bpd). Not only did Turkey obtain part of its domestic supplies from the pipeline, but it was paid a sizable entrepôt fee. Some sources have estimated this fee at US$300 million to US$500 million.

Turkey's economy was battered by the 1991 Persian Gulf War. The UN embargo on Iraq required the ending of oil exports through the Çeyhan pipelines, resulting in the loss of the pipeline fees. In addition, the economy may have lost as much as US$3 billion in trade with Iraq. Saudi Arabia, Kuwait, and the United Arab Emirates (UAE) moved to compensate Turkey for these losses, however, and by 1992 the economy again began to grow rapidly.

The Turkish economy again was plunged into crisis in 1994. The central government's moves in 1992 and 1993 to grant large salary increases to civil servants and to increase transfers to state enterprises enlarged the public-sector borrowing requirement to a record 17 percent of GDP in 1993. This high government spending sharply boosted domestic demand's rate of growth to 6.4 percent in 1992 and 7.6 percent in 1993. In turn, inflation rates went up, with the annual rate peaking at 73 percent in mid-1993. The resulting rise in the real exchange rate translated into increased imports and slowed the expansion of exports. The trade deficit rose in 1993 to US$14 billion, while the current account deficit reached US$6.3 billion, or 5.3 percent of GDP.

Turkey's impressive economic performance in the 1980s won high marks from Wall Street's credit-rating agencies. In 1992 and 1993, the government used these ratings to attract funds to cover its budget deficits. International bond issues over this period amounted to US$7.5 billion. These capital flows helped maintain the overvalued exchange rate. In a market economy, a high level of government borrowing should translate into higher domestic interest rates and even possibly "crowd out" private-sector borrowers, thereby eventually slowing economic growth. But the government's foreign borrowing took the pressure off domestic interest rates and actually spurred more private-sector borrowing in an already overheated economy. Sensing an easy profit opportunity during this period, commercial banks borrowed at world interest rates and lent at Turkey's higher domestic rates without fear of a depreciating currency. As a result, Turkey's foreign short-term debt rose sharply. External and internal confidence in the government's ability to manage the impending balance of payments crisis waned, compounding economic difficulties.

Disputes between Prime Minister Tansu Çiller (1993–) and the Central Bank governor undermined confidence in the government. The prime minister insisted on monetizing the fiscal deficit (selling government debt instruments to the Central Bank) rather than acceding to the Central Bank's proposal to issue more public debt in the form of government securities. The Central Bank governor resigned in August 1993 over this issue. In January 1994, international credit agencies downgraded Turkey's debt to below investment grade. At that time, a second Central Bank governor resigned.

Mounting concern over the disarray in economic policy was reflected in an accelerated "dollarization" of the economy as residents switched domestic assets into foreign-currency deposits to protect their investments. By the end of 1994, about 50 percent of the total deposit base was held in the form of foreign-currency deposits, up from 1 percent in 1993. The downgrading by credit-rating agencies and a lack of confidence in the government's budget deficit target of 14 percent of GDP for 1994 triggered large-scale capital flight and the collapse of the exchange rate. The government had to intervene by selling its foreign-currency reserves to staunch the decline of the Turkish lira. As a result, reserves fell from US$6.3 billion at the end of 1993 to US$3 billion by the end of March 1994. Before the end of April, when the government was forced to announce a long-overdue austerity program following the March 1994 local elections, the lira had plummeted by 76 percent from the end of 1993 to TL41,000 against the United States dollar.

The package of measures announced by the government on April 5, 1994, was also submitted to the IMF as part of its request for a US$740 million standby facility beginning in July 1994. Measures included a sharp increase in prices the public-sector enterprises would charge the public, decreases in budgetary expenditures, a commitment to raise taxes, and a pledge to accelerate privatization of state economic enterprises (SEEs). Some observers questioned the credibility of these measures, given that the tax measures translated into a revenue increase equivalent to 4 percent of GDP and the expenditure cuts were equivalent to 6 percent of GDP.

The government actually succeeded in generating a small surplus in the budget during the second quarter of 1994, mainly as a result of higher taxes, after running a deficit of 17 percent of GDP in the first quarter. The slowdown in government spending, a sharp loss in business confidence, and the resulting decline in economic activity reduced tax revenues, however. The fiscal crisis resulted in a decline in real GDP of 5 percent in 1994 after the economy had grown briskly in 1992 and 1993. Real wages also fell in 1994: average nominal wage increases of 65 percent were about 20 percent below the rate of consumer price inflation.

Analysts pointed out that despite the fragility of the macro-economic adjustment process and the susceptibility of fiscal policy to political pressures, the government continued to be subject to market checks and balances. Combined with a stronger private sector, particularly on the export front, the economy was expected to bounce back to a pattern of faster growth.

Structure of the Economy

In the years after World War II, the economy became capable of supplying a much broader range of goods and services. By 1994 the industrial sector accounted for just under 40 percent of GDP, having surpassed agriculture (including forestry and fishing), which contributed about 16 percent of production. The rapid shift in industry's relative importance resulted from government policies in effect since the 1930s favoring industrialization (see fig. 8). In the early 1990s, the government aimed at continued increases in industry's share of the economy, especially by means of export promotion.

Services increased from a small fraction of the economy in the 1920s to just under half of GDP by 1994. Several factors accounted for the growth of the services sector. Government—already sizable under the Ottomans—expanded as defense expenditures rose; health, education, and welfare programs were implemented; and the government work force was increased to staff the numerous new public organizations. Trade, tourism, transportation, and financial services also became more important as the economy developed and diversified.

Human Resources and Trade Unions

In the early 1990s, Turkey suffered from serious structural unemployment, although the country continued to lack skilled workers and managers. The number of people engaged in subsistence agriculture and in informal labor complicated efforts to make accurate estimates of unemployment and underemployment. In the absence of direct surveys, available statistical data only broadly indicated trends in labor markets (see table 5, Appendix A). In 1992 the civilian labor force totaled almost 18.5 million; the government estimated that unemployment was about 8.7 percent, but unofficial sources put it at 15 percent for 1993. In a study, the State Institute of Statistics estimated that unemployment in urban areas among those aged

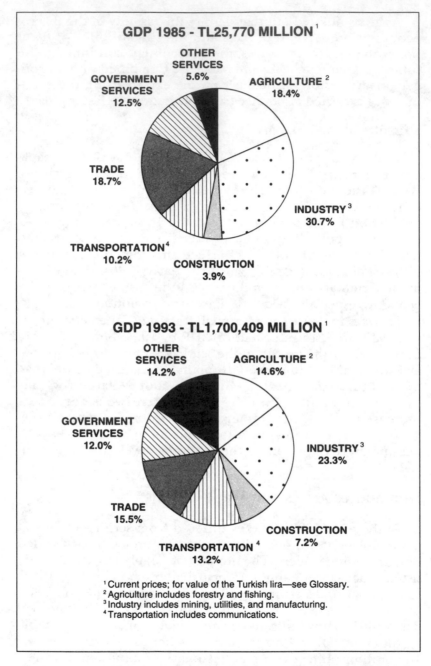

Figure 8. Structure of the Gross Domestic Product (GDP), 1985 and 1993

fifteen to twenty-four was 30.2 percent. According to official figures for 1992, about 44 percent of those employed worked in agriculture—down from more than 75 percent in the early 1960s. Employment in industry and construction amounted to about 20 percent in 1994, and the services sector employed about 35 percent.

During the postwar period, as agriculture modernized and grew more productive, many agricultural workers became redundant. Many now-jobless farmers, attracted by higher wages in the urban economy, migrated to the cities. Although industry and services grew rapidly after 1950, these sectors did not create enough jobs to meet the demand.

Demographic trends portend continued unemployment problems. Population growth rates declined somewhat after the 1970s, but in the mid-1990s demographers were predicting that the active population (those between fifteen and sixty-four years of age) would increase at more than 2 percent per year until at least 2000. The labor force grew at an estimated average annual rate of 2 percent during the 1960s and 1970s, at 1.5 to 2.0 percent during the early 1980s, and at 2.2 percent per year from 1985 to 1992. The several austerity programs since 1980 exacerbated the unemployment situation in the mid-1980s, with an estimated 3 million Turks unemployed in 1985. The recovery of the economy in the late 1980s appeared to improve the overall situation; manufacturing employment increased 3.4 percent per year. However, the economic crisis of early 1994 and the austerity program once again were expected to slow employment growth.

The labor force would have grown even faster during the 1970s and 1980s had it not been for a fall in the work force participation rate from about 73 percent in the 1970s to 35 percent in the early 1990s. This decline resulted from increased enrollments in secondary and postsecondary education and from the tendency of rural women who migrated to the city to refrain from entering the work force. Most demographers believed that participation rates would continue to fall as a result of higher overall school and female education rates. By 1991 the secondary school enrollment ratios, particularly for females, lagged significantly behind primary school enrollment ratios, implying room for higher future enrollment. Even if participation rates continue to fall, however, projected population growth rates will make unemployment a continuing problem.

Unemployment has caused distortions in rural and urban labor markets. Many farmers have remained on unproductive farms to avoid more uncertain fates in the cities. In addition, the large postwar increase in employment in the services sector probably reflects wide-scale underemployment, as unemployed persons resort to working as street vendors and domestic workers. The largest groups of the unemployed include educated youths from urban areas, migrants dislocated from the villages and living in shantytowns, and Turks returning from working abroad.

Emigration has provided a partial safety valve for excess labor, especially during the period between 1969 and 1973, when more than 100,000 workers left each year to seek jobs abroad. The capital-intensive, labor-short countries of northwestern Europe began recruiting workers from southern Europe and the Mediterranean basin in the 1950s. Turkish workers began emigrating to Western Europe in large numbers in the early 1960s, as the demand for labor increased in northern Europe and as the supply from southern Italy dried up because of increased domestic demand. Although Turks worked in many European countries, most went to the Federal Republic of Germany (West Germany). Many Turkish workers also went to France, Austria, and the Netherlands. The number of Turkish workers going abroad peaked near 136,000 in 1973. The oil shock of that year and the 1974–75 recession led to restrictions on new guest workers throughout Western Europe, including a ban in West Germany. These measures caused a sharp decline in Turkish emigration to Western Europe—which averaged only 18,000 per year from 1974 to 1980—and became an important issue between Turkey and the European Community. Despite the restrictions, in 1981 there were still about 1 million Turkish workers in Western Europe, half of them in West Germany.

After the unification of Germany in 1989, pressure mounted to return so-called foreign workers to their home countries even though many had been born in Europe. High unemployment rates, especially in eastern Germany, spurred neo-Nazi political parties to agitate for forced repatriation, and some groups used violence against immigrants. In one celebrated case in Rostock, members of a Turkish family were burned to death in their own home. Other European states also witnessed a rise in hostility toward guest workers, including Turks. In

France, the National Front Party, led by Jean-Marie Le Pen, gained much support for its anti-immigrant stance.

After 1975 Turkish workers went more often to Arab oil states than to Western Europe. Each year from 1980 through 1982, more than 24,000 workers went to Libya and more than 10,000 to Saudi Arabia. During the same period, a yearly average of only 370 Turkish workers went to West Germany. By 1982 about 150,000 Turks were employed in Saudi Arabia, Libya, and the small Arabian Peninsula states. However, economic difficulties faced by oil-producing states in the mid- and late 1980s reduced opportunities for further Turkish emigration.

In general, the Turkish government has looked favorably on worker emigration, despite concerns that skilled workers are being lost because it is better-educated Turks who tend to emigrate. In 1994 an estimated 1.1 million Turkish workers were in Western Europe, of whom about 750,000 were in Germany. More than 200,000 were in Middle Eastern countries. Workers in Europe usually stay abroad several years, remitting funds to relatives in Turkey. Most eventually return with their accumulated savings to start a small business or buy a farm. Turks working in the Middle East, in contrast, tend to work for Turkish construction firms and typically return after each project is completed; these workers tend to remit a larger share of earnings to their families. The flow of workers' remittances became financially significant after 1965, when they reached the equivalent of US$70 million. By the early 1990s, this figure had reached US$3 billion per year.

Like most developing countries, Turkey lacks an adequate number of trained and skilled personnel. In the early 1990s, the demand for educated and skilled workers exceeded the limited number of technically and scientifically trained graduates.

Trade unions play an important role with reference to labor in the more modern sectors of the economy. Most agricultural and service workers do not belong to unions, but a substantial part of the industrial labor force in larger enterprises and some workers in other sectors, such as transportation, trade, and finance, are unionized; public-sector workers are the most likely to join a union. In the 1960s and 1970s, the wage and benefit gains of unionized workers exerted a positive influence on the income levels of nonunionized workers. After the 1980s, however, the labor movement weakened. Not only are unions smaller in terms of membership—Ministry of Labor and Social Security figures for 1985 suggested that unions included about 1.8 million workers, or about 10 percent of the civilian work force—but severe limits on their activities have kept them politically weak. As a result, during the 1980s organized labor suffered large cuts in real earnings.

By the mid-1970s, Turkey had about 800 unions, many of which had memberships in the hundreds. Few were what might be called nationwide unions; several had extensive membership in a particular industry, which gave them a leverage that most unions lacked. Many unions joined national federations to exert more influence. Before the 1980 coup, four main trade union federations with differing political orientations dominated the labor scene. The main union organization, the Confederation of Turkish Trade Unions (Türkiye Isçi Sendikaları Konfederasyonu—Türk-Is) was politically moderate, adhering to legal limits on its activities. The other major union group, the Confederation of Revolutionary Workers' Trade Unions of Turkey (Türkiye Devrimçi Isçi Sendikaları Konfederasyonu—DISK), originated from a faction of Türk-Is in 1967. DISK was much smaller than Türk-Is but more militant. In addition, small numbers of workers belonged to the pro-Islamist Confederation of Turkish Just Workers' Unions (Türkiye Hak Isçi Sendikaları Konfederasyonu—Hak-Is) and the right-wing Confederation of Turkish Nationalist Workers' Unions (Türkiye Milliyetçi Isçi Sendikaları Konfederasyonu—MISK). After the 1980 coup, all union federations except Türk-Is were banned for a period. Subsequently, the government allowed the other union groups to resume their activities.

Figures on trade union membership vary, but Ministry of Labor statistics at least give an idea of the relative sizes of the unions. According to this source, in 1992 Türk-Is had a membership of about 1.7 million, Hak-Is had about 330,000 members, and DISK had about 26,000 members. In addition, Turkey had twenty-four independent unions that did not belong to federations. The size of their memberships was uncertain in early 1995, but organized labor totaled almost 2.2 million workers in 1992. Workers could legally belong to more than one union, which explains some of the confusion surrounding membership statistics.

Established in 1952, Türk-Is includes many workers employed in SEEs and was the only union group actively involved in large-scale collective bargaining in the early 1990s.

Strongly centralized, Türk-Is is dominated by a few large, conservative unions; the social democratic unions that figure among its thirty affiliates have little say in federation affairs. In adherence to the law, Türk-Is has remained technically aloof from party politics but is interested in issues affecting labor. Türk-Is is affiliated with the American Federation of Labor-Congress of Industrial Organizations through its membership in the Asian-American Free Labor Institute, which provides training for union leaders. Since 1980 Türk-Is has generally refrained from calling strikes, perhaps because of fears that labor conflicts might lead to layoffs of surplus SEE personnel.

Against a background of growing labor unrest in 1994, related to deepening economic problems, budget cuts, and privatization, Türk-Is coordinated wage talks with the government at the end of the year. Although accused of earlier and questionable cooperation with the government, Türk-Is faced widespread pressure from affiliated unions and their members not to agree to the increase the government was offering. Both DISK and Hak-Is had strongly opposed a pay increase of 102 percent for the Türk-Is-affiliated Teksif union at the end of 1994 on the grounds that the size of the pay increase did not meet the much higher inflation rates and the agreement was co-optive.

DISK, Türk-Is's chief rival, draws its members primarily from the private sector and from municipal workers. In the mid-1990s, it seemed that supporters of left-wing unions such as DISK were shifting to Islamist-oriented ones. Nonetheless, DISK-affiliated unions continued to exert some influence as part of overall labor pressure to maintain wage and employment levels.

Before 1980 Hak-Is was reportedly tied to the pro-Islamic National Salvation Party (Milli Selamet Partisi—MSP), whereas MISK supported the Nationalist Action Party (Milliyetçi Hareket Partisi—MHP). In 1980 the two federations claimed memberships of 68,000 and 290,000, respectively. After 1984 they played only a minor role in collective bargaining because they lacked sufficient membership to be considered representative under new labor legislation.

The 1980 military intervention severely restricted trade union activities. The 1982 constitution and the laws on union organization, collective bargaining, strikes, and lockouts passed in 1983 have made Turkey's unions the most tightly controlled in noncommunist Europe. To have the right to represent the workers at a given facility, unions must prove that they have the support of at least 10 percent of union membership within the industry and a majority at the particular workplace. Political and general strikes and many forms of industrial action, including secondary strikes, work slowdowns, and picketing, are prohibited. About half of the unionized workers, including those in the gas, water, electricity, mining, and petroleum industries as well as those in banking, urban transit, garbage collection and firefighting, are allowed to strike. Strikes can be called only after a written announcement to the government, which may require a ninety-day cooling-off period followed by compulsory arbitration. Workers who strike illegally may be punished with as much as eighteen months in prison, and those who participate in such strikes can be fired, with the loss of all accumulated financial claims, including pensions.

Following the 1980 coup, the military government prohibited collective bargaining until May 1984, after which time officials continued trying to restrain wage settlements in order to limit inflation. Although private-sector wage settlements in 1984 and 1985 included increases ranging from 25 to 60 percent, pay adjustments generally continued to run behind the inflation rate, resulting in declines in real wages. The government took a more relaxed attitude in the late 1980s, but by 1994 the authorities were once again using antistrike regulations from the early 1980s to stop strikes and other job actions.

In the public sector, the government has been even more successful at holding the line against wage increases, although large increases in 1992–93 led to a sharp jump in government expenditures. With a limited endorsement by the IMF, government employees' wages were targeted as the primary means of achieving budget cuts in 1994 and early 1995. As part of this strategy, Prime Minister Çiller attempted to use illegal strikes as a pretext for liquidating certain public enterprises; unionized workers also would be notified that there were plenty of unemployed people willing to do their jobs for lower pay. In early 1995, unions for public-sector workers outside the public enterprises faced the possibility of being abolished altogether. Also, seasonal workers with part-time jobs working on village roads, irrigation projects, and other infrastructure components were to be placed under the authority of provincial authorities, an arrangement that would cost them their labor rights. People employed with "worker" status, who therefore had certain rights under the law, were reclassified as "public servants" with no right to bargain collectively or to strike. Members of this group fared badly in the mid-1990s, with declining wages accompanying their loss of rights.

Role of Government in the Economy

The Ottoman Empire established a strong tradition of government direction of the economy. Ottoman economic doctrine ascribed to the state both the right and the duty to control the economy for the common good. The state controlled a large proportion of the land and suppressed power centers, blocking the development of a landed aristocracy. One's position in the imperial hierarchy was the primary determinant of income. Because the sultan confiscated his functionaries' wealth when they died, status could be passed on only by means of education. For example, candidates for positions in the bureaucracy were required to have command of the Ottoman language. Peasants and artisans also claimed and received protection from the state, often at the expense of economic modernization. The bureaucracy had little interest in economic growth, which might lead to the rise of a new class that would challenge its dominance. To ensure control of certain urban-based production and service functions, they were reserved for minority groups.

Republican Turkey inherited attitudes and memories from the Ottomans that continue to play a key role in the country's political economy in the late twentieth century. Republican leaders believe that the state has a duty to intervene in the economy, not only to strengthen the nation against foreign intervention but ultimately to further the well-being of the people.

Liberal Interlude

Scholars traditionally have stressed the significance of state intervention in the economy during the early years of the republic, but more recent research indicates that Turkish economic policy was relatively liberal until the 1930s. The government made significant investments in railroad and other infrastructure projects, but the Law for the Encouragement of Industry of 1927 and other measures encouraged private enterprise. Moreover, Turkey's economy was relatively open to international markets during the 1920s. Under the provisions of the Treaty of Lausanne of 1923, the capitulations were abolished, but Turkey could not introduce protective tariffs until August 1929. As a result, tariffs remained low, and the Turkish lira was convertible and floating. Foreign interests invested in both public and private enterprises, helping to initiate industrial development. During these early years, economic growth was satisfactory, but the country ran chronic foreign trade deficits despite the continued fall in the value of the lira.

Turkish economic development reached a turning point with the Great Depression. By 1930 foreign markets for Turkish agricultural products had collapsed, causing sharp declines in the prices of agricultural goods and a corresponding decline in national income. Dissatisfied with the slow development of industry, Turkey's leaders began to look for alternative policies. During the late 1920s and the early 1930s, economic and political thinkers discussed alternative approaches to national economic development. The interventionist trend in Western economic thinking, represented by works such as John Maynard Keynes's *The End of Laissez-Faire* (1926), influenced the theoretical debate. The apparent successes of the Soviet Union's drive to develop heavy industry under its First Five-Year Plan (1928–33) also impressed Turkish thinkers, although in the end Turkish policy borrowed primarily from the West.

Etatism

At its 1931 congress, the Republican People's Party (Cumhuriyet Halk Partisi—CHP) adopted etatism, one of Atatürk's Six Arrows, as its official economic strategy. According to this program, individual enterprise was to retain a fundamental role in the economy, but active government intervention was necessary to boost the nation's welfare and the state's prosperity. The CHP also declared that etatism was an intermediate road between capitalism and socialism. In practice, etatism entailed the promotion of industrialization by means of five-year plans and the creation of public enterprises. Comprehensive protective tariffs also were introduced during the 1930s, establishing a pattern of import-substitution industrialization that would continue for many years.

After World War II, all major parties claimed to support etatism. The sharp reorientation of Turkey's economic policies after 1980 included a repudiation of much etatist doctrine, which, however, still influenced Turkish economic thinking. Inasmuch as Atatürk had declared that once Turkey had reached a satisfactory level of development certain state enterprises could be returned to private control, the post-1980s economic reforms perhaps could be considered a continuation of one aspect of the original etatist program. Moreover, the government continued to use policy tools such as SEEs and development planning that had originated during the etatist period. Nonetheless, by the mid-1990s deepening government indebtedness dictated a faster reduction of the state's economic commitments. Given Turkey's high inflation, job insecurity, and unemployment, etatism could be in vogue again, but in the mid-1990s no major opposition party was calling for the wholesale renationalization of the economy. .

State Economic Enterprises and Privatization

An important tool of etatism to further government economic policies, State Economic Enterprises (SEEs) are variously organized, but the government owns at least a 50 percent share in each of them. SEEs are set up by the government, and each has a board that reflects the ownership of the particular SEE, combining government representatives, who direct the enterprise, with private interests. During the etatist industrialization campaign of the 1930s, the government set up many industrial SEEs. In the mid-1990s, SEEs continue to dominate sectors considered to be of national importance or sectors where private investors have hesitated to invest because capital requirements are too great in light of expected returns. SEEs include national transportation, communications, and energy enterprises; banks that own companies, in particular branches such as textiles or refining; and conglomerates with holdings in many fields. Some SEEs control companies in which ownership is shared with private and foreign investors. In 1964 the State Investment Bank was established to provide long-term investment credits to SEEs. Credits from the Central Bank of Turkey, transfers from the Treasury, and capital markets also finance SEEs.

In the mid-1990s, SEEs accounted for more than 40 percent of value added in manufacturing and employed about 550,000 workers, or about 20 percent of the industrial work force. Until 1980 SEEs set their prices in accordance with government directives, but after the introduction of that year's reform package, they were expected to set prices independently. Nevertheless, prices of some major commodities, such as fertilizers, continue to be determined by the government. SEEs also influence markets, especially those for agricultural goods, by establishing guaranteed minimum prices for commodities.

Aside from their role in industrial development, SEEs are charged with social goals. The farm-support program stabilizes farmers' incomes, while low consumer prices for food, energy, and transportation help the urban poor. SEEs also provide training and employ surplus university graduates and constituents of influential politicians, contributing to overstaffing. Some SEEs are placed in underdeveloped regions to spur industrial development, a practice that increases transportation and infrastructure costs.

One objective of the Özal reforms was to improve SEEs' efficiency and reduce their need for subsidies. By 1982 the government had freed most SEE prices and had given SEE managers greater autonomy and responsibility. The administration favored opening state monopolies to outside competition and decided in 1983 to limit SEE investments in manufacturing. Nevertheless, in the mid-1980s the state sector had to take over several failed banks that had significant industrial holdings, and the low rate of private investment meant that the public share in industrial investment actually rose. By the mid-1990s, SEEs remained a major burden on the public exchequer. Of the fifty SEEs, only fifteen were expected to report profits in 1994. Funding the operating losses of the SEEs—TL90 trillion in 1994 alone—annually cost the Treasury around TL20 trillion (about US$70 billion) in 1993 and 1994; the remainder was borrowed from banks. The total debt stock of the public enterprises by late 1994 was estimated at TL250 trillion, the bulk of which was owed to the Treasury and Central Bank. This debt generated an interest charge of around TL60 trillion in 1994 alone on collective sales of TL550 trillion. Deepening economic problems in the 1990s were part of the reason for the losses. This situation was exacerbated by a requirement that took effect after 1989 stipulating that SEEs borrow at high market rates.

Major plans for privatization of SEEs were supposed to go into effect as early as 1987 but as of early 1995 had not yet occurred. Prime candidates for sale include the state airline, the cement industry, and the textile industry. Almost all SEEs are considered potentially suitable for privatization except for certain infrastructure facilities such as power plants and railroads.

Some SEE managers and unions oppose privatization, fearing that, once under private management, the enterprises will eliminate unprofitable subsidiaries or aggressively reduce overstaffing. Some opposition parties also fear that public assets will be allocated among "friends" of government officials, with the result being the creation of private monopolies. Observers anticipate that certain "strategic" industries, including much mining and defense production, will remain in the public sector and that the best the administration can hope for would be to force them to approximate private- sector practices. Moreover, certain privatization moves, particularly the sale of cement mills belonging to the public enterprise Citosan, and a controlling stake in the airport management company Havas, were reversed by the Constitutional Court on administrative grounds.

After becoming prime minister, Çiller accepted the existing legislation on privatization and even sought wider powers to hasten the process. Law 3291, passed in 1986, had established the Public Participation Administration, which would control SEEs designated for privatization and prepare them for the process. In late 1994, the National Assembly passed a bill introduced by Çiller to revamp the administrative procedures dealing with privatization.

The bill established the Privatization Administration to carry out technical work and a Privatization High Board to make final decisions. The latter would control the Privatization Fund into which revenues were to be channeled. The Privatization High Board would consist of the prime minister, the minister of state "responsible for privatization," and the ministers of finance and industry and trade. The board was also to be responsible for deciding which public enterprises are of special strategic importance and in which the state should retain preference shares. Turkish Petroleum, Ziraat Bank, Halk Bank, Turkish Airlines, and the Soil Products Office Alkaloid Plant were placed in the latter category. Railroads, airports, and the General Management for Trade in Tobacco, Tobacco Products, and Alcoholic Spirits (Tütün, Tütün Mamülleri, Tuz ve Alkol Isletmeleri Genel Müdürlügü—TEKEL) were not designated to be privatized in the mid-1990s. Privatization of telecommunications and the electricity production and distribution board were to be dealt with in separate legislation. All other types of SEEs were again targeted for privatization in various ways, including the sale of all or parts of a company through share offers, block sales, auctions, and the transfer of plants to private domestic and foreign entities and to companies formed by workers and local townspeople. Some of the early candidates were the Eregli Iron and Steelworks, the Turkish Petroleum Refineries Corporation (Türkiye Petrol Refinerileri As— TÜPRAS), the state oil products distributor (Petrol Ofisi), the petrochemicals company (Petkim), the industrial interests of the state holding company, Sumerbank, the national airline (Turkish Airlines), and the airport company (Havas). The bill also set guidelines to prevent the formation of private monopolies and methods for dealing with workers who lose their jobs. Workers made redundant would continue to receive their wages for up to eight months and, depending on length of service, would get pensions or severance pay.

Development Planning

Turkey first introduced five-year plans in the 1930s as part of the etatist industrialization drive. The first five-year plan began in 1934. A second plan was drafted but only partially implemented because of World War II. These early plans were largely lists of desirable projects, but they provided guidance for the development of infrastructure, mining, and manufacturing. During the 1950s, the Democrat Party (DP) eliminated central economic planning, but the 1961 constitution made social and economic planning a state duty. In 1961 the government established the State Planning Organization (SPO), which was given responsibility for preparing long-term and annual plans, following up on plan implementation, and advising on current economic policy. The SPO comes under the prime minister's office and receives policy direction from the High Planning Council (also seen as the Supreme Planning Council), which is chaired by the prime minister and includes cabinet ministers. The Central Planning Organization, the secretariat of the High Planning Council, formulates the strategy and broad targets on which the SPO bases detailed plans. Plan targets are binding for the public sector but only indicative for private enterprises.

SPO plans include—in addition to investment levels—macroeconomic targets, social goals, and policy recommendations for individual subsectors of the economy. Turkey was one of the first countries to develop regional planning, a major challenge given the limited development of eastern and southeastern Anatolia. The SPO has approached planning from a long-term perspective and drew up the First Five-Year Plan (1963–67) and the Second Five-Year Plan (1968–72) in the context of what should be accomplished by the mid-1970s. Similarly, development goals for 1995, including a customs union with the EC, were set in the Third Five-Year Plan (1973–77) and the Fourth Five-Year Plan (1979–83). Successive plans took stock of problems and previous accomplishments, but many policy suggestions were never effectively implemented.

Early plans were heavily weighted toward manufacturing, import substitution, and the intermediate goods sector. The economic and political disorder of the late 1970s, however, made it impossible to achieve plan targets. After the 1980 coup, the Fourth Five-Year Plan was modified to favor the private sector, labor-intensive and export-oriented projects, and investments that would pay for themselves relatively quickly. The Özal administration delayed the Fifth Five-Year Plan (1984–89) for one year to take account of the structural reform program introduced in 1983. Unlike earlier plans, the Fifth Five-Year Plan called for a smaller state sector. According to the plan, the state would take more of a general supervisory role than it had in the past, concentrating on encouraging private economic actors. Nevertheless, the state was to continue an aggressive program of infrastructure investments to clear bottlenecks in energy, transport, and other sectors.

In May 1989, the government published the 1990–95 Development Plan. The plan called for overall economic growth of 7 percent per year. The growth of private-sector investment was targeted at an average of 11 percent per year, whereas the aim was to increase exports 15 percent per year. The inflation rate was targeted at 10 percent per year. As it developed, although high growth rates were maintained during the 1990–95 period, they came at the cost of increased foreign and domestic borrowing, which funded an inflationary government budgetary and monetary policy. Rapid rates of growth also were boosted by foreign direct investment. Excessive borrowing and domestic political problems led to a balance of payments crisis that sharply reduced domestic investment rates and ultimately led to a decline in incomes. Whereas the development plan had called for high growth rates and macroeconomic stability, Turkey actually has experienced high growth rates and macroeconomic instability.

Budget

Public-sector spending is the most important means of state

intervention in the Turkish economy. The consolidated government budget comprises central government spending and a number of annexed budgets of such partially autonomous entities as the State Highway Administration, state monopolies, and some universities and academies. Local budgets and most SEE budgets generally are not included in the consolidated budget, nor are special and extrabudgetary funds. The most important of the latter are the Mass Housing Fund, financed from luxury-import duties; the Defense Industry Support Fund, financed from levies on sales of gasoline, cigarettes, and alcoholic beverages; and the Public Revenue Sharing Schemes Fund. The partially autonomous organizations are included in the calculations for the public-sector borrowing requirement (PSBR).

Since 1983 the Treasury, under the direct control of the prime minister's office, has had sole responsibility to raise domestic tax revenues. The Ministry of Finance and the SPO are mainly responsible for planning spending policies, but the minister of finance presents the annual budget to parliament, which approves the annual government budget and legislates supplementary appropriations as required during the fiscal year, at times making significant modifications.

Turkish governments have persistently run large budget deficits, which have fueled inflation, capital flight, and heavy foreign and domestic borrowing. At the heart of this problem is the political system, which tends to be largely unrepresentative even when democracy is formally operating. Prior to major elections, governments have been prone to boost spending, particularly salaries for government workers. Despite recent modest changes to this system, Turkish governments have been averse to increasing taxes to pay for their high spending. Taxes, excluding social security contributions, are still around 20 percent of GNP—the lowest figure among the member countries of the Organisation for Economic Co-operation and Development.

Prior to 1980, local administrations had limited revenue-earning power and depended heavily on funds transferred from the central government. Even with such transfers, local governments were often short of funds needed to provide services required during a period of rapid urbanization when many city dwellers lacked even the most basic services. After 1980 reforms significantly strengthened the revenue base of municipalities, in part by providing that 5 percent of government tax revenues would be withheld at the local level. In 1994 Çiller also attempted to increase the revenues that local governments might raise.

During the early and mid-1980s, the government made serious attempts to reduce Turkey's inflationary budget deficits, implementing policies to streamline government, improve public resources allocation, and modernize the tax system. The government, for example, designed tax reforms to increase revenues and to reduce inequities. In addition, the introduction of a lump sum tax on small businesses and a new system of income tax payments for self-employed people reduced tax evasion. The government also started to tax farmers' incomes systematically for the first time since the 1920s. Other reforms strengthened tax administration, established new tax courts, and instituted heavier penalties for tax evasion.

Overall, the consolidated budget deficit declined during the 1980s as a result of the reform measures. During the decade, the deficit averaged 3 percent of GNP. However, the deficit went up in the 1990s, reaching 7.4 percent in 1991, 6.1 percent in 1992, 9.8 percent in 1993, and 8 percent in 1994 (see table 6, Appendix A). The 1994 figure includes a first-quarter budget deficit of 17 percent, which was sharply offset in subsequent quarters after the promulgation of the April 5 measures and tight supervision by the IMF. These measures more than reversed some of the increases in wages and other spending made in 1992 and 1993. Public-sector borrowing requirements have been much higher as a percentage of GNP. After averaging around 6 percent during the 1980s, they ranged from about 10 to 17 percent in the 1990s.

Agriculture

Agriculture—the occupation of the majority of Turks—continued to be a crucial sector of the economy in the mid-1990s, although industrial production was rising. Turkey's fertile soil and hard-working farmers make the country one of the few in the world that is self-sufficient in terms of food. Turkey's great variety of microclimates and adequate rainfall permit a broad range of crops. Farming is conducted throughout the country, although it is less common in the mountainous eastern regions, where animal husbandry is the principal activity. In the mid-1990s, crop cultivation accounted for about two-thirds and livestock for one-third of the gross value of agricultural

175

production; forestry and fishing combined contributed a minimal amount.

Agriculture's share in overall income has fallen progressively, declining from almost 50 percent of GDP in 1950 to around 15 percent of GDP by 1993. During the same period, the sector grew only about 1 percent faster than the country's population, and per capita food production declined in absolute terms. The relatively poor showing of the agricultural sector reflected in part government policies that had made rapid industrialization a national priority since the 1930s. In addition, farmers were slow to adopt modern techniques, with agricultural output suffering from insufficient mechanization, limited use of fertilizer, excessive fallow land, and unexploited water resources. The result has been low yields.

Despite agriculture's relative decline in the 1980s as a percentage of GDP, the sector played an important role in foreign trade. Turkey enjoys a comparative advantage in many agricultural products and exports cereals, pulses, industrial crops, sugar, nuts, fresh and dried fruits, vegetables, olive oil, and livestock products. The main export markets are the European Union and the United States—to which Turkey primarily exports dried fruit and nuts, cotton, and tobacco—and the Middle East, which primarily imports fresh fruit, vegetables, and meat from Turkey. As late as 1980, agricultural exports accounted for nearly 60 percent of the total value of exports. In the early 1990s, agricultural products accounted for 15 percent of total exports. Around 50 percent of manufactured exports originate in the agricultural sector; counting these exports, the agricultural sector's contribution to exports again would rise to around 60 percent.

Agriculture has great potential for further development, provided that the state can implement successful agrarian reforms and development projects. Observers believe that to achieve balanced growth, Turkey needs to improve the training of farmers, make better seed available, upgrade livestock herds, standardize products, expand food-processing facilities (including cold storage and refrigerated transport), and reorganize marketing networks. Since 1980 the government has encouraged investments in packaging, processing, livestock, and slaughterhouses, and has imported new seed varieties. These efforts had a modest impact on overall production by the mid-1990s.

Irrigation of an olive grove in the Izmit area
Courtesy Hermine Dreyfuss

Tea plantation near Artvin, northeastern Turkey; olives and tea are major Turkish crops.
Courtesy Hermine Dreyfuss

The failure to exploit the country's great agricultural potential has contributed to Turkey's periodic economic crises and poses serious problems for future development. Glaring inequalities of income between urban and rural residents—and among segments of the farm population—have created social tensions and contributed to emigration from rural to urban areas. Malnutrition continues to threaten segments of the rural population, especially children. The Kurdish insurgency in eastern Turkey has added to problems in some rural areas. Rising incomes in the urban areas have caused increased demand for more "exotic" foodstuffs, especially meat and poultry. Since 1984 Turkey has liberalized its policy on food imports, partly to meet this urban demand and partly to offset domestic price pressure. Many previously banned luxury food imports and imports that compete with domestically produced staples are permitted for these reasons; in turn, the growth of these imports has contributed to pressures on foreign trade accounts. Overall, agricultural output needs to expand along with the rest of the economy to maintain adequate supplies for industry and exports. Longer-term economic growth prospects and macroeconomic stability, therefore, depend on the performance of Turkey's agricultural sector and rural incomes.

Agricultural Policy

By 1980 Turkey was self-sufficient in food, and agricultural output was growing at a respectable rate, albeit more slowly than the economy as a whole. Starting in the early 1970s, crop intensification resulted from a reduction of fallow areas and increased use of fertilizer, fuel, and pesticides. The livestock industry, however, showed little improvement in productivity, and the later years of the decade saw the stagnation of all agriculture. Although production became less dependent on the weather as a result of irrigation and high-yielding varieties of seeds, these methods required adequate supplies of fertilizers, chemicals, equipment, and fuel, much of which had to be imported.

Productivity shortcomings, along with the new export-oriented development strategy, led to the adoption of different agricultural policies after 1980. Under the new approach, the government switched from promoting food self-sufficiency to maximizing agriculture's net contribution to the balance of trade. The incentive system was partially dismantled, fertilizer and pesticide subsidies were curtailed, and the remaining price supports were gradually converted to floor prices. The tight monetary policy limited agricultural credit, but real interest rates on loans to farmers remained negative. Nonetheless, a high proportion of defaults by farmers occurred on loans with high interest rates. In some cases, this led to the confiscation of land, tractors, or other property by the state, prompting one Turkish daily, *Milliyet,* to run an article entitled, "Bailiff Officer: The New Lord of the Peasants." The elimination of export licenses and minimum export prices, along with currency devaluation, an export-incentive system, and flat domestic demand, encouraged agricultural exports. In addition, a wider range of food imports was permitted, providing competition for domestic products.

The government's hope of rapidly increasing agricultural exports was slow in materializing, and total values fell sharply in the mid-1980s. This decline reflected both softer demand abroad (especially in the Arab oil-producing countries) and Turkey's own attempts to increase the share of agricultural products processed prior to export. Still, by the early 1990s agricultural exports had risen, with the most dramatic increase occurring in textiles and clothing, which depend on indigenously grown cotton.

Despite the turn toward liberal agricultural policies, government intervention in agriculture remained pervasive in the mid-1990s. Many of the institutions established between 1930 and 1980 continue to play important roles in the daily life of the farmer, and many old attitudes and practices remain. A large number of ministries, agencies, SEEs, and banks administer government price supports, credit measures, extension and research services, and irrigation projects. In the past, overlapping responsibilities and lack of coordination had often diluted the effectiveness of government activities. Some progress was made in the 1980s, however, when the Ministry of Agriculture, Forestry, and Rural Affairs reorganized its eleven departments into five general directorates. Subsequently, the ministry was divided into the Ministry of Agriculture and Rural Affairs and the Ministry of Forestry.

After 1980 the government reduced budget transfers to agricultural SEEs and decreased the level of price supports, but the state still controlled most markets in the sector. Public marketing agencies and marketing or credit cooperatives administered prices and handled a large share of exports. Several of the SEEs involved in agricultural production had been slated for privatization in the early 1990s. The Meat and Fish Board, the Fodder Industry (Yem Sanayili), and the Milk Industry Board (SEK) were targeted for immediate privatization when they were placed under the control of the Public Participation Administration. However, officials in 1994 stated that they lacked sufficient funds to pay the sizable debts these organizations had accumulated, a necessary step before privatization.

Nearly all farm produce except livestock and fresh fruits and vegetables has support prices, which became more effective when the ministry started announcing them in the fall, giving farmers time to choose which crops would be most profitable. For most crops (except tea, sugar beets, and opium, for which the state is the only buyer), farmers can choose between selling to private buyers or to the state. Supports stabilize crop prices and improve aggregate farm income but add to the disparities of income between large and small farmers. Support prices grew slowly in the 1980s and did not keep up with inflation. However, in the summer of 1991, in anticipation of the forthcoming elections, Özal's Motherland Party government raised all support prices by 60 to 70 percent. Subsequent governments under Demirel and Çiller maintained increases in support prices roughly in line with the high inflation rate. During 1994, however, these increases were not maintained. In addition, the Agricultural Supply Organization provides many farm materials at subsidized prices, including fertilizers, pesticides, and insecticides.

The Agricultural Bank of Turkey (Türkiye Cumhuriyeti Ziraat Bankası—TCZB) provides most loans to farmers and cooperatives and closely watches agricultural credit. Although the TCZB was intended to favor small farmers in the distribution of credit, its loan requirements restrict credit for the many small farmers who either rent or lack a secure title to land or other properties needed as collateral. Much of the bank's lending consists of short-term loans extended to cooperatives for commodity price support. Farmers also obtain credit from merchants, wealthy farmers, and money lenders, often at extortionate interest rates. Much of the World Bank's lending for agricultural projects in Turkey is channeled through the TCZB.

Agricultural extension and research services are poorly organized and generally inadequate because of shortages of qualified advisers, transportation, and equipment. Well-trained personnel willing to work in the field are difficult to find, and agricultural research is fragmented among more than ninety government and university institutes. Research is organized by commodity, with independent units for such major crops as cotton, tobacco, and citrus fruit. Observers note that coordination of the efforts of different research units and links between extension services are inadequate. During the mid-1980s, the government attempted to strengthen and rationalize research and extension services, but the organizational complexity of the entities involved made reform difficult.

Irrigation

Getting enough water to crops is a major problem for many Turkish farmers. Rainfall tends to be relatively abundant and regular in the coastal areas because of the mountains behind them. However, the bulk of the agricultural land is on the Anatolian Plateau, which receives less rainfall because it is ringed by mountains. Although rainfall on the plateau varies considerably among regions, it is barely adequate over large areas. In addition, the amount and time of rains vary sharply from year to year, causing sharp fluctuations in harvests. Since World War II, officials have stressed irrigation as a means of increasing and stabilizing farm output, and irrigation projects have consumed more than half of public investment in agriculture.

In the mid-1980s, observers estimated that private irrigation, depending on weirs and small barrages to direct water into fields, reached up to 1 million hectares. In addition, some farmers pumped water from wells to irrigate their own fields. Development of large-scale irrigation was delayed until the 1960s. Public-sector irrigation systems, built and operated by the General Directorate of State Hydraulic Works (Devlet Su Isleri—DSI) under the Ministry of Energy and Natural Resources, tend to be large and costly. Most provide water for entire valleys, and some large projects—for example, the Southeast Anatolian Project (Güneydogu Anadolu Projesi—GAP)—combine water supplies for urban areas, protection from flooding, hydroelectric power, and irrigation. Irrigation projects are dispersed throughout the country, but most are concentrated in the coastal regions of the Aegean and Mediterranean seas, where the longer growing seasons are particularly favorable to crops. Public irrigation water was available to 3.7 million hectares in the mid-1990s, although the area irrigated with public water totaled about 3 million hectares.

Deficiencies in irrigation included a serious lag between the construction of the main parts of an irrigation system and the completion of land leveling and drainage on farms. Also, crop research and farmer training were inadequate to assure the planting of suitable crops to obtain maximum yields from irrigated land. In the late 1970s, government officials estimated that only one-third of the irrigated land was being cultivated to its full potential. Moreover, low user fees did not initially permit the authorities to regain their initial investments; the fees were adjusted in the 1980s, however.

Major projects were planned to expand the irrigation system because government surveys had indicated that irrigation of up to 8.7 million hectares was possible. The most important project of the late 1980s and early 1990s is the GAP, which is linked with the 2,400-megawatt Atatürk Dam on the Euphrates River and is expected to irrigate 1.7 million hectares when it is completed in 2002. The system consists of a twin-bore 24.6-kilometer tunnel, which will take water from the reservoir to irrigate the plains around Harran, Mardin, and Ceylanpınar in southeastern Turkey. In the GAP region, farmers face a six-month dry season allowing them only one cash harvest per year. Irrigation will probably enable expansion to two or even three harvests. Crop rotation, which is largely unknown in areas without irrigation, has been introduced in the GAP region. Winter vegetables are expected to alternate with cotton as the summer crop. Although wheat and pulses dominate cropping patterns, cotton could take a larger share as access to water increases. The government projects that the GAP will increase Turkish wheat production by more than 50 percent, barley by a similar figure, and the region's production of cotton by more than four times by 2005, thus increasing national cotton production by 60 percent. The value of food surpluses expected to result from this project is estimated at US$5 billion.

Land Use

Turkey's land surface totals about 78 million hectares, of which roughly 48 million hectares were being used for some form of agriculture by 1991. There were almost 24.2 million hectares in field crops, of which 5.2 million lay fallow. Another 3.7 million hectares were in use as vineyards, orchards, and olive groves, and 20.2 million hectares were covered by forests and other woodlands. Other land areas accounted for about 29 million hectares; included in this figure was land classified as lakes, marshes, wasteland, and built-up areas. The "other" category also included about 9 million hectares of permanent pastureland.

During the twentieth century, population pressure resulted in the expansion of farmland. The cultivated area increased from about 8 million hectares in the 1920s to nearly 19 million hectares in 1952 and to almost 28 million hectares by 1991. Using Marshall Plan credits that first became available in 1948, Turkey began to import large numbers of tractors, which made it feasible to expand cultivation of marginal lands, especially on the Anatolian Plateau. Although total production grew rapidly, average yields did not. By about 1970, nearly all arable land was under cultivation.

Cultivation increased primarily at the expense of meadows and grasslands, which diminished from about 46 million hectares in the mid-1920s to about 14 million hectares in the mid-1980s. Although cultivation of the larger area made greater

Pickers of sultana grapes in fields east of Izmir, western Turkey
Courtesy Hermine Dreyfuss

agricultural production possible over the short run, it created long-term problems for livestock production. It also resulted in the destruction of tree cover and the plowing of marginal fields that were too steep and that received barely sufficient rainfall even in normal years. By the early 1960s, government agents were encouraging farmers to practice contour plowing and to take other measures to minimize erosion, but to little effect. By the late 1970s, more than half the country's land was judged to have serious erosion problems, and some plains regions were experiencing dust-bowl conditions. All of Turkey was affected, with the mountainous eastern provinces hit hardest. Some areas lost all topsoil and could support few plants.

In the 1970s, the government conducted land-use studies and found that more than one-fifth of the land should have been used differently to achieve optimum long-term production. Misuse was greatest in rain-fed cropped fields, but some grazing land and wasteland were found better suited to other uses such as cropping and forestry. Turkey's unusually high proportion of fallow land also limited production; in 1981 the government began encouraging double cropping and the planting of feed crops on fallow fields. The government also was considering a broad land-use policy. However, reform proved difficult because of government inefficiency and the lack of alternative crops in areas cut off from markets, where farmers had little choice but to use their land to grow grain to feed their families. Expansion of the road network, irrigation facilities, and extension services continued to offer hope for eventual improvements in land use.

Land Tenure

From the time of Atatürk, it has been generally recognized that land reform would speed rural development. Most attention focused on land redistribution—a highly charged political issue. People who favored land reform pointed to the higher yield achieved by owner-operators and attacked absentee landlords. Opponents pointed out that land reform would not solve the difficulties of the rural population because there was insufficient land to establish farms large enough to support families. Whatever the merits of land reform proposals, large landowners effectively blocked most action, and governments often lacked the will to implement those measures that were enacted. Moreover, landless peasants continued to migrate to the cities in sufficient numbers to reduce the pressure for reform.

Historically, Turkey has been a land inhabited by independent peasants. The Ottoman state restricted the growth of a landowning class; and in the early years of Ottoman rule, the central government retained ownership of most of the land, which was leased to farmers under relatively secure tenure arrangements. To maintain farms large enough to support a family and a pair of oxen, the Ottomans exempted land from Muslim inheritance policy, a practice subsequently reversed as the state reinstituted Islamic inheritance practices, sold land to gain revenues, and authorized land transfers. These changes favored the growth of a class of large landowners during the latter decades of the empire. By 1923 landownership had shifted in favor of a small group with large holdings. However, during the republican period land concentration declined, a development that perhaps reflected the effects of division through inheritance or the attraction of alternative investments. At the same time, the opening of new areas to cultivation made land available to those farmers without holdings.

Because no comprehensive cadastral surveys have been carried out, landownership data are still poor in the mid-1990s, but a general picture of ownership patterns emerges. According to the 1980 agricultural census, about 78 percent of the farms consisted of five hectares or less and together accounted for 60 percent of farmland. About 23 percent of the farms were between five and twenty hectares in size, accounting for another 18 percent of the land. Fewer than 4 percent of the farms covered more than twenty hectares, although these occupied more than 15 percent of the farmland. Few farms exceeded 100 hectares. Although experts believed that landownership was more concentrated than data on farm size implied, it was clear that Turkey had more equal distribution of land than did many other developing countries.

Some observers estimate that, despite widespread leasing and sharecropping, a majority of farms are owner operated. However, tenure patterns vary significantly among regions, reflecting different geographical conditions and historical developments. In general, Islamic inheritance practices, which establish set shares for each male and female child, cause fragmented holdings and make leasing and sharecropping extensive. Joint ownership of land is common, and even very small farms normally consist of several noncontiguous plots. Farmers often rent out some of their own land while leasing or sharecropping other plots in order to till areas reasonably close together and large enough to support their families. Owners of small plots may rent out their land and work on other farms or in town. Owners of large holdings, sometimes whole villages, usually rent out all or most of their land. Between one-tenth and one-fifth of farmers lease or sharecrop the land they till, and landless rural families also work as farm laborers.

Tenancy arrangements are many and complex. Some leaseholds can be inherited, but many tenants lack sufficient security to make a long-term commitment to the soil they till. Sharecroppers generally receive about half of the crop, with the owner supplying inputs such as seed and fertilizer. Grazing rights are often held by groups rather than individuals. Many villages have common pastures open to the village herd. Cultivated areas have expanded as individuals appropriate village pastureland to grow grains, a process that not only has caused village strife but also has worsened erosion.

After 1950 the commercialization of agriculture accelerated changes in land-use and tenure patterns. Many of the large holdings on the coastal plains of the Aegean Sea and Mediterranean Sea were converted to modern farms, often benefiting from irrigation projects and specializing in high-value fruits, or industrial crops. Landless families supplied the labor for such modern farms, while sharecroppers and owners of small farms tilled the adjacent land. In these more fertile areas, a five-hectare farm might produce as much income as a twenty-hectare farm in the semiarid central Anatolian Plateau. Southeastern Anatolia, one of the poorest regions of Turkey, included feudal-style landlords who controlled entire villages and many landless families.

Although Atatürk had stressed the need for upper and lower limits on landownership, the latter to halt the fragmentation process, little in the way of effective land reform had been carried out by the early 1990s. Nevertheless, more than 3 million hectares had been distributed to landless farmers between the 1920s and 1970, most of it state land.

The problems of land tenure remain, and some have worsened. Many farms are too small to support a family and too fragmented for efficient cultivation. Tenancy arrangements foster neither long-term soil productivity nor the welfare of tenants. In many areas, the rural poor are becoming poorer while land better suited to grazing continues to be converted to grain fields. At the same time, however, many large landholdings have been turned into productive modern farms that contribute to the country's improved agricultural performance. Major irrigation projects in the Euphrates River Valley and elsewhere offer the prospect of increasing the supply of productive land. The declining population growth rate has reduced the pressure for land reform, and industrialization offers an alternative for landless farm workers, who prefer city life to that of rural areas.

Cropping Patterns and Production

Turkey's varied ecology allows farmers to grow many crops, yet the bulk of the arable land and the greater part of the farm population traditionally have been dedicated to producing cereal crops, which supply 70 percent of Turkey's food consumption in terms of calories. As of 1992, cereal crops occupied 12.5 million hectares or more than half of the country's cultivated area. Wheat accounted for about 9 million hectares of this area, and barley for about 3 million hectares. Other grain crops include rye, millet, corn, and rice. Grains are produced in most parts of the country (see fig. 9).

Small or subsistence farmers produce most of Turkey's grain. Because most fields depend on rainfall, production varies considerably from year to year. Farmers traditionally have left grain fields fallow for a year to allow water to accumulate in the soil. Although the government encourages planting soybeans as a secondary crop following the wheat crop, farmers have been slow to adopt the practice. The integration of forage crops into crop rotation and the elimination of fallow periods offer the possibility of increased soil fertility and moisture retention.

Wheat has long been the basic food in the Turkish diet, generally eaten in the form of bread—of which Turkish per capita consumption ranks among the highest in the world. Farmers consume about half of the crop; the other half moves through commercial channels. The Soil Products Office buys up to one-fifth of the crop at support prices, which largely determine the prices for the open market, and handles most imports and exports of grain.

Production increases in the late 1970s turned the country into a wheat exporter. After 1980 the country also imported small amounts of high-quality wheat to improve baked products. Steady increases continued in the 1980s, with wheat production averaging 15 million tons. Even in the drought-stricken 1989 harvest, wheat production totaled 16.2 million

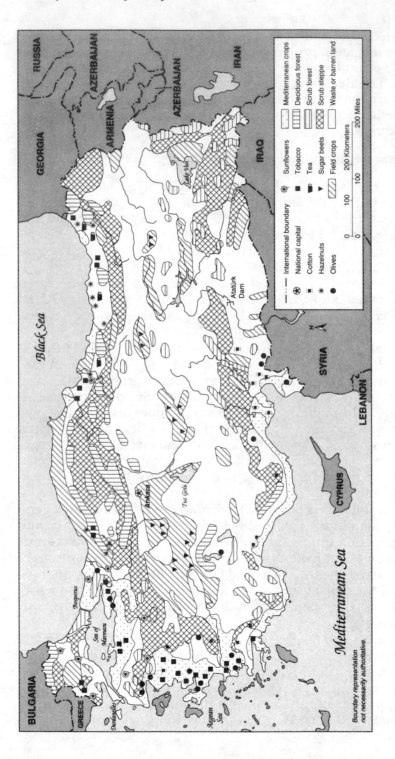

Figure 9. Major Crop Areas and Land Use, 1995

tons. By the early 1990s, wheat production was averaging 20 million tons per year.

Barley production did not rise substantially after the 1960s; crops averaged 6 million tons per year in the 1980s and 7 million tons in the early 1990s. One reason for the slow growth in barley production was a change in dietary habits: whereas barley previously had been a staple food, it came to be used almost exclusively as animal feed or for export. Harvests of corn, which is also used for feed, increased from an average of about 1.1 million tons per year during the 1970s to around 2 million tons per year in the early 1990s (see table 7, Appendix A).

Turkey is the main pulse producer in the Middle East, and pulse output increased dramatically from an annual average of 617,000 tons in the 1970–75 period to more than 1.1 million tons in the 1980–85 period. By the early 1990s, however, pulse output had fallen to about 860,000 tons in 1990 and 610,000 tons in 1992. The country made a major effort to meet the increased demand for dry beans, lentils, and peas in the Middle East, and exported increasing amounts during the 1980s. Nevertheless, declining export demand in the 1990s and better opportunities in raising other crops led to falling output.

Cotton is the major industrial crop in terms of value, supplying seed for vegetable oil and fiber for textiles, a major export. In the 1950s and 1960s, cotton cultivation increased rapidly following the introduction of new varieties and the extension of irrigation. The main cotton areas are on the coastal plains of the south and southwest, where yields have exceeded international averages since the 1950s. Annual output of cotton lint rose from about 145,000 tons in the early 1950s to about 600,000 tons in the early 1990s. Exports averaged 10 percent of production in the early 1990s, having fallen from around 30 percent in the 1980s.

Tobacco is a classic industrial crop, but output rose relatively slowly after World War II, reaching about 200,000 tons per year by the 1980s and 300,000 tons by the early 1990s. European consumers' preference for Virginia tobacco was a factor in the slow expansion, although foreign investment in the domestic tobacco industry in the 1980s spurred production.

Sugar beet production expanded in the 1950s and 1960s, leveling off at a rate sufficient to produce an annual average of 677,000 tons during the first half of the 1970s. The yield met domestic needs and allowed limited exports. Production jumped sharply, to about 1.5 million tons in 1981, and ended the decade at around 11 million tons in 1989. The annual average in the early 1990s was 14 million tons.

Oilseed cultivation expanded during the 1980s and 1990s, but harvests averaging about 2 million tons in the latter half of the 1980s and early 1990s continued to lag behind consumption, causing Turkey to import vegetable oils. Production of sunflower seeds, the main source of edible oil, declined, and the use of degenerated seed resulted in lower oil production. In 1987 Turkey produced 1.1 million tons of sunflower seeds; by 1992 production had declined to 950,000 tons. Olive production has experienced a two-year cycle with small crops every other year.

Cultivation of opium poppies as a field crop traditionally was fairly extensive in parts of the Anatolian Plateau. The opium gum had cash value, and the plant served villagers as food, forage, and thatch. Official figures showed that during the second half of the 1960s, annual production of opium gum averaged about 110 tons per year. During this period, the crop played an important role in the international illegal drug trade. With the United States pushing for a ban on poppy cultivation, after 1974 the Turkish government strictly controlled poppy harvesting, requiring that the mature pod be removed and processed at a state-run plant. During the first half of the 1990s, the area sown with opium ranged from 7,000 to 19,000 hectares, producing between 3,700 and 13,700 tons of opium pods. Most observers believed that government measures were effective in keeping opium derivatives in legal channels without causing undue hardship to farmers.

During the mid-1990s, cultivation of fruit, nuts, and vegetables contributed nearly 33 percent of the value of crop production, although such cultivation occupied only about 13 percent of cultivated land. Improved export possibilities led to the expansion of fruit and vegetable hectarage during the 1980s and 1990s; in 1991 about 593,000 hectares were devoted to green vegetables, tomatoes, and other produce, of which about 20,000 hectares were grown in greenhouses. Turkey is a major producer of high-quality hazelnuts, despite stiff competition in international markets from rising production in Spain, the United States, and Italy. The annual crop averages 400,000 tons per year, roughly half of which is exported. Turkey is also a major producer and exporter of various fruits, including grapes, sultana raisins, citrus fruits, and melons. Total fruit and vegetable exports yielded Turkey nearly US$1 billion per year in the early 1990s.

Livestock

Animal husbandry is an important part of Turkey's agricultural sector and economy. Livestock products, including meat, milk, eggs, wool, and hides, contributed more than 33 percent of the value of agricultural output in the mid-1990s. Sheep and cattle are kept mainly on the grazing lands of Anatolia. Despite growing demand for animal products in Turkey's cities as incomes rose, animal numbers were static in the 1980s and fell in the early 1990s. Although yields were growing, traditional methods kept the livestock industry from achieving its considerable potential. Only 20 percent of cattle, for example, were high-yielding variety breeds. The oil boom in the Persian Gulf, however, led to an expansion of export markets and to major investments in the meat industry of the eastern Turkish towns of Erzurum and Van. In 1992 meat exports totaled US$140 million; exports, however, were being hurt by the UN embargo on Iraq. Wool is also a significant export. Traditional Turkish sheep varieties produce a coarse wool suitable for carpets and blankets rather than clothing. Merino sheep, which produce a finer wool, have been introduced in the Bursa region.

During the 1950s, officials expected that livestock production would decline as grain cultivation increased at the expense of grazing lands. In fact, the period of most rapid expansion of grain cultivation also saw an upswing in the number of farm animals. One result was overgrazing of grasslands, wasteland, forests, and mountain meadows, which damaged the soil, although not enough to reduce the size of herds. Another result was smaller, less productive animals. Cattle, which process coarse forage less efficiently than sheep and goats, suffered most from the loss of grazing land, but nearly all animals produced less meat and milk and fewer offspring.

Farmers made a modest beginning toward improving livestock production techniques in the 1980s, but traditional practices were hard to change. Even if they have no land, most village families own a few animals. Animals essentially scrounge for an existence, foraging on crop stubble, weeds, and grass on fallow land, and on uncultivable grazing areas. Few farmers integrate livestock production with cropping activities or match feed supply to their animals' requirements. Rural families raise livestock on land that lacks alternative uses, but the system does not allow the high levels of production necessary to meet the needs of the rapidly expanding population. Moreover, over-grazing has caused environmental damage that is difficult to repair.

Data on the livestock industry are poor but indicative of general trends. Official statistics reveal that recent years have seen changes in the relative roles of various animals in the farm economy. Given Turkish dietary preferences, sheep have relatively high value and increased in number from about 36.8 million head in 1970 to about 40.4 million head in 1992. The number of goats declined during the same period, from about 18.9 million to about 10.7 million because of grazing restrictions in forests and government policies encouraging herd reduction. The use of tractors probably has caused the decline in the number of oxen. Cattle, which have risen in value as farmers strive to meet the growing urban demand for milk, increased in number from about 2.1 million in 1970 to about 11.9 million in 1992.

Livestock output has increased over the years, although less rapidly than demand. In the early 1980s, the country was essentially self-sufficient in milk products, producing about 5.2 million tons per year. By the early 1990s, milk output had doubled, to 10 million tons per year. Annual meat production averaged 660,000 tons per year; this figure, however, represents only an estimate because most slaughtering occurs outside official slaughterhouses. During the 1980s, the price for red meat increased sharply, leading to a fall in domestic meat demand and an increase in poultry consumption. However, meat demand was partially sustained by exports of live animals—some of them smuggled over borders—to Middle Eastern countries, especially Iran and Iraq. The UN embargo on Iraq hurt domestic meat exporters after 1990.

Poultry production expanded rapidly after 1980 and appears capable of rising with demand as incomes increase and diets begin to include animal products. Poultry exports to Iran and Iraq also grew in the 1980s but fell somewhat in the 1990s. Many Turkish poultry operations are small, producing between 5,000 and 10,000 fowl at a time. However, larger, integrated operations have also been established, particularly in urban areas. One, Yupi of Izmir, claims to be one of the largest poultry producers in the world. By 1992 Turkey had 134 million head of poultry, double the number that it had had in 1987.

Forestry and Fisheries

Forestry contributes little to the economy, but it holds potential for future development. In the early 1990s, Turkey's forests covered an estimated 20.2 million hectares, or 201,990 square kilometers (26 percent of the land area). Official statistics indicate that forests have doubled in size since 1950; the figures do not reflect actual growth in forested areas but rather continuing survey efforts and the inclusion of less productive wooded areas under the jurisdiction of the forestry administration. The most productive lumber area is the Black Sea region, followed by central, western, and southern Anatolia, where mostly pine wood is produced. The forests in the eastern part of the country are in poor condition and yield little besides firewood. Many forests are overmature because of poor management and infrequent cutting, and thus only about 20 percent of the total forested area is commercially exploitable.

By the mid-1950s, the state had taken over all forest areas from private owners. Compensation was largely in the form of access to fuel wood at low prices. The one-third of the rural population that lives in or near forests includes many of the country's poorest families. The bulk of their income comes from farming; forest products provide supplemental income and fuel. The main objective of forest management is control of traditional logging and grazing rights; the lack of alternative fuel supplies makes it impossible to stop illegal wood harvests in state forests.

The General Directorate of Forestry in the Ministry of Forestry has assumed responsibility for logging and reforestation operations and for reducing erosion. Whereas wood production has been substantially below potential, partly because of a lack of equipment and roads, reforestation efforts increased Turkey's wooded area by about 2 percent between 1977 and 1981. During the early 1980s, annual wood production averaged 5.2 million cubic meters of lumber. By 1991 production had risen to about 6.5 million cubic meters.

Despite the country's long coastline and large freshwater bodies, fishing is an underdeveloped industry. The Black Sea and the Sea of Marmara constitute the main fishing grounds. The tonnage of the fishing fleet has increased, but in the early 1990s it still included about 7,000 traditional boats, some 1,500 of which lacked motors. The annual catch rose from around 430,000 tons in 1981 to about 625,200 tons in 1988, but declined to about 365,000 tons in 1991. Frogs' legs, snails, shrimp, and crayfish are exported to Europe.

Industry

Turkish modernizers have long struggled to build an industrial system that would help restore the country's economic power. The import-substitution strategy followed until 1980 was designed to make the country an independent producer of manufactured goods. The result was a striking unfolding of industry, especially between 1950 and 1977, when the sector (including energy and natural resources) grew at an annual average rate of 8.6 percent in real terms, expanding its share of GDP from about 12 percent to about 25 percent. Despite the retrenchment of the early 1980s, the recovery of the industrial sector—which registered an average annual growth rate of 5.9 percent between 1987 and 1992—restored the sector to its pre-1980 proportion of more than 23 percent of GDP in 1993. By the early 1990s, industry was broadly based; the only individual industries accounting for more than 5 percent of industrial output were food processing, petroleum, textiles, and iron and steel.

Under the republic, the Turks have vastly improved their country's infrastructure and have achieved the ability to produce a wide range of products. The country's first factories processed food, such as sugar and flour, and nondurable consumer goods, such as textiles and footwear. Next came intermediate industrial products, including iron and steel, chemicals, cement, and fertilizer. By the end of the 1970s, the country was developing capital goods industries and high-technology products. Production of trucks and buses in cooperation with the West German firm Mercedes-Benz, and of F-16 fighter aircraft with the United States firm General Dynamics, indicated Turkey's industrial ambitions.

The press for rapid industrialization minimized the attention given to efficiency, and excessive protection forestalled competition that would have promoted efficiency; selling in the protected home market was much more attractive than attempting to export. Moreover, the rise of montage industries, which assembled such products as motor vehicles, consumer durables, and electronic goods primarily using imported components, meant that industrial growth required ever more imports. Hence, attempts at import substitution paradoxically tended to aggravate the country's trade balance. The

Fish vendor on the Bosporus
Courtesy Hermine Dreyfuss

Fisherman mending his
net, Trabzon
Courtesy Hermine Dreyfuss

capital-intensive nature of many industrial investments, especially those in the intermediate goods sector, caused employment in industry to grow relatively slowly, contributing to structural unemployment. Dependence on imported petroleum made the country highly vulnerable to increases in oil prices.

By the end of the 1970s, industry had reached a turning point. In the short run, the sector needed to overcome shortages of energy, imported machinery, parts, and processing materials that had caused a decline in industrial output during the last years of the decade. In the longer run, to become more efficient and to enable increased exports, the industrial structure had to be adjusted in accordance with the country's comparative advantages. In effect, industry would have to transfer resources out of uncompetitive industries to favor those that could compete in world markets. The difficult adjustment process started during the early 1980s, and substantial progress was made under the Özal team. Under the new outward-oriented development strategy, as under the old import-substitution policies, industry was to be the leading sector of the economy. Industrial performance—especially in export markets—would determine if that strategy would be successful.

Many of the problems of import substitution had not yet been overcome by the mid-1990s. Much progress had been made in spurring private-sector-led industrialization, particularly in light manufacturing and export promotion, however. Light manufactures and iron and steel accounted for an increasing proportion—and since the 1980s, the majority—of exports. Moreover, foreign investment in the industrial sector, made either directly or through the stock market, had begun to have a positive impact on Turkish industry. However, much of industry was still dominated by the public sector in early 1995, and private-sector companies still depended on crucial inputs from public-sector industries.

Industrial Policy

In line with the shift to an outward-oriented development strategy, in 1980 Turkey's policy makers began to revamp the country's industrial policy. The new policy set forth four related goals for industry: upgrading the role of market signals in decision making, increasing manufacturing exports, enlarging the private share in manufacturing, and reforming the SEEs to reduce inefficiency. In the early 1990s, a fifth goal was added: privatization of public-sector entities. Policy makers were also concerned with obtaining adequate energy supplies and providing enough work for the growing labor force.

Energy

Turkey is relatively well endowed with energy and mineral resources. The extensive mountainous terrain provides numerous hydroelectric sites, although most are far from the main population and consumption centers. The country also has substantial exploitable lignite resources and small reserves of hard coal, petroleum, and natural gas. Commercially exploitable deposits of many minerals have been located, but the territory has been surveyed only partially. Exploitation of these natural resources has occurred relatively slowly.

The combined demands of industrialization and urbanization nearly tripled energy consumption in the 1960s and 1970s. An inappropriate pricing policy, especially the subsidy of petroleum that led to unduly cheap products, was one cause of shifts in the sources of energy that exacerbated shortages. In 1960 more than half of the primary energy consumed came from noncommercial sources, mainly firewood but also manure and other agricultural wastes. These noncommercial sources, plus domestic coal and lignite, accounted for more than 80 percent of all primary energy consumed; oil supplied only 18 percent. By 1980, in contrast, oil supplied about 47 percent of the primary energy consumed, coal and lignite about 21 percent, hydroelectric power 8 percent, and noncommercial sources such as firewood and animal wastes only 23 percent. By 1992, 43.5 percent of final energy came from petroleum, 31.1 percent from lignite and hard coal, 4.1 percent from hydroelectric power, 6.9 percent from natural gas, and 14.4 percent from other energy sources, including solid fuels, geothermal, solar power, and wind power.

During the 1970s, the demand for electricity began to exceed supply, and by the late 1970s the power gap began to constrain industry. After 1977 rotating blackouts affecting industrial, commercial, and residential consumers were necessary to meet demand. By 1979 the shortage of foreign exchange had so restricted imports of crude oil that fuel for cars, trucks, and tractors had to be rationed. In the mid-1980s, in an attempt to deal with the energy shortage the Özal administration launched the build, operate, and transfer (BOT) system, under which foreign investors would provide the capital and technology to build plants, operate them for a number of years with guaranteed revenues, and finally transfer the units to the government when the investment had been fully returned. The Atatürk Dam was a major project designed to increase electricity output. Its first two power units came on line in 1992.

Although Turkey's energy resources remained underdeveloped in early 1995, the country had relatively good energy production potential. One estimate places the economically feasible hydroelectric potential at around 29,500 megawatts, which would allow annual production to reach roughly 100,000 gigawatt-hours in years with normal rainfall. Lignite is the second most important potential source of energy, with proven and probable deposits put around 6.4 billion tons. However, Turkish lignite, containing high amounts of water and sulfur, is hard to burn and pollutes the air. Turkey's proven and estimated petroleum stocks are equivalent to about three years' consumption. Proven reserves are estimated at about 16 million tons, and enhanced oil-recovery techniques may allow extraction of another 30 million tons. Proven reserves of natural gas total about 12.4 billion cubic meters, and reserves of hard coal about 1 billion tons. Turkey's geothermal resources are considerable, but they have not yet been systematically explored.

Imports of petroleum averaged more than 15 million tons per year in the early 1980s and increased to about 23 million tons in the early 1990s. Most of Turkey's oil fields are located in southeastern Anatolia near the borders with Iran, Iraq, and Syria (see fig. 10). Because of the country's fractured substrata, deposits are often contained in small pockets, which makes exploration and extraction difficult. In 1985 exploration proved that Turkey has oil deposits at very deep levels, but it was not known how large the deposits might be. Shell Oil determined that oil at Paleozoic levels would be recoverable, and other investigations proved significant deposits in central Anatolia under the salt flats in the plain north of Konya. In 1991 British Petroleum began exploring for oil in offshore areas of the Black Sea. It is also suspected that the Aegean shelf contains considerable petroleum deposits, but as long as relations with Greece remain strained, conflicting claims to the Aegean seabed limit prospects for exploration. To speed up the exploration process, the Turkish government in 1983 eased regulations on such activities by foreign oil companies, allowing them to export 35 percent of production from fields they discovered in Anatolia and 45 percent from offshore fields. Although several foreign concerns started exploration after the liberalization package went into effect, up to the mid-1990s no major finds had been reported.

The state-owned oil company, Turkish Petroleum Corporation (TPAO), Shell Oil, and Mobil control most petroleum output, which had climbed gradually to a peak of 3.6 million tons in 1969 but declined to about 2.1 million tons in 1985 as deposits were depleted (see table 8, Appendix A.). By the early 1990s, output had increased once again to nearly 4.4 million tons. The main petroleum project during the 1980s was an attempt at secondary recovery at the Bati Raman fields in southeastern Anatolia, which were expected to produce roughly 1.5 million tons a year over a twenty-year period.

TPAO stepped up oil exploration efforts at home and abroad in the hope of raising output. But prospects for new domestic finds were endangered by the escalating conflict with Kurdish rebels in southeastern Turkey. Western operators in the area were nervous after a sharp increase in the number of attacks on oil installations. Mobil suspended operations at its 3,200-bpd Selmo field and other small sites after Kurdish attacks on its staff. In the early 1990s, talks were underway on a possible transfer of the Selmo operation to TPAO. Shell Oil's rig near the 25,000-bpd Batman refinery was also hit, although operations there continued. TPAO reported no attacks. Total Turkish production in 1993 of about 78,600 bpd—down from about 84,500 bpd in 1991—met 17 percent of the country's 458,000-bpd needs. The state firm in 1993 pumped about 60,550 bpd, Shell Oil about 14,500 bpd, Mobil about 3,230 bpd, and Aladdin Middle East about 330 bpd. On several aging fields, rising water content has halved productivity. TPAO drilled sixty exploration wells in 1993, only one of which hit oil. In 1994 it planned to drill eighty-one, stepping up work outside the affected southeast. Meanwhile, Mobil was doing seismic work in central and southern Turkey, and Shell Oil and United States Arco were both exploring in the southeast.

TPAO's joint venture in Kazakhstan, which holds seven concessions, should help to increase the company's oil reserves. In addition, preliminary tests in 1993 near Aktyubinsk and Atyrau were promising. It is expected to be several years, however, before the oil or gas reaches Turkey, given the need to work out export routes or an exchange agreement with Russia. Turk-

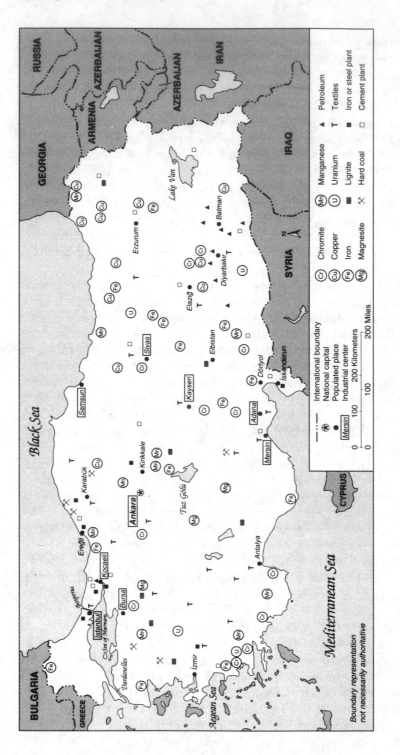

Figure 10. Selected Industries and Minerals, 1995

ish sources are cofinancing the venture with the Kazakh state oil company. The project is TPAO's first major overseas enterprise, although its subsidiary, the Turkish Petroleum International Corporation, holds concessions in Australia, Pakistan, and Egypt.

Five refineries with a total capacity of about 713,000 bpd meet most of the country's need for petroleum products. Until early 1995, about 85 percent of refinery capacity was in public hands in four refineries located at Aliaga near Izmir, Kocaeli, Kirikkale, and Batman. A fifth refinery, jointly owned by Mobil, Shell Oil, British Petroleum, and a Turkish company, is located at Mersin.

In early 1995, Turkey's privatization program appeared to be back on track after a period of wrangling over the legality of the sale of the state refinery company TÜPRAS and the retail company Petrol Ofisi. The sale of part or all of each company is scheduled to take place before the end of 1995.

Petrol Ofisi's 4,000 stations control 56 percent of a domestic gasoline market that since 1987 has grown by an average of 5.5 percent a year to 94,000 bpd. Full privatization is expected by the end of 1995.

A TPAO pipeline extends for nearly 500 kilometers from the oil fields near Batman to Dörtyol on the Mediterranean coast. The corporation also owns and operates the Turkish section of the pipeline from Iraq's Kirkuk fields to a port facility near Dörtyol. This pipeline was enlarged in 1984 to carry 1.1 million bpd, a share of which Turkey purchased at preferential rates. A second, smaller-capacity Kirkuk-Dörtyol pipeline was built in the late 1980s, which increased capacity to 1.5 million bpd. Oil flows through the two pipelines ceased after the UN embargo on Iraq was imposed in 1990. The pipeline cannot be used for domestic oil because according to international law the oil in the pipeline at the time of the embargo must be stored, awaiting UN disposition.

Apart from the country's own oil prospects in the Black Sea, Turkish officials see their nation as a strategic hub bringing oil from Azerbaijan and Kazakhstan to the Mediterranean and connecting Turkmenistan and possibly Iran to the European gas network. Turkish officials have pushed their own brand of pipeline diplomacy, encouraging the nations of Central Asia and the Caucasus—as well as Iran—to cooperate so that they can start exporting their prime resources to the outside world via Turkey.

The Turks are convinced that at least some of the projects eventually will come to fruition, beginning with a projected pipeline to bring Azerbaijani crude to the eastern Mediterranean. In the early 1990s, the governments of Turkey and Azerbaijan officially approved plans for such a line. But a series of obstacles remained to be overcome, including rival pipeline projects that would bypass Turkey, border disputes that would render key intervening areas dangerous, and even a degree of antagonism toward Turkey on the part of some neighboring states. The most immediate challenge was the effort to bring oil from Kazakhstan's Tengiz field to the Russian Black Sea port of Novorossiysk, which would mean an upsurge in tanker traffic not only in the Black Sea, but also in the Bosporus and Dardanelles. Turkey has opposed this project vehemently but is constrained by international conventions that guarantee passage between the Black and the Mediterranean seas. In some places, the straits are only 800 meters wide, and the Bosporus bisects Turkey's largest city, Istanbul. The threat to one of the nation's greatest attractions has turned Turkish officials into ardent environmentalists.

Natural gas became important in the 1980s. Gas tapped in Thrace (Trakya, European Turkey) was piped to the Istanbul region and used to produce electricity, thereby reducing the need for energy imports from Bulgaria. In 1986 Turkey began construction of a pipeline to carry Soviet natural gas from the Bulgarian border to Ankara; the line was completed in the late 1980s. In 1990 government officials announced that they also desired to purchase natural gas from Algeria, a move that would help balance Turkey's large purchases from the Soviet Union.

Policy makers in the early 1970s had targeted lignite as the most abundant domestic source of hydrocarbons, and production grew rapidly from an average of about 7.9 million tons for the 1970–75 period to more than 31 million tons in 1985. Mines operated by the state-owned Turkish Lignite Company are responsible for about two-thirds of output; private firms produce the remainder. Production of hard coal is entirely controlled by the government-owned Turkish Coal Company, which suffers from poor management and outmoded technology. Coal production is also hampered by the great depth of the country's deposits. Hard coal output fell from around 6.5 million tons in 1976 to about 3.8 million tons in 1983, and unit costs exceeded those of coal imports. As a result of these trends, Turkey is beginning to import coal for use in power plants. In 1992 Turkey produced about 12 million tons of coal and imported a net of about 4.2 million tons.

The Turkish Electricity Authority (Türkiye Elektrik Kurumu—TEK) is responsible for most electric power generation and distribution. In Adana the Cukurova Electrical Company produces some electricity privately. In Kepez, a city in Antalya Province, another private company produces electricity. Upgrading of the national distribution grid began in the 1980s, and by 1985 about 70 percent of Turkey's villages were receiving electricity. The Fifth Five-Year Plan (1984–89) called for the completion of village electrification by 1989; by the mid-1990s no village was without electricity.

Demand for electricity has increased rapidly, in large part because of the growth of industry, which consumed more than 56 percent of electricity in 1992. By 1985 thermal plants produced 53 percent of total installed capacity; hydroelectric plants produced the remainder. During the early 1980s, shortages of electricity had to be covered with imports from Bulgaria and the Soviet Union. In 1984 Turkey and the Soviet Union agreed to build a second transmission line that would allow future increases in Soviet electricity deliveries. Although in the 1990s electricity imports meet less than 1 percent of Turkey's needs, the Turks want to be independent of supplies from unreliable neighbors.

Sources for generating such electricity varied. By 1992 electricity generated by coal accounted for 36 percent of total installed capacity, with hydroelectric plants accounting for 40 percent. The rest was generated using petroleum products.

Turkey's chronic energy shortages make development of hydroelectric power imperative. In 1994 the General Directorate of State Hydraulic Works was building or planning to build about 300 hydroelectric plants. The centerpiece of Turkey's ambitious hydroelectric program, the Southeast Anatolia Project, which includes dams on the Tigris and Euphrates rivers, will increase Turkey's irrigable land about 25 percent and its electricity-generating capacity about 45 percent. As of early 1987, the first two of the three large dams in the program (the Keban Dam and the Karakaya Dam, both on the Euphrates, northeast of Malatya) had been built, and the third, the Atatürk Dam, was under construction, completed in 1994. The World Bank refused to help finance the construction of the Atatürk Dam because Turkey had not reached an agreement on sharing the water of the Euphrates River with Syria and Iraq; Turkey, however, arranged independent financing.

Turkish officials had long discussed the possibility that nuclear power might help the country address its energy problems. During the 1980s, the military government drew up a nuclear energy program and established the Nuclear Power Plants Division of the Turkish Electricity Authority to make feasibility studies and to build nuclear plants. Given Turkey's desire to diversify its energy sources, nuclear power was expected to remain on the agenda. By early 1995, however, no electricity had been generated from nuclear power.

Although Turkey has made a good start at addressing its energy problems, some analysts feel that more attention needs to be paid to conservation and pricing policies to limit the growth of demand. Industry is the major consumer of energy, and industrial consumption is expected to grow rapidly if left unchecked. The most energy-intensive sectors of industry, such as iron and steel, food processing, textiles, mining and nonferrous metals, chemicals, cement, and bricks and ceramics, probably could reduce demand significantly if required to do so. However, the government needs to audit major energy users to discover which could cut back consumption. In addition, a shift in relative energy prices to reflect long-run costs might induce industrial restructuring that would take Turkey's energy endowment into account. Moreover, energy policy makers need to improve management of firewood and agricultural wastes, which continue to play an important role in the rural energy economy.

Mineral Resources

Turkey's most important minerals are chromite, bauxite, and copper. The country also exploits deposits of other minerals such as iron, manganese, lead, zinc, antimony, asbestos, pyrites, sulfur, mercury, and manganese. Mining contributed slightly under 2 percent of GDP in 1992, but the subsector provides the raw material for such key manufacturing industries as iron and steel, aluminum, cement, and fertilizers. Turkey exports a variety of minerals, the most important of which are blister copper, chrome, and boron products. Minerals accounted for an average of about 2 percent of export earnings in the mid-1990s. The public sector dominates mining, accounting for about 75 percent of sales. Etibank, set up in 1935 to develop Turkey's natural resources, manages most of

Market in Bodrum, in
central Anatolia
Courtesy Hermine Dreyfuss

Vendor of simit, *the*
traditional bread, in
Istanbul
Courtesy Hermine Dreyfuss

the state's mineral interests, particularly bauxite, boron minerals, chromite, and copper.

Private-sector mining enterprises are generally small, concentrating on lead, zinc, and marble; some operate intermittently depending on market conditions. A 1978 law nationalized all private holdings, but it was only partially implemented before being invalidated by the Constitutional Court. In 1980 the government began to encourage foreign investment, and in 1983 and 1985 mining laws were revised to provide incentives for private investment. Etibank sought to encourage joint ventures with private firms in Turkey and foreign investors. Although some partnerships were struck, mainly for copper production, foreign and private investors in 1995 continued to hesitate to make major investments.

Manufacturing

Turkey's manufacturing industries are diverse and growing. Public-sector entities dominate manufacturing, accounting for about 40 percent of value added. Private-sector firms are dominated by a number of large conglomerates that have diversified across several industries.

The manufacture of textiles is Turkey's largest industry, very competitive in international markets, and the most important foreign-exchange earner. Domestic cotton and wool provide much of the raw material for the industry, but synthetics production has also expanded. The textile sector contributed 20 percent of total manufacturing output and employed 33 percent of all workers in the mid-1990s. Textiles are produced by factories controlled by the country's largest SEE, Sumerbank, and a number of private firms. Installed capacity is equivalent to around 33 percent of that of the EU in terms of cotton spinning and around 11 percent of EU woolen yarn and textiles. In 1994 Sumerbank was identified as a likely candidate for privatization.

Textile exports grew rapidly after 1980, but protectionism in industrial countries, including the EC nations and the United States, threatened the sector's growth. Nonetheless, between 1987 and 1992 textile export values expanded at an average annual rate of 19 percent. By 1992 textiles accounted for 35 percent of total exports. Investment in increased capacity in the 1980s resulted in increased exports of finished products and ready-made garments. In 1990 the administration of President George Bush increased the quota for United States textile imports from Turkey by 50 percent to compensate for Turkey's economic problems caused by sanctions on Iraq.

Agroprocessing is one of the most dynamic branches of Turkish industry, supplying both domestic and export markets. Main product lines are sugar, flour, processed meat and milk, and fruits and vegetables. Processed food exports grew at an average rate of 8 percent per year between 1987 and 1992, accounting for 9 percent of total exports.

SEEs are the most important producers of intermediate goods, although private firms are also active. The iron and steel sector has become more competitive in adjacent Middle Eastern markets, where Turkey's location is an advantage. However, competitiveness results largely from heavy subsidies to the state companies. Two-thirds of Turkey's steel is produced by three public-sector steel mills, which remain heavily subsidized. Twenty smaller private plants produce steel from arc furnace operations. Public plants include the old and outmoded mill at Karabük, the Eregli works completed in 1965, and the plant at

Women crocheting lace edgings on head scarves, Göreme
Courtesy Hermine Dreyfuss

Woman beating and washing wool near Lake Van
Courtesy Hermine Dreyfuss

Iskenderun, which was built with Soviet aid and opened in 1975. The overstaffed Iskenderun plant, although the largest and most modern, performs poorly. Private plants, often more profitable than state plants, tend to use scrap as a raw material and to export to neighboring countries. In December 1994, the government indicated that 51.7 percent of the Eregli Iron and Steel Works would be privatized in 1995. This company was cited as one of the most profitable in Turkey, especially after a US$1.5 billion upgrade designed to raise raw steel capacity by one-third, to about 3 million tons annually.

Capacity use in the iron and steel sector increased rapidly in the 1980s and early 1990s. Total output of crude iron grew from about 3.1 million tons in 1985 to about 4.5 million tons in 1992. Steel ingot output rose from about 7 million tons in 1987 to 10.3 million tons in 1992. The value of exports of iron and steel rose from US$34 million in 1980 to US$1.6 billion in 1992. Such exports accounted for around 10 percent of total exports.

The demand for cement also increased in the late 1980s and early 1990s as a result of an upswing in domestic construction stimulated by infrastructure and housing projects. The cement industry consists of a large SEE, the Turkish Cement Corporation, and a number of smaller companies. Until 1970 the country imported most of its cement, but it has since become self-sufficient. Total output increased from 22.7 million tons in 1987 to 28.5 million tons in 1992. Exports of cement, especially to the Middle East, grew rapidly in the early 1980s because of the construction boom in that region.

The chemical industry, one of the country's largest in terms of value, is concentrated in a few large state enterprises, including the Petrochemical Corporation (Petrokimya Anonimsirketi—Petkim) and Etibank, and some 600 private enterprises. Chemicals produced in Turkey include boron products, caustic soda, chlorine, industrial chemicals, and sodium phosphates. The high quality of the country's minerals gives it a comparative advantage in several products. Chemical exports increased during the second half of the 1980s but fell sharply in the early 1990s, mainly because of increasing competition and lower prices elsewhere. In the late 1980s, petrochemical production, dominated by Petkim, started with a complex at Yarmıca, near Kocaeli, followed by a second at Aliaga, near Izmir. The complex includes twelve plants, seven subplants, a thermal power station, and a water supply dam. These plants supply small private-sector plants, which in turn manufacture finished products. The sector's goal is to make the country self-sufficient in petrochemicals rather than to export. In 1992 Turkey produced about 144,000 tons of polyvinyl chloride, about 238,000 tons of polyethylene, about 85,000 tons of benzine, and about 32,000 tons of carbon black.

Turkey's automobile industry, established in the mid-1960s, was gradually exposed to imports after 1980. Although the sector recovered from low production levels after 1983, domestic producers remain weak. Industry observers believe that Turkey's automobile makers are too numerous and too inefficient, but market prospects appear fairly favorable because of the low per capita ownership of cars. Car output rose from about 55,000 units in 1985 to about 300,000 units in 1993. Including trucks, buses, and tractors, Turkey produced about 345,000 units in 1992. Some 60,000 vehicles were imported in that year, a figure that should increase in the near future if Turkey gains entrance into the European customs union. Turkish producers benefit from a 20 percent tariff on foreign imports.

The Turkish automobile industry in 1995 consisted of three producers, each affiliated with a foreign manufacturer: Tofas, which assembles Fiat passenger cars; Oyak Renault, which assembles Renaults; and General Motors, builder of Opel Vectras. Toyota in partnership with local conglomerate Sabançı Holding completed a plant in 1994 designed to produce 100,000 cars per year, and a Hyundai factory that would produce 100,000 units is scheduled to open in 1996.

Construction

Turkey has several relatively large, internationally competitive construction firms, some of which specialize in particular types of projects such as dam or pipeline construction. During the late 1970s and early 1980s, domestic demand was relatively weak, but Turkish firms were quite successful at selling their services abroad, especially in the oil-producing states of the Middle East. However, by the mid-1980s construction projects in the Middle East had slowed down because of falling oil prices. Fortunately, Turkey's major infrastructure program and housing projects saved contracting firms from financial ruin. For example, the establishment of the Mass Housing Fund in the 1980s offered opportunities to Turkish contractors. A number of large infrastructure projects—particularly the GAP and the construction of state highways—provided enormous contracts for local builders. With the demise of the Soviet Union, Turkish contractors set their sights on Central Asia and Russia, with estimates of potential business in this region around US$700 million. The end of the Iran-Iraq War in 1988 also promised new opportunities for Turkish contractors; however, the Iraqi invasion of Kuwait and subsequent Persian Gulf War damaged such hopes. Contractors estimated their combined losses as a result of the crisis at US$800 million. Nonetheless, the external market accounted for a substantial portion of the industry's revenues. At the end of 1992, Turkish contractors had contracts worth US$20.6 billion; Libya accounted for US$10.3 billion, Saudi Arabia US$5.4 billion, and the republics of the former Soviet Union US$1 billion.

Policy makers have made housing—perhaps the most deficient sector of the economy—a priority. The combination of rapid population growth and high rates of urbanization has overwhelmed available housing. In the mid-1980s, perhaps more than half of the inhabitants of urban centers lived in shanties lacking sewers, water, and electricity. According to a tradition dating back to Ottoman rule, shelters built overnight had been tolerated by the authorities. These shanties, or *gecekondus* (see Glossary), had been a problem since the 1950s. In the early 1980s, the government took several steps to improve the housing situation. A law was passed transferring ownership of existing *gecekondus* to their inhabitants but declaring that any new structures would be destroyed. In addition, a housing fund, set up in 1984 and financed by a tax on tobacco, liquor, and luxury imports, offered financing for the construction of up to 100,000 houses a year. Monies could be used to improve existing *gecekondus* or for new construction and could be lent to homeowners, cooperative associations, or contractors. Analysts believed it unlikely that the fund would grow fast enough to eliminate the *gecekondus*, although it might stem their proliferation.

Services

After seventy years of development, the services sector has grown to account for more than half of the labor force but nevertheless remains relatively unproductive. In addition to traditional enterprises, services include modern activities such as banking and engineering. The development of government services has been significant, but the state has paid little attention to increasing the efficiency of private-sector service enterprises. Services have traditionally produced only a small fraction of exports; however, after 1980 the government encouraged development of service earnings and allowed foreign enterprises to enter previously protected markets such as those in finance.

Banking and Finance

The government, banks, and industry form a complex system through which legislation and government policies direct credit flows. Most state-owned banks were established to finance particular industries, whereas private banks generally have intimate connections with large industrial groups. The Central Bank of Turkey often provides credit to other banks at negative real interest rates. Banks, in turn, funnel credit to industries or groups they serve. The amounts available to particular sectors of the economy thus depend largely on the

*Man making brooms,
Trabzon
Courtesy Hermine Dreyfuss*

*Rug vendor displaying his
wares, central Anatolia
Courtesy Hermine Dreyfuss*

resources available to the institutions for that sector, rather than on market assessments.

The Central Bank set up a system of quarterly reporting in the mid-1980s, enabling timely warning of banks in difficulties. This reform was a start toward making banking more transparent, but it is still difficult to assess the condition of the banks. Strong political pressures to keep weak industries and groups afloat during the adjustment period make it likely that several years will pass before standard accounting rules can be systematically applied. Legislation introduced in 1993 sought to bring the Turkish banking sector into line with European standards on capital adequacy and other prudential ratios. However, in December 1993, the Constitutional Court blocked this legislation because the executive had enacted it without approval of the legislature. No further action had occurred as of early 1995.

Despite some setbacks, the government's new policies have effected rapid changes in the financial sector. The banking system in early 1995 consisted of the Central Bank and fifty-eight banks, including twenty-one foreign banks, divided between Ankara, where most state-owned banks are located, and Istanbul, the center for most privately owned banks. Turkey also had three state investment and development banks. The Development Bank is funded from the Treasury and invests in the private sector. The Export Credit Bank of Turkey (Türkiye Ihracat Kredi Bankası) provides export finance. The Municipalities Bank (Iller Bankası) supports local institutions. In 1995 nine merchant banks also operated in Turkey, six domestically owned and three foreign owned.

The Central Bank, founded in the early 1930s, has the usual central bank responsibilities, such as issuing banknotes, protecting the currency, and regulating the banking system and credit. The Central Bank also finances the government's budget deficits and makes loans to public and private banks. Starting in 1983, however, the Central Bank began to reduce lending and stepped up its supervisory functions.

Six of Turkey's commercial banks are in the public sector, and twenty-one are partly or wholly foreign owned. Of the banking sector's assets, 46 percent are concentrated in four banks: the oldest and largest public bank, the Agricultural Bank of the Republic of Turkey (Türkiye Cumhuriyet Ziraat Bankası—TCZB); the Real Estate Bank (Türkiye Emlâk Bankası As); and two private banks, Isbank and Akbank TAS. The

TCZB has many branches in rural areas, a strong deposit base, and favored access to state credits, which it uses partly for the agricultural commodity price-support program. After 1983 the TCZB was forced to take over other banks that had failed, a move that reduced earnings.

Much as in Germany and Japan, the major private banks are closely linked to industrial groups. Yapi ve Kredi Bankası, Pamukbank, and Interbank are owned by the Cukurova Group conglomerate. Akbank, reputed to be the most profitable private bank in Turkey, is owned by the Sabançı Group. Partially publicly traded Kocbank is owned by the Koç Holding Company. Tütünbank is owned by the Yasar Holding Corporation.

Before 1980 there were only four foreign banks in Turkey, but their numbers grew rapidly during the 1980s as the government liberalized conditions. Several joint ventures were created in the 1980s, as well as two Islamic banks specializing in trade finance.

Private banks remain the most vulnerable sector of the banking system because the public banks enjoy de facto state guarantees. During the 1980s, most private banks engaged in trade financing or in sales of state bonds because investment activity was depressed. The largest private banks maintained their ties to Turkey's major corporations despite a 1983 banking law enacted to discourage such links. Although a few private banks were able to eliminate nonperforming loans, many remained vulnerable to their customers' difficulties. By 1986 private-bank balance sheets began to improve, as several years of high-interest earnings made it possible for banks to write off bad loans.

Although the government, public enterprises, and private undertakings increased their use of stocks and bonds after 1970, capital markets remained underdeveloped in the 1970s. After the passing of the Capital Markets Law in 1982, a Capital Markets Board was established to issue regulations for institutions marketing bonds and other financial instruments. Most Turkish corporations were closely held and tended to finance expansion through their own funds from their small circles of stockholders. But in the 1980s, companies were allowed to issue profit-and-loss-sharing certificates with liability limited to the face value of the certificate. The Özal administration also took steps to revive Istanbul's stock market, which had closed down in the late 1970s. The Istanbul Stock Exchange (ISE) reopened in December 1985. With the rise of "emerging market" funds, trading on the ISE expanded rapidly in the early 1990s; indeed, it was the best performing of any market in 1993. Foreign investment accounted for 25 percent of the daily trading volume. In early 1994, however, the stock market crashed in the wake of the currency and balance of payments crisis. Plans for privatization of SEEs were expected to revive the stock market, if foreign investment and confidence in the government's attempts to stabilize the macroeconomic situation increased.

Government securities are quite liquid in secondary markets; this has been true especially since the Treasury began issuing T-bills in 1986 and an interbank market was established in 1987. Government T-bill issues jumped in the early 1990s as the budget deficit exploded. In 1986 the public snapped up revenue-sharing certificates used to finance the Keban hydroelectric project on the Euphrates; the Oymapınar Dam, also on the Euphrates south of Malatya; and a second bridge across the Bosporus. Such certificates were popular, in part because they conformed to Islamic strictures prohibiting interest. Low returns discouraged the government from using such certificates in the 1990s.

Transportation and Telecommunications

Under the Ottomans, foreign companies constructed the portion of the Berlin-to-Baghdad railroad that crossed Turkey, as well as a few other lines used mostly for mining development and the export of agricultural products. Atatürk and the nationalists took an active interest in the development of the railroad system for strategic reasons, setting up the Turkish Republic State Railways (Türkiye Cumhuriyeti Devlet Demiryolları Isletmesi Genel Müdürlügü—TCDD) in 1920. The nationalists set two priorities for railroad development: extending lines to major areas, such as eastern Anatolia and the new capital at Ankara, and buying out foreign railroad interests. The TCDD invested large sums during its first two decades, bringing all railroads under state control by 1948 and increasing track lengths from 4,018 kilometers in 1923 to 7,324 kilometers in 1950. By 1950 the rail system linked the major areas and accounted for about three-quarters of surface freight traffic.

After 1950 the railroads received only small investments and insufficient maintenance because of increasing emphasis on road transport. By the 1970s, the tracks and rolling stock were in poor condition and the TCDD was running chronic deficits, partly because of its low rate structure. In the 1970s, as mining expanded to support the metalworking and fuel industries, the railroads received additional funds to expand and upgrade service.

Between 1985 and 1992, the rail network grew modestly, from 8,193 kilometers of track to 8,430 kilometers. Almost all rail was single-tracked and nonelectrified. Although rail lines linked most important cities, there were few cross connections between lines, and routes were often circuitous. Passengers preferred other means of transport because the railroads were slow and unsafe; in 1982 there were 210 train collisions and 737 derailments. As a result of increased use of trucks, the railroads carried only one-quarter of surface freight, mostly long-haul bulk commodities.

After World War II, transportation development concentrated on the road system. As a result, by early 1995 Turkey had nearly 59,770 kilometers of all-weather highways, of which about 27,000 kilometers were paved. There were also some 308,000 kilometers of gravel and earth roads in rural areas. The government planned to build 3,000 additional kilometers by the year 2000 and to upgrade existing roads.

The Özal administration in the early 1980s began a major project that was expected to result in highways that would traverse the country, making it possible for Turkey to handle increased levels of freight between Europe and the Middle East. This project, along with the second bridge across the Bosporus, would form a 3,600-kilometer link in a 10,000-kilometer trans-European highway going from Gdansk on the Baltic Sea to cities on the Caspian Sea and the Persian Gulf.

Several road and highway improvements were underway in the mid-1990s. The four-lane highway linking Ankara, Istanbul, and Edirne is complete except for a thirty-kilometer stretch under construction west of Bolu (see fig. 11). Another four-lane highway in the southeast, designed to link Gaziantep with Mersin via Adana, lacks about eighty kilometers west of Gaziantep. Another offshoot of this highway that would connect with Iskenderun via Dörtyol is under construction. Other highways in the planning stage include improved links between Iskenderun and Antalya, Ankara and Adana, and Istanbul and Izmir. Additional highways are needed because traffic is extremely dense around major cities in western Anatolia, creat-

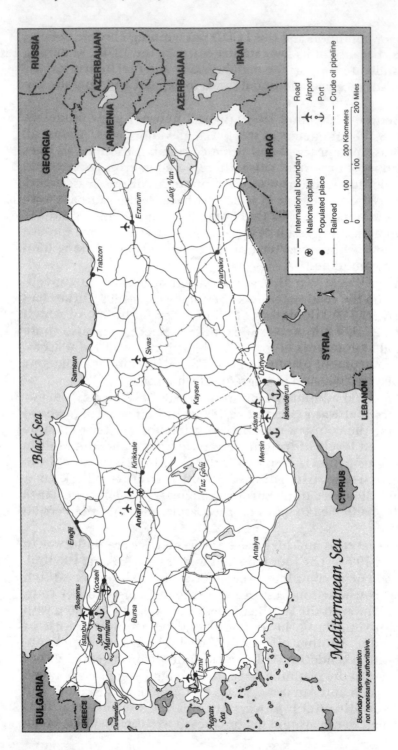

Figure 11. Transportation System and Crude Oil Pipeline, 1995

ing frequent traffic jams and contributing to a high accident rate.

Truck transport of surface freight increased from about 25 percent of the total of such freight in 1950 to more than 75 percent by the mid-1980s. According to one source, in 1984 trucks carried about 40 percent of exports by tonnage. As the oil boom hit the Persian Gulf states and imports clogged their ports during the mid-1970s, heavy truck traffic passed through Turkey. By 1985, however, transit traffic had fallen off somewhat as a result of the fall in demand from oil-exporting countries and a cutback on purchases by Iran and Iraq. The end of the Iran-Iraq War modestly helped revive transit traffic, which was disrupted again by the 1990 Iraqi invasion of Kuwait and the resulting UN embargo. In the mid-1990s, goods moved by truck accounted for 27 percent of total export tonnage.

Shipping is much less important than land transport, but capacity expanded rapidly in the early 1990s. The Özal administration encouraged the growth of Turkey's merchant marine by granting tax rebates to companies registering their ships under the Turkish flag. As a result, the fleet grew from about 1.7 million gross registered tons (GRT) in 1975 to about 2.5 million GRT in 1983. In 1990 the merchant marine's 2,996 cargo ships had a combined capacity of about 3.8 million GRT. A large number of these ships were owned by the Maritime Bank (Denizcilik Bankası) and Deniz Nakliyati, a large private company. In the 1980s and early 1990s, private cargo lines expanded rapidly. Aside from the ferry across Lake Van, internal shipping is insignificant because few of Turkey's rivers are navigable.

Five ports handle the bulk of the country's sea freight. Istanbul is the most important port, followed by Mersin, Izmir, Iskenderun, and Kocaeli. There are also many small ports along the country's extensive coastline; coastal shipping is substantial, particularly of such bulk commodities as coal and iron ore. Cargo handling is slow and storage limited, however. The main oil terminals near Iskenderun handle both domestic and Iraqi crude. In 1992 ships brought 60 million tons of cargo to Turkey; 26 million tons were exported by sea.

Turkey has 105 usable airports, sixty-nine of which have paved runways. Turkish Airlines (Türk Hava Yolları—THY), plagued by a poor safety record in the 1970s, fought its way back to profitability during the 1980s, although heavy capital expenditures in the 1990s put it back in the red. By 1995 it was a prime candidate for partial privatization, which was expected to net the government US$300 million. By 1985 Turkish Airlines was serving thirty-six international and sixteen domestic destinations with a fleet that had been recently augmented by the purchase of several Airbus Industrie A–310 passenger aircraft. Much of the company's international business involves serving the many Turks who work in Europe and the Middle East. Domestic flights are popular because surface travel between major cities is time consuming; THY's domestic services probably will be further upgraded. In 1992 the total number of passengers carried to, from, or within Turkey on all airlines landing in Turkey reached about 13.8 million (about 2.8 million domestic and 11 million international); the domestic carrier transported about 2.4 million passengers within Turkey and about 1.7 million international passengers. Private airlines entered the market in the 1980s; Istanbul Airlines and Green Air handle both domestic and foreign routes.

Turkey's archaic telecommunications system, which had long been overloaded, received expanded domestic and international lines in the 1980s and early 1990s. Until the 1980s, more than half of Turkey's villages lacked telephone connections, and customers had to wait years to get telephones installed. In the early 1980s, authorities designed a program to eliminate the waiting list for telephones; make service available to all of the country's settlements; and install countrywide automatic dialing, a new telex system, and a connection with the European telecommunications satellite. The number of telephones increased from about 351,000 in 1966 to an estimated 7.96 million by the end of 1991.

The Turkish Radio-Television Corporation (Türkiye Radyo-Televizyon Kurumu—TRT) has flagship radio stations in Ankara and Istanbul, with subsidiary networks in fifteen other urban centers. Frequency modulation (FM) transmitters are located in ten cities, including Ankara and Istanbul. In addition to Turkish, broadcasts are made in Albanian, Arabic, Azerbaijani, Bulgarian, Chinese, English, French, German, Greek, Hungarian, Persian, Romanian, Serbo-Croatian, and Urdu. Turkish television has two main channels that reach more than forty population centers. The Istanbul area has three additional channels. In early 1995, the Turkish population had some 8.8 million radios and some 10.53 million television sets.

Tourism

Turkey's long and varied sea coast, high mountains and lakes, and its many historical, religious, and archaeological sites (possibly including more Greek ruins than survive in Greece) give the country unrivaled tourist potential. Until the 1980s, Turkish tourism lagged far behind its counterparts in other Mediterranean countries, and visitors tended to stay for shorter periods of time and spend less money than in countries such as Spain, Portugal, and Greece. The Özal government's promotion of tourism in the 1980s led to dramatic change. The number of visitors grew rapidly during the 1980s and early 1990s, and Turkey was able to appeal to tourists from many different countries. Including business travelers, Turkey hosted about 1.3 million visitors in 1983 and 2.1 million in 1984, whereas Greece during the same period received at least 6 million and Spain 40 million visitors annually. By 1987 visits to Turkey had increased to about 2.9 million, and by 1992 close to 7 million.

In the early 1980s, most tourists came from European countries, especially Greece and West Germany, but the number of Middle Eastern tourists also increased. Even in the late 1980s, however, European tourists accounted for nearly 61 percent of total arrivals. By 1992 the European proportion had fallen to 45 percent. The largest increase was registered in tourists from the republics of the former Soviet Union. By 1992 they accounted for 43 percent of tourists, whereas the Middle Eastern share had shrunk from 11 percent to 8 percent.

Regional origin is a good predictor of the type of tourism and destination. Middle-class Turks, who started to take vacations in the early 1980s, usually prefer the beach resorts on the Aegean and Mediterranean seas. Tourists from Western Europe, Israel, and the United States tend to visit beaches and historical sites. East European tourists, particularly from the former Soviet Union, typically come to Istanbul or Black Sea towns to shop or barter goods. Tourists from Iran and other Middle Eastern countries generally take longer holidays in Istanbul and Bursa, also coming to shop in Turkey.

Although tourism earnings reached US$770 million in 1985 and jumped to US$3.6 billion by 1992, the industry has been plagued by political, economic, and environmental problems. The fallout from the nuclear power plant disaster at Chernobyl in the Soviet Union, terrorist attacks by Kurdish insurgents, and economic problems in Europe and the Middle East have tended to discourage tourism. Turkey has attempted to overcome these impediments by improving domestic services. The number of beds for visitors rose from about 49,000 in 1980 to about 206,000 in 1992, for example. The total will probably reach 600,000 by the end of the 1990s. One important effort, the South Antalya Project, involves transforming a seventy-four-kilometer stretch of Mediterranean beaches into a base for resort villages. Istanbul, the main tourist center, still lacks sufficient beds, however, and there is a tendency to concentrate on luxury hotels that are too expensive for middle-class tourists. Nevertheless, the mid-1990s saw a noticeable improvement in the average spending per day by tourists: US$141 compared with the world average of US$70-US$100. Shopping tours helped raise the average significantly.

Foreign Economic Relations

Foreign Trade

Trade played a minor role in the economy until 1980 but grew rapidly thereafter, the sum of exports and imports reaching about 49 percent of GNP by 1985. By 1994 this total had fallen somewhat, to 42 percent of GNP. The trend toward increased trade had begun in the 1970s as imports increased—primarily as a result of the rise in oil prices—and limited incentives for exports were implemented. The turning point came after 1980, when a realistic exchange rate, strict monetary policy, and efforts to strengthen bilateral cooperation with the country's trading partners led to sharply increased exports. Improvements in the balance of trade, in turn, allowed gradual liberalization of the import regime.

Turkey's trade policy traditionally has been subordinate to the country's etatist development strategy. The demand for imports historically has exceeded the country's supply of foreign currency, forcing the government to set up extensive controls to mobilize foreign exchange for products deemed essential for investment or production. As Turkish industry developed, the proportion of finished goods declined as a share of imports. Despite liberalization of import regulations after 1980, in the mid-1990s petroleum, machinery, and industrial raw materials continued to account for the bulk of Turkish imports.

Turkey's export performance since 1980 has been particularly striking. Traditionally, Turkey has exported agricultural products and minerals. As of 1980, total merchandise exports

Old and new forms of transportation: cattle-drawn wagon in central Anatolia and modern vehicle in Istanbul
Courtesy Hermine Dreyfuss

221

amounted to about US$2.9 billion, or 5 percent of GNP, of which 58 percent was agricultural products, 22 percent processed agricultural products and textiles, and 6.5 percent mineral products. By 1992, when exports reached 17 percent of GNP, the share of processed and manufactured products had risen to 82 percent, whereas the share of agricultural exports had declined to 15.0 percent and that of minerals to 1.7 percent (see table 9, Appendix A). The shift in the structure of exports resulted largely from the trend toward domestic processing of agricultural products before exportation, which caused them to be reclassified as industrial exports. Textile exports also increased during the 1980s, becoming twice as important as agricultural exports by 1992. Observers had expected that limitations on textile imports implemented by industrialized countries would hamper growth in textile exports during the late 1980s, but special concessions by the United States in 1990—related to compensation for Turkey's effort in the Persian Gulf crisis—helped open export markets even further. Industrial diversification has enabled Turkey to export a wide range of products, including rubber, plastics, petroleum products, glass, ceramics, and cement.

Turkey's trade is largely with Organisation for Economic Cooperation and Development (OECD) members, particularly the European countries, notwithstanding a sharp upswing in trade with Middle Eastern oil-producing countries in the early 1980s. Exports to the EC increased from 35 percent of total exports in 1950 to almost 45 percent in 1992, while imports from the EC grew from 33 percent to about 40 percent during the same period. Turkey's most important trading partner, Germany, accounted for 15 percent of imports and 24 percent of exports in 1993. Trade with Middle Eastern countries increased considerably after 1970, partly as a result of Turkey's increased expenditures for petroleum imports, and peaked in 1982 at 45 percent of total trade, declining to about 15 percent by the early 1990s. Turkey's commerce with Iran and Iraq was important because they bought food and other products and provided petroleum to Turkey in exchange (see table 10, Appendix A). Turkey remained neutral in the Iran-Iraq War, hoping for further improvement in trade when the two countries made peace. The embargo on Iraq after its invasion of Kuwait dramatically reduced Turkish-Iraqi trade. In 1988 Turkey sent 8.8 percent of its exports to Iraq and bought 10 percent of its imports from that country. Trade between the two countries was almost nonexistent in 1994.

Trade with the United States was much greater in the 1950s and 1960s than in the 1970s and 1980s. In 1992 imports from the United States constituted a little over 11 percent of Turkey's total imports, but exports to the United States represented only 6 percent of Turkey's exports (see table 11, Appendix A). Although trade with the Soviet Union began in the 1930s and the Soviet Union supplied much aid, in 1992 imports from the former Soviet Union constituted less than 1 percent of Turkey's imports, while exports were about 5 percent of the total. Historically, trade with the Soviet Union and Eastern Europe had increased to more than 10 percent of total trade during periods, such as the late 1970s, when Turkey experienced balance of payments difficulties.

After 1980 Turkey shifted its emphasis in trade policy from strictly limiting imports to actively encouraging exports. In March 1985, Turkey signed the General Agreement on Tariffs and Trade (GATT), which committed the country to abolishing most export subsidies over a three-year period. In January 1993, in accordance with its commitments under the GATT agreement, Turkey consolidated and reduced most import charges.

Turkey and the EC entered into an association agreement on December 1, 1964, with the aim of full membership for Turkey after the implementation of a customs union, which the Turkish government hoped would occur in 1995. Turkey's record in meeting the European body's tariff-reduction schedule has undergone several permutations. It was adhered to until 1976, when it was abandoned, only to be reinstituted in December 1987. Several Turkish industries—in particular the automobile industry—fear total integration, whereas the EU in the mid-1990s fears the competitive strength of the Turkish textile industry.

Balance of Payments

Throughout the twentieth century, Turkey has suffered from a shortage of foreign exchange, a problem that has continued despite the improved export performance of the 1980s and the early 1990s. During the 1950–80 period, three balance of payments crises followed periods of rapid economic growth. After the crisis of the late 1950s, brought on by inflationary financial policies and excessive use of short-term commercial credits, Turkey received substantial aid from an OECD consortium, and the country's external debt had to be rescheduled. The foreign-exchange shortage of the 1960s was less the result of inflation than of increased demand for imports. The 1970 devaluation, along with increased workers' remittances during the early 1970s, sufficed to overcome the problem. Turkey's improved balance of payments status during the first half of the 1970s allowed the government to resort to foreign borrowing to finance rapid economic growth. However, the 1970 devaluation, government deficits, and the 1973 oil price increase worsened inflation. After 1976 Turkey tried several reform packages, none of which effectively addressed the underlying causes of the deficits. In 1979 Turkey's creditors had to reschedule some US$14 billion in debt in an arrangement that delayed repayments of principal for five years.

The policy package introduced after 1980 enabled growth to resume, largely by improving the balance of trade. Exports grew at an annual average rate of more than 20 percent from 1980 to 1985, much more rapidly than imports, reducing the trade deficit from more than US$4.6 billion in 1980 to an average of slightly less than US$3 billion a year from 1983 to 1985. Nevertheless, Turkey's merchandise trade balance remained in deficit because of continued high levels of imports.

In 1993–94, Turkey experienced its fourth major balance of payments crisis in the past forty years, despite a decade of reforms and structural adjustment. An expansionist fiscal and monetary policy had led to a sharp deterioration in the trade balance in 1993 as imports soared to US$29 billion, while exports lagged sharply behind at US$15.6 billion (see table 12, Appendix A). A draconian adjustment program accompanied by an IMF standby agreement helped sharply reduce imports in 1994, but the trade deficit remained around US$4 billion and was projected at about the same level for 1995.

Economic reforms had strengthened the services account of the balance of payments in the 1980s, although this increase was insufficient to offset the periodic deterioration of the trade account in the 1990s. Meanwhile, remittances from Turkish workers abroad remained an important source of foreign exchange. Remittances averaged roughly US$2 billion annually from 1980 to 1985 but fell during that period from a peak of almost US$2.5 billion in 1981 to US$1.7 billion in 1985. In the late 1980s, they once again recovered, reaching a level of US$3 billion during the first half of the 1990s. The flow of remittances through legal channels is very sensitive to the real exchange rate and to foreign-exchange regulations.

Tourism was a relatively small source of services income until 1985 when earnings jumped to US$770 million, reaching around US$4 billion in 1994 as investments in this sector paid off. Interest payments on Turkey's foreign debt, which averaged about US$1.5 billion from 1980 to 1985, grew to US$3.2 billion in 1990 and were US$3.6 billion in 1994. They remained a major burden on the services account.

Turkey's deficit on the current account declined from US$3.4 billion in 1980 to about US$1 billion in 1985 as a result of the decline in the trade deficit and the increased surplus on the services account. Despite fluctuations mid-decade, by the end of the 1980s the current- account deficit was sharply reduced, although 1990 saw the deficit at US$2.6 billion as a result of high oil prices and loss of income stemming from the Persian Gulf War. Aid payments and certain policy measures led to a small surplus in 1991, but a lax fiscal and monetary policy by 1993 pushed the deficit to its highest level at US$6.4 billion. The policy measures enacted in coordination with the IMF helped the current account register a surplus of US$3 billion in 1994.

Turkey's capital account suffered from the heavy foreign-debt payments that came due in increasing amounts after 1985. Heavy borrowing in the late 1980s and early 1990s pushed principal payments up to US$4.4 billion in 1993, US$5.9 billion in 1994, and a projected US$7.7 billion in 1995. As a percent of exports of goods and services, Turkey's debt-service ratio rose to 33 percent in 1994, close to crisis levels.

Domestic savings were insufficient for the country's development plans, making continued foreign borrowing necessary. Direct foreign investment averaged only US$70 million from 1980 to 1985, as foreign investors hesitated to put money into the country. The growth of emerging market funds in the developed countries, combined with Turkey's economic- and financial-sector reforms, had led to a sharp increase in foreign direct and portfolio investment in the 1990s. In 1994 such investments were estimated at US$300 million. However, the country's 1994 balance of payments crisis was expected to dampen near-term enthusiasm for Turkish stocks and bonds.

Turkey's short-term debt increased in the mid- and late 1980s as the country scrambled to meet debt payments. In 1985 Turkey broke off negotiations with the IMF concerning a standby agreement and turned to commercial banks for short-term loans. In 1986 alone, Turkey's outstanding short-term debt increased by more than 40 percent to at least US$9.4 billion. As a result, short-term debt amounted to about 33 percent of total foreign debt, a development that sparked concerns abroad. By early 1987, it was reported that some foreign banks were limiting long-term loans to Turkey pending the outcome of the 1987 local elections. A similar situation transpired in 1993 in the run-up to the 1994 local elections. Short-term debt jumped from US$9.5 billion in 1990 to US$12.7 billion in 1992 and US$18.5 billion in 1993. The austerity measures enacted by the government and a surplus on the current account helped reduce the short-term debt to US$12.6 billion by the end of 1994, when long-term debt was US$52.8 billion. A little more than half of this amount was owed to private-sector creditors, which was a sign of the success of the economic reforms of the 1980s. Nonetheless, bilateral and multilateral creditors accounted for nearly US$18 billion. The relative shares of private and public creditors were expected to change during the mid-1990s as Turkey was obliged to borrow more from international agencies to stabilize its balance of payments.

Regional Economic Integration

After 1980 Turkey's need for foreign markets led the country to try to strengthen cooperation with trading partners worldwide. Trade ties with the Middle East received particular attention under Özal, but Turkish businesspeople also worked to improve trade with countries in North America, East Asia, and Eastern Europe. In the protectionist climate of the mid- and late 1980s, policy makers also took up proposals for regional integration with the economies of Turkey's West European and Middle Eastern neighbors.

For many years, Turkish policy makers and politicians had expressed interest in closer multilateral cooperation with other Islamic countries, especially with oil-producing Middle Eastern states. Starting in the late 1970s, Turkey's increased attention to Middle Eastern markets boosted exports of manufactured goods and construction services, attracted tourists from Middle Eastern countries, and provided additional sources of foreign direct investment and commercial financing. During the early 1980s, exports to Iran, Iraq, Libya, and Saudi Arabia grew rapidly but then declined again after 1982 as oil revenues fell. In

Fatih Bridge over the Bosporus in Istanbul
Courtesy Hermine Dreyfuss

the mid-1980s, Turkey served as a conduit for West European exports to Iran under a countertrade arrangement according to which Turkey received oil and other commodities in exchange for manufactures. Trade with Iraq was reduced after the latter announced in late 1985 that it could not make more than US$1.2 billion in payments, thereby forcing credit from Turkey. Although the Turks remained open to discussions of an "Islamic common market," disappointment with Middle Eastern markets in the mid-1980s refocused their attention on upgrading economic ties with Western Europe.

During the early 1970s, both European countries and Turkey adhered to the terms of a 1973 protocol for reducing trade barriers. The EC began granting preferential treatment to most Turkish agricultural imports, and Turkey was given a period of twenty-two years to align its agricultural policies with the EC's Common Agricultural Policy (see Glossary). In 1977, however, Turkey stopped reducing tariffs on EC goods because of the deterioration of the domestic economy. By the late 1970s, relations had deteriorated between Turkey and the EC. The EC imposed quotas and other restrictions on certain Turkish imports, including cotton yarn and T-shirts; in retaliation, Turkey applied levies on imports of European iron and steel. In 1980 the military coup froze relations between Turkey and the EC, although the EC continued to apply the commercial provisions of the association agreement. After 1981 the EC suspended financial assistance in the amount of 600 million European Currency Units (see Glossary) because of reservations concerning human rights violations under Turkey's military government.

After Turkey's return to civilian government in 1983, political relations between Turkey and the EC countries began to improve, and in September 1986 the EC-Turkey Association Council held its first meeting since the 1980 coup. In early 1987, West European diplomats seemed to be united in urging Turkey to pursue the advantages offered by the association agreement, including the provision for a customs union by 1995, before making an application for membership. In April 1987, the Özal government overrode both Turkish hesitation and European misgivings and made a formal application for EC membership. The European Commission issued an official opinion on the Turkish application in December 1989, which was later adopted unchanged by the community's Council of Ministers. In this opinion, the commission proposed that negotiations should not begin until 1993. Negotiations thereafter led the EU to vote for Turkey's inclusion in the free-trade area in 1995.

Some observers have postulated that the EU will never admit Turkey. In addition to criticizing Turkey's human rights policies, they cite three main reasons. First, the level of industrialization in Turkey lags behind that of the European economies. Second, the degree of budgetary transfers from the EU necessary to lift Turkey to the levels of even the poorest European countries would place a huge burden on Europe's resources. Third, given that entry into the union permits labor mobility, Turkey's economic structure, relatively high unemployment, and low wages particularly discourage Europeans at a time when violence in Europe against foreigners has increased dramatically, mainly as a result of high levels of joblessness there.

Since the fall of the Soviet Union, Turkey has shown a keen interest in developing strong economic ties with the states of Central Asia, the Caucasus, and the Black Sea region. In 1990 Turkey and the other states—Armenia, Azerbaijan, Bulgaria, Georgia, Greece, Moldova, Romania, Russia, and Ukraine—surrounding the Black Sea initiated the Black Sea Economic Cooperation (BSEC) project to broaden and deepen cooperation and trade relations among themselves, nonmember states, and other regional structures. Despite obstacles, on June 24, 1992, a basic structure, including concrete plans for integration, was articulated. The most ambitious aspect of the BSEC is an attempt to create a free-trade area to promote easy movement of capital, labor, and goods. The wide range of generally complementary economies in the BSEC area is seen as a factor encouraging integration. Nonetheless, one important difference among the economies—particularly between the Turkish economy and those of the republics of the former Soviet Union—is that many of them are only in the early stages of transition from statist structures. Some observers consider this an impediment to smooth integration. Another major project of the BSEC is the creation of a development bank to finance projects in the region. Some observers, however, have noted that in a capital-poor area the ability of such an institution to mobilize sufficient funds from within the region must be doubted.

Outlook

Regionally, Turkey faces a host of potential political and security threats, largely as a consequence of the end of the Cold War and conflicts in the Middle East, which have forced the government to devote extensive resources to the military. Also, Turkey's attempts to forge regional cooperation arrangements and exploit economic opportunities have been largely stillborn. Strong nationalist sentiment at home, combined with a poor human rights record, also contributes to an uncertain domestic economic future. The Kurdish insurgency has taken its toll on government resources and foreign confidence. Turkey's long-standing attempt to integrate its economy into that of Europe has been jeopardized by the opposition of European governments to Turkey's incursion into Iraq in late 1994 and its repression of its Kurdish population.

Despite setbacks, the steady liberalization of the economy and integration into the world economy begun by former President Özal has continued without interruption. Turkey's trade sector accounts for a growing proportion of GDP, and foreign funds are a major source of investment. Despite crises in mid-1994 such as the devaluation of the currency, the stock market crash, and a number of bank failures, Turkey has been designated a major emerging market by the main international financial centers. And because a large proportion of foreign investments has gone into industrialization, most observers have expressed confidence in the economy and the government's ability to steer it carefully toward the objective of making Turkey a major regional and international industrial power.

*   *   *

The OECD's annual economic survey, *Turkey*, is an authoritative and readily available summary of the Turkish economy that includes up-to-date statistical tables. The International Energy Agency's *Energy Statistics and Balances of OECD Countries* provides energy sector data on Turkey. Economic data on Turkey can also be found in the publications of the World Bank and the International Monetary Fund.

The Turkish weekly journal *Briefing* provides insightful, lively, and independent analysis of the Turkish economy. Among non-Turkish journals, regular economic and political coverage can be found in the *Financial Times*, *Middle East Economic Digest*, and the Economist Intelligence Unit's annual *Country Profile: Turkey*. The *Middle East Journal* and *Middle East Report* offer in-depth articles on Turkey. Three excellent books on Turkey that include discussion of the economic and political consequences of structural adjustment are Ziya Onis and James Riedel's *Economic Crises and Long-Term Growth in Turkey*, F.T. Nas and Mehmet Odekon's *Liberalization and the Turkish Economy*, and *The Political and Socioeconomic Transformation of Turkey* by Atila Eralp et al. (For further information and complete citations, see Bibliography.)

Chapter 4. Government and Politics

Double-headed eagle, symbol of the ancient Seljuk Turks

TURKEY'S POLITICAL SYSTEM faced four distinct but intertwined challenges in early 1995: accommodating the disaffected Kurdish ethnic minority; reconciling the growing differences, expressed with increasing stridency, between the secular elite and groups using traditional Islamic symbols to manifest their opposition to the political status quo; establishing firm civilian control over the military, which had a long history of intervening in the political process; and strengthening weak democratic practices and institutions. Turkey displays the trappings of a Western-style democratic government: a legislature whose deputies are elected by secret ballot, multiple and competitive political parties, and relatively free news media. However, Turkey also is a country where, on three occasions since 1960, military coups have overthrown elected civilian governments. The most recent military government, which seized power in September 1980, governed for three years. During the period of military rule, strict limits were imposed on personal and political rights and liberties. Political parties were banned, and prominent civilian politicians were barred from participating in political activity for up to ten years. The military justified its intervention on the premise that it was returning the country to the principles of Kemal Atatürk (see Atatürk and the Turkish Nation, ch. 1).

The supervised restoration of civilian rule began in November 1983 with National Assembly elections for which every candidate needed to obtain military approval. A civilian government with Turgut Özal as prime minister was formed after Özal's Motherland Party (Anavatan Partisi—ANAP) won a majority of the seats in the new assembly. Özal worked with the president, General Kenan Evren, a leader of the 1980 coup, to reestablish the primacy of civilian authority. By November 1987, martial law decrees had been repealed in most of Turkey except Istanbul and the predominantly Kurdish provinces of the southeast, and the military refrained from interfering in the selection of candidates for National Assembly and local elections.

The strengthening of democratic practices, however, was hindered by a lack of consensus within the political elite on the issue of granting cultural freedom and local government autonomy to the country's Kurdish minority. The Kurdish question began to reemerge in 1984 after the Kurdistan Workers' Party (Partiya Karkere Kurdistan—PKK) initiated armed struggle against the state by attacking rural police posts in southeastern Turkey. The military's inability to suppress the militant PKK, combined with the international media attention generated in 1988 by the arrival of tens of thousands of Iraqi Kurdish refugees fleeing chemical weapons attacks by their own government, made the Kurdish situation a leading topic of public discourse. Özal, whom the National Assembly elected president in 1989, became the first prominent politician to acknowledge openly that the Kurds were not merely "mountain Turks" but a separate ethnic group whose culture merited respect. Kurdish politicians opposed to the violent tactics and separatist ideology of the PKK responded by participating actively in the Social Democratic Party (Sosyal Demokrat Parti—Sodep) and the Social Democratic Populist Party (Sosyal Demokrat Halkçı Parti—SHP). Following the October 1991 National Assembly elections, a group of SHP-aligned Kurdish deputies, who previously had formed the People's Labor Party (Halkın Emek Partisi—HEP) to promote the full equality of Kurds and Turks within Turkey, organized themselves as a separate parliamentary party. However, many Turkish leaders were unable to distinguish between a separate Kurdish political party and a Kurdish separatist movement, and they campaigned to have the HEP banned and its members arrested, even though HEP deputies enjoyed parliamentary immunity. In a severe blow to democratic procedures, seven Kurdish deputies were arrested in March 1994; they were sentenced to long prison terms in December after being convicted of "crimes against the state."

During the late 1980s and early 1990s, the intensification of the PKK insurgency in southeastern Turkey tended to enhance the status of the military as the guardian of the country's territorial integrity and security. Consequently, Turkish politicians tended to treat the armed forces cautiously, apparently as part of a strategy to dissuade senior officers from initiating yet another coup. Civilian wariness was evident in the government's acquiescence to a number of extrajudicial measures that violated basic due process rights, for example, military censorship of news coverage of operations against the Kurdish guerrillas. In 1993 and 1994, scores of Turkish journalists whose reportage was perceived by the military as endangering state security were detained for trials in special military courts. The military also forcibly deported more than 150,000 Kurds from some 850 villages in the southeast. Most of the evicted villagers subsequently resettled in the cities of western Turkey, where as many as one-half of the country's Kurdish minority was estimated to be residing in 1994. The presence of so many Kurds in Ankara, Istanbul, Izmir, and other large cities has contributed to a transformation of the Kurdish situation from a regional problem to a national one, whose characteristics include increasing ethnic polarization between Kurds and Turks.

Another cause of polarization is the ideological competition between Turkey's elite, which is imbued with the secular philosophy of Atatürk, and a new generation of grassroots leaders, influenced by Islamic ideas. Islamic political activists began organizing in 1983, after the government authorized the formation of political parties, and subsequently founded the Welfare Party (Refah Partisi—RP; also seen as Prosperity Party). Its candidates competed in both national and local elections, campaigning in middle- and lower-class urban neighborhoods with a consistent message. They blamed the country's economic and political problems on the alleged indifference of secular leaders to Muslim values. The Welfare Party steadily increased its share of the popular vote, and won more than sixty seats out of a total of 450 in the 1991 National Assembly elections. In nationwide local elections held in March 1994, Welfare Party candidates won 19 percent of the total vote, placing the party third behind the ruling True Path Party (Dogru Yol Partisi—DYP) of President Süleyman Demirel and Prime Minister Tansu Çiller and the main opposition Motherland Party. The Welfare Party's electoral successes included winning the mayor's office in Ankara, Istanbul, and twenty-seven other major cities, as well as in 400 smaller municipalities, including almost all the towns in the Kurdish provinces of the southeast.

In early 1995, Turkey was still in the process of trying to redefine its regional foreign policy in the wake of the two major international developments on its borders during 1991: the Persian Gulf War fought by the United States-led international coalition against Iraq and the unexpected collapse of the Soviet Union. Turkey's de facto participation in the Persian Gulf War—Ankara permitted United States aircraft to use a Turkish air base for bombing missions over Iraq—helped to strengthen ties with the United States, a fellow member of the North Atlantic Treaty Organization (NATO—see Glossary). However, the aftermath of that same war—hundreds of thousands of Iraqi Kurds trying to flee into Turkey following the collapse of their uprising against the Iraqi government—was one of the factors that contributed to the intensification of the Kurdish problem within Turkey. The military efforts to suppress the PKK and the political efforts to silence Kurdish political leaders prompted international human rights organizations to accuse the Turkish government of systematic human rights violations. These charges complicated relations with the European Union (EU—see Glossary), an economic organization that Turkey aspired to join as a full member, because several EU countries opposed Turkish membership on grounds that the country's practice of democracy fell short of EU standards. In addition, Turkey and its neighbor Greece, an EU state and a member of NATO, had failed to resolve their dispute over the status of Cyprus and their conflicting offshore claims in the Aegean Sea.

The consequences of the Soviet Union's dissolution potentially are more promising for Turkish diplomacy than the consequences of the Persian Gulf War. The fifteen countries that replaced the Soviet Union include five Asian states whose peoples speak Turkic languages. Özal and his successor as president, Demirel, promoted Turkey as a political and economic model for these Turkic-speaking countries. In keeping with this role, they sought to expand Turkey's influence through numerous bilateral agreements pertaining to cultural and economic relations. However, the long-term success of Turkey's efforts is not assured because both Iran and Russia are trying to extend or maintain their respective influence in Azerbaijan and Central Asia. Initially, Turkish leaders seemed to welcome the prospect of competition with Iran for influence in the region, and they confidently asserted the superiority of their secular state over Iran's Islamic model. By the end of 1993, however, Turkey—perhaps out of concern about Russian intentions—began to stress the need to work with Iran through multilateral regional arrangements such as the Economic Cooperation Organization.

The Constitutional System

The government of Turkey functions in accordance with the constitution of 1982, which was drafted and adopted during the period of military rule following the September 1980 coup. The National Security Council (NSC—see Glossary), composed of the commanders of the army, navy, air force, and gendarmerie, and headed by the president, established a Consultative Assembly in June 1981 to draft a new constitution. This assembly consisted of 160 members, forty of whom were appointed directly by the NSC and the remaining 120 selected from a list of about 10,000 names compiled with the aid of provincial governors. In July 1982, a fifteen-member constitutional committee of the Consultative Assembly produced a draft that subsequently was amended by the Consultative Assembly and the NSC. The constitution was submitted to a public referendum on November 7 and approved by 91.4 percent of the voters; 91.3 percent of the registered electorate cast ballots. A factor in this high turnout was Provisional Article 16 of the constitution, which stipulated that registered voters who failed to vote would lose their electoral rights for five years.

The 1982 constitution replaced the constitution of 1961, which also had been drafted following a military coup (see The Armed Forces Group and Interim Rule, 1960–61, ch. 1). Under the 1961 constitution, an elaborate system of checks and balances had limited the authority of the government; the powers of the president were curtailed, and individual rights and liberties were given greater emphasis. In contrast, the 1982 constitution expands the authority of the president and circumscribes the exercise of individual and associational rights. The 1982 constitution also limits the role and influence of political parties, which are governed by more detailed and restrictive regulations than under the 1961 document. For example, political parties are required to obtain a minimum percentage of the total vote cast before any candidates on their lists can qualify for seats in the National Assembly. The 1982 constitution also provides for the enactment of electoral laws to regulate the formation of parties and the rules for their participation in elections.

Provisions of the 1982 Constitution

Article 2 of the 1982 constitution stipulates that the Republic of Turkey is a "democratic, secular, and social state governed by the rule of law," respecting human rights and loyal to the political philosophy of Kemal Atatürk. Article 5 vests sovereignty in the nation, stipulating that it is not to be delegated to "any individual, group, or class." The fundamental objective and duty of the state is defined as safeguarding the independence and integrity of the democratic Turkish nation and ensuring "the welfare, peace, and happiness of the individual and society." The constitution divides the powers of the state among the three branches of government. The legislative branch consists of a unicameral parliament, the National Assembly, composed of 400 members (later increased by amendment to 450) elected to five-year terms. The executive branch consists of the president, who is elected to a seven-year term by the National Assembly, and a prime minister, who is appointed by the president from among National Assembly deputies. The prime minister heads the Council of Ministers, members of which are nominated by the prime minister and appointed by the president. The judicial branch is independent of the legislature and the executive.

Like its predecessor, the 1982 constitution includes a detailed bill of rights covering the social, economic, and political rights and liberties of citizens. According to Article 5, all individuals are equal before the law and possess "inherent fundamental rights and freedoms which are inviolable and inalienable." However, articles 10 through 15 authorize the government to restrict individual rights in the interest of safeguarding the "integrity of the state" and "the public interest." The government may impose further limitations on individual rights "in times of war, martial law, or state of emergency."

Articles 28 and 67 of the 1982 constitution stipulate that the individual is entitled to privacy and to freedom of thought and communication, travel, and association; that the physical integrity of the individual must not be violated; that torture and forced labor are prohibited; that all persons have access to the courts and are assumed innocent until proven guilty; that all Turkish citizens over twenty years of age have the right to vote in elections and to take part in referenda; and that the news media are free and not liable to censorship, except by a court order when national security or the "indivisible integrity of the state" are threatened. According to articles 35, 44, and 46, all citizens have the right to own and inherit property. The state is obligated to provide land to landless farmers or to farmers with insufficient land, and, if the public interest so requires, the state may expropriate private property, provided that compensation is paid in advance.

Articles 49 through 54 of the 1982 constitution pertain to labor. The constitution stipulates that it is the right and duty of all people of working age to work and that all have the freedom to work in the field of their choice. The state is given responsibility to take necessary measures to raise the standard of living of workers, to protect them, and to create suitable economic conditions for the prevention of unemployment. Workers have the right to rest and leisure; minors, women, and people with disabilities are to be provided special protection at work. Workers and employers are free to form labor unions and employers' associations without prior permission, but no one may be compelled to join a union or association. Workers are allowed to bargain collectively and to strike, but not in a manner "detrimental to society." General and politically motivated strikes are prohibited.

According to Article 42, primary education is compulsory and free in public schools. Only Turkish may be taught as the primary language, and all schools must follow the principles and reforms of Atatürk. Education is to be based on "contemporary science and education methods" and is provided under the supervision and control of the state. The state provides scholarships and other means of assistance "to enable students of merit lacking financial means to continue their education."

Article 24 guarantees freedom of religion, provided that the exercise of this right does not threaten the "indivisible integrity of the state." No one may be compelled to worship or to participate in religious ceremonies or rites. Primary and secondary schools are required to provide religious instruction under state supervision and control. Secularism, a primary principle of Atatürk's reforms, is reaffirmed in the provision forbidding "even partially basing the fundamental, social, economic, political, and legal order of the state on religious tenets."

Articles 68 and 69 of the 1982 constitution stipulate that citizens may form or join political parties without prior permission from the government. However, political parties must act according to the principles of the constitution and may be dissolved by the Constitutional Court if that body determines that their activities "conflict with the indivisible integrity of the state." Political parties may not have ties with any association, union, or professional organization. Judges, teachers at institutions of higher education, students, civil servants, and members of the armed forces may not join political parties.

Other articles of the constitution obligate citizens to pay taxes and to render national service in the armed forces or elsewhere in the public sector, grant them the right to petition competent authorities and the National Assembly for redress of complaints, and stipulate that the constitutionality of all laws and decrees is subject to review by the Constitutional Court. To amend the constitution, at least one-third of the members of the National Assembly first must propose an amendment. The actual proposal then must win the votes of a two-thirds majority of all members of the assembly. If the amendment is vetoed by the president, the votes of a three-quarters majority of the members are required to override the veto.

The 1982 constitution also included a set of provisional articles, the first of which stipulated that the chair of the NSC and head of state would become president of the republic for seven years following approval of the constitution in a referendum. Another provisional article stipulated that the NSC would be transformed into an advisory Presidential Council after the formation of a civilian government following elections for the National Assembly. This Presidential Council would function for a period of six years and then be dissolved. Yet another provisional article made permanent a 1981 NSC decree that barred more than 200 politicians from joining new political parties or becoming candidates for a period of ten years. Some of the provisional articles were later rescinded.

Once the 1982 constitution had been approved but before it was implemented, the NSC in April 1983 issued a Political Parties Law (Law No. 2820) that placed further restrictions on political activities. This law, which was intended to regulate the formation of political parties in advance of the November 1983 National Assembly elections, stipulates that political organizations cannot be based on class, religion, race, or language distinctions. To qualify for registration, a political party is required to have at least thirty founders, each of whom must be approved by the minister of interior. New political parties are prohibited from claiming to be continuations of any parties in existence before 1980. The law also requires each party to establish organizations in at least half the country's provinces and in one-third of the districts within those provinces. Political parties are prohibited from criticizing the military intervention of September 1980 or the actions or decisions of the NSC. The Political Parties Law empowers the NSC and its successor, the Presidential Council, to investigate all party members and candidates for office and to declare any unsuitable.

Electoral System

The 1982 constitution stipulates that elections are to be held on the basis of free universal suffrage with direct, equal, and secret balloting. Ballots are to be sorted and counted publicly under the supervision of judicial authorities. The Supreme Electoral Council, composed of eleven judges elected by the Court of Appeals (also known as the Court of Cassation) and the Council of State from among their own members, has jurisdiction over all electoral proceedings. The Supreme Electoral Council is empowered to rule in cases of complaints concerning the validity of elections and may declare a particular election invalid. The executive and legislative branches of the government are prohibited from exercising any control over the electoral process.

Prior to the first elections under the new constitution, the NSC issued the Electoral Law of June 1983 (Law No. 2839), which stipulates that only parties obtaining 10 percent or more of the total national vote can be represented in the National Assembly. Law No. 2839 maintains the system of proportional representation on a provincial basis, but subdivides the more populous provinces for electoral purposes so that no single constituency can elect more than seven deputies. Each province automatically is assigned at least one seat, regardless of population. These measures work to the advantage of the larger parties and the rural provinces.

Government

Following the military coup of September 1980, Turkey was ruled by the NSC, a five-member collective body representing all branches of the armed forces. The NSC scheduled the first elections under the 1982 constitution for November 1983. The new National Assembly convened soon after the elections, and subsequently a civilian government consisting of a prime minister and a Council of Ministers was formed. In late 1983 and early 1984, the NSC turned over its executive and legislative functions to these new institutions.

National Assembly

The 1982 constitution vests the power to enact legislation in the unicameral National Assembly (Millet Meclis). The first National Assembly, consisting of 400 deputies, was elected in November 1983 to a five-year term. The new Motherland Party headed by Turgut Özal won a majority of seats (211) and formed Turkey's first civilian government since the 1980 coup. In 1987 Özal convinced the National Assembly to adjourn itself one year short of its five-year mandate and hold new elections, a procedure that is permitted under the constitution. Prior to these elections, the assembly approved two constitutional amendments that affected its future structure and composition. One amendment expanded the assembly from 400 to 450 seats. A second amendment repealed the provisional article of the constitution that had banned more than 200 political leaders from all political activity for a ten-year period ending in 1991. This article had permitted the military to retain a degree of control over the electoral process, both at the national and local levels. Its repeal enabled Turkey's best-known politicians, including Süleyman Demirel and Bülent Ecevit, to participate openly in the electoral process. Consequently the National Assembly elections held in November 1987 constituted the first genuinely free balloting in the country since the 1980 coup.

Özal's party won a majority (292 of 450 seats) in the 1987 assembly elections, and he continued to head the government until 1989, when he was elected president. In 1991 the National Assembly again voted to schedule elections one year early. However, as a result of the October balloting, the Motherland Party won only 24 percent of the vote, coming in second behind Demirel's True Path Party, which obtained 27 percent of the vote. Because none of the political parties had won a clear majority, Demirel obtained the agreement of the Social Democratic Populist Party to form a coalition government. The next National Assembly elections are due to be held in October 1996.

Although the constitution stipulates that by-elections to fill vacant seats may be held once between general elections— unless the number of vacancies reaches 5 percent of the total assembly membership—the National Assembly has not scheduled such elections on a regular basis. The assembly holds a convocation following elections, but does not open its annual legislative term until the first day of September. By law, it cannot be in recess for more than three months in a year. Article 93 of the constitution empowers the president during an assembly adjournment to summon the deputies for an extraordinary session, either on his or her own initiative or at the written request of one-fifth of the members.

The National Assembly's powers include exclusive authority to enact, amend, and repeal laws. It also can pass legislation over the veto of the president. The assembly supervises the Council of Ministers and authorizes it to issue government decrees. The assembly is responsible for debating and approving the government's budget and making decisions pertaining to the printing of currency. In addition, the assembly approves the president's ratification of international treaties and has authority to declare war. The constitution stipulates that the assembly can request that the executive respond to written questions, investigations, and interpellations, and can vote the Council of Ministers out of office.

According to Article 76 of the constitution, every Turkish citizen over the age of thirty is eligible to be a National Assembly deputy, provided that he or she has completed primary education and has not been convicted of a serious crime or been involved in "ideological and anarchistic activities." In addition, men are required to have performed their compulsory military service. Members of higher judicial and education institutions as well as civil servants and members of the armed forces must resign from office before standing for election. Article 80 of the constitution stipulates that deputies represent the whole nation, not just their own constituencies.

Articles 83 and 84 of the constitution grant deputies parliamentary immunities, such as freedom of speech and, with some qualifications, freedom from arrest. These freedoms were put to a severe test in March 1994, when the National Assembly voted to strip the parliamentary immunities of seven deputies who had spoken out within the assembly on behalf of civil rights for the country's Kurdish minority. The seven deputies were arrested at the door of the National Assembly building in Ankara and charged with making speeches that constituted "crimes against the state."

Articles 83 and 84 also provide for a deputy to be deprived of membership in the National Assembly by vote of an absolute majority of its members. Furthermore, a deputy who resigns from his or her political party after an election may not be nominated as a candidate in the next election by any party in existence at the time of that resignation.

As was also the case before the 1980 coup, deputies in the National Assembly in early 1995 typically were fairly young, well-educated members of the elite, with as many as two-thirds having college degrees. However, since 1983 there has been a shift in occupational representation away from a predominance of government officials. In the three assemblies elected starting in 1983, a large percentage of deputies were lawyers, engineers, businesspeople, and economists (see The Changing National Elite, ch. 2).

President, Council of Ministers, and Prime Minister

The 1982 constitution vests executive authority in the president, who is the designated head of state. The president ensures implementation of the constitution and the orderly functioning of the government (see fig. 12). The president serves a seven-year term and cannot be reelected. Under a provisional article of the constitution, General Evren, who was chair of the NSC, automatically assumed the presidency when the constitution took effect at the end of 1982. Article 102 of the constitution provides the procedures for electing subsequent presidents, who must be chosen by the National Assembly from among its members. A deputy nominated for the presidency must obtain a two-thirds majority vote of the assembly. If a two-thirds majority cannot be obtained on the first two ballots, a third ballot is held, requiring only an absolute majority of votes. If a presidential candidate fails to obtain a majority on the third ballot, a fourth and final ballot is held, the choice being between the two candidates who received the greatest number of votes on the third ballot. If this procedure fails to produce a winner, new assembly general elections must be held immediately.

When Evren's seven-year term ended in November 1989, the assembly failed to produce a two-thirds vote for any candidate on the first two ballots. Prime Minister Turgut Özal won a majority on the third ballot and became Turkey's second president under the 1982 constitution. Özal died of a heart attack in April 1993 before completing his term in office. In the subsequent assembly vote for a new president, no candidate won a two-thirds majority on the first two ballots. Süleyman Demirel, who had become prime minister in November 1991, garnered the simple majority required for the third ballot and became the country's third president since the 1980 coup.

A candidate for president must have completed secondary education and must be at least forty years old. Articles 101 and 102 of the constitution provide that a presidential candidate can be nominated from outside the membership of the National Assembly if the candidate meets the stipulated qualifications and if the nomination is presented to the assembly in the form of a written resolution that has the endorsement of at least one-fifth of the deputies. In accordance with the requirement that the president-elect terminate relations with his or her political party, both Özal and Demirel resigned as heads of their respective parties following their election to the presidency.

The 1982 constitution gives the president a stronger and more extensive role than did the 1961 constitution, under which the presidency was a largely ceremonial office. The president is empowered to summon meetings of the National Assembly, promulgate laws, and ratify international treaties. The president also may veto legislation passed by the National Assembly, submit constitutional amendments proposed by the assembly to popular referenda, and challenge the constitutionality of assembly laws and cabinet decrees. The president's responsibilities include appointing the prime minister, convening and presiding over meetings of the Council of Ministers, and calling for new elections to the National Assembly. The president also is authorized to dispatch the Turkish armed forces for domestic or foreign military missions and to declare martial law.

The constitution also provides the president with appointive powers that he or she may exercise independently of the Council of Ministers. For example, the president is empowered to appoint the members of the Constitutional Court, one-quarter of the members of the Council of State, all diplomatic representatives, the chief of the General Staff, members of the Supreme Military Administrative Court, the Supreme Council of Judges and Public Prosecutors, the State Supervisory Council, the Council of Higher Education, and all university presidents.

The president may be impeached for high treason at the recommendation of one-third of the members of the National Assembly and removed from office by the vote of a three-quarters majority. Otherwise, Article 105 of the constitution stipulates that "no appeal shall be made to any legal authority, including the Constitutional Court, against the decisions and orders signed by the president of the Republic on his own initiative." The constitution also provides for the establishment of a State Supervisory Council to conduct investigations and inspections of public organizations at the president's request.

The president presides over the National Security Council, a body that contains civilian as well as military members. It should not be confused with the former NSC, an all-military body, which ruled the country following the 1980 coup and subsequently became the advisory Presidential Council. The present National Security Council is composed of the prime

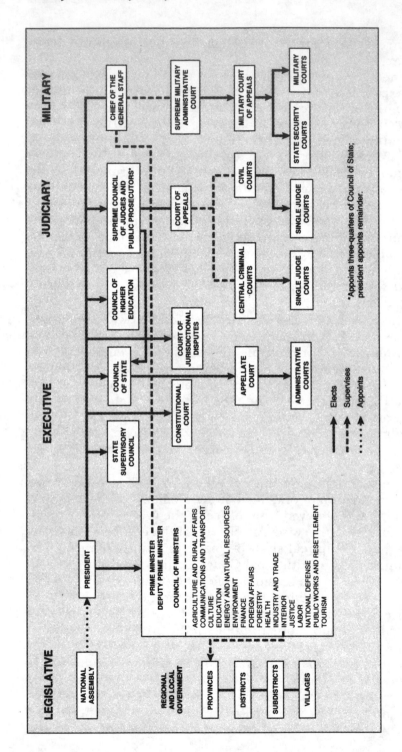

Figure 12. Government Structure, 1995

minister, the chief of the General Staff, the ministers of national defense, interior, and foreign affairs, and the commanders of the branches of the armed forces and the gendarmerie. This body sets national security policy and coordinates all activities related to mobilization and defense. An advisory Presidential Council, composed of the armed forces commanders who had joined Evren in the 1980 military coup and the military government that lasted until 1983, continued to advise the president until 1989. At that time, in accordance with the provisional articles appended to the 1982 constitution, the Presidential Council was dissolved (see Political Developments since the 1980 Coup, this ch.).

The Council of Ministers, or cabinet, is headed by the prime minister, who is appointed by the president from among the elected deputies of the National Assembly. In practice, the president asks the head of the party with the largest number of deputies to form a government. The prime minister then nominates ministers for appointment by the president. Within one week of being selected, each new cabinet must be presented to the full assembly for a vote of confidence; a simple majority is required. If at any time during the Council of Ministers' tenure an absolute majority of the assembly should support a motion of no confidence, the ministers must resign. In the event that no party obtains a majority in National Assembly elections, a coalition of parties is allowed up to six weeks to form a government. If no new cabinet can be formed within forty-five days, the president may dissolve the assembly and call for new elections.

The prime minister supervises the implementation of government policy. Members of the Council of Ministers have joint and equal responsibility for the implementation of this policy. In addition, each minister is responsible for the conduct of affairs under his or her jurisdiction and for the actions of subordinates. In early 1995, the prime minister was Tansu Çiller, the first woman to hold this office. Her cabinet consists of a deputy prime minister and the following ministers: agriculture and rural affairs, communications and transport, culture, education, energy and natural resources, environment, finance, foreign affairs, forestry, health, industry and trade, interior, justice, labor, national defense, public works and housing, and tourism. Çiller's Council of Ministers also includes a number of ministers of state with cabinet rank.

247

In the area of national defense, the Council of Ministers is responsible to the assembly for national security and for the readiness of the armed forces. However, the president normally serves as commander in chief of the armed forces. With the president as chair, the cabinet is empowered to declare martial law or a state of emergency and to issue decrees without restriction during such periods.

The 1982 constitution strengthens the role of the Council of Ministers vis-à-vis the National Assembly by empowering the cabinet to issue regulations pertaining to the implementation of laws. However, the cabinet also is weakened in terms of its relationship to the president. The constitution grants the president the right to dismiss any minister upon the suggestion of the prime minister. In effect, individual ministers are subject to removal at the discretion of either the president or the prime minister.

Judiciary

Since legal reforms instituted in 1926, Turkey's judicial system has been based on the Swiss Civil Code, the Italian Penal Code, and the Neuchâtel (Swiss) Code of Civil Procedure. The 1982 constitution guarantees judicial independence and prohibits any government agency or individual from interfering with the operations of the courts and judges. Members of the National Assembly also are not allowed to discuss or make statements concerning pending court cases. Although trials normally are held in open court, the constitution provides that they can be closed "for reasons of public morality or public security."

Headed by the minister of justice, the High Council of Judges and Public Prosecutors is the principal body charged with responsibility for ensuring judicial integrity. This council acts on matters pertaining to the careers of judges, including appointments, promotions, transfers, and supervision. The high council is empowered to remove judges and abolish courts and the offices of judges and public prosecutors. However, judges themselves are protected against arbitrary removal from office by a constitutional provision stipulating that they cannot be dismissed without due cause or retired involuntarily before age sixty-five.

In early 1995, Turkey's legal system consisted of three types of courts: judicial, military, and administrative. Each system includes courts of first instance and appellate courts. In addition, a Court of Jurisdictional Disputes rules on cases that cannot be classified readily as falling within the purview of one court system.

The judicial courts form the largest part of the system; they handle most civil and criminal cases involving ordinary citizens. The two supreme courts within the judicial system are the Constitutional Court and the Court of Appeals.

The Constitutional Court reviews the constitutionality of laws and decrees at the request of the president or of one-fifth of the members of the National Assembly. Its decisions on the constitutionality of legislation and government decrees are final. The eleven members of the Constitutional Court are appointed by the president from among candidates nominated by lower courts and the High Council of Judges and Public Prosecutors. Challenges to the constitutionality of a law must be made within sixty days of its promulgation. Decisions of the Constitutional Court require the votes of an absolute majority of all its members, with the exception of decisions to annul a constitutional amendment, which require a two-thirds majority.

The Court of Appeals (also known as the Court of Cassation) is the court of last instance for review of decisions and verdicts of lower-level judicial courts, both civil and criminal. Its members are elected by secret ballot by senior judges and public prosecutors. Below the Court of Appeals are the ordinary civil and criminal courts. At the lowest level of the judicial system are justices of the peace, who have jurisdiction over minor civil complaints and offenses. Single-judge criminal courts have jurisdiction over misdemeanors and petty crimes, with penalties ranging from small fines to brief prison sentences. Every organized municipality (a community having a minimum population of 2,000) has at least one single-judge court, with the actual number of courts varying according to the total population. Three-judge courts of first instance have jurisdiction over major civil suits and serious crimes. Either of the parties in civil cases and defendants convicted in criminal cases can request that the Court of Appeals review the lower-court decision. The Turkish courts have no jury system; judges render decisions after establishing the facts in each case based on evidence presented by lawyers and prosecutors.

The administrative court system consists of the Council of State, an appellate court, and various administrative courts of first instance. The Council of State reviews decisions of the lower administrative courts, considers original administrative disputes, and, if requested, gives its opinion on draft legislation submitted by the prime minister and the Council of Ministers. The president appoints 25 percent of the Council of State's judges. The other 75 percent are appointed by the High Council of Judges and Public Prosecutors.

The military court system exercises jurisdiction over all military personnel. In areas under martial law, the military also has jurisdiction over all civilians accused of terrorism or "crimes against the state." The military court system consists of military and security courts of first instance, a Supreme Military Administrative Court, an appellate State Security Court, and the Military Court of Appeals, which reviews decisions and verdicts of the military courts. The decisions of the Military Court of Appeals are final.

Provincial and Local Government

The 1982 constitution retains Turkey's centralized administrative system. Each province is administered by a governor (*vagi*) appointed by the Council of Ministers with the approval of the president. The governors function as the principal agents of the central government and report to the Ministry of Interior. The constitution grants governors extraordinary powers during a state of emergency, powers similar to those of military authorities in areas under martial law. The constitution also stipulates that the central administration oversee elected local councils in order to ensure the effective provision of local services and to safeguard the public interest. The minister of interior is empowered to remove from office local administrators who are being investigated or prosecuted for offenses related to their duties.

In early 1995, Turkey was divided into seventy-six provinces (*vilayetlar*). Each province was further subdivided into an average of about eight districts, or *kazalar*, each roughly equivalent in size to a county in a United States state. Each district was segmented into an average of 493 subdistricts, or *bucaklar*. Each provincial capital, each district seat, and each town of more than 2,000 people is organized as a municipality headed by an elected mayor. Government at the provincial level is responsible for implementing national programs for health and social assistance, public works, culture and education, agriculture and animal husbandry, and economic and commercial matters.

As chief executive of the province and principal agent of the central government, each governor supervises other government officials assigned to carry out ministerial functions in his or her province. Civil servants head offices of the national government that deal with education, finance, health, and agriculture at the provincial level. In each province, these directors form the provincial administrative council (*vilayet genel meclisi*), which, with the governor as chair, makes key administrative decisions and, when necessary, initiates disciplinary actions against errant provincial employees.

The governor also heads the provincial assembly and several service departments concerned mainly with local trade and industrial matters. The provincial assembly, which advises and works closely with the provincial administrative council, is elected every five years and, with the governor chairing, meets annually to approve the provincial budget and to select one person from each district to serve on the province's administrative commission. With the governor presiding, the administrative commission meets weekly for mutual consultation. Provincial budgets derive their income from rents, payments for services, fines, state aid, and a 1 percent share of national tax revenues. In most provinces, provincial funds are spent primarily on agricultural and reforestation programs, irrigation, and schools.

Each district in a province has its own administration based in the district seat. The district administration consists of a district chief (*kaymakam*), central government representatives, and a district administrative board. The more than 500 district chiefs are appointed by the president upon nomination by the minister of interior. Each district chief is responsible to the governor, serving essentially as his or her agent in supervising and inspecting the activities of government officials in the district. The district in which a provincial capital is located may not have a district chief but instead be headed directly by the governor. Each subdistrict director (*bucak mudur*) is appointed by the minister of interior on the nomination of the governors. The subdistrict directors, who number about 40,000, are responsible for law enforcement in the villages. They are assisted by officials in charge of rural security; land titles; vital statistics; schools; and postal, telephone, and telegraph services.

Municipal governments exist in each provincial and district capital, as well as in all communities with at least 2,000 inhabitants. Municipal governments are responsible for implementing national programs for health and social assistance, public works, education, and transportation. Each municipality (*belediye*) is headed by a mayor (*belediye reisi*), who is elected by the citizens to a five-year term and is assisted by deputy directors of departments and offices. Municipal councils, also elected for five years, vary in size according to each town's population. Municipal councils meet three times a year to decide on such issues as the budget, housing plans, reconstruction programs, tax rates, and fees for municipal services. A variety of municipal standing committees, appointed by the mayor and municipal department directors or selected by municipal council members from among themselves, deal with financial issues and decide on the appointment and promotion of municipal personnel.

The smallest unit of local government in Turkey is the village (*köy derneg*), a locality with fewer than 2,000 inhabitants. The principal authority in a village, the headman (*muhtar*), is chosen by an assembly of all the village's adults. This informal assembly also makes decisions pertaining to village affairs and elects a council of elders (*ihtiyar meclisi*) that includes the village schoolteacher and the imam (see Glossary). The headman supervises the planning and operation of communal projects and services and administers directives from higher authorities. The headman receives government officials, maintains order, collects taxes, and presides at civil ceremonies. The village council supervises village finances, purchases or expropriates land for schools and other communal buildings, and decides on the contributions in labor and money to be made by villagers for road maintenance and other community improvements. The village council also arbitrates disputes between villagers and imposes fines on those who fail to perform the services allotted to them.

Civil Service

Since the early years of the Turkish republic, the civil bureaucracy has played an important role in politics. It became one of the bases of Atatürk's power and was a key instrument of his reform policy, which emphasized adherence to the "Six Arrows" of secularism, republicanism, populism, nationalism, etatism (see Glossary), and reformism (see Atatürk's Reforms, ch. 1). During the 1930s and 1940s, a consistently high percentage of parliament members had a civil service background. However, the power and social prestige of the official elite declined with the emergence of competitive political parties in the late 1940s and early 1950s. Civil bureaucrats generally believed they worked in the service of the entire nation, and they tended to view politicians, especially those affiliated with the Democrat Party (Demokrat Partisi—DP), as being too partisan to comprehend the difference between policies beneficial to the nation and those merely serving special interests. Democrats and their Justice Party (Adalet Partisi—AP) successors did not appreciate these attitudes, and consequently bureaucrats lost credibility and influence among these politicians, who tried, generally with little success, to restrict the autonomy of the civil service.

The military regime that seized power in 1980 was less tolerant of an independent bureaucracy than its predecessor had been in 1960. Accordingly, it took measures designed to reduce the bureaucracy's autonomy and involvement in partisan politics. For example, civil servants lost the right to challenge or appeal decisions made by members of the Council of Ministers or the Council of State. Martial law commanders were empowered to remove or reassign civil servants under their jurisdiction at their own discretion. In April 1981, a Supreme Board of Supervision was established to oversee the bureaucracy. Its investigations resulted in a large number of officials receiving administrative or penal punishments and prompted many senior bureaucrats to leave government service. The tension between the military government and the civil service did not cease with the end of military rule. When Turgut Özal became prime minister at the end of 1983, he proclaimed that streamlining the bureaucracy was part of the fundamental administrative reform he intended to implement. Gradually, however, cooperation between bureaucrats and political leaders was restored; by the early 1990s, it was no longer fashionable to blame civil servants for the country's problems.

In early 1995, the civil service operated in accordance with provisions stipulated in the 1982 constitution and subsequent regulations. For example, civil servants are appointed for life on the basis of competitive examinations and can be removed from their posts only in exceptional cases. They must remain loyal to the constitution and may not join political parties. If a public employee wishes to compete in National Assembly elections, that individual first must resign from government service. All disciplinary decisions pertaining to civil servants are subject to judicial review.

Political Dynamics

Since the military coup of 1960, Turkish politics have been characterized by two opposing visions of government. According to the "rule from above" view, which has been dominant among the military elite and some of the civilian political elite, government is an instrument for implementing the enduring principles of Kemalism. Thus, if a government fails to carry out this mandate, it must be replaced by those who are the guardians of Atatürk's legacy, which is identified as synonymous with Turkish nationalism. In contrast, the "rule from below" view, which predominates among more populist-oriented politicians and thinkers, tends to regard government as an instrument for protecting the civic rights and individual freedoms of Turkish citizens. Thus, if elected leaders fail in their responsibilities, they should be voted out of office. Supporters of the first view tend to interpret democracy as a political order in which all Turks share common goals and national unity is not disrupted by partisan politics. When they perceive partisan politics as threatening this democratic ideal, they back military intervention as a corrective measure. Those favoring rule from below tend to accept diversity of opinion, and its organized expression through competitive political parties, as normal in a healthy democracy. These two very different conceptions of government have contributed significantly to Turkey's political history since 1960, an era in which periods of parliamentary democracy have alternated with periods of military authoritarianism.

The legacy of military intervention, in particular a general fear among politicians that it may recur, has adversely affected democratic practices in Turkey. For instance, the successor civilian governments have lifted only gradually the harsh restrictions imposed on political rights by the 1980–83 regime. In early 1995, various restrictions on the formation of political parties and free association remained in effect; civilians accused of "crimes against the state" continued to be remanded to military courts for detention, interrogation, and trial.

Political Developments since the 1980 Coup

Immediately following the September 1980 coup, the military government arrested Turkey's leading politicians, dissolved the bicameral Grand National Assembly, declared

Painting of Atatürk, the
father of modern Turkey
Courtesy Hermine Dreyfuss

martial law, and banned all political activity (see Military Interlude, ch. 1). In October 1981, all political parties then in existence were disbanded and their property and financial assets
confiscated by the state. In April 1983, the NSC issued regulations for the formation of new political parties—which could
have no ties to the disbanded parties—in anticipation of elections for a new single-chamber National Assembly to be held
later that year. Subsequently, the ban on political activity was
lifted, except for 723 politicians active before the coup who
were forbidden to participate in politics. About 500—former
deputies and senators of the dissolved Grand National Assembly—were barred until 1986. The remaining group of more
than 200 was not allowed to be involved in politics until 1991.
In addition to these restrictions, each party had to submit its
list of candidates for NSC approval in order to compete in the
assembly elections. Although fifteen parties were established by
August 1983, the NSC disqualified all but three of them on the
grounds that they had ties to banned political leaders such as
Süleyman Demirel and Bülent Ecevit. For a variety of other
political reasons, the NSC also vetoed several proposed candidates on the lists presented by the three approved parties.

The parties allowed to participate in the November 1983
National Assembly elections were the Nationalist Democracy
Party (Milliyetçi Demokrasi Partisi—MDP), headed by retired

general Turgut Sunalp, an ally of NSC chair and president Kenan Evren; the Motherland Party, led by Turgut Özal, a civilian who had served in the military government from 1980 to 1982 as deputy prime minister for economic affairs; and the Populist Party (Halkçı Partisi—HP), led by Necdet Calp. The military publicly supported Sunalp's party and expected it to win a majority of seats in the new assembly. However, the elections proved to be a stunning repudiation of the military government: the Nationalist Democracy Party won only 23.3 percent of the total votes cast and obtained only seventy-one of the assembly's 400 seats. Özal's Motherland Party won an absolute majority of seats (211 total); subsequently, Evren asked Özal to form a new government, which took office in December 1983.

The restoration of civilian government did not mean an immediate restoration of civilian rule. Although the NSC had dissolved itself, Evren, as president of the republic, was in a position to veto any policies that might displease the military. In addition, most of Turkey remained under martial law, which meant that military officers retained ultimate decision-making authority at the local level. Although Özal proceeded cautiously to reassert civilian authority, he recognized that easing various military-imposed restrictions was essential to improve Turkey's international image, especially in Western Europe.

Following the 1980 coup, the members of the European Community, which Turkey aspired to join, had frozen relations with Ankara. The pan-European parliament, the Council of Europe, had cited the military regime's record of human rights violations as justification for banning Turkish participation in 1982 (see Foreign Relations, this ch.). To demonstrate his commitment to democracy, Özal allowed three political parties whose participation in the 1983 general elections had been vetoed by the military to contest the municipal elections his government had scheduled for March 1984. All three parties seemed to be obvious continuations of dissolved precoup parties, and they did not try very hard to disguise their ties to banned politicians. For example, the True Path Party had been formed by former members of the Justice Party, and its de facto leader was widely acknowledged to be Süleyman Demirel. Supporters of the old Republican People's Party (Cumhuriyet Halk Partisi—CHP) had formed the Social Democratic Party (Sosyal Demokrat Parti—Sodep) under the leadership of Erdal İnönü, the son of İsmet İnönü, a former president and close political ally of Atatürk. The Welfare Party (Refah Partisi—RP) was headed by Necmettin Erbakan, an Islamic activist whose political views had been irksome to the military since the early 1970s.

The local elections held on March 25, 1984, constituted a further repudiation of the military, with Sunalp's Nationalist Democracy Party obtaining less than 10 percent of the vote. At the level of local politics, Sodep and the True Path Party emerged as the second and third strongest parties behind Özal's Motherland Party, which won 40 percent of the vote. The Populist Party, which had the second largest contingent in the National Assembly, did poorly in the municipal elections, probably because most of its potential support went to Sodep, a party with which it shared ideological affinities, as well as common origins in the old Republican People's Party. Subsequently, in November 1985 a majority of Populist Party deputies voted to dissolve their party and merge with Sodep to form a single party, the Social Democratic Populist Party (Sosyal Demokrat Halkçı Parti—SHP). The local elections and the lifting of martial law in several Turkish provinces had a positive effect on some European governments, and in May 1984, the Council of Europe voted to readmit Turkey as an associate member of the European Community.

Following the 1984 municipal elections, former political leaders challenged restrictions on their activities by appearing at political meetings and making public speeches. Demirel and Ecevit were the most prominent of the leaders who openly defied the bans on political activities. The Özal government was under pressure from the military to enforce the bans but under equal pressure from both domestic public opinion and international human rights organizations to relax the restrictions on the country's former leaders. The government responded with alternating tolerance and legal harassment. Inconsistency also characterized the government's treatment of other democratization issues. For example, by the end of 1987 martial law had been lifted in most of Turkey's provinces, but the number of civilians being tried in military courts actually had increased. In addition, the government was embarrassed by reports published by Amnesty International and similar organizations charging the continuation of systematic torture in Turkish prisons, press censorship, and the denial of civil rights for the Kurdish minority. Although the Özal government

257

dismissed these reports, they tended to complicate already delicate relations with members of the European Community.

In 1986 the expiration of the law banning political activity by some 500 minor politicians of the precoup era served to highlight the anomalous situation of a self-proclaimed democracy that continued to deny the right of political participation to more than 200 major political figures, including former prime ministers and cabinet members. Özal persuaded President Evren and the other senior military officers who supported the ban that the issue should be put to a referendum. The vote took place in September 1987, with a large majority of voters approving repeal. Demirel and Ecevit almost immediately assumed leadership of the parties they had controlled from behind the scenes, respectively the True Path Party and the Democratic Left Party (Demokratik Sol Partisi—DSP), and began campaigning for the National Assembly elections scheduled for November.

The 1987 National Assembly elections were held under the most democratic conditions since the 1980 coup. In contrast to its actions during the 1983 election, the government proscribed no political parties or individual candidates on party lists. From the perspective of the individual parties, the only drawback was the requirement that each must win at least 10 percent of the national vote in order to obtain a seat in the assembly. Parties competing in the elections included the Democratic Left Party, the Motherland Party, the Nationalist Labor Party (Milliyetçi Çalisma Partisi—MÇP), the SHP, the True Path Party, and the Welfare Party (see Political Parties, this ch.). However, only three parties exceeded the 10 percent threshold to qualify for assembly seats. Özal's Motherland Party upheld its dominance in parliament by winning 36 percent of the national vote—slightly less than the 40 percent it had won in 1983—and more than 60 percent of the assembly seats—292 out of a total of 450. Inönü's SHP, a 1985 merger of Sodep and the Populist Party (the latter had won the second highest number of seats in 1983), ranked second with ninety-nine seats. Demirel's True Path Party, which had not been allowed to participate in the 1983 elections, ranked third with fifty-nine seats.

The four years following the 1987 elections witnessed the political comeback of Demirel, who had been prime minister at the time of the 1980 military coup. Following the takeover by the armed forces, he and other members of his government had been arrested. His Justice Party and all other parties subsequently were forcibly dissolved. During Demirel's eleven-year exclusion from politics, his former protégé, Özal, emerged as the country's most prominent civilian politician. Because Özal had been a rising star in the Justice Party prior to the coup and had been chosen to take charge of the government's economic reform program, Demirel resented Özal's initial cooperation with the military and his later establishment of the Motherland Party, which competed directly with the True Path Party for the allegiance of former Justice Party supporters. Consequently, once the ban on his political activities was lifted, Demirel campaigned tirelessly against Özal and the Motherland Party. Demirel's persistent criticism of Özal's policies probably was an important factor in the major electoral setback suffered by the Motherland Party in the March 1989 municipal council elections. The Motherland Party's share of the popular vote fell to 22 percent—compared with 26 percent for Demirel's True Path Party—and it lost control of several municipal councils, including those in the country's three largest cities: Istanbul, Ankara, and Izmir. Whatever satisfaction Demirel may have derived from his party's electoral edge over the Motherland Party, the True Path Party nevertheless did not receive the largest plurality of ballots. That distinction went to the SHP, which obtained 28 percent of the total vote (see fig. 13).

Encouraged by the results of the municipal council elections, Demirel devoted the next two-and-one-half years to building up his party for the National Assembly elections. His goal was for the True Path Party to win a majority of seats, a victory that would enable him to reclaim the post of prime minister from which he had been ousted so unceremoniously in 1980. Özal may have provided unintentional support for Demirel's efforts when he decided at the end of 1989 to be a candidate for president to replace General Evren, whose seven-year term was expiring. Because Özal's Motherland Party still controlled a majority of seats in the assembly, his nomination was approved, albeit on the third ballot. However, in accordance with the constitution, Özal had to sever his political ties to the Motherland Party upon becoming president. Because he had been so closely identified with the party and because none of its other leaders, including Yildirim Akbulut, who succeeded Özal as prime minister in November 1989, had achieved national prominence, Özal's departure tended to weaken the Motherland Party politically.

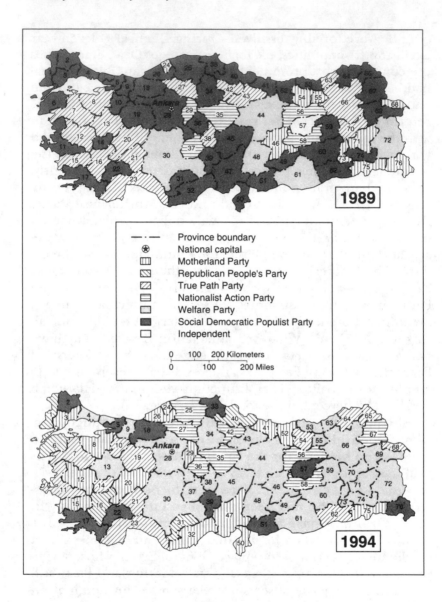

Figure 13. Provincial Elections, 1989 and 1994

The decline—at least temporarily—of the Motherland Party was demonstrated in the October 1991 National Assembly elections. The party received only 24 percent of the total vote and won only 115 seats. In comparison to four years earlier, these results represented a severe defeat. However, the Motherland Party remained a serious competitor in the political arena, falling only from first to second place in terms of overall parliamentary representation. Whereas the True Path Party emerged from the elections with the largest number of votes and the greatest number of assembly seats, its overall performance—27 percent of the total vote and 178 assembly seats—was less impressive than Demirel had hoped and insufficient to give the party the 226 seats needed for parliamentary control. For Demirel to become prime minister, it would be necessary for the True Path Party to form a coalition with the Motherland Party—a very unrealistic prospect—or at least one of the three other parties that had obtained 10 percent or more of the total vote and thus qualified for representation in the assembly. The three parties were the SHP, eighty-eight seats; the Welfare Party, sixty-two seats; and the Democratic Left Party, seven seats. In November 1991, Demirel announced a DYP-SHP coalition government, with himself as prime minister and SHP leader Inönü as deputy prime minister. Thus, eleven years after being overthrown by the military, Demirel returned as head of government. More significantly, in May 1993 the National Assembly elected Demirel president of the republic following the unexpected death of Özal.

The Welfare Party and other parties also perceived the Motherland Party's weakness and shared Demirel's hope of benefiting from it. The Welfare Party built steady support in middle- and lower-class urban neighborhoods by focusing on widespread dissatisfaction with government policies and attributing official abuses of authority to the failure of leaders to adhere to traditional religious values. It had received 10 percent of the total vote in the 1989 municipal council elections and won control of several small town councils. In the October 1991 National Assembly elections, the party obtained 16.9 percent of the total vote and won sixty-two seats. Its base in the assembly provided the Welfare Party with a strong platform from which to criticize the DYP-SHP coalition government, which Welfare Party leaders accused of being as insensitive on issues of social injustice and civil rights abuses as its Motherland predecessor. In the March 1994 municipal elections, the Welfare Party demonstrated its ability to draw some of the support base of the DYP, whose share of the total vote fell to 22 percent. In contrast, the Welfare Party won 19 percent of the total vote—placing it a very close third after the DYP and the

Motherland Party. Its mayoralty candidates won in both Ankara and Istanbul, the country's two most secular cities, as well as in scores of other cities and towns.

Political Parties

Prior to 1950, the Republic of Turkey was essentially a one-party state ruled by the Republican People's Party, which had been created by Atatürk to implement the Six Arrows of Kemalism. Although there had been abortive experiments with "loyal opposition" parties in the mid-1920s and in 1930, it was not until 1946 that the CHP permitted political parties to form and contest elections, albeit in a politically controlled environment. The Democrat Party was founded in 1946 by CHP members who were dissatisfied with the authoritarian style of the CHP but who otherwise supported the party's Kemalist principles. The DP emphasized the need to end various restrictions on personal freedom so that Turkey could become a democracy. Reform of laws governing political parties and electoral activities—measures that would enable the DP to compete on an equal basis with the CHP—were enacted prior to the 1950 parliamentary elections. Consequently, those elections were the first free ones since the founding of the republic in 1923. The DP won a large majority of seats in the assembly and thus took over the government from the CHP.

The DP retained control of the government throughout the 1950s, a period during which it enacted legislation that restricted news media freedom and various civil liberties. As the DP steadily became less tolerant of dissent, the CHP gradually moved in the opposite direction, abandoning its authoritarian stance and becoming an advocate of civil rights. The DP's efforts to suppress opposition to its policies provoked a political crisis that culminated in a May 1960 military coup. The DP subsequently was dissolved, but the Justice Party, which was established in 1961, was widely perceived as its successor and attracted most of its supporters. In the 1961 parliamentary elections that led to the restoration of civilian government, the Justice Party won the second largest number of seats and thus established itself as the principal competitor of the CHP, which had won a plurality of seats. In the subsequent nineteen years, the rivalry between the Justice Party and the CHP remained a significant feature of Turkish politics. Although both parties proclaimed their loyalty to Kemalist ideals, they evolved distinct ideological positions. Süleyman Demirel, who became leader of the Justice Party in 1964, favored economic policies that benefited private entrepreneurs and industrialists. In contrast, Bülent Ecevit, who became leader of the CHP in 1965, believed in a form of democratic socialism that included government intervention aimed at regulating private business and protecting workers and consumers. The views of these two men and the positions of their respective parties became increasingly polarized after 1972.

The inability of either the Justice Party or the CHP to win parliamentary majorities and the refusal of both Demirel and Ecevit to cooperate politically necessitated the formation of numerous coalition and minority-party governments. These governments proved ineffective at devising policies to cope with Turkey's economic and social problems, which became steadily more serious throughout the 1970s. Various groups on the extreme right and the extreme left formed illegal political organizations that resorted to violence in pursuit of their objectives, which for certain groups included the overthrow of the government. The apparent inability of governments—whether dominated by the Justice Party or by the CHP—to control increasing terrorism in urban areas contributed to a general sense of insecurity and crisis and served as the catalyst for the 1980 coup. Blaming politicians for the country's political impasse, the military sought to end partisan politics by dissolving the old parties and banning all activity by the politicians deemed responsible for the crisis. Although the formation of new parties was authorized in 1983, none was allowed to use the name of any of the banned parties from the precoup past. Nevertheless, most of Turkey's existing parties in early 1995 were transparent continuations of earlier parties.

True Path Party

In January 1995, the True Path Party (Dogru Yol Partisi—DYP) was the senior partner in Turkey's coalition government. It was a continuation of the Justice Party, and its leader from 1987 until 1993 was Demirel. Because Demirel was barred from political activity prior to late 1987, his close associate, Hüsamettin Cindoruk, became the party's titular chair when the True Path Party was established in 1983. However, Demirel was the driving force behind the party, raising money and campaigning on its behalf despite being banned from political action. Demirel promoted economic policies similar to those he had advocated as leader of the Justice Party, updated, however, to

263

reflect changing economic conditions resulting from international political developments between 1989 and 1991.

The True Path Party's rise from political pariah to ruling party was gradual. In 1983 the military government prohibited the party's participation in the parliamentary elections, effectively shutting it out of the legal political process. However, a gain of thirty-five seats in the National Assembly resulted in 1986 when the Nationalist Democracy Party dissolved itself and most of its deputies joined the True Path Party. Subsequently the party won fifty-nine seats in the 1987 parliamentary elections, and Demirel returned to the National Assembly as a deputy for the first time since the military coup. The party's performance four years later was even more impressive: the True Path Party tripled its representation to 178 seats and emerged from the 1991 elections with a plurality in the assembly. Demirel, who had served three times as prime minister before the 1980 coup and twice had been deposed by the military, succeeded in forming his fourth government by negotiating a coalition agreement with the SHP.

When the Demirel government assumed office in November 1991, it faced several political and economic challenges. Two important political issues eluding resolution were the increasing militancy of Kurdish demands for civil rights and the growing stridency of the confrontation between religious and secular elements of society. Although the True Path Party had no sympathy for Kurdish aspirations, its SHP partners tended to support cultural freedom for the Kurds and had a relatively strong political base in the Kurdish provinces. However, the SHP's ability to influence overall government policy on the Kurdish issue was limited because the military had assumed de facto decision-making authority for matters pertaining to southeastern Turkey and expected that civilian politicians would accept this role. There was also no consensus among either True Path Party or SHP leaders on how to handle Islamist aspirations. Whereas some True Path Party members believed it was possible to accommodate Islamist concerns, militant secularists opposed any concessions to those whom they termed "Islamic fundamentalists."

After President Özal suffered a fatal heart attack in April 1993, Demirel decided he wanted to be president. In accordance with the constitution, which mandated that the president be nonpartisan, Demirel resigned as the True Path Party's secretary general in May, after the National Assembly had elected him president. In June 1993, the party's deputies in the assembly chose as their new leader Tansu Çiller (b. 1946), the first woman to head a Turkish political party. Çiller, who had done graduate studies in economics in the United States, put together a new DYP-SHP coalition government that was approved by the assembly in July 1993, enabling her to become Turkey's first female prime minister.

Social Democratic Populist Party

In early 1995, the junior partner in the Çiller government was the Social Democratic Populist Party, known by the Turkish acronym SHP, for Sosyal Demokrat Halkçı Parti. The SHP was one of several parties formed since 1983 that presented itself as an heir to the CHP. In fact, the SHP leader, Erdal İnönü, was the son of Ismet Inönü, a close associate of Atatürk and a cofounder of the CHP. The SHP had been created in 1985 when Inönü's Sodep (disqualified by the military from participating in the 1983 parliamentary elections) merged with Necdet Calp's Populist Party, which had been allowed to take part in the 1983 elections and had won the second largest number of assembly seats.

The decision to join the True Path Party in a coalition government brought to the fore the internal divisions within the SHP. Civil rights activists, both Turkish and Kurdish, opposed the SHP's participation in the government because they associated Demirel with government abuses of human rights during the late 1970s and doubted his willingness to terminate martial law in the Kurdish provinces. Consequently eighteen SHP deputies resigned from the party and, led by Ahmet Türk, established the People's Labor Party (Halkın Emek Partisi—HEP) in 1990 as a separate group in the National Assembly, although they agreed to continue voting with the SHP on certain issues. Because the HEP emphasized civil rights issues, its primary appeal was among Kurds, and a majority of the party's executives were Kurdish. The alliance with the HEP enabled the SHP to broaden its support base—the urban working-class neighborhoods of western and northeastern Turkey—to include the Kurdish areas of the southeast. Meanwhile the security situation in the southeast deteriorated as guerrillas affiliated with the PKK intensified attacks on government sites and personnel as part of a proclaimed effort to create a separate Kurdish state.

Many Turkish leaders, both civilian and military, tended not to distinguish between the HEP, which was committed to working for civil rights within the political process, and the PKK, which aimed to overthrow the political system through armed struggle. When the military initiated proceedings against HEP founders in 1992 for allegedly promoting "separatist propaganda," the HEP deputies accused the SHP of not actively protecting them from official persecution. The Constitutional Court outlawed the HEP in 1993 and its successor, the Democracy Party (Demokrasi Partisi—DEP), the following year. These developments, plus the arrest of DEP deputies in the National Assembly in March and June 1994, adversely affected the SHP's image, especially among its Kurdish supporters. Consequently the SHP did very poorly in the 1994 municipal council elections—virtually all SHP incumbents in the cities and towns of southeastern Turkey lost. It remained unclear in early 1995 whether the SHP could regain the confidence of its Kurdish base. A failure to do so would diminish the SHP's chances in the 1996 parliamentary elections to maintain its status as the third largest party in the National Assembly.

Motherland Party

In early 1995, the Motherland Party (Anavatan Partisi—ANAP) was the main parliamentary opposition party, after having served as the governing party from 1983 to 1991. Turgut Özal founded the Motherland Party in May 1983, and his personality and energy were instrumental to the party's subsequent success. Even after Özal officially resigned as party leader in 1989 to become president, his influence—and that of his wife and brothers—continued in Motherland Party affairs. For example, Özal handpicked his successor as party leader, Yildirim Akbulut. However, after Akbulut proved ineffective, both as party chair and as prime minister, Özal pressured him to resign in June 1991. In anticipation of the forthcoming parliamentary elections, Özal approved the younger and more dynamic Mesut Yilmaz as Akbulut's successor. Yilmaz campaigned energetically, used his position as prime minister to woo voters with incentives such as wage increases for public-sector employees, and performed well against other political leaders in Turkey's first-ever televised political debate. However, the Motherland Party's total share of the national vote in the October 1991 balloting fell by 12 percent compared to 1987, and the party won sixty-three fewer assembly seats than its rival, the True Path Party.

The Motherland Party's policies and constituency were similar to those of the True Path Party, but the intense personal rivalry between Demirel and Özal had precluded political cooperation between the two parties prior to Özal's death in 1993. The president's death represented both a major loss and a potential opportunity for the Motherland Party. The party's cohesion had depended on the force of Özal's personality, and in early 1995 it was unclear whether Yilmaz would succeed in transforming the Motherland Party into an effective organization based on a coherent political program and ideology. In addition, because the party's past electoral strength had derived from Özal's own popular appeal, it was not evident what long-term impact his death would have. Despite Yilmaz's relative youth and limited political experience, he appeared to be the party's chief asset, and even before Özal's death he had been trying to chart a course independent of the party's influential founder. Nevertheless, many members were dissatisfied with Yilmaz's leadership; in late 1992 and early 1993, more than fifteen Motherland Party deputies, citing differences with Yilmaz, resigned from the party in a move that reduced its overall strength in the National Assembly to fewer than 100 seats. More than fifty former deputies, including five founding members of the party, also resigned to demonstrate their opposition to Yilmaz. Yilmaz now faced the challenge of developing a new party identity that would appeal to a broader constituency; otherwise the Motherland Party would expend all its energies competing with the ideologically similar True Path Party.

Welfare Party

The Welfare Party (Refah Partisi—RP), which had received only 7 percent of the total vote in the 1987 parliamentary elections and thus had not qualified for assembly seats, was the main electoral surprise in the 1991 balloting. Nearly 17 percent of the electorate voted for the Welfare Party, enabling it to win sixty-two seats in the National Assembly. The Welfare Party was widely considered an Islamic party. Its leader, Necmettin Erbakan, had been identified with Islamic political activism since the early 1970s. He was the founder in 1972 of the National Salvation Party (Milli Selamet Partisi—MSP), which became the third largest party in parliament in 1973. The MSP openly supported a religious political agenda calling for the restoration of traditional "morals and virtues" and a reduction of economic ties to the Christian countries of Western Europe. In 1974 the

267

MSP gained a measure of political legitimacy by participating in a CHP-led coalition government. In fact, Turgut Özal briefly was a member of the MSP in the 1970s and was at one time an unsuccessful candidate on its parliamentary list.

Following the 1980 coup, the military not only dissolved the MSP, along with other political parties, but also prosecuted Erbakan and other MSP leaders for violating a law forbidding the use of religion for political purposes. When new political parties were authorized in 1983, Erbakan founded the Welfare Party on a platform stressing themes similar to those espoused by the defunct MSP. The ruling generals—and most civilians—perceived the Welfare Party as a continuation of the MSP. It was therefore disqualified from participation in the 1983 parliamentary elections. However, the party did sponsor candidates in the 1984 municipal elections and since then has steadily expanded its support base.

The Welfare Party's strength is in middle- and lower-class urban neighborhoods and in the Kurdish areas of the southeast. This strength was first demonstrated during the municipal elections of 1989, when the party's candidates for mayor won in five large cities and 100 towns. The 1991 parliamentary elections provided further evidence of the Welfare Party's growing popularity and its ability to consolidate an electoral base. Inspired by the party's achievements in 1991, Welfare Party activists, including a new generation of university students, campaigned tirelessly to recruit new supporters. As a result of these efforts, the Welfare Party's share of the total vote increased to 19 percent in the municipal elections of March 1994. The symbolic importance of the 1994 balloting because of its religious implications, probably exceeded the actual significance of the party's turnout. Tayyip Erdogan, the Welfare Party's candidate for mayor of Istanbul, and Melih Gokchek, its mayoral candidate for Ankara, both won. In addition, Welfare Party candidates for mayor won in twenty-seven other cities and in 400 towns, including almost all of the predominantly Kurdish municipalities in the southeast.

The Welfare Party's electoral appeal stems from the popularity of its call for a return to traditional values—widely interpreted as meaning Islamic morals and behavior. Its slogans are sufficiently vague with respect to specific policies to attract diverse support. Thus, self-identified Welfare Party loyalists range from professionals who dress in expensive Western fashions and interpret Islam liberally to individuals, especially women, who adopt a contemporary version of traditional Islamic dress and give Islam a fundamentalist interpretation. Whereas the Welfare Party has adopted certain well-defined positions, such as opposition to Turkey's goal of full membership in the European Union, its adherents tend to hold divergent views on most economic and political issues. However, they share a common interest in religious practices such as daily prayers, fasting during the Islamic holy month of Ramazan (Ramadan in Arabic), avoiding behavior harmful to others, and reading the Kuran (Quran in Arabic). Furthermore, the Welfare Party's emphasis on common religious bonds tends to bring together, rather than to divide, Turkish-speaking and Kurdish-speaking Muslims and has impressed secular Kurds who have become disillusioned with other political parties.

Democratic Left Party

The Democratic Left Party, known by the Turkish acronym DSP (for Demokratik Sol Partisi), was the smallest parliamentary party in January 1995. Because the party received almost 11 percent of the vote in the 1991 elections, DSP leader Bülent Ecevit and six other party officials took seats in the National Assembly. Ecevit considered the DSP the legitimate successor to the CHP, which he headed prior to the 1980 coup. When the DSP was founded in November 1985—with Ecevit's wife serving as chair because he remained barred from political activity—Ecevit made known his low opinion of the SHP, which also presented itself as the heir to the CHP, and its leader, Erdal Inönü. Ecevit's personal animosity toward Inönü prevented DSP-SHP cooperation, even though the parties had similar programs and appealed to the same constituency. In both 1987 and 1991, Ecevit spurned efforts by Inönü and other SHP leaders to persuade him to join an electoral alliance. Ecevit condemned the SHP's participation in the Demirel and Çiller governments as evidence that the party had abandoned social-democratic principles and betrayed the working class.

Other Parties

Several small parties existed in early 1995. Two post-1991 splinters from parliamentary parties included Unity and Peace (Birlik ve Baris), whose members left the Welfare Party in 1992, and the Freedom and Labor Party (OZEP), formed from a breakaway faction of the SHP in 1992. The Nationalist Labor Party (Milliyetçi Çalisma Partisi—MÇP), founded in 1985 by the controversial nationalist of the 1970s, Alparslan Türkes, espoused pan-Turkism in foreign policy and cooperated with the Welfare Party in domestic politics. Deniz Baykel, a politician disillusioned by the partisan sniping between the SHP and the True Path Party, announced the reactivation of the CHP in September 1992 and called on its former members to rejoin. Thirteen SHP deputies joined the new CHP, providing it with an immediate base in the National Assembly. The former Democrat Party, banned following the 1960 coup, also was reactivated in 1992. It consisted of politicians who supported the economic policies of the Motherland Party and the True Path Party but distrusted both Özal and Demirel.

In addition to the legal parties, several illegal political organizations operated clandestinely in Turkey in 1995. These parties were considered illegal either because they never had registered as required by law or because they had been proscribed by judicial authorities. Many of these parties advocated armed struggle, although some were nonviolent. The illegal parties fell into three categories, which reflected the intertwined security and ideological concerns of the Turkish military since 1980: separatist parties, a term used to describe all Kurdish groups; communist parties, a term used to describe all organizations espousing various versions of Marxism; and *irtica* (religious reaction) parties, a term used to describe all groups pushing for the establishment of an Islamic government in Turkey. The most important of the illegal parties was the Kurdistan Workers' Party (Partiya Karkere Kurdistan—PKK), which in 1984 had initiated a steadily escalating armed struggle against the government. By mid-1994 at least 12,000 persons were estimated to have been killed in southeastern Turkey, where the government maintained at least 160,000 troops in combat readiness against as many as 15,000 guerrillas. With the exception of the Revolutionary Left Party (Devrimçi Sol—Dev Sol), the illegal communist and Islamic groups were not well organized; they functioned in small cells that carried out mainly isolated but sensational acts of terrorism in various cities. One of the more notorious actions was the January 1993 car bomb assassination of the nationally prominent journalist Ugur Memçu, for which an extreme Islamist group claimed responsibility (see Internal Security Concerns, ch. 5).

Political Interest Groups

The decades following World War II saw a proliferation of

interest groups that evolved into increasingly active and politically conscious associations. The growth of these groups was part of a general trend toward a more politicized and pluralistic society. This trend resulted primarily from factors such as the advent of multiparty politics, economic development and the accompanying expansion of opportunity, and improvements in communications (see Mass Media, this ch.). Increasing urbanization, rising literacy rates, rapid industrial expansion, and the exposure of hundreds of thousands of Turkish guest workers—most from villages and lower-class urban areas—to new ideas and customs in Western Europe also contributed to the politicization of the populace. As a consequence, a growing number of voluntary associations sprang up to promote specific interests, either on their own, through representatives in parliament, or through the cabinet and senior bureaucrats. These associations enabled various social groups to exercise a degree of influence over political matters. The activities of groups such as labor unions, business associations, student organizations, a journalists' association, and religious and cultural associations promoted public awareness of important issues and contributed to a relatively strong civil society.

The autonomy of civic groups vis-à-vis the state has been a persistent political problem since 1960. During periods of military rule and martial law, the independence of such groups often was circumscribed (see Crisis in Turkish Democracy, ch. 1). Following the military takeover in September 1980, for example, strict limits were placed on the political activities of civic associations; some of these restrictions remained in force in early 1995. For example, the 1982 constitution, like that of 1961, affirms the right of individuals to form associations but also stipulates that the exercise of this right must not violate the "indivisible integrity of the state." Furthermore, associations are prohibited from discriminating on the basis of language, race, or religion, or from trying to promote one social class or group over others. Civic associations also are forbidden to pursue political aims, engage in political activities, receive support from or give support to political parties, or take joint action with labor unions or professional organizations. In addition, legislation enacted in 1983 prohibits teachers, high school students, civil servants, and soldiers from forming associations, and bans officials of professional organizations from participating actively in politics.

Military

By dint of the influence it has exerted on politics since the early days of the Turkish republic, the military constitutes the country's most important interest group. Atatürk and his principal allies all were career officers during the final years of the Ottoman Empire. Although Atatürk subsequently endeavored to separate the military from political affairs, he nevertheless considered the army to be the "intelligentsia of the Turkish nation" and "the guardian of its ideals." By the time of Atatürk's death in 1938, the military had internalized a view of itself as a national elite responsible for protecting the Six Arrows of Kemalism. Prior to 1960, the military worked behind the scenes to ensure that the country adhered to the guidelines of the Kemalist principles. However, in 1960 senior officers were so alarmed by government policies they perceived as deviating from Kemalism that they intervened directly in the political process by overthrowing the elected government and setting up a military regime. The military saw its mission as putting the country back on the correct path of Kemalism. Believing by October 1961 that this goal had been achieved, the officers returned to the barracks, whence they exercised oversight of civilian politicians.

The 1960 coup demonstrated the military's special status as an interest group autonomous—if it chose to be—from the government. On two subsequent occasions, in 1971 and 1980, the military again intervened to remove a government it perceived as violating Kemalist principles. The 1980 coup resulted in a longer transition period to civilian government and the imposition of more extensive restrictions on political rights than had the earlier interventions. At the start of 1995, some fourteen years after the coup, senior officers in the armed services still expected the civilian president and Council of Ministers to heed their advice on matters they considered pertinent to national security. For instance, the military defines many domestic law-and-order issues as falling within the realm of national security and thus both formulates and implements certain policies that the government is expected to approve.

Universities

College teachers and students have acted as a pressure group in Turkey since the late 1950s, when they initiated demonstrations against university teaching methods, curricula, and administrative practices that they alleged resulted in an inade-

View of Ankara, showing the National Assembly building,
and view of the interior of the National Assembly
Courtesy Turkish Information Office

quate education. The violent repression of student demonstrations in the spring of 1960 was one of the factors that prompted that year's military coup. In 1960 both teachers and students generally were held in high public esteem because the universities were viewed as the centers where the future Kemalist elite was being trained. During the 1960s and 1970s, however, the universities became the loci of ideological conflicts among a multitude of political groups espousing diverse political, economic, and religious ideas. As students became progressively more radicalized and violent, armed clashes among rival student groups and between students and police increased in frequency and magnitude. By 1980 the military regarded the universities as a source of threats to Kemalist principles.

One of the aims of the military government that assumed power in 1980 was to regain state control over the universities. The regime created a Council of Higher Education, which was intended to provide a less autonomous, more uniform system of central administration. The regime purged ideologically suspect professors from the faculties of all universities and issued a law prohibiting teachers from joining political parties. Student associations lost their autonomy, and students charged with participating in illegal organizations became subject to expulsion. A cautious revival of campus political activity began in the 1990s, mainly around foreign policy issues. However, as of early 1995 the government's possession of the means and will to punish campus activists appeared to be intimidating most faculty and students.

Labor

The legalization of unions under the Trade Union Law of 1947 paved the way for the slow but steady growth of a labor movement that evolved parallel to multiparty politics. The principal goal of unions as defined in the 1947 law was to seek the betterment of members' social and economic status. Unions were denied the right to strike or to engage in political activity, either on their own or as vehicles of political parties. In spite of these limitations, labor unions gradually acquired political influence. The Confederation of Turkish Trade Unions (Türkiye Isçi Sendikaları Konfederasyonu—Türk-Is) was founded in 1952 at government instigation to serve as an independent umbrella group. Under the tutelage of Türk-Is, labor evolved into a well-organized interest group; the organization also functioned as an agency through which the government could restrain workers' wage demands (see Human Resources and Trade Unions, ch. 3). The labor movement expanded in the liberalized political climate of the 1960s, especially after a union law enacted in 1963 legalized strikes, lockouts, and collective bargaining. However, unions were forbidden to give "material aid" to political parties. Political parties also were barred from giving money to unions or forming separate labor organizations.

The labor movement did not escape the politicization and polarization that characterized the 1960s and 1970s. Workers' dissatisfaction with Türk-Is as the representative of their interests led to the founding in 1967 of the Confederation of Revolutionary Workers' Trade Unions of Turkey (Türkiye Devrimçi Isçi Sendikaları Konfederasyonu—DISK). DISK leaders were militants who had been expelled from Türk-Is after supporting a glass factory strike opposed by the Türk-Is bureaucracy. Both Türk-Is and the government tried to suppress DISK, whose independence was perceived as a threat. However, a spontaneous, two-day, pro-DISK demonstration by thousands of laborers in Istanbul—the first mass political action by Turkish workers—forced the government in June 1970 to back away from a bill to abolish DISK. For the next ten years, DISK remained an independent organization promoting the rights of workers and supporting their job actions, including one major general strike in 1977 that led to the temporary abolition of the military-run State Security Courts. By 1980 about 500,000 workers belonged to unions affiliated with DISK.

Following the 1980 coup, the military regime banned independent union activity, suspended DISK, and arrested hundreds of its activists, including all its top officials. The government prosecuted DISK leaders, as well as more than 1,000 other trade unionists arrested in 1980, in a series of trials that did not end until December 1986. The secretary general of DISK and more than 250 other defendants received jail sentences of up to ten years. Meanwhile, the more complaisant Türk-Is, which had not been outlawed after the coup, worked with the military government and its successors to depoliticize workers. As the government-approved labor union confederation, Türk-Is benefited from new laws pertaining to unions. For example, the 1982 constitution permits unions but prohibits them from engaging in political activity, thus effectively denying them the right to petition political representatives. As in the days prior to 1967, unions must depend upon Türk-Is to mediate between them and the government. A law issued in May 1983 restricts the establishment of new trade unions and places constraints on the right to strike by banning politically motivated strikes, general strikes, solidarity strikes, and any strike considered a threat to society or national well-being.

The government's restrictions on union activity tended to demoralize workers, who generally remained passive for more than five years after the 1980 coup. However, beginning in 1986 unions experienced a resurgence. In February several thousand workers angered by pension cutbacks held a rally—labor's first such demonstration since the 1980 coup—to protest high living costs, low wages, high unemployment, and restrictions on union organizing and collective bargaining. A subsequent rally in June drew an estimated 50,000 demonstrators. Since 1986 workers have conducted numerous rallies, small strikes, work slowdowns, and other manifestations of dissatisfaction. By the early 1990s, an average of 120,000 workers per year were involved in strike activity. Türk-Is has mediated these incidents by bailing detained workers out of prison, negotiating compromise wage increase packages, and encouraging cooperative labor-management relations.

Business

The Turkish Trade Association (Türkiye Odalar Birligi—TOB) has represented the interests of merchants, industrialists, and commodity brokers since 1952. In the 1960s and 1970s, new associations representing the interests of private industry challenged TOB's position as the authoritative representative of business in Turkey. Subsequently the organization came to be identified primarily with small and medium-sized firms. The Union of Chambers of Industry was founded in 1967 as a coalition within TOB by industrialists seeking to reorganize the confederation. The Union of Chambers of Industry was unable to acquire independent status but achieved improved coordination of industrialists' demands. By setting up study groups, the union was able to pool research on development projects. In addition, the union organized regional Chambers of Industry within TOB.

Business interests also were served by employers' associations that dealt primarily with labor-management relations and were united under the aegis of the Turkish Confederation of Employers' Unions (Türkiye Isveren Sendikaları Konfederasyonu—TISK). This confederation was established in 1961, largely in response to the development of trade unions, and was considered the most militant of employers' associations. By the end of 1980, TISK claimed 106 affiliated groups with a total membership of 9,183 employers. Although membership in TISK was open to employers in both the private and public sectors, it was primarily an organization of private-sector employers. When the military regime took power in 1980, labor union activities were suspended, but TISK was allowed to continue functioning. Employers supported the subsequent restrictive labor legislation, which appeared to be in accord with TISK proposals.

Another representative of business interests, the Turkish Industrialists' and Businessmen's Association (Türk Sanayiçileri ve Is Adamları Dernegi—TÜSIAD), was founded by the leaders of some of Turkey's largest business and industrial enterprises soon after the March 1971 military coup. Its aim was to improve the image of business and to stress its concern with social issues. At the same time, TÜSIAD favored granting greater control of investment capital to the large industrialists at the expense of the smaller merchant and banking interests usually supported by TOB. TÜSIAD's leaders also were concerned with the widening economic inequalities between regions and social classes and opposed TISK's extreme antilabor policies, which they perceived as jeopardizing Turkey's chances of entering the European Union.

Religious Interests

Turkey officially has been a secular state since 1924. Atatürk viewed attachment to religion as an impediment to modernization and imposed rigorous restrictions on the practice of Islam (see Secularist Reforms, ch. 2). Until the late 1940s, the separation of mosque and state was rigidly enforced by the authoritarian, one-party government. However, secularism remained an elite ideology, whereas Islam, the nominal religion of 98 percent of the population, continued to be a strong influence on most of the people, especially in rural areas and lower-class urban neighborhoods. The advent of competitive politics in 1950 enabled religion to reacquire a respected public status. Initially the Democrat Party, then most other parties, found it politically expedient to appeal to religious sentiments in election campaigns. As the government gradually became more tolerant of religious expression, both public observance of religious festivals and mosque construction increased. In addi-

277

tion, there was a resurgence of voluntary religious associations, including the *tarikatlar* (sing., *tarikat*—see Glossary). Prior to 1970, however, religion was not a political issue.

The formation of the MSP in 1972 as Turkey's first republican party to espouse openly Islamic principles inaugurated the politicization of the religious issue (see Retreat from Secularism, ch. 2). The MSP attracted a following by providing an Islamic defense of traditional values that were eroding as a consequence of the economic and social changes the country had begun to experience in the late 1960s. In effect, religion became a vehicle for expressing popular discontent. The inability of the major political parties to agree on policies to counteract this discontent tended to enhance the influence of minor parties such as the MSP. Indeed, in 1974 the main exponent of Kemalist secularism, the CHP, invited the MSP, by then the third largest party in parliament, to join it in a coalition government. Its participation in the government provided the MSP, and the Islamic movement more broadly, with an aura of political legitimacy. Subsequently, the MSP sponsored an Islamist youth movement that during the late 1970s engaged other militant youth groups—both socialists on the left and secular nationalists on the right—in armed street battles. In the mosques, numerous voluntary associations were formed to undertake religious studies, devotional prayers, charitable projects, social services, and the publication of journals. Even the minority Shia (see Glossary) Muslims organized their own separate groups (see The Alevi, ch. 2).

The 1980 coup only temporarily interrupted the trend toward increased religious observance. Initially, the military regime arrested Erbakan and other MSP leaders and put them on trial for politically exploiting religion in violation of Turkish law. However, the senior officers, although committed to secularism, wanted to use religion as a counter to socialist and Marxist ideologies and thus refrained from interfering with the *tarikatlar* and other voluntary religious associations. Furthermore, the generals approved an article in the 1982 constitution mandating compulsory religious instruction in all schools. When political parties were allowed to form in 1983, Özal's Motherland Party welcomed a large group of former MSP members, who probably were attracted to the party because Özal and some of his relatives had belonged to the MSP in the 1970s. One of Özal's brothers, Korkut Özal, held an important position in the Naksibendi *tarikat,* the oldest and largest organized religious order in Turkey.

The military regime was preoccupied with eliminating the threat from "communists," a term freely applied to anyone with socialist ideas. Thousands of persons lost jobs in state offices, schools, and enterprises because they were perceived as "leftists," and leftist organizations virtually disappeared. Religiously motivated persons assumed many of the vacated positions, especially in education, and Islamic groups filled the political vacuum created by the state's successful assault on the left. At the same time, the policies of neither the military regime nor its civilian successors effectively addressed the economic and social problems that continued to fuel popular discontent.

Without competition from the left, the religious orders and the religiously oriented Welfare Party enjoyed almost a monopoly on the mobilization of discontent. One *tarikat,* the boldly political Fethullahçı, actually tried to recruit cadets in the military academies. By 1986 the increasingly vociferous and militant activities of religious groups had forced on the defensive the concept of secularism itself—a bedrock of Kemalist principles for sixty years.

In 1987 the military had become persuaded that what it called "Islamic fundamentalism" was a potentially serious threat to its vision of Kemalism. In January 1987, President Evren publicly denounced Islamic fundamentalism as being as dangerous as communism. Initially, the secular political elite, with the exception of the SHP, was not persuaded by his arguments. Özal, then prime minister, seemed to support the Islamic wing of his party, which was pushing for the repeal of the remaining laws restricting religious practices. The True Path Party characterized the trend toward religious observance as a healthy development and stressed freedom of practice. However, as clandestine religious groups began to carry out attacks on noted secularists in the late 1980s, True Path Party leaders became concerned, and then alarmed, by the influence of Islamism (sometimes seen as fundamentalism).

The Welfare Party disassociated itself from violent attacks by both organized and unorganized religious fanatics, but such attacks increased in both frequency and severity in the 1990s. The most sensational attack occurred in July 1993, when a mob leaving Friday congregational prayers in the central Anatolian city of Sivas firebombed a hotel where Turkey's internationally renowned author, self-proclaimed atheist Aziz Nesin, and dozens of other writers were staying while attending a cultural festival. Although Nesin escaped harm, thirty-seven persons were killed and 100 injured in that incident. Several weeks before the attack, Nesin's newspaper, *Aydinlik,* had published translated excerpts of British author Salman Rushdie's controversial 1988 novel, *The Satanic Verses,* which many Muslim religious leaders had condemned as blasphemous. Following publication of the excerpts, the newspaper's offices in Istanbul and other cities were attacked by groups of Islamic militants.

Turkey's religious revival has foreign policy implications because the *tarikatlar* tend to link with religious groups in other Muslim countries. Saudi Arabia, for example, has been an important source of the extensive financial support that has enabled the *tarikatlar* to proselytize and to operate charitable programs that enhance their political influence. Turkish political leaders also fear the influence of neighboring Iran, where an Islamic government replaced the secular regime in 1979, and since 1987 have tended to blame incidents of religious violence on Iranian agents. However, Turkey's religious activists are Sunni (see Glossary) Muslims who tend to display suspicion and prejudice toward Shia Muslims—who make up more than 90 percent of the Iranian population—and there has been scant evidence to support the existence of significant ties between the Turkish Sunni and Iran.

Minorities

At least 15 percent of Turkey's population consists of ethnic and religious minorities. The Kurds are the minority group with the greatest impact on national politics. Since the 1930s, Kurds have resisted government efforts to assimilate them forcibly, including an official ban on speaking or writing Kurdish. Since 1984 Kurdish resistance to Turkification has encompassed both a peaceful political struggle to obtain basic civil rights for Kurds within Turkey and a violent armed struggle to obtain a separate Kurdish state. The leaders of the nonviolent struggle have worked within the political system for the recognition of Kurdish cultural rights, including the right to speak Kurdish in public and to read, write, and publish in Kurdish. Prior to 1991, these Kurds operated within the national political parties, in particular the SHP, the party most sympathetic to their goal of full equality for all citizens of Turkey. President Özal's 1991 call for a more liberal policy toward Kurds and for the repeal of the ban on speaking Kurdish raised the hopes of

Kurdish politicians. Following the parliamentary elections of October 1991, several Kurdish deputies, including Hatip Dicle, Feridun Yazar, and Leyla Zayna, formed the HEP, a party with the explicit goal of campaigning within the National Assembly for laws guaranteeing equal rights for the Kurds.

Turkey's other leaders were not as willing as Özal to recognize Kurdish distinctiveness, and only two months after his death in April 1993, the Constitutional Court issued its decision declaring the HEP illegal. In anticipation of this outcome, the Kurdish deputies had resigned from the HEP only days before and formed a new organization, the Democracy Party (Demokrasi Partisi—DEP). The DEP's objective was similar to that of its predecessor: to promote civil rights for all citizens of Turkey. When the DEP was banned in June 1994, Kurdish deputies formed the new People's Democracy Party (Halkın Demokrasi Partisi—HADEP).

The PKK initiated armed struggle against the state in 1984 with attacks on gendarmerie posts in the southeast. The PKK's leader, Abdullah Öcalan, had formed the group in the late 1970s while a student in Ankara. Prior to the 1980 coup, Öcalan fled to Lebanon, via Syria, where he continued to maintain his headquarters in 1994. Until October 1992, Öcalan's brother, Osman, had supervised PKK training camps in the mountains separating northern Iraq from Turkey's Hakkâri and Mardin provinces. It was from these camps that PKK guerrillas launched their raids into Turkey. The main characteristic of PKK attacks was the use of indiscriminate violence, and PKK guerrillas did not hesitate to kill Kurds whom they considered collaborators. Targeted in particular were the government's paid militia, known as village guards, and schoolteachers accused of promoting forced assimilation. The extreme violence of the PKK's methods enabled the government to portray the PKK as a terrorist organization and to justify its own policies, which included the destruction of about 850 border villages and the forced removal of their populations to western Turkey.

In March 1993, the PKK dropped its declared objective of creating an independent state of Kurdistan in the southeastern provinces that had Kurdish majorities. Its new goal was to resolve the Kurdish problem within a democratic and federal system. The loss of PKK guerrilla camps in northern Iraq in October 1992, following defeat in a major confrontation with Iraqi Kurdish forces supported by Turkish military intervention, probably influenced this tactical change. At the same time, Öcalan announced a unilateral, albeit temporary, cease-fire in the PKK's war with Turkish security forces. The latter decision may also have reflected the influence of Kurdish civilian leaders, who had been urging an end to the violence in order to test Özal's commitment to equal rights. Whether there were realistic prospects in the spring of 1993 for a political solution to the conflict in southeast Turkey may never be known. Özal suffered a fatal heart attack in April, and his successor, Demirel, did not appear inclined to challenge the military, whose position continued to be that elimination of the PKK was the appropriate way to pacify the region. Fighting between security forces and PKK guerrillas, estimated to number as many as 15,000, resumed by June 1993.

In early 1995, Turkey's other minorities—Arabs, Armenians, other Caucasian peoples, Circassians, Georgians, Greeks, and Jews—tended toward political quiescence. Arabs, who are concentrated in the southeast to the west of the Kurds and north of the border with Syria, had demonstrated over language and religious issues in the 1980s. Because most of Turkey's Arabs belong to Islam's Alawi branch, whose adherents also include the leading politicians of Syria, Ankara's often tense relations with Syria tend to be further complicated.

The Armenian issue also adds tension to foreign affairs. The 60,000 Armenians estimated to be living in Turkey in the mid-1990s had refrained from attracting any political attention to their community. However, along with Armenians residing in Lebanon, France, Iran, and the United States, the Republic of Armenia, which borders Turkey's easternmost province of Kars, has embarrassed Turkey with highly publicized annual commemorations of the Armenian genocide of 1915–16—which the Turkish government denies ever occurred (see World War I, ch. 1). The Turkish government also condemns as harmful to overall relations the periodic efforts by the United States Congress and the parliaments of European states to pass resolutions condemning the mass killings. Various clandestine Armenian groups—of which the most prominent is the Armenian Secret Army for the Liberation of Armenia (ASALA)—have claimed responsibility for assassinations of Turkish diplomatic personnel stationed in the Middle East and Europe. Such assassinations have continued to occur in the 1990s. Unidentified Turkish government officials frequently have leaked reports to the news media accusing Armenia, Lebanon, and

Syria of allowing Armenian terrorists to receive training and support within their borders.

Mass Media

The Turkish news media consist of a state-operated radio and television broadcasting system and privately owned press and broadcasting operations. Newspapers are not subject to prior censorship, but a 1983 press law restricts them from reporting information deemed to fall within the sphere of national security and prohibits the publication of papers that promote "separatism." Violations of these restrictions result in the closing down of newspapers and the prosecution of journalists. Except for official press releases, most reports on military operations in southeastern Turkey and almost all accounts of public speeches calling for Kurdish cultural rights prompt state prosecutors to come before security courts calling for judicial investigations of possible press law violations. Amnesty International has documented the detention of scores of journalists who wrote independent articles about conditions in the southeast during 1991–92; in some instances, journalists were injured during interrogations or held for prolonged periods without access to attorneys. Twenty-eight journalists were tried and sentenced to prison in the first six months of 1993 alone. Many of them worked for the Istanbul daily *Ozgur Gundem*, which has regularly featured stories on conditions in the Kurdish areas and has carried interviews with both PKK guerrillas and Turkish soldiers. In an apparent attempt to halt publication of such articles, the government arrested the newspaper's editor in chief, Davut Karadag, in July 1993 and charged him with spreading separatist propaganda. Subsequently, editors at *Medya Gunesi, Aydinlik*, and other newspapers were detained on similar charges.

The publication of materials thought to offend public morals is also grounds for suspending a periodical or confiscating a book. The Censor's Board on Obscene Publications has responsibility for reviewing potentially offensive material and deciding on appropriate action. The weekly *Aktuel* frequently questions the value of, and need for, such a board in a democracy, using biting satire to deliver its message. In 1993 the editor of the weekly and one of its freelance columnists were arrested and charged with insulting the board.

Newspapers and Periodicals

In 1994 there were more than thirty daily newspapers in Turkey. The mass-circulation dailies are based in Istanbul and are distributed nationally. These include the country's largest newspaper, *Hürriyet* (Freedom), which has a circulation of more than 850,000, and three other papers, each with daily circulations ranging from 200,000 to 300,000: *Günaydın* (Good Morning), *Tercuman* (Interpreter), and *Milliyet* (Nationality). A smaller paper, *Cumhuriyet* (Republic), is influential because it is read widely by the country's economic and political elite. In all, more than a dozen dailies are published in Istanbul. Nine dailies are published in Ankara and three in Izmir. Other major cities, including Adana, Bursa, Diyarbakır, Gaziantep, Konya, and Mersin, have at least one local daily newspaper. In addition to the newspapers, twenty weeklies and a variety of biweekly, monthly, bimonthly, and quarterly journals also are published.

The main news agency in Turkey is the official Anadolu Ajansi (Anatolian Agency), founded by Atatürk in 1920. Its primary function is to issue news bulletins and printed information within the country and for distribution abroad. As do most newspapers, Turkish radio and television depend on the agency as a primary source of domestic news. In 1994 it had regional offices in Turkey's major cities as well as correspondents throughout the country. It also had foreign correspondents in all major world cities. In addition to the Anatolian Agency, several private agencies serve the press.

Radio and Television

The government of Turkey began radio broadcasting in 1927. Atatürk and his colleagues perceived radio as a means to promote modernization and nationalism and thus created a Bureau of the Press Directorate to oversee programming and ensure that it served national goals. In 1964 the government established the Turkish Radio and Television Corporation (Türkiye Radyo Televizyon Kurumu—TRT) to expand radio facilities and develop public television. Subsequently, the transmission power of radio stations greatly increased, as did the number of licensed receivers. (The government required purchase of a license for ownership of radios, and later of televisions.) By 1994 almost the entire nation had radio coverage, with thirty-six transmitters beaming a total power of 5,500 kilowatts to an estimated 10 million receivers. TRT also broadcasts programs abroad in Turkish and in several foreign languages, including Arabic, Bulgarian, Greek, and Persian.

Television developed more slowly than radio, mainly because the government considered it a luxury. Television broadcasting began through a technical-assistance agreement between Turkey and the Federal Republic of Germany (West Germany). With the aid of the equipment and technical personnel provided under this agreement, TRT inaugurated the country's first public television station in Ankara in 1968. Gradually new stations were opened in Istanbul, Izmir, and other cities. Investment in television facilities accelerated after 1972, and during the following decade television replaced radio as the country's most important mass medium. By 1994 the estimated number of television sets—10 million—equaled the number of radio receivers.

TRT had a constitutionally mandated monopoly on radio and television broadcasting prior to 1993. It financed its operations through limited allocations it received from the government's general budget and income derived from radio and television license fees. TRT news presentations and documentaries tended to avoid controversy; television viewers often criticized the programs as dull. Dissatisfaction with public television prompted proposals beginning in the late 1980s to amend the constitution to permit private, commercial broadcasting. Opposition to private broadcasting came from the military and other groups that feared loss of government control over programming. It was not until 1993 that the National Assembly approved legislation to authorize private radio and television in tandem with public broadcasting. Even before their legalization, however, private stations had begun to broadcast programs, many of which disturbed officials in the national security bureaucracy. For example, in the summer of 1993 the State Security Court opened an investigation into a public affairs program of a private Istanbul channel, charging that the program had spread separatist propaganda by including Kurdish guests.

Foreign Relations

Turkey began reevaluating its foreign policy in 1991, when the United States-led war against Iraq and the collapse of the Soviet Union totally upset patterns of international relations that had been relatively consistent for more than forty years. Both of these developments intimately affected Turkey because the former Soviet Union was its neighbor to the north and east, and Iraq its neighbor to the south. Political instability has plagued both these regions since 1991, causing some Turkish national security analysts to fear possible negative consequences for their own country. However, other Turks believe that the international changes since 1991 offer their country a unique opportunity to reassert its historical role as a bridge between two regions in which it has had only a marginal presence since 1918.

Dissolution of the Soviet Union

Since the end of World War II, Turkey had regarded the Soviet Union, the superpower with which it shared a 590-kilometer frontier, as its principal enemy. Fear of Soviet intentions was powerful enough to persuade Turkish leaders to join the United States-European collective defense agreement, the North Atlantic Treaty Organization (NATO), in 1952. Participation in NATO made Turkey a partisan on the side of the West in the Cold War that dominated international politics for more than forty years. Turkish suspicions of the Soviet Union gradually eased during the era of détente that began in the 1960s, paving the way for several bilateral economic cooperation agreements in the 1970s. However, the Soviet invasion of Afghanistan in 1979 revived Turkish concerns about Soviet expansionism and led to a cooling of relations that lasted more than five years. Beginning in the mid-1980s, Turkish fears again eased. Ankara and Moscow concluded a number of agreements, including plans for a pipeline to carry natural gas from Soviet gas fields to Turkey. Economic and diplomatic ties between the two countries were being expanded when the Soviet Union dissolved into fifteen independent nations.

For Turkey the practical consequence of the Soviet Union's demise was the replacement of one large, powerful, and generally predictable neighbor with five smaller near neighbors characterized by domestic instability and troubling foreign policies. Like most states, Turkey perceives Russia as the principal inheritor of Soviet power and influence. Turkish officials likewise share in the widespread uncertainty over Russia's role in the Commonwealth of Independent States (CIS), formed at the end of 1991, and thus try to avoid policies that might antagonize a traditional adversary. Diplomatic contacts with Russia and the CIS have focused on the renegotiation of numerous Soviet-era economic and technical cooperation agreements that were in force when the Soviet Union was dissolved. Turkey also has initiated multilateral discussions with the five states that now border the Black Sea—Russia, Georgia, Ukraine, Bulgaria, and Romania—on an economic cooperation project originally proposed before the demise of the Soviet Union. The inaugural meetings of the new group called for ambitious plans to increase trade among member states, encourage labor mobility, and establish a development bank.

In Transcaucasia and Central Asia, regions where Turkey is most keen to project its influence, Ankara has tended to defer to Moscow whenever such a course seems prudent. Turkey's efforts to make its presence felt in nearby Transcaucasia have been limited not so much by Russia as by the political realities that emerged in Transcaucasia itself after December 1991. All three new countries in the region—Armenia, Azerbaijan, and Georgia—share land borders with Turkey; thus political and economic leaders view them as natural partners for trade and development projects. Both President Özal's Motherland Party and Prime Minister Demirel's True Path Party embraced the idea of expanding ties with Azerbaijan, an oil-producing country whose people speak a Turkic language closely related to Anatolian Turkish.

Almost all the major parties have expressed reservations about an independent Armenia, probably on account of the historical bitterness between Armenians and Turks. In the mid-1990s, the revival of Ottoman-era animosities seemed inevitable because Armenia and Azerbaijan had become independent while fighting an undeclared war over the Azerbaijani province of Nagorno-Karabakh, whose ethnic Armenian majority has been trying to secede. Turkey adopted an officially neutral position in the conflict, although its sympathies lie with Azerbaijan. Popular opinion against Armenia became especially intense in 1992 and 1993, when military successes by Armenian forces caused tens of thousands of Azerbaijani refugees to enter Turkey. Turkey responded by applying temporary economic pressure on Armenia, such as closing the transborder road to traffic bringing goods into the landlocked country and cutting Turkish electrical power to Armenian towns. However, Turkey's membership in NATO and the Conference on Security and Cooperation in Europe (from January 1995, the Organization for Security and Cooperation in Europe), its concerns about overall regional stability—adjacent Georgia was engulfed in its own civil war in 1993—and fears of unpredictable Iranian and Russian reactions all combined to restrain Turkey from providing direct military assistance to Azerbaijan.

Disappointment over the inadequacy of Turkish support was one of the factors that prompted the 1993 coup against Azerbaijan's staunchly pro-Turkish government. This unexpected political change in Baku represented a major blow to Turkish policy. The new regime in Azerbaijan was not only cool toward Turkey but also determined to cultivate friendlier relations with Iran and Russia. These developments provoked opposition deputies in Turkey's National Assembly to accuse the Çiller government of having "lost" Azerbaijan. As of late January 1995, Ankara's political influence in Baku still was limited, although Turkey's overall cultural influence in Azerbaijan seemed strong.

Turkey's policy in Central Asia has proved more successful than its Transcaucasian policy. As with Azerbaijan, a feeling of pan-Turkic solidarity has prompted Turkish interest in expanding ties with the countries of Kazakhstan, Kyrgyzstan, Turkmenistan, and Uzbekistan. In April 1992, in his first year as prime minister, Demirel traveled to the region to promote Turkey as a political and developmental model for the Central Asian states. He explicitly represented Turkey not only as a successful example of what an independent Turkic country could achieve but also as a more appropriate model than the Islamic alternative offered by Iran, which he perceived as Turkey's main rival for influence in the region. Subsequently, Turkey concluded numerous cultural, economic, and technical aid agreements with the Central Asian states, including non-Turkic Tajikistan. Turkey also sponsored full membership for the Central Asian countries and Azerbaijan in the Economic Cooperation Organization, a regional trade pact whose original members were Iran, Pakistan, and Turkey. In practice, however, Turkey lacks adequate economic resources to play the pivotal role in Central Asia to which it aspires. Because Iran also has insufficient capital for aid to and investment in the region, the anticipated rivalry between Iran and Turkey had failed by the mid-1990s to develop into a serious contest. By the time President Özal followed Demirel's trip with his own tour of the region in April 1993, Turkey recognized, albeit reluctantly, that Russia, rather than Turkey or Iran, had emerged as the dominant political force in Central Asia, and that this situation would prevail indefinitely. Nevertheless, the new countries have professed friendship toward Turkey and welcomed its overtures. In response, Turkey has reoriented its policies to focus on strengthening bilateral cultural ties and encouraging Turkish private entrepreneurs to invest in the region. As of early 1995, Turkey enjoyed close diplomatic relations with the four Turkic republics of Central Asia and good relations with Persian-speaking Tajikistan.

Closely related to the dissolution of the Soviet Union was the collapse of the communist regimes in Eastern Europe. This development had positive consequences in terms of Turkey's relations with Bulgaria, which borders the Turkish province of Thrace. Relations between Turkey and Bulgaria had been badly strained between 1985 and 1989 as a result of Bulgaria's campaign of forcibly assimilating its Turkish minority, estimated at 900,000 and comprising approximately 10 percent of the country's total population. Efforts by Bulgaria's ethnic Turks to protest government policies requiring them to change their Turkish and Muslim names to Bulgarian and Christian ones, end all Islamic teaching and practices, and stop speaking Turkish in public had led to increasingly severe repression. This repression culminated in the summer of 1989 with a mass exodus of an estimated 320,000 Turkish Bulgarians, who fled across the border into Turkey during a seven-week period in July and August. The exodus overwhelmed Turkey's refugee facilities and provoked an international crisis as well as an internal crisis within Bulgaria that contributed to the fall of the communist government. Subsequently, Bulgaria's new democratic government repealed the controversial assimilation decrees and invited those who had fled to return home. Relations between Turkey and Bulgaria steadily improved during the early 1990s, and the two countries have concluded several bilateral trade and technical assistance agreements. A similar spirit of cooperation was evident in the agreements signed with other East European countries, in particular Hungary and Romania.

In contrast to the generally positive evolution of relations with Bulgaria, the international politics surrounding the disintegration of Yugoslavia proved frustrating for Turkish diplomacy. The plight of the Muslim population of Bosnia and Herzegovina during the civil war that followed Bosnia's 1992 declaration of independence aroused popular sympathy in Turkey and support for interventionist policies to help the Bosnian Muslims. Although the government supported the United Nations (UN) peacekeeping force in Bosnia and an auxiliary

NATO military role, Ankara criticized these efforts as inadequate. In the mid-1990s, Turkey favored firmer measures against Bosnian Serbs and the government of Serbia, which Turkey, like other countries, had accused of providing military aid and other assistance to the Bosnian Serbs. However, as of early 1995, Turkey was not prepared to take unilateral steps in Bosnia that might antagonize its NATO partners.

The Middle East

Turkey shares borders with three major Middle Eastern countries: Iran, Iraq, and Syria. Turkey ruled much of the region during the Ottoman Empire, but between 1945 and 1990 Turkish leaders consciously avoided involvement in various Middle Eastern conflicts. President Özal broke with that tradition in 1990 when he sided with the United States-led coalition confronting Iraq following its invasion and annexation of Kuwait. To comply with the economic sanctions that the UN imposed on Iraq, Özal closed down the two pipelines used to transport Iraqi oil through Turkey to the Mediterranean Sea. Although Turkey did not formally join the military coalition that fought against Iraq, it deployed about 150,000 troops along its border with Iraq, which caused Baghdad to divert an equivalent number of forces from the south to the north of the country. Furthermore, Turkey authorized United States aircraft to use the military air base at Incirlik for raids over Iraq. A likely motive for Turkish support of the war against Iraq was a desire to strengthen ties with the United States and other NATO allies at a time of considerable uncertainty—at least in Turkey—about post-Cold War strategic relations.

The Persian Gulf War's main consequence for Turkey was the internationalization of the Kurdish issue. Following Iraq's defeat by the United States-led coalition at the end of February 1991, Iraq's Kurdish minority, which constituted approximately 15 percent of the approximately 19 million population, rebelled against the government of Saddam Husayn. Government forces repressed the rebellion within three weeks, precipitating a mass exodus of almost the entire Kurdish population of northern Iraq toward the Iranian and Turkish borders. Unable to deal with the refugee flood, Turkey closed its borders in April after more than 400,000 Kurds had fled into Hakkâri and Mardin provinces. Turkish soldiers prevented about 500,000 more Kurdish refugees on the Iraqi side of the border from crossing over to Turkey, forcing them to remain in makeshift camps; an additional 1 million other Kurds fled into Iran. The humanitarian crisis and the international publicity surrounding it posed a major dilemma for Turkey, which was reluctant to absorb hundreds of thousands of Kurdish refugees. Furthermore, Turkey opposed the creation of permanent refugee camps, believing such camps would become breeding grounds for militant nationalism, as had happened in the Palestinian refugee camps established during the war that followed Israel's creation in 1948.

Turkey's preferred solution to the Kurdish refugee crisis has been for the Kurds to return to their homes in Iraq with guarantees for their safety within a political environment that would encourage their integration into a united Iraq. Negotiations with Britain, France, and the United States produced an agreement in June 1991 to establish an interim protected zone in northern Iraq in which all Iraqi military activities would be prohibited. Turkey would permit its allies to use the Incirlik Air Base for armed reconnaissance flights over the protected zone. The interim period originally was intended to last for six months but could be extended for an additional six months at the discretion of the National Assembly. Although the agreement created a de facto safe haven in Iraq's three northern provinces and prompted a majority of the Kurdish refugees to return home, it did not resolve the political problem between the refugees and the Iraqi government. On the contrary, Baghdad responded by imposing a blockade on the north, effectively making the Kurds economically dependent on Iran and Turkey. The Western powers saw Iraq's attitude as justifying prolongation of the safe-haven agreement; as of January 1995, it was still in force.

Turkey has opposed the creation of an autonomous Kurdish government in northern Iraq. However, Iraq's intransigence toward the UN after the Persian Gulf War and the determination of the United States to limit its involvement in the safe-haven zone to air patrols made the formation of a local administration inevitable. Turkey reluctantly acquiesced after Iraqi Kurdish leaders reassured Ankara that an autonomous government would not pursue independence for the Kurds but would cooperate with all Iraqi opposition groups to create a democratic alternative to Saddam Husayn's regime. Following elections for a representative regional assembly in May 1992, an autonomous government claiming to operate in keeping with the Iraqi constitution was established at Irbil. Turkey has accepted this government as the de facto authority in northern Iraq, but has not recognized it as a de jure provincial government. Turkey has made its continued cooperation with this autonomous government contingent on the Kurds' support of Iraq's territorial integrity and their assistance in controlling PKK camps in northern Iraq.

The Kurdish issue also assumed an important role in Turkey's relations with both Iran and Syria beginning in 1991. Ankara was concerned that Damascus and Tehran might exploit the Kurdish issue to put pressure on Turkey to compromise on other issues over which there were deep disagreements. For example, although Turkey had enjoyed relatively close political and diplomatic relations with Iran for more than fifty years following the establishment of the Republic of Turkey in 1923, these ties were strained after 1979 when the Iranian Revolution brought to power an Islamic theocratic regime that frequently cites secular governments such as Turkey's as an evil that Muslims should resist. Although bilateral trade remained important to both countries throughout the 1980s and early 1990s, their economic ties have not prevented the regular eruption of tension. One source of intermittent friction has been the presence in Turkey of thousands of Iranians who fled their country during the 1980s because they opposed the religious government, preferred not to live under its puritanical legal codes, or wanted to evade military service during the Iran-Iraq War (1980–88). Tehran has periodically protested that Ankara allows "terrorists" (i.e., members of various Iranian opposition groups) to reside in Turkey. Turkish security officials in turn suspect that Iranian diplomats in Turkey have been involved in assassinations of Iranian opposition leaders and also have assisted some of the militant Turkish Islamists who began resorting to violence in the late 1980s. With respect to international concerns, Turkey resents Iran's criticism of its membership in NATO, distrusts Iran's alliance with Syria and its cooperation with Armenia, and perceives Iran as a competitor for influence in Azerbaijan and Central Asia. Above all, Turkish leaders believe that Iran supports the PKK and even provides sanctuary and bases for it in the area of northwest Iran that borders Kars, Agri, Van, and Hakkâri provinces.

Turkish suspicions of Iranian support for the PKK probably originated in 1987, when Iran strongly protested Turkey's bombing of Iraqi Kurdish villages that Ankara claimed were bases for PKK guerrillas. At the time Iran condemned this violation of Iraqi sovereignty, Iran and Iraq were at war, with Iranian forces occupying parts of southern Iraq. Iran's protest may have been prompted by the fact that the area Turkey bombed was controlled by an Iraqi Kurdish opposition group to which Iran was allied. This group not only helped Iran by fighting against Saddam Husayn's regime but also cooperated with Iran to suppress Iranian Kurdish opposition. From Turkey's perspective, however, this same Kurdish group was too friendly toward the PKK.

This complex intertwining of domestic and international Kurdish politics continued to cause misunderstanding between Turkey and Iran for more than five years. However, beginning in 1992, Turkish and Iranian views on the Kurdish issue gradually converged as Iranian Kurdish opposition groups initiated operations in Iran from bases in territory controlled by the Kurdish autonomous authority in northern Iraq. Iran not only ceased protesting Turkish actions in Iraq, but it even followed Turkey's example in bombing opposition bases in Iraq. During 1993 Iran also responded favorably to Turkish proposals pertaining to security cooperation in the region along their common border and joined Turkey in affirming opposition to an independent Kurdish state being carved out of Iraq.

Syria joined Iran and Turkey in declaring support for the territorial integrity of Iraq, and representatives of the three states met periodically after 1991 to discuss mutual concerns about developments in northern Iraq. Nevertheless, Turkey has had serious reservations about Syria's motives; some Turkish officials believe that if an appropriate opportunity presented itself, Syria would use the Kurdish issue to create a Kurdish state in parts of both Iraq and Turkey. Such pessimistic views stem from Syria's long support of the PKK. Turks believe that Syria permits the PKK to maintain a training base in Lebanon—where Syrian troops have been stationed since 1976—and allows PKK leaders to live freely in Damascus. Tensions between Turkey and Syria actually had been accumulating long before the eruption of the PKK "dispute" in 1984. Like Iraq, Syria was an Ottoman province until 1918. Subsequently, it was governed by France as a League of Nations mandate. In 1939 France detached Hatay (formerly Alexandretta) province from Syria and ceded it to Turkey, an action bitterly opposed by Arab nationalists. Syria thus became independent in 1946 with an irredentist claim against Turkey. The Arab-Israeli conflict soon developed as another source of Syrian antagonism toward Turkey, which extended diplomatic recognition to Israel in 1948. Syria's staunch Arab nationalists also condemned Turkey's participation in NATO and other Western defense arrangements during the 1950s and 1960s.

Turkey's adoption in 1974 of a more evenhanded policy toward the Arab-Israeli conflict failed to impress Syria. Much to Turkey's disappointment, Syria supported the Greeks in the conflict between the Greek and Turkish communities on the island of Cyprus. By the mid-1970s, Turkey was convinced that Syria was facilitating Armenian terrorist operations against Turkish diplomats abroad. Given the coolness and mutual suspicions that have characterized their relations, neither Syria nor Turkey was prepared to be sensitive to the other's interests. One reflection of this attitude was Turkey's decision to proceed with plans for a major dam project on the Euphrates River, apparently without adequate consultation with Syria. The Euphrates rises in the mountains of northern Anatolia, and Syria's territory is bisected by the river before it enters Iraq on its way to the Persian Gulf. Upon completion of the project, Turkey demonstrated the way control of the flow of water to downstream users in Syria could be used for political purposes, provoking a minicrisis in already tense relations. Thus the dam became yet another source of tension between the two countries.

Turkey's relations with other Arab countries, including Iraq prior to 1990, have been more positive than those with Syria. In early 1995, trade seemed to be the most important aspect of overall relations. Ankara had hoped that its support of the United States-led coalition in the Persian Gulf War would produce economic rewards. In fact, some Turkish business interests won contracts for construction projects in the Persian Gulf region, albeit not to the extent anticipated. Turkey's regional exports prior to 1990 had gone primarily to Iraq and secondarily to Iran. The loss of the Iraqi market because of Turkish compliance with sanctions initially represented a severe blow to export-dependent businesses and probably contributed to an economic recession in 1991. Beginning in 1992, however, Turkey gradually increased the level of its exports—particularly processed food and manufactured goods—to Kuwait and other Persian Gulf states. Although the prospects for expanding trade with Egypt and Israel appear limited because Turkey and these countries export similar products that compete in international markets, Turkey, nevertheless, has consolidated its political ties to both countries. Since 1992, for example, Israeli and Turkish investors have undertaken several joint-venture development projects in Central Asia. Turkey also imports most of its oil from Middle Eastern countries, particularly Libya.

European Union

Since 1963, when it was accepted as an associate member of the European Community (EC), Turkey has striven for admission as a full member of that body, now called the European Union (EU—see Glossary), the association of fifteen West European nations that comprises the world's wealthiest and most successful trading bloc. The Özal government, which had formulated its economic policies with the goal of meeting certain EC objections to a perceived lack of competitiveness in Turkish industry, formally applied for full membership in 1987. Much to Turkey's disappointment, the decision was deferred until 1993—or later—on grounds that the EC could not consider new members until after the implementation of tighter political integration scheduled for the end of 1992. The unexpected end of the Cold War and the dissolution of the Soviet Union actually delayed integration by one year, primarily to allow time for the EU to adjust to West Germany's absorption of East Germany. The new Demirel government, which strongly supported Özal's goal of joining the EC, was disappointed in 1992 when the EC agreed to consider membership applications from Austria, Finland, Norway, and Sweden without making a decision on Turkey's long-standing application. By then it seemed obvious that the EC was reluctant to act on Turkey's application. In fact, most EC members objected to full Turkish membership for a variety of economic, social, and political reasons.

The principal economic objections to Turkish membership center on the relative underdevelopment of Turkey's economy compared to the economies of EC/EU members and Turkey's high rate of population growth. The latter issue is perceived as a potentially serious problem because of free labor movement among EU members and the fact that Turkey's already large population is expected to surpass that of Germany—the most populous EU member—by 2010. Closely related to the concern about there being too many Turkish workers for too few jobs is the social problem of integrating those workers into European culture. Throughout Western Europe, the early

1990s witnessed a rise in anti-immigrant feeling directed primarily against Muslim workers from North Africa and Turkey. For the most part, EU governments have not developed policies to combat this resurgence of prejudice.

The political obstacles to EU membership concern Turkey's domestic and foreign policies. Because the European body prides itself on being an association of democracies, the 1980 military coup—in a country enjoying associate status—was a severe shock. The harshness of repression under the military regime further disturbed the EC—many EC leaders knew personally the former Turkish leaders whom the military put on trial for treason. The EC responded by freezing relations with Turkey and suspending economic aid. A related body, the Council of Europe, also expelled Turkey from its parliamentary assembly. The restoration of civilian rule gradually helped to improve Turkey's image. In 1985 Germany's prime minister signaled the EC's readiness to resume dialogue with Turkey by accepting an invitation to visit Ankara. The following year, the EC restored economic aid and permitted Turkey to reoccupy its seats in European deliberative councils. Nevertheless, frequent veiled threats by Turkey's senior military officers of future interventions if politicians "misbehaved" did not inspire confidence in Europe that democracy had taken permanent root in Turkey. As late as 1995, some Europeans remained apprehensive about the possibility of another military coup, a concern that was shared by various Turkish politicians.

EU members have also expressed reservations about Turkey's human rights record. Amnesty International and Helsinki Watch, two human rights monitoring organizations supported by the EU, have reported the persistence of practices such as arbitrary arrests, disappearances, extrajudicial killings, torture in prisons, and censorship. The Turkish Human Rights Association, itself subject to harassment and intimidation tactics, has prepared detailed chronologies and lists of human rights abuses, including the destruction of entire villages without due process, and has circulated these reports widely in Europe. The documented reports of human rights abuses, like the coup rumors, sustained questions about Turkey's qualifications to join a collective body of countries that have striven to achieve uniform standards for protecting citizen rights.

In terms of foreign policy, the main obstacle to EU membership remains the unresolved issues between Turkey and EU member Greece. The most serious issue between the two countries is their dispute over the island of Cyprus, which dates back to 1974. At that time, Turkish troops occupied the northeastern part of the island to protect the Turkish minority (20 percent of the population), which felt threatened by the Greek majority's proposals for unification with Greece. Years of negotiations have failed to resolve a stalemate based on the de facto partition of Cyprus into a Turkish Cypriot north and a Greek Cypriot south, a division that continues to be enforced by a Turkish force estimated at 25,000 troops in early 1995 (see Conflict and Diplomacy: Cyprus and Beyond, ch. 1).

Following the November 1983 declaration of independence of the Turkish Republic of Northern Cyprus—a government recognized only by Turkey in early 1995—Greece persuaded fellow EU members that progress on settling the dispute over Cyprus should be a prerequisite to accepting Turkey as a full member. Despite Ankara's position that such an obvious political condition was not appropriate for an economic association, once the EC agreed in 1990 to consider an application for membership from Cyprus, diplomatic efforts aimed at convincing individual EC members to veto the condition became futile. Since 1990 Turkey has supported UN-mediated talks between Greek Cypriot and Turkish Cypriot leaders that are aimed at devising procedures for the island's reunification. As of January 1995, these intermittent discussions had made little progress, and the prospects for a resolution of the Cyprus problem appeared dim.

Equally as serious as the Cyprus issue is Turkey's dispute with Greece over territorial rights and interests in the Aegean Sea. Although both Greece and Turkey are de jure allies in NATO, their conflicting claims brought them to the brink of war in 1986 and 1987. A fundamental source of contention is exploration rights to minerals, primarily oil, beneath the Aegean Sea. International law recognizes the right of a country to explore the mineral wealth on its own continental shelf. Greece and Turkey, however, have been unable to agree on what constitutes the Aegean continental shelf. Turkey defines the Aegean shelf as a natural prolongation of the Anatolian coast, whereas Greece claims that every one of the more than 2,000 of its islands in the Aegean has its own shelf. The issue is complicated further by Greece's claim to the territorial waters surrounding its islands. Turkey rejected Greece's attempts to extend its six-nautical-mile territorial claim around each island to twelve nautical miles on grounds that such a move would enable Greece to control 71 percent, rather than 43 percent, of the Aegean. Thus, it would be impossible for Turkish ships to reach the Mediterranean Sea without crossing Greek waters.

The issue of the right to control the airspace over the Aegean appears similarly intractable. Greece, which was granted control of air and sea operations over the entire Aegean region by various NATO agreements, closed the Aegean air corridors during the 1974 Cyprus crisis and only reopened them early in 1980 as part of the compromise arrangement for Greek reintegration into NATO. Disputes over the median line dividing the Aegean into approximately equal sectors of responsibility remain unresolved. In addition, Turkey refuses to recognize the ten-mile territorial air limit decreed by Greece in 1931; this line extends from the coast of Greece's mainland as well as from its islands. These unresolved issues contribute to the tensions over Cyprus and mineral exploration rights in the Aegean Sea.

Prime Minister Özal recognized the potential of Greece to block Turkish admission to the EC even before his government formally submitted its application. Thus, early in 1987 he attempted to defuse tensions by initiating a meeting with his Greek counterpart in Switzerland—the first meeting between Greek and Turkish heads of government in ten years. Their discussions resolved an immediate crisis over oil drilling in the Aegean and established channels for further diplomatic discussions. In June 1988, Özal accepted an unprecedented invitation to visit Athens, the first state visit by a Turkish leader in thirty-six years. Although Özal's initiatives did much to clear the political atmosphere, leaders in both countries remain unable to overcome their mutual suspicions. Thus, no progress has been achieved in resolving outstanding differences, although both countries are showing more restraint in their rhetoric and actions. Beginning in 1989, dramatic political developments in Eastern Europe and the Middle East caused Turkey and Greece to focus their attention beyond the Aegean Sea and the Mediterranean Sea.

The United States

In early 1995, Turkey's most important international relationship was with the United States. Turkey's association with the United States began in 1947 when the United States Congress designated Turkey, under the provisions of the Truman Doctrine, as the recipient of special economic and military

assistance intended to help it resist threats from the Soviet Union (see Politics and Foreign Relations in the 1960s, ch. 1). A mutual interest in containing Soviet expansion provided the foundation of United States-Turkish relations for the next forty years. In support of overall United States Cold War strategy, Turkey contributed personnel to the UN forces in the Korean War (1950–53), joined NATO in 1952, became a founding member of the Central Treaty Organization (CENTO) collective defense pact established in 1955, and endorsed the principles of the 1957 Eisenhower Doctrine. Throughout the 1950s and 1960s, Turkey generally cooperated with other United States allies in the Middle East (Iran, Israel, and Jordan) to contain the influence of those countries (Egypt, Iraq, and Syria) regarded as Soviet clients.

The general tendency for relationships between nations to experience strain in the wake of domestic and international political changes has proved to be the rule for Turkey and the United States. The most difficult period in their relationship followed Turkey's invasion of northern Cyprus in 1974. In response to the military intervention, the United States halted arms supplies to Turkey. Ankara retaliated by suspending

United States military operations at all Turkish installations that were not clearly connected with NATO missions. The Cyprus issue affected United States-Turkish relations for several years. Even after the United States Congress lifted the arms embargo in 1978, two years passed before bilateral defense cooperation and military assistance were restored to their 1974 level.

During the 1980s, relations between Turkey and the United States gradually recovered the closeness of earlier years. Although Ankara resented continued attempts by the United States Congress to restrict military assistance to Turkey because of Cyprus and to introduce congressional resolutions condemning the 1915–16 massacre of Armenians, the Özal government generally perceived the administrations of President Ronald Reagan and President George H.W. Bush as sympathetic to Turkish interests. For example, Washington demonstrated its support of Özal's market-oriented economic policies and efforts to open the Turkish economy to international trade by pushing for acceptance of an International Monetary Fund (IMF—see Glossary) program to provide economic assistance to Turkey. Furthermore, the United States, unlike European countries, did not persistently and publicly criticize Turkey over allegations of human rights violations. Also, the United States did not pressure Özal on the Kurdish problem, another issue that seemed to preoccupy the Europeans. By 1989 the United States had recovered a generally positive image among the Turkish political elite.

The end of the Cold War forced Turkish leaders to reassess their country's international position. The disappearance of the Soviet threat and the perception of being excluded from Europe have created a sense of vulnerability with respect to Turkey's position in the fast-changing global political environment. Özal believed Turkey's future security depended on the continuation of a strong relationship with the United States. For that reason, he supported the United States position during the Persian Gulf War, although Turkey's economic ties to Iraq were extensive and their disruption hurt the country. After the war, he continued to support major United States initiatives in the region, including the creation of a no-fly zone over northern Iraq, the Arab-Israeli peace process, and expanded ties with the Central Asian members of the CIS. Özal's pro-United States policy was not accepted by all Turks. United States use of Turkish military installations during the bombing of Iraq in 1991 led to antiwar demonstrations in several cities, and sporadic attacks on United States facilities continued in 1992 and 1993. Nevertheless, among Turkey's political elite a consensus had emerged by January 1995 that Turkey's security depended on remaining a strategic ally of the United States. For that reason, both the Demirel and Çiller governments undertook efforts to cultivate relations with the administrations of presidents George H.W. Bush and William J. Clinton.

*　　*　　*

George S. Harris analyzes Turkey's governmental framework, political dynamics, and foreign policy from both historical and contemporary perspectives in *Turkey: Coping with Crisis*. Frank Tachau describes the tension among authoritarianism, democracy, and economic development in *Turkey: The Politics of Authority, Democracy, and Development*. Insight into the breakdown of Turkish democracy and the framing of a new constitution is provided in Clement H. Dodd's *The Crisis of Turkish Democracy* and in Lucille W. Pevsner's *Turkey's Political Crisis*.

Religion and religious movements in contemporary Turkey are examined in *Religion and Social Change in Modern Turkey*, by Serif A. Mardin, and in a volume edited by Richard Tapper, *Islam in Modern Turkey: Religion, Politics, and Literature in a Secular State*. Information on patterns of political participation through specialized associations can be obtained from Robert Bianchi's detailed study, *Interest Groups and Political Development in Turkey*. David Barchard examines aspects of Turkey's foreign policy in *Turkey and the West*. The complicated relationship between Turkey and Greece and it simplications for the United States are examined in Theodore A. Couloumbis's *The United States, Greece, and Turkey* and Monteagle Stearns's *Entangled Allies: United States Policy Toward Greece, Turkey, and Cyprus*. (For further information and complete citations, see Bibliography.)

Chapter 5. National Security

The Rumeli Hisar or castle guards the Bosporus and Istanbul.

THE ARMED FORCES have figured prominently in Turkish national life for centuries. Under Ottoman rule, the government and the military establishment were virtually indistinguishable. After World War I, the army commander, Mustafa Kemal, later called Atatürk (meaning Father Turk), evicted the occupying forces of the victorious Allies from Anatolia and formulated the principles underlying the modern Turkish state. On three occasions since then, the military leadership has intervened to protect the nation's democratic framework. The third interlude of military rule, which lasted from 1980 to 1983, was welcomed by many Turkish citizens because it ended the terrorism of the 1970s. The military's actions, however, also limited the democratic process.

A member of the North Atlantic Treaty Organization (NATO) since 1952, Turkey long had the vital mission of anchoring the alliance's southern flank against the military power of the Warsaw Pact and the Soviet Union. Turkish armed forces defended the Bosporus and Dardanelles straits and Turkey's northeastern border with the Soviet Union in the Transcaucasus region. Vessels of the Soviet Union's Black Sea fleet had to transit the Turkish-controlled straits to enter the Mediterranean.

The disintegration of the Soviet Union in 1991 fundamentally changed Turkey's security environment. Fear of Soviet aggression no longer looms over the nation, yet Turkey remains at the center of a region seething with political and economic discord. The stability of Turkey's borders is threatened by turbulence among the newly independent republics of the Caucasus and by hostile states in the Middle East. Turkey's concern over the fortunes of the Turkic states of Central Asia could bring it into conflict with Russia or Iran. Turkey is an advocate of the interests of Muslim peoples in the Balkans, but its modest military role as part of the United Nations (UN) Protection Force in Bosnia has generated controversy because of memories of the Ottoman Empire's long involvement there.

The Turkish government has taken sweeping measures to restructure and modernize the armed forces to deal with the new conditions, in which Soviet military might has been superseded by a multiplicity of threats near Turkey's eastern and southern borders. The new strategy emphasizes the ability to perform a variety of missions, move forces rapidly from one region to another, and mount firepower sufficient to meet any foreseeable threat. Undergoing the most radical reorganization have been the land forces, which were reduced from about 525,000 troops in 1990 to about 393,000 in 1994. For added flexibility, the army has adopted a brigade structure in place of the previous divisional pattern. The army's stocks of tanks and armored vehicles have been enlarged and improved; self-propelled howitzers and multiple rocket launchers also have been added. Troop-carrying helicopters will ensure greater mobility.

An expanded Turkish defense industry has played a major role in the modernization of the armed forces. Under joint-venture programs with United States manufacturers, combat aircraft, armored vehicles, rocket systems, and tank upgrades have been supplied. Submarines and other vessels have been produced in cooperation with the German shipbuilding industry. The centerpiece of the modernization effort has been the United States-Turkey F–16 coproduction project, which is expected to add 240 high-performance fighter aircraft to the Turkish inventory during the 1990s.

Turkey and the United States developed many defense links and common goals after United States military and economic assistance began in 1947 in response to the threat of Soviet expansion. For instance, Turkey has permitted the United States to use forward bases and intelligence installations on Turkish territory. During the Cold War, these installations were of vital importance in monitoring military activity and weapons testing by the Soviet Union. Following the end of the Persian Gulf War in 1991, Turkish bases enabled the United States and coalition forces to conduct Operation Provide Comfort, an effort to supply humanitarian relief to Kurds in northern Iraq and enforce a "no-fly zone" in the area against Iraqi aircraft.

Overshadowing all external threats to Turkish security is the Kurdish insurgency, which began in 1984 in the southeastern region of the country. This movement, which involves only a small minority of Turkey's Kurdish population, is led by the extremist Kurdistan Workers' Party (Partiya Karkere Kurdistan—PKK). The conflict became particularly violent beginning in 1992. Some 4,000 Kurds and government security personnel were killed in 1993 alone, many of them noncombatants. The activities of the PKK complicate Turkey's relations with Syria, Iraq, and Iran, where the PKK insurgents have maintained supply and training bases. By early 1995, the Turkish government

306

had deployed nearly 200,000 soldiers and police to the region, and had adopted a policy of forcibly evacuating and often burning Kurdish villages believed to be aiding the insurgents. These measures apparently dampened the insurgency, but at the cost of alienating large numbers of Kurds not involved in the separatist movement.

Historical Role of the Armed Forces

The professional armed forces of Turkey trace their origins back more than five centuries, to a permanent body of men recruited to form the nucleus of the much larger armies mobilized to conduct annual campaigns against selected objectives. A unique feature of the Ottoman military organization was the janissary army, whose members were conscripted as youths from among the empire's non-Muslim subjects in the Balkans, converted to Islam, and given military training. Gradually acquiring high status, prominence, and privilege, the janissaries ultimately constituted a reactionary palace guard resistant to reforms and of little military value to the reigning sultan.

Military conquest permitted the spread of the Ottoman Empire through the Middle East, North Africa, the Balkans, and most of Eastern Europe. The sequence of Ottoman victories was finally halted and a gradual military eclipse ensued after the failure of the siege of Vienna in 1683 (see Köprülü Era, ch. 1). Vast territories were relinquished as a result of a century of setbacks in battles with the European powers.

The need to modernize a military system engaged in a losing struggle to maintain Ottoman control over the Mediterranean littoral and the Middle East was recognized by the first of the reforming sultans, Selim III (r. 1789–1807). He introduced French instructors to train the soldiers of a new volunteer army organized along the lines of contemporary European armed forces. However, his efforts were successfully resisted by the janissaries, who concluded that reform foreshadowed an end to their traditional privileges. Rising up in 1807, the janissaries precipitated the sultan's abdication and the dismantling of the new army. Mahmud II (r. 1808–39) eventually became strong enough to challenge the power of the traditional military caste. He reinstituted the reformed army and, in 1826, crushed the janissaries with a massive artillery barrage aimed at their barracks.

The internal decay of the Ottoman Empire during the late nineteenth century was accompanied by growing disaffection and turmoil among younger military officers and civil servants. Coming together as the Committee of Union and Progress (better known as the Young Turks), and operating as secret cells within military units, the dissidents instigated a series of upheavals and mutinies within the military that culminated in the revolution of 1908 and the fall of Sultan Abdül Hamid II (see The Young Turks, ch. 1). Divided between nationalist and liberal factions, the Young Turk officers could not prevent foreign powers from seizing portions of the empire's Balkan holdings. After the empire's defeat at the hands of Bulgaria, Greece, Italy, and Serbia in the Balkan Wars of 1912–13, a military dictatorship emerged, under the nominal control of the sultan. Motivated by their fear of Russia, the nationalist officers made the fateful error of joining the Central Powers in World War I. Initially, the Turkish army was successful, stubbornly resisting the landing of British and Australian forces at Gallipoli in 1915 and forcing their withdrawal the following year. But operations against Russia went badly, and tsarist forces advanced onto Turkish soil. In Mesopotamia and Palestine, British and Arab units also prevailed against the Turks (see World War I, ch. 1).

A new contingent of Young Turks led by the war hero Atatürk resisted the postwar occupation of most of Turkey by Greek, French, Italian, and British forces. A series of defeats were administered to the Greek troops, resulting in their withdrawal in 1922. The Turks subsequently forced the occupying Allies to accede to a peace treaty recognizing the present borders of Turkey and enabling the proclamation in 1923 of the Republic of Turkey, with Atatürk as its president (see War of Independence, ch. 1).

Atatürk envisioned Turkey as a modern, secular democracy in which the army would distance itself from the civil functions of government. The army nevertheless preserved the right to intervene as the ultimate guardian of the state if the political system became deadlocked or Atatürk's reforms were endangered. Although active-duty officers were forbidden to engage in politics, the interests of the military did not go unrepresented. Until 1950 many influential leadership posts and at least 20 percent of the seats in the Grand National Assembly were held by individuals with military backgrounds. For nearly thirty years, the nation was governed by two military heroes of the War of Independence—first Atatürk and then, after his death in 1938, Ismet Inönü—and a single political party in which retired senior officers were heavily represented.

The Armed Forces and Society

The armed forces traditionally have enjoyed a distinguished position in Turkish national life. Soldiers receive widespread respect as symbols of Turkish national identity and as legatees of the country's long martial traditions. A leading Turkish journalist has written that "the army is always praised, never criticized, and, in an emergency, it is seen as the nation's savior." Over the centuries, the army has been perceived as a civilizing and humanizing factor in society. In the modern era, it is considered the embodiment of the enlightened, progressive forces that inspired the revolution of 1908 against Ottoman rule and later prevented the nation's dismemberment by driving out the occupying armies after World War I. The army also has received credit for rescuing the nation from the turmoil and violence of the late 1970s.

Turks recognize that a career in the armed forces provides the opportunity for a quality education at no cost, followed by a lifetime of secure and respected employment. Although some members of the middle and upper classes hold the view that the specialized education and isolated life of the officer produce individuals inflexibly committed to a set of values remote from the real world, such criticism is rarely expressed openly. In any event, a career in the armed forces has become less of a lifetime commitment than in the past. Because of the superior technical education it provides, military service is often seen as an avenue to a successful civilian career.

Because of the large number of applicants for places in the military high schools and service academies, the standards for officer candidates remain high. In the course of their military education, students learn the values of Kemalism (the precepts of Atatürk) and are taught to take pride in the role of the military in protecting the democratic state against the extremes of left and right and the appeal of radical Islamism. Officers tend to develop an outlook that is nationalistic and hierarchical. In the early 1960s, a minority of junior officers had left-wing sympathies, but strict background checks, together with the emphasis on cohesiveness and discipline, are believed subsequently to have produced an officer corps immune to radicalism. The military maintains intense vigilance against the infiltration of leftist thought, as well as against Islamic activism (also seen as fundamentalism).

The officer corps enjoys certain privileges, but the military makes efforts to keep these from becoming conspicuous enough to provoke civilian criticism. Officers consider clubs, attractive housing, vacation resorts, and sports facilities as necessary to compensate for the modest pay and other disadvantages of career military service. Officers are also expected to meet high standards of personal probity.

Most individuals entering the service academies are drawn from the lower-middle and middle classes. The results of one survey showed that about 40 percent of army and air force cadets and 55 percent of naval cadets were sons of military service members, gendarmes, or civil servants, in particular teachers. This suggests, one analyst has noted, a perpetuation of the sense of kinship with the spirit of Atatürk and the revolution of 1908. Less than 10 percent of those entering the army and air force academies in the early1980s were from rural families; naval cadets with an agricultural background were almost unknown. Geographically, central Anatolia and areas adjacent to the Aegean Sea and the Sea of Marmara were overrepresented, whereas southeastern Turkey was most underrepresented, supplying only 1 to 2 percent of cadets (see fig. 1). Resistance to assimilation by Kurdish- and Arabic-speaking minorities in the southeast and strict political screening may account for the limited recruitment from this area to the officer corps.

In contrast to officer candidates, enlisted personnel, especially conscripts, are preponderantly from peasant households. At least 80 to 85 percent are ethnically Turkish, and the vast majority are Sunni (see Glossary) Muslims. Once rare, efforts to evade the draft or obtain unjustified deferments apparently are becoming more common (see Conditions of Service, this ch.). Nevertheless, for a young soldier facing doubtful employment prospects, active duty means a nutritious diet, access to medical care, and perhaps an opportunity to further one's education and acquire a useful job skill. Military service offers an interlude from the unvarying pace of village life and is a source of pride, linking one to the warrior tradition of Turkish society.

Politics and the Military

Since the founding of the Turkish Republic in 1923, six of the nation's nine presidents have had armed forces backgrounds. Until 1950 Atatürk and his successor and closest military associate, Inönü, ruled what was an essentially a one-party political system with a strong martial flavor. Atatürk encouraged the military to abjure politics, but the armed forces intervened on three occasions—in 1960, 1971, and 1980. Although they did so under different circumstances in each case, their justification was their sworn duty to uphold national unity and the democratic order.

The military regime of 1980–83 was the longest lasting, and represented the armed forces' most serious effort to transform traditional political behavior. The changes the regime introduced were intended to break what had become a cycle of decennial military interventions. The constitution introduced by the coup leaders in 1982, which forbade political activism in the universities and trade unions, abolished pre-existing parties, and banned political activity by pre-1980 party leaders, was the centerpiece of the military's efforts to curtail the factionalism and polarization that had stalemated the previous civilian government (see Political Developments since the 1980 Coup, ch. 4).

The leader of the 1980–83 junta, General Kenan Evren, remained as president after the return of civilian government, but the generals disavowed any desire for a continuing political role for the military. The public failed to respond to Evren's appeal to vote for the party favored by the generals, the Nationalist Democracy Party (Milliyetçi Demokrasi Partisi—MDP). A new grouping of retired officers and other leading citizens, the MDP had the same interests and goals as the military regime. Although disappointed by the party's lack of success, military leaders established good working relations with the victorious Motherland Party (Anavatan Partisi—ANAP) of Turgut Özal. By promptly relinquishing control over public life, the military preserved its reputation as the ultimate protector of Turkish democratic institutions.

On two occasions, Özal prevailed when differences arose with the armed forces. In 1987, as prime minister, he overrode the military's choice of an army commander as the new chief of the General Staff, reportedly out of dissatisfaction with the conduct of the campaign against the Kurdish insurgency. In 1990, after Özal became president, the chief of staff resigned as a result of undisclosed disagreements assumed to have sprung from Özal's activist stance against Iraq's takeover of Kuwait but did not make a public issue of his difference with Özal.

Imbued with the concept that its mission is to safeguard Atatürk's heritage, the military establishment has often shown its impatience with political bickering and compromises that appear to slight Kemalist objectives. Civilian politicians indifferent to those goals or embracing other ideologies are viewed with suspicion or even as subversive. Much of the military education system is concerned with instilling the Kemalist spirit through study of the 1919–22 War of Independence, the concept of patriotism as embodied by Atatürk, and the values and principles of Kemalism, particularly the "Six Arrows" of secularism, republicanism, populism, etatism (see Glossary), reformism, and nationalism, as guidance for the future of the Turkish state.

A democratic system is fully accepted as the best form of government by the professional military. However, young career officers are indoctrinated with the view that the proper working of democracy demands discipline, organization, constructiveness, unity of purpose, and rejection of self-interest. Thus, the military has little tolerance of politicians whom it perceives as putting personal ambition before the good of the state or of political parties or groups acting in ways it considers to be dictated by a struggle for power and economic advantage.

From a career point of view, it is said to be unwise for an officer to express opinions that can be construed as liberal or otherwise unorthodox. The armed forces have shown particular sensitivity to the threat of radical Islamism to military order. In 1991 the general staff disclosed that in the preceding decade 357 officers and seventy-one noncommissioned officers (NCOs) had been dismissed on charges of involvement in extreme leftist or separatist (presumably Kurdish) activities. During the same period, thirty-seven officers and 188 NCOs were discharged for involvement in extreme rightist or Islamist activities.

External Security Concerns

Throughout the Cold War, Turkey's security situation was shaped by the country's vulnerability to Soviet military strength. It was obliged to contend with the threat of twenty divisions of Soviet land forces close to the common border of more than 500 kilometers in the Transcaucasus region of northern Turkey. Turkey's heavily populated areas were within easy range of Soviet fighter aircraft and bombers; Soviet naval vessels and submarines were well positioned to dominate the Black Sea.

Turkish suspicion of Soviet motives had historical roots in the efforts of imperial Russia to extend its influence beyond the Black Sea to the eastern Mediterranean and the Middle

Soldiers, armored unit, and mobile antiaircraft passing in review,
Republic Day parade (October 29)
Courtesy Embassy of Turkey, Washington

East. The Soviet naval presence in the Mediterranean was linked tactically and logistically to the Soviet Black Sea fleet. Transit of the Turkish-controlled Bosporus was essential to the projection of Soviet naval power in the Mediterranean.

For Turkey, perhaps the most important consequence of the 1991 breakup of the Soviet Union was that it no longer shares a border with Russia and that the risk of conflict with the Russians has greatly receded. The appearance of several newly independent nations at Turkey's borders, however, has resulted in a less settled security environment because Turkey now feels a greater potential threat from other powers in the area such as Greece, Syria, and Iraq.

Although buffered by other new nations in the Black Sea and Caucasus regions, Russia remains a compelling presence in the minds of Turkish military planners. With Moscow increasingly willing to intervene in conflicts near Turkey's borders, concern has grown that a resurgent Russian nationalism might seek pretexts to gain control of former republics of the Soviet Union. Russia has repositioned to its southern flank some of the ground weapons withdrawn from Central Europe under the terms of the Conventional Forces in Europe (CFE) Treaty of 1990. Although the treaty placed a ceiling on the number of tanks, armored vehicles, and artillery pieces that could be redeployed to the North Caucasus Military District, the Russians have exceeded this limit, citing concerns over instability in their border regions.

Close to Turkey's northeastern border, three former republics of the Soviet Union—Georgia, Armenia, and Azerbaijan—are beset by dissidence and fighting. Turkey has historical, cultural, religious, and linguistic ties with Azerbaijan and supported Azerbaijan in its war with Armenia. From the Turkish perspective, Armenia committed aggression against Azerbaijan by seizing the Nagorno-Karabakh region, which is inhabited mostly by ethnic Armenians. Russia issued veiled warnings against Turkish involvement in the Armenian situation, which could pit Turkey against Russia. Turkey has ruled out the use of force, wary of a wider conflict between Christians and Muslims in the region.

Middle Eastern Conflicts

Despite its location, Turkey generally has been successful in pursuing a policy of noninterference and noninvolvement in Middle Eastern conflicts. For instance, Turkey refrained from supporting either belligerent in the Iran-Iraq War of 1980–88. Although both sides violated Turkish airspace, Turkey took no defensive action and sought to mediate an end to hostilities.

In the first days after Iraq's occupation of Kuwait in August 1990, the Turkish government tried to preserve its traditional neutral stance in what it perceived as an inter-Arab dispute. Ankara was quickly obliged to depart from this position, however, in light of the strong reaction in the UN against the invasion. Turkey responded to the UN Security Council's call for an embargo against Iraq by closing the Kirkuk-Yurmurtalik oil pipeline linking the two countries and halting trade with Iraq. These measures were crucial to the economic campaign against Saddam Husayn but imposed severe economic hardship on Turkey. The direct cost to its balance of payments was estimated at US$2 billion to US$2.5 billion annually. This burden was eased somewhat by aid from the United States and the Persian Gulf countries. Firm opposition in parliament and the cabinet prevented President Özal from offering a Turkish contingent for the coalition forces in the Persian Gulf. However, some 150,000 Turkish troops were deployed near the southeastern border with Iraq, tying down eight or nine Iraqi divisions. Turkey requested and received a defensive deployment of NATO air forces in the area to discourage attack by the Iraqi air force, which could easily outmatch the fighter aircraft and antiaircraft defenses that Turkey could muster. A total of forty German, Italian, and Belgian aircraft were dispatched to Turkey. In addition, United States and Dutch Patriot missile batteries were deployed against a possible Iraqi missile attack.

When the coalition air strikes on Iraq were launched in January 1991, ninety-six United States aircraft and several British bombers operated from the United States air base at Incirlik, refueling at Batman, a base about 150 kilometers from the Iraqi border. Sorties continued from Incirlik until the ceasefire on February 28, 1991, without provoking retaliation from Saddam Husayn.

The major consequence of the Persian Gulf War from the standpoint of Turkish security was the uprising of the Kurds in northern Iraq and the exodus of Kurds toward Turkish territory to escape Saddam Husayn's brutal suppression of the rebellion. Turkey was decidedly reluctant to accept the Kurds as refugees, considering them a potential destabilizing factor in its struggle with domestic Kurdish dissidents. As an alternative, Turkey supported the UN-approved Operation Provide Comfort, which distributed relief and set up a safe haven in northern Iraq whose security was guaranteed by a coalition force of 2,000 soldiers from five countries. Incirlik served as the base for a rapid deployment of air forces to enforce a no-fly zone in the region.

The Iraqi government's loss of control over Iraqi Kurdistan and elections in the area in May 1992 produced what was in effect an autonomous Kurdish government. Although Turkey permitted the lifeline to the Iraqi Kurdish enclave to originate on its territory, the Turks feared what they saw as the emerging outlines of an independent Kurdish state in Iraq. For this reason, Turkey resisted any international action that could lead to Iraq's dismemberment and thus endanger the regional status quo.

Syria

Several disputes make relations between Syria and Turkey uneasy. However, Syria's limited military potential and the alignment of Syrian forces on the Israeli front preclude any immediate threat along the 900-kilometer border between Turkey and Syria.

Syria has never abandoned its claim to the Turkish province of Hatay, which includes the city of Iskenderun. France, the mandatory power over Syria from 1920 to 1941, ceded the area to Turkey in 1939 after a disputed plebiscite, in violation of its League of Nations mandate.

Tensions with Syria are compounded by Turkey's control over distribution of the waters of the Euphrates River. Turkey's huge Southeast Anatolian Project, with its dams and hydroelectric plants, threatens to deplete Syria's water resources. In addition, Syria has a history of permitting hostile political movements—Armenian, Marxist, and Kurdish—to conduct anti-Turkish operations from Syrian-controlled territory in Lebanon's Bekaa Valley. To a considerable degree, the issues of access to water and Syria's support for the Kurdish insurgency are linked. To the extent that Turkey attempts to accommodate Syria on water sharing, Syria limits its backing of the Kurds. In December 1993, the Syrian government took into custody the Kurdish rebel leader, Abdullah Öcalan, in what was seen as an attempt to strengthen Syria's hand in water negotiations.

Iran

Frictions with the Tehran government stem largely from

competing philosophies—the secularism at the root of the Turkish system and the Shia (see Glossary) orientation of Iran. The Turkish government has refrained from accusing Iran of direct responsibility for incidents of Islamist terrorism. However, the Turkish minister of interior declared in 1993 that the perpetrators of a series of murders of well-known secularist figures had been trained in Iran and helped by the staff of the Iranian Cultural Center in Ankara. Turkey considers such attacks a threat to national security because the government and laws of the modern Turkish state are so closely identified with its secular tradition.

Another source of potential tension is Turkey's support of Azerbaijan in its conflict with Armenia. Tehran fears that a nationalistic Azerbaijan friendly to Turkey could encourage unrest in northern Iran, which has a considerable Azerbaijani population. Turkey estimates that about 800 Kurdish guerrillas are based in Iranian territory. Tehran has denied supporting them, and in December 1993 the two countries announced that an agreement had been reached to prevent the guerrillas from using Iran as a sanctuary.

The Balkans

As the principal successor state to the Ottoman Empire, which controlled the Balkans for centuries until its defeat in the Balkan Wars of 1912–13, Turkey retains a keen interest in the fate of the Muslims of Bosnia and Herzegovina, the former Yugoslav Republic of Macedonia (FYROM—the name under which independent Macedonia was recognized by the United Nations in 1993), and Albania. Turkey opposed the dissolution of Yugoslavia, fearing the resulting instability could create broader regional conflict. With the outbreak of war in Bosnia in 1992 and Serbian human rights violations, Turkey advocated Western military measures to contain the Serbs. It pressed for an end to the UN arms embargo to enable Bosnian Muslims to defend themselves more effectively against Serbian attack. Turkey contributed ships to the NATO naval force blockading Serbia and Montenegro and dispatched a squadron of eighteen F-16 aircraft to Italy to help enforce the no-fly zone over Bosnia. Unilateral Turkish military aid to Bosnia was impractical because of the interposition of Greek and Bulgarian territory in between. A Turkish offer of troops to the UN Protection Force in Bosnia was at first rejected by the UN Security Council because of Ankara's strong sympathies for the Bosnian Muslims and memories of the Ottoman role in the Balkans. In April 1994, however, after experiencing difficulties in obtaining force commitments, the UN accepted a Turkish deployment of about 1,500 soldiers in spite of objections by the Bosnian Serbs, Serbia, Greece, and Bulgaria.

Albania also is receiving attention from Turkey. Once Albania ended its long isolation as a Stalinist state, Turkey proposed military cooperation accords that included officer training. The possibility of Serbian action against FYROM, whose independence Turkey recognized, and against Kosovo, a Serbian province largely populated by Albanians, is a concern of both Albania and Turkey. It seems unlikely, however, that Turkish military help will be forthcoming if the conflict in former Yugoslavia widens to Kosovo and FYROM.

Mutual distrust has long characterized Turkey's relations with Bulgaria, which, like Greece, has a short but strategically significant border with Turkish Thrace, the European region of Turkey. A major cause of friction was the Balkanization program instituted by the communist government of Bulgaria, which caused a mass migration of Bulgarian Turks to Turkey in the spring of 1989. After the communists fell in late 1989, Turkey moved to improve its security ties to Bulgaria's new government. A series of agreements were reached on formal notification of military movements, exchanges of military visits, and the establishment of a military security zone extending sixty to eighty kilometers on each side of the common border. Talks were also held in 1993 on cooperating in the production of military equipment, and the two countries conducted a joint military exercise with Romania.

Greece and Cyprus

In their first foreign combat operations since the Korean War, Turkish troops intervened in Cyprus in 1974 with the professed aim of protecting the Turkish minority population after a Greek-inspired coup brought a threat of union of the island with Greece. Against determined resistance by the lightly armed Greek Cypriot National Guard, the Turkish troops occupied the northern third of the island. The Turkish intervention force, which consisted of about 40,000 soldiers and 200 tanks, subsequently was reduced to a garrison of 30,000 troops. It greatly outnumbers the contingent of Greek national forces on the island, which is supplemented by the Greek Cypriot

National Guard. Air reinforcement of the Turkish troops can be effected, if necessary, within hours.

Ankara does not consider Cyprus one of its most pressing security issues because of Turkey's military superiority over Greece and the more serious strategic problems posed in the east. Nevertheless, the unresolved dispute over Cyprus complicates Turkish participation in NATO and remains an obstacle to NATO's effectiveness in the region. In addition, the question of the rights of 120,000 Muslims of Turkish ancestry in Grecian Thrace arouses Turkish sympathies, contributing to long-standing distrust between Greece and Turkey.

Other differences between the two NATO members contribute to contention. Greece, basing its claim on the Convention on the Law of the Sea passed by the UN in November 1994, which extends territorial waters from six to twelve nautical miles, seeks to claim this limit around each of the more than 2,000 Greek islands in the Aegean Sea. Such a claim, if implemented, would give Greece about 70 percent of the Aegean Sea. Greece also claims a ten-nautical-mile airspace around each island. Turkish military aircraft and ships do not respect these claims. In addition, Turkey claims an Exclusive Economic Zone that is disputed by Greece.

Turkey maintains the Aegean Army, a force separate from its NATO-committed troops, ostensibly to defend the southwestern coastal areas. The force is a response to Greece's militarization of its islands close to the Turkish coast, which Turkey asserts violates the 1923 Treaty of Lausanne that set Turkey's present borders. The Aegean Army is considered a largely symbolic force; most of the troops assigned to it are kept in training status.

Turkey's Participation in NATO

Turkey's decision to seek Western assistance after being confronted by Soviet territorial demands at the conclusion of World War II and its subsequent participation in NATO's collective defense system have been the principal factors influencing the country's modern military evolution. In 1950 Turkey demonstrated its gratitude for the military aid received from the United States when it sent a brigade of 4,500 troops to serve under the UN command in Korea. The brigade became known for its valor on the battlefield after suffering proportionately the highest casualty rates of any UN element engaged in the fighting.

Turkey's admission to NATO, effective in February 1952, was preceded by extensive study and debate of the strategy of extending the alliance's southern flank to include the eastern Mediterranean. Changes were needed in the wording of the treaty to expand its territorial reach to include Turkey. The admission of Turkey gave NATO a much longer land frontier with the Warsaw Pact (see Glossary), as well as a treaty interest in Turkey's Black Sea coast and the straits through which the Soviet Union had access to the Mediterranean. At the same time, Turkey brought to the alliance its second largest body of military manpower after that of the United States, in addition to access to sites for forward deployment and intelligence gathering.

Under the provisions of the alliance, most of the Turkish armed forces are committed to NATO command in the event of hostilities. Turkish land, sea, and air units then come under the Commander in Chief Allied Forces Southern Europe (AFSOUTH), with headquarters in Naples. The largest of NATO's four military regions, AFSOUTH encompasses Italy, Greece, Turkey, the Black Sea, and the Mediterranean Sea (including the Adriatic Sea, the Aegean Sea, the Ionian Sea, and the Tyrrhenian Sea). AFSOUTH develops joint contingency plans and conducts training exercises of assigned units.

One of the five principal subordinate commands under AFSOUTH, the Allied Land Forces Southeastern Europe (LANDSOUTHEAST) is headquartered at Izmir under a Turkish lieutenant general, with a United States general officer as deputy. About 90 percent of Turkish land forces are committed to this command. The two other commands with Turkish forces assigned to them are Allied Air Forces Southern Europe (AIRSOUTH), under a United States general officer, and Allied Naval Forces Southern Europe (NAVSOUTH), under command of an Italian vice admiral. Both commands have headquarters in the Naples area. Still under dispute is the matter of establishing LANDSOUTHCENT in Larissa, Greece. Initially, Turkey agreed and Greece objected, but in early 1995 Turkey objected unless a Turkish general were to command the center.

Important air, naval, and intelligence-gathering facilities are made available on Turkish soil to United States combat aircraft and to units of the United States Sixth Fleet committed to NATO (see Military Cooperation with the United States, this ch.). A detachment of NATO's Airborne Early Warning Force was installed at the Konya Air Base in southwestern Turkey in 1983, using NATO-owned Airborne Warning and Control System (AWACS) aircraft to provide low-level radar coverage and regional air and sea surveillance.

In the mid-1990s, Turkey allocated a mechanized infantry division consisting of one mechanized brigade and one armored brigade, as well as one combat engineering company, to the Allied Command Europe Rapid Reaction Force formed as part of NATO's restructuring. One commando brigade was earmarked for the southern multinational division, along with brigades from Italy and Greece. These forces remain under national command at their home bases until released to NATO.

Despite rapid changes in the European security environment that have replaced the NATO-Warsaw Pact confrontation with a less definable set of missions for the alliance, Turkey remains a strong partisan of the NATO linkage. Turkish participation gives the country a voice in major strategic decisions by Western democracies and a framework for multilateral cooperation in matters critical to its own security. Nevertheless, with NATO strategy based on the management of multidimensional threats rather than deterrence of the now-defunct Soviet Union, and with the admission of former members of the Warsaw Pact into a partnership relation with NATO, the importance of Turkey to European security has become less obvious. From a Turkish perspective, the protection of Turkey's eastern borders demands a continued high level of NATO involvement. In the shifting European security order, however, Turkey's geostrategic position could become a liability, potentially exposing the alliance to military action in an area where its commitments are ill defined.

Armed Forces

Composed of elements of regular cadre and conscripts, the armed forces in 1994 had an active-duty strength estimated by *The Military Balance, 1994–1995* at 503,800 officers and enlisted personnel. Of this total, some 93,600 were regulars in career assignments; the remaining 410,200 were draftees. The staffing level already had been reduced by 6 percent from that in 1990 as a consequence of forces reorganization.

Article 117 of the constitution stipulates that the president of the republic is the commander in chief of the armed forces. Responsibility for ensuring security and military preparedness is delegated to the prime minister and the Council of Ministers (the cabinet), who are appointed by the president but are subject to a legislative vote of confidence. Article 118 of the constitution prescribes that the National Security Council (NSC—see Glossary) shall submit its views to the Council of Ministers on pending decisions and shall coordinate the formulation, establishment, and implementation of the state's national security policy. A joint body of the chief civilian and military officials concerned with national defense and internal security, the NSC meets twice monthly. Its meetings are chaired by the president or, in his or her absence, by the prime minister (see fig. 14).

In the view of one Turkish observer, the NSC has not been particularly successful as a forum for the armed forces and the government to debate and agree on security policies. At the meetings, the military speaks with a single voice, having worked out differences beforehand. Such unanimity is not conducive to an open dialogue, yet the military is disappointed when it fails to elicit concrete responses from the civilian leadership. Civilians sometimes have found the military insensitive to the government's problems in dealing with the bureaucracy, parliament, and the public when facing difficult decisions.

The constitution designates the chief of the General Staff as the commander of the armed forces. In wartime that officer also exercises the duties of commander in chief on behalf of the president. The chief of the General Staff is appointed by the president upon nomination by the Council of Ministers and is responsible to the prime minister in the exercise of his duties. In early 1995, the chief of the General Staff was General Ismail Hakki Karadayi, who was appointed in August 1994. The extensive authority of the Turkish chief of the General Staff contrasts strikingly with that of his counterparts in most NATO countries. He holds one of the highest positions in the government after the prime minister and is chosen strictly on the basis of seniority. As of 1994, the chief of the General Staff had always been an army officer, although an air force or naval officer might also be selected.

By law the chief of the General Staff determines the principles and policies of major programs concerned with operations, training, intelligence, and logistics. His views must be sought with respect to the military implications of proposed international treaties. He has the final say in the allocation of the military budget among programs and service branches.

The General Staff, a prestigious body that implements the decisions and guidance of the chief of the General Staff, in effect constitutes a joint headquarters with authority over the commanders of the service branches. It thus differs materially from the United States Joint Chiefs of Staff, who act as the immediate military staff of the secretary of defense, subject to the latter's authority and direction, and whose chair functions as presiding officer and spokesperson for the service commanders. The Turkish General Staff headquarters is administered by the deputy chief of the General Staff, who is responsible for preparing directives representing orders emanating from the General Staff, and for assuring their proper implementation.

The General Staff organization follows the same pattern as the United States system in most respects. Its departments are J-1 (personnel, including appointments and promotions), J-2 (internal and foreign intelligence), J-3 (operations, training, organization, war planning, and exercises), J-4 (logistics), J-5 (strategic-military policies, threat planning, targeting, budget allocations, and military agreements), J-6 (communications and electronics), and J-7 (studies of military history and strategy). The Turkish representative to NATO and the Turkish military representative to the Supreme Headquarters Allied Powers Europe (SHAPE) are both attached to the office of the deputy chief of the General Staff.

A separate body, the Supreme Military Council, consists of eighteen members, including the prime minister as chair, the chief of the General Staff as vice chair, the minister of national defense, the three service commanders, and other commanders of four-star rank. All promotions and other appointments to higher military positions are decided in this council, as are many internal policy matters affecting the military services. In practice, the chief of the General Staff initiates the appointments of service chiefs after consulting the civilian leadership and promotions to general rank after consulting the respective service chiefs.

The Ministry of National Defense executes defense policies and programs determined by the chief of the General Staff with respect to conscription, procurement of weapons and equipment, logistical needs, and other services such as health care, construction, infrastructure, and finances and auditing. The ministry compiles, coordinates, and steers the annual budget request through the National Assembly. The ministry is

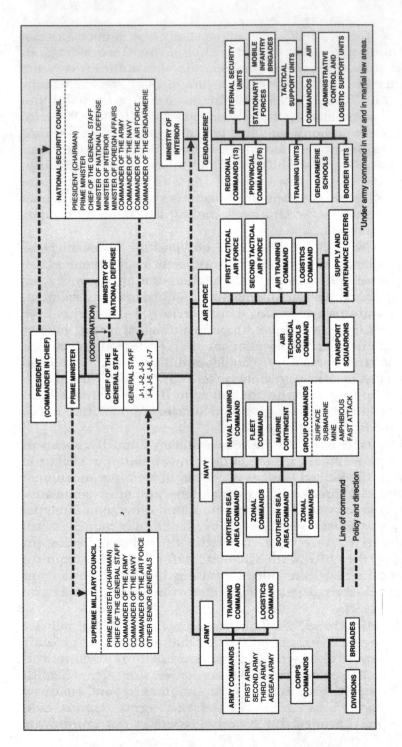

Figure 14. Organization of the National Security Establishment, 1995

responsible for negotiating with other countries for military assistance and arms supplies but is not involved in discussions concerning the allocation of foreign aid among the service branches. The Ministry of National Defense reflects lesser civilian influence than its United States counterpart; many ministry staff officers are military officers, and the undersecretary of national defense is a general on active duty.

Defense Spending

The high cost of maintaining a credible military establishment in an age of rapidly changing technology has required heavy expenditures by the Ministry of National Defense in relation to other demands on the government's revenue. As a result, the Turkish government has allocated funds to defense in disproportion to widely acknowledged needs for social and economic development. In the decade between 1981 and 1991, defense was the largest category in the national budget, averaging in most years close to 20 percent of total government expenditures and 4 to 5 percent of the country's gross domestic product (GDP—see Glossary). The next largest budget category—education—commanded little more than half of the resources earmarked for defense.

Until the mid-1970s, the military budget covered only the domestic cost of maintaining the large armed forces establishment; most equipment costs and much of the expense of training military specialists were borne by the United States. A sharp increase in defense spending by Turkey itself was necessitated by the 1974 intervention in Cyprus. The immediate cost of the Cyprus operation, estimated at between US$350 million and US$700 million, was overshadowed by the burden of compensating for the embargo on military assistance imposed by the United States until 1978.

The Defense Industry Support Fund, which is separate from the regular defense budget, finances a US$15 billion military modernization program with earmarked taxes and assessments. The modernization fund is supplemented by a so-called Gulf Fund of grants from Saudi Arabia, Kuwait, the United Arab Emirates, and the United States to compensate Turkey for the cost of maintaining the embargo against Iraq and the lost income from the closing of the Kirkuk-Yumurtalik oil pipeline. By 1993 the Gulf Fund had accumulated more than US$4.8 billion (see Domestic Arms Industry, this ch.).

According to NATO estimates, personnel expenditures constituted almost exactly 50 percent of total defense expenditures in 1993. Equipment expenditures made up 25 percent of the total, infrastructure expenditures 3.2 percent, and other operating expenses the remaining 21.6 percent. The share of the budget going to personnel was lower than in most NATO countries, although higher than in the United States (38.6 percent in 1993). Low-paid conscripts who make up the bulk of the armed forces accounted for only 11 percent of overall personnel costs.

Equipment purchases absorbed 9.2 percent of defense outlays from 1980 to 1984 and 18.2 percent from 1985 to 1989. Such expenditures rose to 25.6 percent in 1993 because Turkey was obliged to assume an increasing share of the cost of new armaments, munitions, and supplies.

United States and German aid has been indispensable to Turkey's efforts to introduce advanced weapons systems. United States assistance has enabled Turkey to continue its modernization program in spite of the weakness of the Turkish lira (for value of the lira—see Glossary). The aid reached a high level during the Persian Gulf crisis, but tapered off with the end of the Cold War, its basis shifting from grants to concessionary loans.

The Military Balance, 1994–1995 has estimated the Turkish defense budget at US$4.1 billion in 1992, US$4.5 billion in 1993, and US$4.6 billion in 1994. Based on the NATO definition of military spending, the 1992 budget was US$6.1 billion, the 1993 budget US$7.1 billion, and the 1994 budget US$7.3 billion. Separate data published by the United States Arms Control and Disarmament Agency (ACDA) depict moderate real growth in Turkey's actual defense spending during most of the 1980s, from US$3.19 billion in 1981 to US$4.13 billion in 1989 (both expressed in constant 1991 dollars). Expenditures rose sharply to US$5.2 billion in 1990 and US$5.7 billion in 1991, largely as a result of the Persian Gulf War. The shrinkage of the armed forces was expected eventually to produce economies, but the initial effect was an increase in the defense budget to acquire and support more advanced weapons.

The country's economic sacrifice in building a strong defense establishment has been greater than that of its more affluent NATO partners. In 1991 Turkey's military expenditures were 5.4 percent of gross national product (GNP—see Glossary); this was roughly the same proportion as a decade earlier, although defense spending had dropped to as low as 3.9 percent of GNP in 1988. Military spending constituted 20.3 percent of total central government expenditures in 1990 and 17.9 percent in 1991 by ACDA's calculations. The budget of the Ministry of National Defense, which excludes some defense-related costs, was 10.4 percent of the entire budget in 1993 and was scheduled to fall to 9.4 percent in 1994. Within NATO only the United States expended a larger percentage of government outlays on defense, and only Greece spent as high a share of GNP on defense. However, Turkey's defense expenditures per capita, amounting to US$97 annually, were the lowest among NATO countries.

Sources and Quality of Personnel

As expressed in Article 72 of the constitution, "National service is the right and duty of every Turk. The manner in which this service shall be performed, or considered as performed, either in the armed forces or in the public service, shall be regulated by law." The required period of active-duty service has been scaled back periodically, from two years to eighteen months and, in 1992, to fifteen months. Male citizens who pass a physical examination are called up during their twentieth year, but induction can be deferred until completion of an education program.

University and college graduates may fulfill their military obligation as reserve officers with an eighteen-month period of active service following some previous preparation at their education institution. Four months of the service period consist of cadet training, followed by fourteen months of service in the branch to which the individual is appointed. With the dwindling need for reserve officers, complete professionalization of the officer corps is contemplated. Most university graduates would serve as conscripts in the regular army, but their active duty would be limited to nine months. An exception would be made for graduates of technical universities who could be called up for longer periods of specialized service.

Reserve officers seem not to be held in high esteem in the services, being regarded as less dependable than regulars, lacking in motivation, and inadequately trained. Regulars are reluctant to accept reservists as equals in personal and social relations. Reservists, on the other hand, tend to look down on regulars as narrowly educated.

After completing four months of basic training, conscripts are sent to their assigned units for more training and unit exercises. Recruits who have graduated from senior high school are eligible to serve as sergeants after NCO training. Promising but less educated recruits can become corporals after a two-week training course. In 1993 a program was introduced to increase the number of career NCOs. The intent was to enlist 100,000 regulars as privates and corporals in the course of the first year. As inducements, the maximum age of enlistment was raised from thirty to thirty-five, and new financial and social benefits were introduced.

The period of active service is an important educational experience for many young men. In addition to mastering weapons, they learn personal hygiene, table manners, and the basics of social conduct. They receive a wholesome diet and, in most cases, better medical and dental care than they will have at any other time in their lives. Literacy classes were formerly an important feature of military training, but by the 1980s fewer than 5 percent of recruits needed to be taught to read and write.

Many conscripts are taught useful skills, such as truck driving and machinery repair. The army's training of technicians and artisans may rival the contribution of civilian technical secondary schools, which produce only about 100,000 graduates a year.

Draft evasion apparently had become a serious problem by the mid-1990s, perhaps because of young men's reluctance to risk their lives against Kurdish insurgents. In December 1993, the chief of staff said that 30 percent of all men of draft age had deferred their service (in many cases in order to complete higher education), 22 percent were evading conscription, and 7 percent were medically unfit. The total of those who had avoided conscription came to about 250,000 but, as the chief of staff pointed out, the armed forces did not have facilities to induct all these men even if they were available. Desertions were also said to have increased, although military leaders were unwilling to confirm this fact.

After completing their active-duty obligation, conscripts are subject to recall in periods of national emergency until age forty-six if physically fit and not otherwise exempted. In practice, it is only for a few years after discharge that conscripts are considered part of the reserve system with specific unit assignments. In 1994 the number in this category was reported to be

Infantry exercises in Kocaeli Province
Courtesy Embassy of Turkey, Washington

about 952,300 (831,700 in the army, 55,600 in the navy, and 65,000 in the air force).

Turkey has always had an ample supply of personnel to meet its military needs. In 1994 roughly 3 million men were between the ages of eighteen and twenty-two. The annual call-up for all branches totaled about 300,000 but was likely to shrink rapidly with the reduction of the army complement and the effort to enlist more regulars. Nevertheless, in January 1994 all discharges were frozen for three months to ensure that the army had enough trained soldiers for operations against the Kurdish guerrillas.

Military discipline is strict. Turkish officers are taught to believe that softness is a sign of weakness, which soldiers will quickly take advantage of. Discipline is considered necessary to ensure quality performance and to prevent the slackness that officers feel pervades the civilian labor force. Corporal punishment is strictly prohibited under the Law of the Armed Services. Yet beatings and slappings, although not common, appear to be accepted forms of punishment. NCOs and sometimes second lieutenants are those most likely to employ corporal punishment for acts considered disruptive of discipline. The alternative is to institute legal proceedings for minor offenses. Such proceedings can be delayed so long that they have little deterrent effect; they may also be perceived as reflecting poorly on the effectiveness of the officer involved. Major offenses, such as theft, desertion, or prohibited ideological activities, are normally the subject of courts-martial.

From the squad level up, soldiers engage in daily training exercises. The armed forces hold a number of combined exercises and participate in several NATO exercises each year. Nevertheless, in the mid-1990s Turkish observers felt that the quality of training still suffered from shortcomings. They noted, for example, that training often has a theoretical quality, traceable in part to the need to conserve ammunition, vehicles, and aircraft.

Since 1955, when the government opened certain military specialties to women, moderate numbers have volunteered for active duty. Recruitment of women was suspended for a time but was resumed in the early 1980s when some female university graduates were again taken in as pharmacists, doctors, dentists, and administrative or communications specialists. No women were accepted in the enlisted ranks or for assignments that could expose them to combat or hazardous duty. In 1992 access to military service was increased when 154 women were allowed to enter the service academies, half of them as army cadets.

Education and Training

The sole source of regular commissioned officers is the army academy at Harbiye, near Istanbul; the naval academy at Tuzla, on the Sea of Marmara near Istanbul; and the air force academy at Istanbul. Cadets who complete officer training receive commissions as second lieutenants or naval ensigns. The three services also operate five military high schools, from which half or more of the cadets are recruited. The selection process is highly selective, based on school grades, especially in the sciences, an oral interview in which appearance and demeanor are appraised, graded fitness tests, and a confidential investigation of the political background of the applicant and his or her family.

The military high schools have superior facilities, and classes are as little as one-third the size of those in civilian high schools. Scholastic performance is closely monitored. A summer camp is devoted to sports and military instruction.

Armed forces personnel engaged in landing exercise
Courtesy Embassy of Turkey, Washington

The selection process for the military academies is even more rigorous than for the military high schools. Only about one in seven applicants is successful. A further weeding out occurs after an initial one-month adaptation course. The academies offer the opportunity of a free higher education under conditions of instruction that cannot be matched at civilian universities. Classroom and laboratory equipment is much superior, and sports facilities are unequaled elsewhere.

Candidates for the academies must be high-school graduates under twenty years of age and must have studied the sciences and a foreign language. Candidates must also score well in the regular university entrance examinations. An academy appointment is not offered until test scores are available. Applicants who score high enough for a place at a leading university often shift to a civilian career path. Each of the service academies must accept at least one cadet from each of Turkey's seventy-six provinces.

Founded on Prussian principles of military education, the service academies since the 1950s have been strongly influenced by the United States approach to officer training. The emphasis of the curriculum has been modified from time to time, often to ensure an acceptable ideological outlook among students. Since the late 1970s, the curriculum has been 56 percent military, including sports, and 44 percent academic. The political and economic areas have been strengthened and managerial training added. Foreign languages are stressed; some classes are taught in English. It is estimated that 20 percent of the curriculum is devoted, directly or indirectly, to study of the principles and reforms of Atatürk. Much attention is given to appearance, social polish, and a proper public deportment. Available books and periodicals have an orthodox outlook; left-wing and religious publications are forbidden. To limit exposure of cadets to political theories inconsistent with the Atatürk model, the academies permit conservative guest lecturers only. Many cadets are expelled for ideological reasons, primarily if they are suspected of leftist sympathies, given that graduates of Islamic high schools are not admitted in the first place. The role played by the army academy in the 1960 coup and in the abortive coup of 1962 led to the expulsion of 1,400 cadets, as a result of which there were no army graduating classes in 1963 and 1964.

The most prestigious training assignment for career officers is to one of the staff academies, which usually occurs after about six years of service, at the rank of captain or the equivalent. There are separate land, air, and naval staff academies, but they share a location in an Istanbul suburb. The staff academies constitute a self-sufficient town with modern accommodations for all officers, day care for the children of officers whose spouses have jobs, and complete sports facilities.

Only 120 to 130 officers are accepted into the staff academies each year for the two-year program. About 60 percent of the curriculum is devoted to military subjects—the principles of war, strategy, and weapons technology—and the remainder to administrative and management skills and general cultural subjects at a postgraduate level. An officer completing the course is credited with an extra three years of seniority, receives a higher salary, progresses faster, and is more likely to be offered a coveted foreign posting. About 75 percent of those reaching the rank of general are staff officers.

Within ten years of commissioning, staff officers who have attained the rank of major or lieutenant colonel or their equivalents are expected to attend the Armed Forces Academy. This academy has a program twice a year for about seventy-five staff officers in subjects such as joint operations, campaign planning, strategy, global conflict, and new concepts and doctrines.

A five-month course is presented once a year at the National Security Academy to twenty civilians and ten officers, usually colonels and sometimes brigadier generals or the equivalent. The civilians typically include high-level civil servants, ambassadors, provincial governors, and subgovernors. Presented in seminar form, the program deals with international political, economic, and military trends, joint planning, and national security problems. Like the staff academies, the Armed Forces Academy and the National Security Academy are located outside Istanbul.

Conditions of Service

The average military academy graduate serves at least ten years in the three lowest officer grades in a combination of training and field assignments as a platoon or company commander. The pace of promotion is usually fairly steady through the rank of colonel or its equivalent, assuming satisfactory performance reports graded by three superior officers. A particularly high rating can advance a promotion by a year. In normal times, an army officer can expect at least two "eastern" assignments, once while a lieutenant or captain and once between the ranks of major and colonel or their equivalents. A post in eastern Turkey is considered undesirable because of its isolation, the severe weather, and the lack of medical and education facilities for families. Since the early 1990s, a much larger part of the army has been deployed in the east to deal with the Kurdish insurgency. Personal influence has little effect on where people in the military are posted.

Most career officers can expect to retire with the rank of colonel or the equivalent. With the number of generals and admirals ranging between 280 and 300, only forty-eight of the hundreds of colonels and navy captains are promoted to flag rank each year. People being considered for general officer rank are subjected to a minute review of their entire service record. General officers must not be involved in political activities and must show discretion and conservatism in social and domestic life. Treated with great deference in civilian society, general officers are entitled to full-time use of an official car and chauffeur, as well as the services of an adjutant and several orderlies. Protocol activities take up much of a general officer's time. A general serving as a field commander exercises authority and responsibility comparable to those of a provincial governor.

Except during periods of high inflation, the net salary of career officers is slightly more than the pay of civil servants of comparable standing, although the difference narrows at higher ranks. The living standards of career officers clearly surpass those of other government workers when special benefits are included. Quarters are provided for more than 70 percent of permanent military personnel. Rents, deducted directly from salaries, may be no more than one-eighth of equivalent civilian rents. Security and the maintenance of grounds and buildings, duties assigned to enlisted personnel, are of high quality.

Salaries of noncareer soldiers are very low and during the first half of the 1990s were eroded by inflation. As of January 1994, the monthly wage of a private was TL37,000, then equivalent to only US$2.25. A corporal earned TL57,000 and a sergeant, TL75,000. Pensions for families of soldiers who had died in service were minimal; compensation for the widow of a private came to about US$37 a month.

Military hospitals provide medical care to all active-duty and retired officers and enlisted personnel and their families. Reservists are eligible on a space-available basis. The quality of treatment and personnel at military hospitals is at least as good as at university hospitals, and superior to what is available in general hospitals.

There are officers' clubs in about forty of the provinces, most with excellent facilities for leisure and recreation, as well as temporary accommodations for officers and their families. The clubs are heavily patronized by retired officers as well. Prices are far lower than in comparable commercial establishments. NCO clubs traditionally were much more modest, but a program was initiated in the mid-1980s to bring them up to officers' club standards. Twenty-five rest camps enable service members and their families to enjoy two-week holidays at a fraction of the cost of commercial resorts. Accommodations are awarded on a point system ensuring an opening at least every four years.

An unusual feature of the national defense establishment is the existence of a semiautonomous foundation known as the Army Mutual Aid Association (Ordu Yardimlasma Kurumu—OYAK), which is essentially a military social security organization. Career officers and warrant officers contribute 10 percent of their basic salaries to the association's fund. Reserve officers contribute 5 percent. OYAK's business activities, which include holdings in eight major companies, have an annual turnover of US$5 billion, and are tax exempt. Participants may obtain housing loans from OYAK and may purchase homes built by OYAK's own construction companies at prices well below commercial rates. Upon retirement, OYAK makes a lump sum payment to career (but not reserve) officers, based on the members' investment plus accrued interest and dividends. OYAK also operates post exchanges selling items at 15 percent below prices at civilian outlets and offering durable consumer goods on highly favorable credit terms.

Army

The army (officially referred to as the Turkish Land Forces) is by far the largest of the three service components. During 1992 the army introduced a sweeping reorganization, shifting from a predominantly divisional and regimental structure to one based on corps and brigades. The personnel strength of the army was reduced in 1994 to about 393,000 (including about 345,000 conscripts). Major equipment acquisitions have enabled the army to upgrade firepower and mobility while enhancing command and control.

Until the dissolution of the Warsaw Pact in 1990, the army had a static defense mission of countering Soviet and Warsaw Pact forces in the Caucasus and any possible attack on Thrace. When the General Staff attempted to shift 120,000 troops to the frontier with Iraq in 1990, they discovered that there were serious deficiencies in the army's ability to respond to crises that could erupt suddenly in distant regions. The army was even less prepared for a situation requiring the deployment and logistical support of forces in operations beyond Turkey's borders.

Prior to the army reorganization, the principal tactical units consisted of sixteen infantry divisions and one armored division, plus twenty-three independent brigades, of which six were armored and four mechanized. Under the reorganization, all divisions except three were dismantled. The existing nine corps were retained, with brigades directly responsible to the corps commands. The brigades were reconfigured as seventeen mechanized infantry brigades, fourteen armored brigades, nine infantry brigades, and four commando brigades. Each armored brigade consisted in late 1994 of six battalions: two armored, two mechanized, and two artillery. The mechanized brigades consisted of one armored battalion, two mechanized battalions, and one artillery battalion, plus a reconnaissance squadron. The infantry brigades consisted of four infantry battalions and one artillery battalion. Each commando brigade consisted of three commando battalions and one artillery battalion.

The Military Balance, 1994–1995 also lists a Presidential Guard regiment, an infantry regiment, five border defense regiments, and twenty-six border defense battalions. The fate of these independent units under the reorganization remained unclear in early 1995.

General Hikmet Bayar, the commander of Turkish land forces in early 1995, operated from headquarters in Ankara. The capital is also the home of the Ankara garrison and of the training and logistics commands. The country is divided into four military sectors on the basis of strategic conditions of terrain, logistics, communications, and the potential external threat. The sectors are assigned to four field armies, the first three of which would come under NATO command in the event of a NATO reinforced alert (see fig. 15).

The First Army, with headquarters in Istanbul, is widely deployed in the European part of Turkey known historically as Thrace, with responsibility for the defense of that province, the Bosporus and Dardanelles straits, and the Kocaeli Peninsula. The Second Army, headquartered at Malatya, is deployed in southeastern Anatolia with a defensive mission facing Syria, Iraq, and Iran. The Third Army, with headquarters at Erzincan, is deployed throughout the rugged mountains and deep valleys of eastern Anatolia, covering the borders with Georgia and Armenia and the historical invasion routes from the east. During the buildup preceding the Persian Gulf War, the Second Army was deployed along the Iraqi border along with some units from the Third Army. Under the new structure, most of the armored, mechanized, and commando brigades are

located in the central region with the mission of rapidly rein-
forcing brigades in each theater as required.

The Aegean Army (sometimes called the Fourth Army) was
organized in the mid-1970s in response to tensions with Greece
in the Aegean Sea. Headquartered in Izmir, it is responsible for
the vast area facing the Aegean coast from the Dardanelles in
the north to the southernmost Greek offshore islands. Turkish
commanders describe the Aegean Army as composed simply of
training elements from which the major army units are supplied. They presumably would have the mission of defending
the Aegean coast and keeping lines of communication open in
the Aegean district in an emergency, although their capability
for this mission seems highly limited. The Turkish corps on
Cyprus is within the Aegean Army command structure. Known
as the Cyprus Turkish Peace Force, it is said in *The Military Balance, 1994–1995* to consist of 30,000 troops, equipped with 235
M-48 tanks, 107 armored personnel carriers (APCs), and
numerous pieces of towed and self-propelled artillery.

In late 1994, in addition to 1,500 troops who served with the
United Nations Protection Force in Bosnia, a contingent of
about 300 Turkish soldiers had participated in the UN operation in Somalia. The overall commander of the UN force in
Somalia in 1993 was Turkish general Cevik Bir.

Accompanying the reorganization of the land forces was a
significant upgrading of weapons systems, armor, and transport. Under the NATO harmonization program adopted
under the CFE Treaty, considerable equipment subject to
removal from the central front was passed on to other NATO
armies, notably those of Greece and Turkey. Turkey's share
included more than 1,000 United States M-60 and German
Leopard main battle tanks and some 700 armored combat vehicles, as well as self-propelled howitzers and United States Cobra
attack helicopters.

Under the CFE Treaty, NATO and Soviet Union/Warsaw
Pact countries also were to reduce the size of their conventional forces. Russia has sought to change this commitment on
the grounds that it needs forces for "police" actions and to
assist former member states of the Soviet Union, such as Armenia, where Russian troops are stationed. Turkey has endeavored to prevent Russia's backing out on its commitment
because, among other reasons, Turkey shares a border with
Armenia.

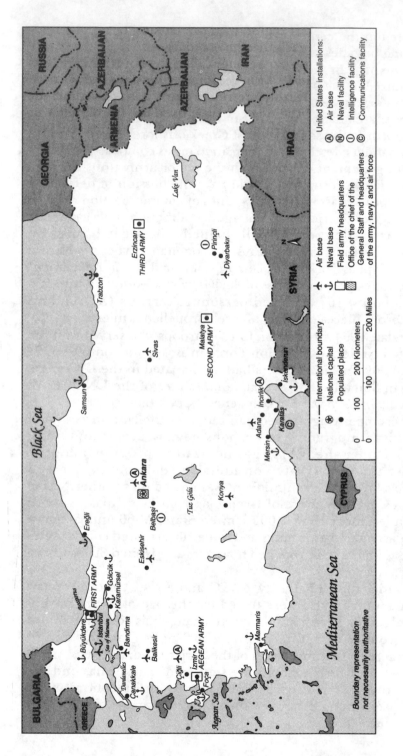

Figure 15. Disposition of Major Units of the Turkish Armed Forces and Major Military Installations Used by the United States, 1995

In addition to the arms received as a result of the CFE Treaty, Turkey's arsenal of more than 3,000 M–48 tanks was being upgraded with advanced fire controls. By 1994 deliveries had begun of armored infantry fighting vehicles, large numbers of which were to be supplied under a Turkey/United States coproduction program. Procurement of a multiple-launch rocket system was proceeding under a similar program (see table 13, Appendix A).

Turkey acquired 300 Russian BTR–60 APCs for use in the struggle against the Kurds because weapons of NATO origin were not approved for this purpose. In spite of the fact that the engines and transmissions of the BTR–60s had to be replaced after brief use, Ankara announced in 1994 that it had acquired 110 BTR–80s. These APCs were assigned to the gendarmerie, who were actively engaged in the war against the Kurds (see Police System, this ch.).

More effective employment of commando and infantry units would become possible with the United States UH–1H Iroquois (of which Turkey had ninety-six in 1994) and other modern troop-lift helicopters entering the army aviation inventory. The addition of missile-armed Cobra AH–1 (Bell 209) assault helicopters and five Super Cobras promised by the United States was expected to improve antitank capabilities.

Air Force

The Turkish air force is the youngest of the three branches of the armed services. Founded in 1911, it saw action in the Balkan Wars and World War I, as well as the War of Independence. The first Turkish pilots were trained in France. The air force has a high priority in Turkey's strategic planning because control of the air would be indispensable for successful defense against a ground attack by well-equipped forces. Moreover, reinforcement and supply of Turkish ground forces by Turkey's NATO allies would not be feasible without control of the air. The air force role in interdicting an invasion force would be to provide close support of ground troops in tactical defensive actions and to airlift troops and supplies. Upon declaration of a NATO reinforced alert, the Turkish air force would be committed to action as part of NATO's Sixth Allied Tactical Air Force (SIXATAF) headquartered at Izmir.

In late 1994, the air force was staffed by about 56,800 officers and enlisted personnel. It is organized around two basic combat elements operating east and west of the thirty-fifth meridian of longitude. The First Tactical Air Force has its head-quarters at Eskisehir Air Base in western Turkey. It defends the Turkish straits and provides air cover in the First Army's area of operations. The Second Tactical Air Force, commanded from its headquarters at Diyarbakır in eastern Turkey, is charged with defending the Third Army and part of the Second Army. Separate air training and logistics commands with their own aircraft squadrons are headquartered at Ankara. The air transport units are assigned directly to specific air force commands. Air force headquarters is located at Ankara; the air force commander in 1994 was General Halis Burhan.

The air force in late 1994 was organized tactically into four-teen fighter-ground attack squadrons, six fighter squadrons, four transport squadrons, two reconnaissance squadrons, one antisubmarine warfare squadron, and three training squadrons. The fighter-ground attack squadrons and three of the four transport squadrons are assigned to NATO. There are eight surface-to-air missile (SAM) squadrons. In 1994 six of the SAM squadrons were equipped with 128 obsolete United States Nike-Hercules missiles; the remaining two were supplied with twenty-four Rapier SAMs of British manufacture. Many Turkish bases and large cities are within range of Russian, Chinese, and North Korean missile systems possessed by Syria and Iran. Iraq supposedly has relinquished its longer-range missiles but still may have some Scud-Bs from North Korea. Turkish officers acknowledge their limited ability to defend against these threats.

In the mid-1990s, Turkey was phasing in advanced F–16 fighter aircraft produced domestically under a cooperative program with the General Dynamics and General Electric corporations. An initial shipment of 160 aircraft was to be supplemented with a second package of eighty aircraft. The F–16s were to replace a combat fleet of obsolete F–5s and F–104s; the force also included somewhat more up-to-date F–4Es (see table 14, Appendix A).

In 1994 the air force's fixed-wing transport squadrons consisted of United States-manufactured C–130E Hercules and German C–160D Transall medium transports and CN–235 light transports. Fifty-two CN–235s coproduced with a Spanish manufacturer have replaced the United States-manufactured C–47s for troop-transport and cargo missions.

Upon completion of the four-year air force academy program, air force pilots are trained for two to two-and-a-half years on a variety of United States propeller and jet training aircraft. The Italian SF–260 coproduced in Turkey is being introduced as an advanced combat trainer. Nonflying officers are trained by the Air Technical Schools Command. NCOs are also trained in twelve- to eighteen-month programs in administrative and technical skills at specialized institutions of this command.

Upgrading of the air force flight inventory is expected to include acquisition from the United States of two surplus KC–135A tanker aircraft—scaled back from seven for financial reasons—that would permit air refueling and thus dramatically increase the range of fighter aircraft. The air force also hopes to receive airborne early warning aircraft and airborne command and control aircraft. The planned transfer of fifty surplus United States A–10 attack aircraft for close support of ground troops was canceled because Turkey's tight foreign-exchange situation did not permit acquisition of the needed reconditioning and support equipment. Ankara considers the acquisition of United States Patriot missiles essential to reducing Turkey's vulnerability to conventional air and missile attack, but in early 1995 such an acquisition did not appear imminent.

Navy

Numbering 54,000 individuals in late 1994, nearly 70 percent conscripts, the navy is responsible for defending the country against seaborne attack in time of war, for safeguarding the Turkish straits at all times, and for patrol and coastal protection along the extensive coastline that borders about two-thirds of the nation. The navy has an assigned NATO role in which it is responsible to the alliance's commander of NAVSOUTH in Naples. The commander of Turkish naval forces serves concurrently as commander, North-East Mediterranean (COMEDNOREAST), under NAVSOUTH. The Turkish navy shares in NAVSOUTH's mission of protecting a line of communications through the Mediterranean and the Black Sea and conducting antisubmarine operations in the event of a general war.

Turkish strategists feel that the creation of new countries in the Black Sea area, following the end of the Cold War, has imposed new missions on the navy. They point out that, whereas there were previously four littoral states on the Black Sea, since the breakup of the Soviet Union there are seven—Bulgaria, Georgia, Moldova, Romania, Russia, Turkey, and Ukraine. Russia retains the major share of the former Soviet Black Sea fleet, but Ukraine claims a number of vessels and base facilities. Because Turkey considers the Central Asian republics likely to make heavy use of the Black Sea for foreign trade, the maintenance of open sea-lanes is expected to become more important. Turkey foresees a greater flow of oil from the Caucasus, Central Asia, and Russia via pipelines to terminals at Iskenderun in the eastern Mediterranean, imposing additional requirements on the navy to ensure the safety of ports and sea-lanes in an increasingly strategic area.

The navy has three operational commands: the Northern Sea Area Command, based at Istanbul; the Fleet Command at Gölcük; and the Southern Sea Area Command at Izmir. The Fleet Command, the largest of the naval components, consists of specialized elements: the war fleet, the submarine fleet, the mine fleet, and the landing units. The zonal commands are the Black Sea (headquartered at Eregli), the Aegean (headquartered at Izmir), two straits commands (headquartered at Istanbul and Çanakkale), and the Mediterranean (headquartered at Mersin). The commander in chief of the Turkish navy in early 1995 was Admiral Vural Bayazit.

The Naval Training Command is based at Karamürsel on the southern coast of the Sea of Marmara. The naval academy near Istanbul is colocated with the Naval Lyceum, a four-year secondary school. Graduates of the lyceum and other high schools who are accepted as midshipmen at the naval academy are promoted to subensign after the four-year program, and then are assigned to sea duty for two probationary years before being commissioned in the regular navy. Entrance to the lyceum is highly competitive; only a small percentage of applicants pass the qualifying examinations.

The Petty Officers School at Istanbul receives applicants at age twelve for four years of secondary and naval preparatory instruction. Graduates are then admitted as petty officer candidates and, after four years of specialist training, are designated career petty officers at the entry grade. Conscripts assigned to the navy receive about four months of basic training and are then assigned to sea or shore duties for the balance of their required service.

The navy's inventory of ships is well maintained, and its officers and crews are considered to possess high levels of professionalism and readiness. Turkey participates in NATO exercises in its region and frequently takes part in national exercises of other NATO members. Its relations with other Black Sea naval powers are good. Mutual high-level naval visits

F–16 aircraft used by Turkish Air Force
Turkish naval vessel on patrol
Courtesy Embassy of Turkey, Washington

have been exchanged with Russia, and negotiations have been opened on agreements to prevent incidents on and over the high seas with both Russia and Ukraine. Turkey conducted joint mine and search-and-rescue exercises with Bulgaria in 1993.

The main categories of Turkish fighting ships are destroyers, frigates, submarines, and fast-attack craft (see table 15, Appendix A). Most of the older ships are of United States origin. More modern units have been supplied by Germany or constructed in Turkish shipyards with German technical assistance and components. The largest vessels are United States destroyers, most of them launched at the close of World War II. They are considered obsolete and incapable of operating with other NATO ships in battle-group formations. One of the destroyers, the *Muavenet*, was hit by two Sea Sparrow surface-to-surface missiles (SSMs) launched accidentally by a United States warship during exercises in 1992. The Turkish captain and four other personnel were killed and a number injured. The destroyer subsequently was scrapped. In 1993 and 1994, eight newer Knox-class frigates were transferred to Turkey by the United States.

In 1994 four MEKO–200 class frigates of German design were in the inventory, and an additional four modernized MEKO–200 frigates are to be delivered between 1995 and 1998. Construction is split, with the first four frigates having been built in Germany and four being built at the naval ship-yard at Gölcük, with German equipment packages. The vessels are armed with five-inch guns, Harpoon SSMs, and Sea Sparrow SAMs.

The submarine force consisted originally of United States World War II-era diesel-powered attack vessels of the Guppy class. Seven of these were still listed in 1994, but their utility was doubtful. Since 1975 Turkey has been acquiring German 20-class (type-1200) submarines, quiet-running craft smaller than the Guppies but suitable for defending the approaches to the straits as well as Turkey's coastal waters. The first three of the six vessels were built in Germany and the next three were built at Gölcük. Four additional 209-class submarines of the more advanced type-1400, armed with sub-Harpoon SSMs, are to be added between 1994 and 1998.

The sixteen missile-armed fast-attack craft in the Turkish fleet in 1994 were a mixture of older and newer technologies. The most up-to-date units were eight Dogan-class vessels equipped with Harpoon SSMs. They were built in Turkey along the lines of the German Lürssen 57. Two more fast-attack craft of the Yildiz class are to be delivered in 1995. These high-speed vessels would be especially effective against ships attempting to transit the confined waters in and around the Turkish straits.

The amphibious force of sixty-six vessels in the inventory at the end of 1994 would be sufficient to land Turkish infantry and tanks in individual operations or in conjunction with other NATO assault forces. The inventory of twenty-nine minelayers and minesweepers would have the task of implementing a NATO decision to seal off the Black Sea. Turkish officers are considered to be highly qualified in such operations, but in the mid-1990s minesweepers and minelayers were due for modernization.

In 1994 the naval air arm included fourteen Italian-built Agusta-Bell AB–204 and AB–212 antisubmarine helicopters, which could be flown off frigate flight decks. United States-manufactured Grumman S–2E Tracker aircraft, flown by air force personnel and used for land-based antisubmarine and marine reconnaissance, were due to be replaced. The marine contingent of some 3,000 officers and troops was organized as a brigade of three infantry battalions and one artillery battalion, plus support units.

Uniforms, Ranks, and Insignia

Uniforms worn in Turkey's three military services are similar in design to those worn by United States military personnel and by troops of other NATO countries. The army winter service dress uniform is a shade of olive drab; a khaki shirt and trousers are worn in summer. Troops wear a field-gray shirt and trousers for winter field duty, and a camouflaged battle-fatigue uniform during the summer. The navy wears a black uniform in winter and a white one in summer. The air force uniforms are the same shade of blue worn by the United States and British air forces.

Army and air force officers wear their rank insignia on shoulder straps. Generals are identified by a red lapel patch; their rank is denoted by a shoulder device combining a wreath with star and crescent and superimposed crossed sabers, plus one to four gold stars. Field-grade officers have one to three gold stars with a wreath and star and crescent. Company-grade officers wear one to three gold stars on plain shoulder straps (see fig. 16).

A red backing to an army officer's wreath indicates general's rank. Among officers at lower grades, the backing's color indicates service corps; for example, green for infantry, dark blue for artillery, black for armor, and light blue for signals. The same wreath device forms part of the badge on the peaked cap. Variations in the cap's peak and chin strap decorations provide further indications of rank. The air force's method of displaying rank is virtually the same as the army's. Naval officers' ranks are indicated by gold stripes around the lower sleeves of their jackets (the upper stripe looped as in the British navy), on shoulder boards, and on the chin straps of visored caps.

TURKISH RANK		ASTEĞMEN	TEĞMEN	ÜSTEĞMEN	YÜZBAŞI	BİNBAŞI	YARBAY	ALBAY	TUĞGENERAL	TÜMGENERAL	KORGENERAL	ORGENERAL	MARESAL
ARMY AND AIR FORCE													
U.S. RANK TITLE		2D LIEUTENANT		1ST LIEUTENANT	CAPTAIN	MAJOR	LIEUTENANT COLONEL	COLONEL	BRIGADIER GENERAL	MAJOR GENERAL	LIEUTENANT GENERAL	GENERAL	GENERAL OF THE ARMY/AIR FORCE
TURKISH RANK		ASTEĞMEN	TEĞMEN	ÜSTEĞMEN	YÜZBAŞI	BİNBAŞI	YARBAY	ALBAY	TUĞAMİRAL	TÜMANİRAL	KORAMİRAL	ORAMİRAL	BÜYÜKAMİRAL
NAVY													
U.S. RANK TITLE		ENSIGN		LIEUTENANT JUNIOR GRADE	LIEUTENANT	LIEUTENANT COMMANDER	COMMANDER	CAPTAIN	REAR ADMIRAL LOWER HALF	REAR ADMIRAL UPPER HALF	VICE ADMIRAL	ADMIRAL	FLEET ADMIRAL

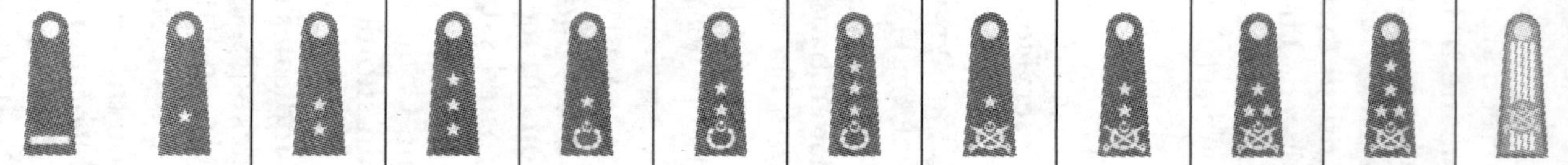

Figure 16. Officer Ranks and Insignia, 1995

TURKISH RANK	ER	NO RANK	NO RANK	ONBAŞI	ÇAVUŞ	ASTSUBAY ÇAVUŞ	ASTSUBAY KIDEMLI ÇAVUŞ	ASTSUBAY USTÇAVUŞ	ASTSUBAY KIDEMLI USTÇAVUŞ	ASTSUBAY BAŞ ÇAVUŞ	ASTSUBAY KIDEMLI BAŞ ÇAVUŞ
ARMY AND AIR FORCE	NO INSIGNIA										
U.S. RANK TITLE	BASIC PRIVATE / AIRMAN BASIC	PRIVATE / AIRMAN	PRIVATE 1ST CLASS / AIRMAN 1ST CLASS	CORPORAL/SPECIALIST / SENIOR AIRMAN/SERGEANT	SERGEANT / STAFF SERGEANT	STAFF SERGEANT / TECHNICAL SERGEANT		SERGEANT 1ST CLASS / MASTER SERGEANT		MASTER SERGEANT, FIRST SERGEANT / SENIOR MASTER SERGEANT	SERGEANT MAJOR/ COMMAND SERGEANT MAJOR / CHIEF MASTER SERGEANT
TURKISH RANK	ER	NO RANK	NO RANK	ONBAŞI	MUKELLEF ÇAVUŞ	ASTSUBAY ÇAVUŞ	ASTSUBAY KIDEMLI ÇAVUŞ	ASTSUBAY USTÇAVUŞ	ASTSUBAY KIDEMLI USTÇAVUŞ	ASTSUBAY BAŞ ÇAVUŞ	ASTSUBAY KIDEMLI BAŞ ÇAVUŞ
NAVY	NO INSIGNIA										
U.S. RANK TITLE	SEAMAN RECRUIT	SEAMAN APPRENTICE	SEAMAN	PETTY OFFICER 3C CLASS	PETTY OFFICER 2D CLASS	PETTY OFFICER 1ST CLASS		CHIEF PETTY OFFICER		SENIOR CHIEF PETTY OFFICER	MASTER CHIEF PETTY OFFICER

Figure 17. Enlisted Ranks and Insignia, 1995

NCO ranks are denoted by arm chevrons (see fig. 17). Insignia of the army and air force are almost identical in design, resembling those of the United States Air Force, with a star and crescent rather than a star at the center. Enlisted personnel wear tabs colored to indicate service corps on their lapels and service caps.

Military Cooperation with the United States

During the postwar era, Turkey's foremost ally has been the United States. Because of Turkey's strategic location in the Middle East, its proximity to the Soviet Union's military installations and test sites, and its control of the Black Sea straits, military ties with the United States were a crucial factor in the East-West confrontation. The alliance originated soon after the end of World War II, when Soviet dictator Josef V. Stalin made a series of demands on Turkey that the Turkish government and the Western powers interpreted as a possible prelude to military action. The begrudging withdrawal of Soviet occupation forces from northern Iran in May 1946 and communist guerrilla warfare in Greece heightened fears of a Soviet drive into the Middle East. The United States responded with proclamation of the Truman Doctrine in March 1947. Both Greece and Turkey were provided with aid to resist the Soviet threat.

Because of concerns over extending a United States military commitment to the Middle East, the United States initially was not convinced that Turkey's admission to NATO should be approved. Turkish troops' noteworthy participation in the Korean War changed this view; Turkey entered NATO in 1952.

In accordance with bilateral defense arrangements under NATO auspices, the United States has developed and maintained several major military installations on Turkish bases. Of particular significance are several electronic intelligence posts considered vital for monitoring Russian weapons and Moscow's compliance with strategic arms limitation agreements. A long-range radar system has been established at Pirinçlik, near Diyarbakır, to monitor Russian missile testing. At Belbasi, near Ankara, nuclear testing can be monitored by means of seismic data collection.

No United States combat forces are based in Turkey, but elements of two United States Air Force fighter squadrons based in Italy are rotated periodically to Incirlik—the West's farthest forward-based tactical combat aircraft in the eastern Mediterranean. Çigli, a Turkish air base north of Izmir, is used by United

States Air Force units in connection with NATO exercises. Three bases in eastern Turkey—at Erzurum, Batman, and Mus—were upgraded following a 1982 agreement to make them available for forward deployment of United States tactical aircraft under conditions of a NATO alert. Aircraft operating from them could cover the entire Turkish-Iranian-Transcaucasian border region without aerial refueling.

A Defense Cooperation Agreement (DCA), first negotiated in 1969 and renewed numerous times, consolidated various bilateral accords governing the United States military presence in Turkey. As a result of its 1988 renegotiation, the agreement is now known as the Defense and Economic Cooperation Agreement (DECA). Under the DECA, the number of United States personnel, including dependents, in Turkey—which had reached a peak of 25,000 in 1968—was reduced to 16,000 in 1970 and 9,000 by 1980. In 1991 the total was slightly above 10,000. Since that year, nearly all of the communications and naval facilities have been closed. In late 1994, United States personnel remained only at the air stations at Incirlik, Ankara, and Çigli, the intelligence posts at Pirinçlik and Belbasi, and a communications station at Karatas, near Incirlik. The number of United States personnel had been reduced to about 4,000.

It is common practice to refer to installations staffed by United States personnel—even those solely connected with the NATO mission—as "American." Turkey has never waived its sovereignty over them; they have Turkish commanders and are officially regarded as joint-use facilities. Even so, Turkish sensitivity about their control and the conspicuous United States presence have at times provoked incidents and disputes. Extremist political factions tend to exploit these issues for their own purposes.

Turkey regarded the arms embargo imposed by the United States Congress after the Cyprus invasion of 1974 as a serious affront. Put into effect in 1975, the embargo was opposed by the executive branch of the United States government, which considered it an obstruction in the quest for an equitable settlement of the Cyprus situation. Turkey retaliated by abrogating the 1969 DCA and suspending operations of United States-used installations not clearly linked to the NATO mission. The intelligence collection sites were closed down, and the United States Navy was denied use of its loran (long-range) navigation station in Turkey. The embargo ended in 1978 when Congress repealed its earlier restrictions, although the president of the

United States was required to make periodic certifications that Turkey was contributing to efforts to settle the Cyprus issue.

Turkish public opinion has been sensitive to suggestions that United States rapid deployment forces or other units might make use of facilities on Turkish territory for non-NATO purposes. The only Muslim country in NATO, Turkey is determined to avoid giving open support to controversial or unpopular actions by the United States in the Middle East. The Turkish government did not permit use of the bases for United States operations during the Arab-Israeli wars of 1967 and 1973 and allowed only nonmilitary supplies to be shipped via Turkey to the United States-led multinational contingent in Lebanon in 1983.

Repeated attempts by members of Congress to pass resolutions commemorating the Ottoman government's massacre of Armenians during World War I have prompted strong reactions by the Turkish government. For instance, in 1989, after such a resolution was approved in the Senate Judiciary Committee, Turkey prohibited some United States training flights, reduced port calls, and halted military construction.

Military assistance has been an intrinsic feature of the defense relationship between Turkey and the United States. Turkey's limited economic resources, juxtaposed against its heavy NATO obligation to contain Soviet power in the eastern Mediterranean, made such support indispensable until the Soviet threat receded in the late 1980s. Between 1950 and 1991, the United States provided military assistance valued at US$9.4 billion, of which about US$6.1 billion was in grant form and US$3.3 billion was on a concessional loan basis.

At the insistence of Congress, the appropriation of military funds for Greece and Turkey has for many years been on a seven-to-ten ratio. The Turkish government regards the aid formula as inequitable given that Turkey has a population about six times that of Greece, has correspondingly heavier NATO commitments, and is host to many NATO and United States military facilities. In 1994 the United States Congress held back 10 percent of the funds appropriated for Turkey until the Department of State could verify improvement of Turkey's human rights record and progress on confidence-building measures in Cyprus. Turkey considered this interference in its internal affairs and made no effort to have the funds restored.

Turkey nevertheless has been the third largest recipient of United States military aid, after Israel and Egypt. Despite the end of the Soviet threat, Turkey's military needs during the Persian Gulf crisis resulted in a rise in the level of grant aid to US$500 million in fiscal year (FY—see Glossary) 1991. Although the administrations of presidents George H.W. Bush and William J. Clinton sought to maintain a similar level in subsequent years, citing heavy United States reliance on Turkish air bases for support of the Iraqi Kurds in Provide Comfort II. Congress approved only US$450 million in FY 1993 and shifted the financing from grants to loans. In FY 1994, a move in Congress to charge interest at market rather than concessional rates was barely deflected. Such a change would have been a blow to Turkey, which was already saddled with heavy foreign debts. Ultimately, US$405 millon in low-interest loans was approved. The Department of Defense also provides training to about 160 Turkish officers each year. These include students at the United States Army Command and General Staff College, as well as individuals assigned to technical schools and those receiving specialized training in management, language instruction, medical logistics, and air-traffic control.

Domestic Arms Industry

Since the mid-1980s, Turkey has been engaged in a wide-ranging program to develop a modern defense industry based on cooperation with firms in other countries. Previously, Turkey's economic and industrial capacity was insufficient to produce weapons as sophisticated as those of Western Europe. In the early years of the republic, the government sponsored a number of arms factories intended primarily to supply basic infantry weapons and ammunition. After World War II, Turkey's efforts to bring its military establishment up to modern standards depended almost totally on military assistance and credits from its NATO partners. After the imposition of the limited embargo by the United States in 1975, Turkey launched a series of projects to reduce its dependence on imports of major military items. Initial results took the form of a broader range of domestically produced light weapons and artillery and the development of an electronics industry oriented toward battlefield communications and the requirements of military aircraft.

In 1985 new legislation centralized efforts to launch an up-to-date arms industry under a new agency—the Defense Industry Development and Support Administration (later the Ministry of National Defense Undersecretariat for Defense Industries, known as SSM) with its own source of capital, the Defense Industry Support Fund. The fund does not depend on national defense budget appropriations but receives earmarked revenues directly—10 percent of taxes on fuel, 5 percent of individual and corporate income taxes, and taxes on alcohol and tobacco. Most of the major projects encouraged by SSM have been international joint ventures and coproduction enterprises. In most cases, the foreign partner must agree to an offset provision, that is, a commitment to purchase some part of the resulting production, or components or other goods manufactured in Turkey.

The Turkish defense industry employs about 50,000 individuals at 110 firms, many of them state owned. About 1,000 additional firms participate in defense business as subcontractors. The largest producer of weaponry in Turkey, with about 12,000 employees, is Makina ve Kimya Endüstrisi Kurumu (MKEK), controlled by the Ministry of Industry and Trade. MKEK meets the requirements of the Turkish armed forces for light arms (including the M–3 and MG–3 rifles and a machine gun of German design), ammunition, and explosives. It also produces antiaircraft and antitank guns.

In 1988 rocket and missile production was shifted from MKEK to a new company, Roket Sanayii (ROKETSAN). ROKETSAN has the largest share in the production of the propulsion system and rocket assembly for the four-country European consortium manufacturing the Stinger SAM. The company also plans to produce multi-launch rocket systems (MLRS) in partnership with a United States firm, the LTV Corporation. A consortium formed by a United States firm, FMC Corporation, and a Turkish firm, Nurol, is projected to produce 1,700 APCs and armored fighting vehicles by 1997.

Turkish arms manufacturers' most ambitious undertaking has been a consortium with United States firms to produce F–16 fighter aircraft. Under this arrangement, airframes for the F–16s are produced in a factory at Mürted Air Base near Ankara by TÜSAS (Türk Uçak Sanayi Sirketi) Aerospace Industries, with 51 percent ownership by Turkish interests, 42 percent by General Dynamics, and 7 percent by General Electric. The engine plant near Eskisehir is a joint venture with General Electric.

The project, whose total cost is projected at US$4.2 billion, is expected to result in the delivery of 240 F–16C/Ds to the Turkish air force between the late 1980s and the late 1990s.

Additional funds were pledged to the Turkish Defense Fund (TDF) after the Persian Gulf War by the United States, Saudi Arabia, Kuwait, and the United Arab Emirates, to be paid over a five-year period. Under an October 1994 agreement, Turkey requested that the TDF, which thus far amounted to some US$1.8 billion, be transferred to Turkey. Most of the TDF funds are to be used to cover the cost of eighty F–16 aircraft, of which forty were agreed upon in March 1992 and forty more in February 1994. Through offset arrangements, F–16 components and engines produced in Turkey are exported to the United States. Egypt ordered forty-six F–16s to be delivered between 1993 and 1995.

Communications equipment and electronic warfare systems for the Turkish military are produced by ASELSAN Military Electronics Industries, a state-owned company whose dominant shareholder is OYAK. ASELSAN manufactures under license a United States-designed family of manpack and vehicular battle-field radios and voice scramblers. It supplies the inertial navigation systems and fire control for the TÜSAS F–16 project and produces components for the Stinger missile program.

In addition to its coproduction role in the F–16 project, TÜSAS has contracted with Agusta, the Italian aircraft manufacturer, to produce forty SF–260 trainers at the Mürted plant. A contract with Construcciones Aeronáuticas, S.A. (CASA) of Spain calls for joint production of fifty-two CN–235 light transport aircraft. A US$1.1 billion agreement was concluded in 1992 with Sikorsky covering direct procurement of forty-five Black Hawk helicopters, with an additional fifty helicopters to be coproduced in Turkey by 1999.

Much of Turkey's indigenous naval construction has been carried out with cooperation from German shipbuilders. Four frigates of the MEKO–200 class were being built in 1995 at the main naval shipyard at Gölcük where three submarines of the 209-class (type-1200) had been built; four type-1400 submarines are scheduled to be commissioned between 1994 and 1998. Dogan-class fast-attack boats armed with Harpoon missiles have been produced in Turkish yards, as well as destroyer escorts, patrol boats, landing craft, and auxiliary craft. In 1993 private shipyards were invited to bid on construction of mine-sweepers and patrol boats.

The effort to create a modern defense industry on a narrow technological base was risky for Turkish defense planners. However, it appears to have been successful in enabling Turkey to rely on domestic sources to meet an increasing portion of its advanced equipment needs. The results have included reductions in costs and in the demand for foreign exchange, as well as the opening of foreign markets, mainly through offset provisions. As of the mid-1990s, the anticipated development of a Middle Eastern market for finished products did not appear to have occurred, based on available arms export data. A broader goal was to set new standards for quality and productivity in Turkish industry generally and thus increase the country's competitiveness through the lead established by the defense industry.

Internal Security Concerns

Since the late 1960s, Turkey has been plagued by recurrent political violence. Radical groups responsible for terrorism have included movements of both leftist and rightist orientation, as well as ethnic and religious extremists. By far the most serious source of violence since the mid-1980s has been the Kurdish separatist insurgency, which by the mid-1990s had nearly assumed the character of a civil war in the southeastern area of the country bordering Syria and Iraq.

During the 1970s, various political groups—particularly ones on the left—used violence in the hope that civil disorder and the consequent suppression by the state might lead to revolution. In the months preceding the assumption of power by Turkey's generals in September 1980, the toll of political killings rose to more than twenty a day. The government's repression of political activism and the detention of an estimated 30,000 persons suspected of terrorism were accompanied by arrests of union members, university students, and journalists. The stern measures of the military commanders were vehemently criticized by Turkish intellectuals and foreign observers; however, the measures did reduce the violence.

Even after civilian rule was restored in 1983, the continuation of martial law in certain areas, the expansion of police powers, and legal constraints on political movements dampened politically inspired violence. Terrorist incidents continued to occur in urban areas, but these were for the most part individually targeted bombings and assassinations, including attacks on United States installations and personnel. The number of such incidents peaked at seventy-five in 1991, most of them attributed to leftist protests against Turkey's strategic role in the international coalition against Iraq. Nevertheless, the preoccupying security issue for the Turkish government continued to be the mounting separatist insurgency of the Kurdistan Workers' Party (Partiya Karkere Kurdistan—PKK). The uprising of Kurds in northern Iraq after the Persian Gulf War focused attention on the condition of Kurds in general; the PKK used the occasion to intensify its military operations in the Kurdish region of southeastern Turkey.

Kurdish Separatists

The Kurdish national movement dates back at least to 1925, when Atatürk ruthlessly suppressed a revolt against the new Turkish republic motivated by the regime's renunciation of Muslim religious practices. Uprisings in the 1930s and 1940s prompted by opposition to the modernizing and centralizing reforms of the Turkish government in Ankara also were put down by the Turkish army. Kurdish opposition to the government's emphasis on linguistic homogeneity was spurred in the 1960s and 1970s by agitation in neighboring Iran and Iraq on behalf of an autonomous Kurdistan, to include Kurds from Turkey, Iran, Iraq, and Syria. The majority of Kurds, however, continued to participate in Turkish political parties and to assimilate into Turkish society.

The best known and most radical of the Kurdish movements, the PKK, which does not represent the majority of Kurds, seeks to establish an independent Marxist state in southeastern Turkey where the Kurdish population predominates. Beginning in 1984, a resurgence of Kurdish attacks attributed to the PKK necessitated the deployment of Turkish army units and elite police forces. Fighting in the mountain terrain favored the insurgents, who could intimidate local Kurdish families and ambush regular troops. The violence has mounted since 1991, with PKK guerrillas from camps in Syria, Iran, and Iraq, as well as from inside Turkey itself, attacking Turkish military and police outposts and targeting civilian community leaders and teachers. In 1993 PKK gunmen sought military targets outside the southeastern region; they also conducted coordinated attacks in many West European cities, particularly in Germany where more than 1 million Kurds live, against Turkish diplomatic installations and Turkish businesses, often operated by Kurds. Such attacks on commercial firms can be seen as efforts at intimidation to gain contributions to PKK fundraising.

Increased numbers of security forces were mobilized in 1994 against the Kurds in a government campaign of mounting intensity. One government strategy has been the forced evacuation and in a number of instances burning some 850 Kurdish villages to prevent them from harboring PKK insurgents. Although militarily successful, the evacuations have caused great hardship to the villagers.

The government has been accused of harassment, destruction of villages, and the slaying of Kurds believed to be sympathetic to the PKK. Its tactics have resulted in hundreds of civilian casualties and turned thousands into refugees, who have crowded into major Turkish cities. The insurgents, in turn, have targeted villages known to be sympathetic to the government, murdering state officials, teachers, government collaborators, and paramilitary village guards. In an especially cruel incident in May 1993 that ended a two-month cease-fire announced by the PKK, a PKK unit executed thirty unarmed military recruits after ambushing several buses.

As of early 1994, about 160,000 Turkish troops and gendarmerie had been mobilized for operations against the PKK. Some 40,000 civilians formed a village guard of progovernment Kurds. A new mobile security force of about 10,000 troops was undergoing special training in antiguerrilla operations. The United States Department of State estimated that there were 10,000 to 15,000 full-time PKK guerrillas, 5,000 to 6,000 of whom were in Turkey and the others in Iran, Iraq, and Syria. There were thought to be an additional 60,000 to 75,000 part-time guerrillas.

The number of deaths since the war's outbreak in 1984 had risen beyond 12,000 by 1994. According to official figures, more than 1,500 PKK guerrillas were killed and 7,600 captured during the first eleven months of 1993. During the same period, the number of government security personnel killed came to 676. Civilian deaths totaled 1,249, more than double the 1992 total.

The PKK cause was not helped by the Kurds of Iraq, who depended on Turkey to keep their enclave protected from the forces of Iraqi president Saddam Husayn. In October 1992, Iraqi Kurds and the Turkish army carried out a joint offensive against PKK bases in Iraqi Kurdistan, forcing the surrender of more than 1,000 PKK fighters. Turkey also enlisted Syria's cooperation in closing the PKK base in the Bekaa Valley of Lebanon. The government's flexibility in seeking a negotiated solution to the conflict was limited by the growing anger of the Turkish public over PKK terrorism and the killing of troops in the southeast and by the military's uncompromising anti-Kurdish stance.

Terrorism of the Left

Marxists and other groups of the extreme left have never been more than marginal factors in national politics, even during those periods when they were permitted to function as legal parties. Just before the military crackdown in 1980, four of the seven Marxist-oriented parties legally recognized at the time contested local elections but were able to gather a total of only 1 percent of the national vote. During the 1970s, the leftist movement turned increasingly to violence and terrorism; at the same time, left-wing ideologies became popular in the universities and among alienated and often unemployed urban youth.

In 1987 the leaders of the banned Turkish Workers' Party and of the Turkish Communist Party returned from exile to form a new Turkish United Communist Party. Both politicians were arrested and charged under the provision of the penal code that specifically outlawed communist organizations and the dissemination of Marxist-Leninist theories. After being decriminalized in 1991, the Turkish United Communist Party was again proscribed after the Constitutional Court upheld a ban on the grounds that it had violated Article 14 of the constitution, which prohibits "establishing the hegemony of one social class over another."

The most active of the left-wing terrorist groups is the Revolutionary Left Party (Devrimçi Sol—Dev Sol). Virulently anti-American and anti-NATO, Dev Sol was responsible for most of the attacks against United States targets and other political violence during the Persian Gulf War. In one incident, two United States civilians working for a United States defense contractor were killed. The Turkish government reacted vigorously, conducting raids against Dev Sol safe houses and enacting new antiterrorist legislation. Dev Sol is believed to have several hundred members, including several dozen armed militants. Because of police raids and internal factionalism, attacks by Dev Sol have been less numerous since 1991. Sympathizers among the foreign Turkish population in Western Europe have helped fund the organization; training support is believed to come from radical Palestinians in Lebanon.

The Turkish Workers' and Peasants' Liberation Army and the Marxist-Leninist Armed Propaganda Unit committed numerous acts of terrorism in the 1970s and early 1980s, including bank robberies and bombings of businesses, courts, and key government offices. Members of the latter group were sentenced in 1984 after convictions for eighty-seven killings, including the murders of five United States servicemen in 1979. Since 1990, however, the other extremist groups of the left have been overshadowed by Dev Sol.

Armenian Terrorism

The primary objective of Armenian terrorists during the 1970s and 1980s was to inflict revenge for the massacres of Armenians during World War I. Armenians regard these killings as systematic genocide, but Turks claim they were the unfortunate outgrowth of deportations intended to prevent Armenians from assisting the invading Russian armies. Terrorist groups also demanded that Turkey admit its guilt for crimes committed against Armenians and provide reparations in the form of money and territory for an Armenian homeland.

Most of the violence by Armenian terrorists has been inflicted on Turkish agencies and representatives outside Turkey. The best known of these groups, the Armenian Secret Army for the Liberation of Armenia (ASALA), apparently was formed in 1975 among leftist Armenians living in Beirut, Lebanon, with the help of sympathetic Palestinians. In reaction, rightists from the Armenian community in Lebanon formed the Justice Commandos of the Armenian Genocide (JCAG). A number of other groups claimed responsibility for terrorist acts, but ASALA and JCAG were judged to be the two main groups. It was not clear whether lawful Armenian political blocs in Lebanon sponsored these terrorist units, but they did not openly condone the terrorist acts of their offshoots.

Among the Armenian diaspora, numbering more than 6 million worldwide, probably fewer than 1,000 persons belong to terrorist factions. Members generally are young, recent immigrants to their countries of residence, or reside in places such as Lebanon where political violence is common. Assassination and bombing are the principal techniques used by the two main terrorist organizations. However, JCAG has limited its attacks to Turkish embassy officials in the United States, Canada, and Western Europe, refraining from indiscriminate violence to avoid alienating Western public opinion. Since 1983 responsibility for most of the attacks has been claimed by a group called the Armenian Revolutionary Army, possibly a cover name for JCAG.

ASALA has carried out a number of bombings of ticket offices and airport counters of United States airlines in Western Europe. Following the bombing of a Turkish airline counter at Orly Airport in Paris in 1983, which resulted in several deaths and injuries, a split developed within ASALA over the rationale of indiscriminate terrorism in advancing the Armenian cause. An offshoot, the ASALA Revolutionary Movement (ASALA-RM), regarded indiscriminate terrorism as counterproductive, while ASALA-Militant (ASALA-M) continued to favor unrestricted violence against both Turkish and "imperialist" targets. After the split, the ASALA membership appeared to become preoccupied with its internal differences and has since been relatively inactive.

Islamists

A legal, nonviolent Islamic political movement exists in Turkey. Its main locus is the Welfare Party (Refah Partisi—RP; also seen as Prosperity Party), which obtained the votes of 16.9 percent of the electorate in the 1991 general elections and captured 19 percent in the municipal elections of 1994. The Welfare Party also won mayoral contests in Ankara, Istanbul, and twenty-seven other large cities. The party stresses economic goals; to cast its appeal in religious terms would bring it into conflict with the constitutional ban on the organization of parties on the basis of religion, ethnicity, or political ideas considered authoritarian.

Turkey's political system is more open than those of most Middle Eastern states, and to a large extent it has been able to accommodate Muslim political expression while marginalizing its radical elements. Nevertheless, radical Muslim groups are considered a threat to the secular political establishment. Although a link with the Iranian government has not been proven, Iranian mullahs are believed to give support and encouragement to extremist Muslims.

Radical Islamic activism—sometimes described as fundamentalism—has been the source of some terrorism, in particular the murders of journalists, politicians, and academics who were outspoken defenders of Turkish secularism. Several Islamic groups have claimed responsibility for these deaths, among them the Islamic Movement Organization, about which little is known. Another obscure group, composed of local Islamists linked to the Iranian government, has targeted external enemies of Iran. One of the worst incidents of religious violence occurred in the city of Sivas in 1993 when religious fanatics set fire to a hotel where a well-known author and translator of Salman Rushdie's *The Satanic Verses* was staying. The author escaped, but thirty-seven people perished and 100 were injured. Anxious to avoid unnecessary tension in relations with Iran, Turkish officials have avoided placing blame directly on the Tehran government for sponsoring terrorist activity. Evidence, however, has been presented to Iran implicating extremists within the revolutionary power structure, if not the Iranian government itself.

Since 1991 a shadowy group known as Hizballah-Contra has sprung up in Kurdish areas, carrying out a campaign of assassination and terrorism against the PKK and its sympathizers. The organization is not connected to Hizballah (Party of God, also known as Islamic Jihad), a Shia terrorist movement dedicated to establishing an Iranian-style government in Lebanon. Although the Turkish government denies any link to Hizballah-Contra, the group's hit squads are believed to be tolerated by the police and gendarmerie, along with other Kurdish groups violently hostile to the PKK.

The leadership of Turkey's armed forces is highly sensitive to the possibility of soldiers becoming exposed to extremist Islamic influences. Orders issued in 1991 instructed troops to avoid "illegal, destructive, separatist trends, either from the right or left, which threaten the military's discipline." Commanders were urged to be especially careful with regard to staff members living outside military compounds in large cities where they could come into contact with Islamist groups. They were ordered to take stern measures—in some cases, expulsion—against officers and NCOs who adopted strong religious views, who refrained from certain social activities on religious grounds, or whose spouses wore Islamic garb.

Police System

The principal agencies devoted to internal security and law enforcement are the National Police and the gendarmerie, both headquartered in Ankara and both administered by the Ministry of Interior. Broadly, the National Police handles police functions (including traffic control) in the cities and towns, and the gendarmerie serves principally as a rural constabulary. In times of crisis, the prime minister can direct the chief of the General Staff to assist the police and gendarmerie in maintaining internal security. The gendarmerie is regarded as a military security force; during wartime or in areas placed under martial law, it functions under the army.

National Police

The territorial organization of the National Police corresponds roughly to Turkey's administrative subdivisions (see Provincial and Local Government, ch. 4). Below the general directorate are police directorates in all of the country's seventy-six provinces and police posts (district commands) in most of the administrative districts. Despite their wide territorial distribution, a very large proportion of the police are clustered in the major cities. No reliable data are available on the size of the police force, whose members are believed to number more than 50,000. Regardless of its size, the force does not appear large enough to keep up with the need generated by Turkey's urban growth and ordinary crime and traffic problems.

The laws establishing the organization of police at the provincial and local levels distinguish three categories of functions: administrative, judicial, and political. In this context, the administrative police perform the usual functions relating to the safety of persons and property: enforcement of laws and regulations, prevention of smuggling and apprehension of smugglers, quelling of public disorder, fingerprinting and photographing, public licensing, controlling traffic and inspecting motor vehicles, apprehending thieves and military deserters, locating missing persons, and keeping track of foreigners residing or traveling in Turkey. Film censorship is also considered an administrative responsibility. In some cases, municipalities provide all or part of the funding for administrative police functions in their localities.

The judicial police work closely with the administrators of justice. Attached to the offices of public prosecutors, the judicial police assist in investigating crimes, issue arrest warrants, and help prosecutors assemble evidence for trials. The political police combat activities considered subversive and deal with those groups whose actions or plans are identified as contrary to the security of the republic.

To carry out the police's broad and sometimes overlapping functions, specialized squads focusing on such problems as smuggling and the narcotics trade are located in the larger commands. At the other end of the scale, the police employ unskilled auxiliaries in many towns and in some neighborhoods of larger communities. These are selected local men, not armed, who are engaged to prevent local theft and to give the alarm in case of emergency.

Police ranks range from constable through sergeant, lieutenant, captain, superintendent second and first class, and several grades of police chief. A commissioner of police commands each of the seventy-six provincial directorates of police. Provincial directorates are divided into district police commands headed by superintendents.

In earlier years, an entrant to the lowest police grade was expected to have completed junior high school. But police authorities recognized that the low education level of the force contributed to violations of legal rights and mistreatment of prisoners. Thus, recent recruits have been required to have completed secondary school. Training consists of a six-month basic course at one of five police schools. Candidates for higher rank are sent to a police college (equivalent to a senior high school offering university preparation) and then to the Police Institute at Ankara, from which students graduate as sergeants after a three-year course.

The performance of the Turkish police has been the subject of persistent criticism for violations of fundamental human rights. These problems, which have received growing international and domestic attention, involve torture during questioning, incommunicado detention, politically motivated disappearances, "mystery killings," and excessive use of force. Successive governments have repeatedly promised to curb abuses by the security forces, but little if any improvement has been recorded (see Individual Rights, this ch.).

Gendarmerie

Primarily a rural police force, the gendarmerie maintains public order outside the municipal boundaries of cities and provincial towns and guards Turkey's land borders against illegal entry and smuggling. It has jurisdiction over 90 percent of the territory of Turkey and 50 percent of the population. The gendarmerie's recruits are supplied through the military conscription system, and its officers and NCOs are transferred from the army. New career junior officers are obtained by quotas from the graduating classes of the Turkish army academy.

Policeman directing traffic, Istanbul
Courtesy Hermine Dreyfuss

In late 1994, the gendarmerie's headquarters in Ankara was commanded by Aydin Ilter, a four-star general. Subordinate to the commanding general's chief of staff, a two-star general, are typical military staff sections for personnel, intelligence, operations, and logistics, as well as the headquarters commandant. The major operational category consists of the internal security units, divided into stationary forces and mobile infantry brigades. These forces may be supplemented by air units and commando units equipped with Russian APCs and towed artillery weapons. In 1994 Turkey announced the purchase of nineteen Russian helicopters to assist in operations against the PKK. Elite fighting formations that distinguished themselves in Cyprus in 1974, the commando units execute many of the operations against the PKK in the southeast. The gendarmerie also includes headquarters and border forces, administrative control and logistical support units, and training staff.

The total number of gendarmes was estimated at 70,000 active members and 50,000 reserves in late 1994. They are organized into thirteen regional commands encompassing the seventy-six provinces. In each province, the principal gendarmerie commander, a colonel or lieutenant colonel, advises the governor on matters of security and maintains direct charge of the district gendarmerie commands, usually headed by captains. Below the district commanders are commanders of the administrative subdistricts, each of whom controls the fixed posts in his area. There are some 3,600 posts, exclusive of border posts, usually located at intervals along the main roads and staffed by a sergeant and six or more gendarmes. To foster detachment from local groups and their interests and quarrels, gendarmes are usually assigned away from their home areas.

The administrative functions of the gendarmerie correspond roughly to those of the National Police but include such distinctive requirements as enforcing hunting and fishing laws, fighting forest fires, and patrolling borders. The gendarmes' judicial tasks include guarding prisons and assisting in investigations and preparations for trial. They also have military duties: serving as adjuncts to the army in emergencies, enforcing conscription, apprehending military deserters, and working in military courts.

Gendarmerie officers are chosen from cadets during the second year of training at the military academy, an aptitude for law being a prime factor in the selection. After completing their academy training, officers attend the infantry school for six months and the commando school for four months. Further professional training follows at the Gendarmerie Schools Command. NCOs are selected by examination from army personnel who have already served at least one year. They are then trained at the Gendarmerie Schools Command for five months. Basic military training is given to conscripts by the Gendarmerie Schools Command, followed by specialized training in various areas.

Writing in the late 1980s, the noted political journalist Mehmet Ali Birand commented that the gendarmerie had had an unfavorable reputation since its founding in 1839 and its later reorganization on the pattern of the French gendarmerie. It began as the agent of brute force for the government, putting down civil conflicts, pursuing criminals, and collecting taxes. From the early days of the republic, the gendarmerie was the only body available to subdue unrest, enforce the principles of Atatürk, suppress opposition, and collect levies.

The gendarmerie has relatively few officers and NCOs; the main burden of the service falls on ordinary conscripts who predominate in the force of 70,000. The conscripts are poorly trained in matters of law and regulations and in the manner of enforcing them, contributing to the harsh image of the gendarmerie. As Birand notes, in contrast to Turkish gendarmerie operations, operations of the French, Belgian, and Italian gendarmeries are carried out primarily by officers and NCOs, privates being assigned sentry duty and other tasks that will not bring them into contact with the public.

The commander of the gendarmerie said in 1993 that efforts were being made to tailor the personnel structure to enable the force to perform its missions more effectively. Specialized sergeants were being recruited instead of conscripts. No longer standardized, unit training was being tailored to conditions in various regions and particular types of missions. New equipment had been introduced to improve air transportation and surface movement, and to provide mobile command, control, communications, and intelligence capabilities.

Formed in 1982 as the maritime wing of the gendarmerie, the coast guard is now separate but also reports to the Ministry of Interior. With a personnel strength of about 1,100, the coast guard is responsible for maintaining the security of the coast and territorial waters, for conducting missions to protect its Exclusive Economic Zone in the Aegean—the boundaries of which are under dispute with Greece—for search-and-air-rescue operations, and for protecting the marine environment. The coast guard is organized into four area commands: the Black Sea, the Sea of Marmara and adjacent straits, the Aegean Sea, and the Mediterranean Sea. Surface patrols are carried out by fifty-two patrol vessels and smaller craft. The most effective of these are fourteen search-and-rescue vessels of 220 tons, all built within recent years in Turkish shipyards. Smaller 150-ton and 70-ton patrol boats of German origin were nearing obsolescence in the mid-1990s. An ambitious construction plan foresaw a major strengthening of the service with eight new vessels of 350 to 400 tons and forty-eight ships of 180 to 300 tons. A number of helicopters and aircraft were to be acquired to expand a small maritime air unit of three United States-manufactured OH–58 (Jet Ranger) helicopters.

Intelligence Services

Intelligence gathering is the primary responsibility of the National Intelligence Organization (Milli Istihbarat Teskilati—MIT), which combines the functions of internal and external intelligence agencies. In 1993 a career diplomat, Sonmez Koksal, was named undersecretary in charge of MIT, the first civilian to head the organization. Each branch of the military has its own intelligence arm, as do the National Police and the gendarmerie. Military intelligence activities in martial law areas aim to prevent seditious activities against the state. Intelligence personnel also engage in electronic eavesdropping and rely on reports of overseas military attachés and exchange information with foreign intelligence services.

Military and civil intelligence requirements are formulated by the National Intelligence Coordination Committee. This committee includes members of the staff of the National Security Council, to which it is directly responsible. Nevertheless, a lack of coordination among the intelligence services is said to be a weakness that hampers MIT effectiveness.

MIT has no police powers; it is authorized only to gather intelligence and conduct counterintelligence abroad and to uncover communist, extreme right-wing, and separatist—that is, Kurdish and Armenian—groups internally. The MIT chief reports to the prime minister but was in the past considered close to the military. MIT has been charged with failing to notify the government when it became aware of past plots, if not actual complicity in military coup attempts. The organization functions under strict discipline and secrecy. Housing and headquarters offices for its personnel are colocated in a compound in Ankara.

Kurdish groups in Western Europe have charged the Turkish intelligence service with fomenting dissension and unrest among their various factions. Although these claims have not been verified, it seems likely that infiltration of the Kurdish separatist movement is a high priority for MIT. Members of the agency are also suspected of having acted as agents provocateurs in leftist organizations during the 1970s. Dev Sol is believed to have been infiltrated by intelligence agents, as raids on its establishments in the early 1990s seemed to demonstrate.

Crime and Punishment

The Turkish court system and judicial procedures are based on European models adopted after the establishment of the republic. For example, the system of criminal justice that replaced the Islamic justice system of the Ottoman Empire derives from the Italian penal code, and civil law follows the Swiss model (see Secularist Reforms, ch. 2).

Crimes are defined as either felonies or misdemeanors, the latter including minor infractions such as traffic violations. Felonies include premeditated homicide, theft, arson, armed robbery, embezzlement of state property, perjury, and rape.

Punishments for felonies fall into the categories of strict imprisonment, ordinary imprisonment, and heavy fines. Under the Criminal Code of 1926, as amended, certain crimes against the state and premeditated murder were punished with the death penalty. In practice, executions were suspended in 1984. More than 1,000 death sentences were pending when blanket commutations were granted in 1986, and capital punishment ended formally with passage of the Anti-Terror Law of 1991. Strict imprisonment entails labor for between one year and life and, for a recidivist, could begin with a period of solitary confinement. Ordinary imprisonment can range up to twenty years and also requires labor. In serious cases, convictions may disqualify a person from holding public office and from practicing a profession or trade. Withdrawal of the right to vote and payment of damages or restitution also may result from conviction for a felony. In 1986 the Execution of Sentences Act halved the time for prisoners then serving jail sentences. Life sentences were reduced to twenty years and death sentences commuted to thirty-year terms.

Procedures in Criminal Law

When the police (or gendarmerie) believe that a person has committed a crime, the suspect is taken to the nearest police station for registration and interrogation. A police magistrate informs the suspect of the charges and questions the suspect and any witnesses to determine whether a prima facie case exists. A warrant of arrest is issued when detention of the accused is indicated. In principle, individuals can be detained pending trial only when there is a strong presumption that they have committed the offense with which they are charged and when there is reason to believe that they intend to escape, to destroy traces of the crime, to induce accomplices or witnesses to make false statements, or to evade the obligation to testify.

Important changes in the treatment of suspects occurred in 1992 with the introduction of the Criminal Trials Procedure Law. This law affirms the right of common criminal suspects to immediate access to legal counsel and the right to meet with an attorney at any time. Permissible prearraignment detention was shortened to twenty-four hours for common individual crimes and to four days for common crimes involving conspiracy. The practical effect of the new law has been improved attorney access for those charged with common crimes.

The 1991 Anti-Terror Law nullified the "thought crimes" articles of the penal code. However, it introduced a broad and ambiguous definition of terrorism, enabling the government to use the law not only to combat alleged terrorism but also to impose sentences of two to five years on ordinary citizens for written and oral propaganda, meetings, and demonstrations aimed at "damaging the indivisible unity of the state."

Persons detained for individual crimes under the Anti-Terror Law must be brought before a judge within forty-eight hours. Anyone charged with crimes of a collective political or conspiratorial nature may be detained for up to fifteen days and up to thirty days in the ten southeastern provinces under a state of emergency in early 1995. The law does not guarantee access to counsel in such cases, leaving this decision to prosecutors, who routinely deny access.

Cases involving minor offenses are tried by a justice of the peace, a single judge who has limited penal and civil jurisdiction. Somewhat more serious offenses are tried by courts of first instance, with a single judge. Central criminal courts that have a president and two judges deal with crimes punishable by more than five years' imprisonment. Three-judge commercial courts also exist.

Ordinary defendants have the right to a public trial and must be provided with free counsel if they are indigent. However, the constitution does provide for closed trials in the interest of "public morality and public security." There is no jury system; all cases are decided by a judge or panel of judges. The constitution requires that judges be independent of the executive in the discharge of their duties, and, in practice, judges are not subject to government interference. Defense lawyers have access to the prosecutor's files after arraignment and prior to the trial. Release may be granted after arraignment upon payment of bail or presentation of an appropriate guarantee.

Eight state security courts, each composed of five members—two civilian judges, one military judge, and two prosecutors—may try defendants accused of terrorism, drug smuggling, membership in illegal organizations, or espousing and disseminating prohibited ideas. The state security courts mainly handle cases under the Anti-Terror Law. As of the end of 1993, a total of 3,792 persons had been detained under the law, and 811 persons were serving sentences under its provisions. In addition to the longer prearraignment detention the law permits, the state security courts can hold closed hearings and may admit testimony gathered during police interrogation in the absence of counsel. Verdicts of the courts may be appealed to a special State Security Court of Appeals.

Martial law courts established after the 1980 coup continue to function in those provinces under martial law. Military courts hear cases involving infractions of military law by members of the armed forces. A separate military court appeals system applies. In late 1993, two television journalists received two-month sentences from a military court for presenting a program on military deserters and draft evaders in the first known case of civilians tried in a military court while Turkey was under civilian rule.

Incidence of Crime

The incidence of ordinary crime is considered low in comparison to rates in other Middle Eastern and some West European countries. As in many other countries with even better data-gathering capabilities, the statistics on criminal acts may be unreliable. The penal registry maintained by the Ministry of Justice offers only a partial indication of the actual extent of crime. Moreover, in much of rural Turkey acts formally considered police matters may be addressed in the local community without coming to the attention of the gendarmerie.

Official statistics indicate a doubling of prison admissions between 1984 and 1991. This increase was due almost entirely to a rapid rise in the number of persons jailed "according to special laws," meaning presumably those convicted of terrorism or illegal political activity. In numerous categories of ordinary crime, the number of prison admissions actually fell from 1984 to 1991. Nevertheless, it is generally believed that the incidence of ordinary crime has been growing because of the economic, social, and cultural stresses associated with relatively rapid urbanization and the weakening of traditional social controls among urban immigrants.

According to the *Statistical Yearbook of Turkey, 1993*, the number of convicts entering prisons in 1991 was 53,912, and the number discharged was 72,885. In most years, the number of admissions and discharges is nearly equal; the higher rate of discharges in 1991 was probably a result of the release of those convicted under political clauses of the penal code repealed that year. Among the most common felonies resulting in incarceration in 1991 were crimes against property (8,360), crimes against individuals (5,879), and crimes against "public decency and family order" (2,681). The numbers of persons admitted to prison bore little relation to the number of cases brought before the various criminal courts. According to official statistics, more than 52,000 new cases were brought before the central criminal courts, 632,000 before the criminal courts of first instance, and 493,000 before the justices of the peace.

The number entering prisons under special laws rose rapidly, from 7,514 in 1985 to 32,645 in 1991. Although Turkish sources offer no explanation of the increase, the period corresponds to the spiraling Kurdish dissidence and the strict laws then in effect dealing with "thought crimes."

Narcotics Trafficking

Turkey plays a major role in the narcotics trade, primarily as a natural route for the movement of hashish from Pakistan, Afghanistan, and Iran to destinations in Europe. The disintegration of the Soviet Union has resulted in a loss of control over drug production in Central Asia and Afghanistan. Unrest in Azerbaijan and Georgia facilitates smuggling from the Caucasus area. Turkish police maintain that the PKK is heavily involved in the heroin trade. The use of air and sea routes for narcotics transshipment through Turkey has grown as the conflict in former Yugoslavia has disrupted the traditional overland routes through the Balkans.

Turkey is an important processing point for morphine base and heroin base imported into the country. Also, the Turks traditionally have grown the opium poppy for medicinal purposes. The government effectively controls the cultivation and production of opiates, paying high prices for the crop and carefully monitoring growing areas. Local drug consumption and abuse are considered minor problems, although there are some indications that heroin and cocaine use is increasing among the more affluent segments of the population.

Nationwide there are more than 1,000 narcotics law enforcement officers. The principal law enforcement agencies concerned with narcotics are the National Police and the gendarmerie. Turkish customs agencies have lacked a professional cadre of narcotics interdiction agents, but in the mid-1990s were working toward creating such a body with United States training assistance. The coast guard has also begun playing a larger role in interdiction. In spite of Turkey's efforts, it is believed that little of the heroin passing through the country is seized because of insufficient staff to screen cargoes adequately, particularly at the key transfer point of Istanbul.

There is no evidence of widespread corruption among senior officials engaged in drug law enforcement. In some cases, however, drug investigations have been compromised by corruption at lower levels of the criminal justice system, as well as within the judicial system once traffickers have been apprehended. Because Turkey has no legislation prohibiting money laundering, it is almost impossible to track inflows of drug profits. However, the Turkish government has indicated its intention to introduce laws to deal with this practice.

Data on seizures of heroin and hashish show an upward trend in the five-year period between 1989 and 1993. Hashish seizures increased from 6.9 tons in 1989 to 28.7 tons in 1993. However, a major factor was a single seizure of more than 2.7 tons of morphine base and 13.5 tons of hashish aboard a Turkish merchant ship in January 1993.

Individual Rights

Under the martial-law regime established after the 1980 coup, Turkey's citizens suffered a serious curtailment of normal civil rights. Starting in 1983, when parliamentary elections were held, the government gradually lifted restraints on individual liberties and progressively withdrew martial law from major cities and provinces. Restrictions on the press were removed in 1985, making it permissible to publish all views except those banned by the penal code. The 1987 state of emergency declared in ten southeastern provinces where the government faced terrorist violence allowed the civilian governor to exercise certain powers verging on martial law, including warrantless searches and restrictions on the press.

Although progress has been made in reducing human rights abuses since the military government period, mistreatment by the police in the form of beatings and torture has remained a seemingly intractable problem. Reports of illegal practices, in some cases extrajudicial killings, deaths in custody, and disappearances, have become more widespread since 1992, when violence resulting from the Kurdish insurgency reached unprecedented levels. The Turkish government has renewed previous pledges to end the use of torture by the security forces, but little has been achieved in curbing the excesses of the police and military.

The widespread evidence of torture and severe ill-treatment of detainees has been condemned by numerous international groups, such as the Council of Europe's Committee for the Prevention of Torture and the United Nations Committee on Torture. Within Turkey, illegal police activities have been monitored by the Human Rights Association since that organization received official approval in 1987. The association subsequently attracted a membership of about 20,000 and opened branches in fifty of the provincial capitals. The companion Human Rights Foundation of Turkey, established in 1990, operates torture-rehabilitation centers in Ankara, Izmir, and Istanbul, and serves as a clearinghouse for human rights information. Besides enduring government-imposed restrictions, the Human Rights Association has seen nine people associated with the organization slain. The group's leadership has charged that nearly half of its offices have been forced to close because of police pressure.

The Human Rights Foundation has claimed that government security forces were responsible for ninety-one extrajudicial killings during the first nine months of 1993, and that security forces were implicated in many of the 291 "mystery killings" during the same period. Perhaps twenty persons died in official custody, some allegedly as a result of torture. Other killings occurred during raids on terrorist safe houses, or when deadly force was used against unarmed civilians participating in peaceful demonstrations.

Turkish human rights advocates believe that most persons charged with political crimes undergo torture, usually while in incommunicado detention in the hands of the police or gendarmerie before being brought before a court. About half of the ordinary criminal suspects are thought to undergo torture while under police interrogation. In the event that law enforcement officers are charged in torture cases, the sentences imposed are generally light or the cases drag on for years.

The constitution guarantees inviolability of the domicile and privacy of communications except upon issuance of a judicial warrant. However, in the southeastern provinces that are under state of emergency the governor may authorize warrantless search. In these areas, security personnel at roadblocks regularly search travelers and vehicles in an effort to apprehend smugglers and terrorists.

University students and faculty members may not be members of political parties or become involved in political activities. Youth branches of political parties are forbidden, and the university rector must grant permission for a student to join any association. Political activity by trade unions is also banned. Thus, unions may neither endorse candidates nor make contributions to their campaigns; they are, however, able to make known their opposition to or support of political parties and government policies. Collective bargaining and strikes are strictly regulated. Unions must have government permission to hold meetings and rallies but are permitted to organize workplaces freely and to engage in collective bargaining (see Human Resources and Trade Unions, ch. 3; Political Interest Groups, ch. 4).

In March 1994, seven Kurdish legislators were arrested on the parliament grounds. Indictments were prepared against them for writings and speeches deemed supportive of Kurdish separatism. The incident aroused considerable controversy both domestically and internationally; all seven assembly members were given long prison terms in late 1994.

Freedom of conscience and religious belief is guaranteed by the constitution, as is private dissemination of religious ideas. However, religious activity is strictly supervised in accordance with the principles of secularism and separation of church and state. No political party advocating a theocracy or government founded on religious principles is permitted. The operation of churches, monasteries, synagogues, and schools must be approved by the state. Armenian and Greek churches are carefully monitored, and prosecutors have brought charges of proselytism against Islamists and evangelical Christian groups deemed to have political overtones. Courts have not been sympathetic to such charges, but the police have acted against some evangelical Christians by refusing to renew their residence permits and expelling them.

Penal System

The civil penal system is administered by the General Directorate of Prisons and Houses of Detention in the Ministry of Justice. There is a prison or jail in almost every town and at least one in every district. The older penal institutions include most of the town and district jails and the larger provincial prisons in use since Ottoman times. These are gradually being supplemented by newer "penitentiary labor establishments" whose distinguishing feature is the availability of equipment for labor. Prison labor is compulsory for all in old and new prisons. Prisoners are allowed to send up to one-half of their prison earnings to a dependent; part is withheld for rations, and the remainder goes to the prisoner upon discharge. Prisons were previously known to be overcrowded, but the apparent reduction in jail sentences for common crimes and the commutation of longer sentences may have mitigated the problem.

According to official data, the number of convicts in prisons declined from more than 46,000 in 1984 to 10,656 in 1991. The drop in the prison population took place mainly between 1986 and 1991, when mass releases occurred. When the large number sentenced to prison is compared with the small prison population at any one time, it appears that many convicts serve sentences of only a few months. Persons classified as political prisoners or terrorists are apparently regarded separately because more than 32,000 were incarcerated in 1991 under the "special laws" category.

By and large, Turks accept the Muslim view that crime is a willful act and thus regard penalties as punishment for the act and as a means to deter similar acts, not as instruments of rehabilitation or reeducation. There has been a trend among some specialists and Turkish officials to view criminal acts as the product of social conditions and therefore to emphasize rehabilitation, but this view has had only limited influence on penal practice.

Whereas torture of both political and ordinary prisoners by security forces is a deep-rooted problem, much of it occurs prior to court hearings. Incidents arising from mistreatment in prisons have been decreasing in recent years. However, in two cases mentioned in 1992 by the international human rights group Amnesty International, large numbers of prisoners were beaten, some seriously, for protesting against prison disciplinary measures.

After widespread hunger strikes in 1989, the minister of justice introduced a number of reforms to improve prison conditions, including an end to corporal punishment, bread-and-water diets, and solitary confinement in unlighted cells. The government, however, continued to be faced with domestic and international criticism and subsequently announced a prison reform bill in 1993. At the end of 1994, parliament had not enacted promised prison reforms.

*   *   *

Discussion in this chapter of the size, organization, and armaments of the Turkish armed forces is based in part on *The Military Balance, 1994–1995,* published by the International Institute for Strategic Studies in London, and on *Jane's Fighting Ships, 1994–95* Additional material can be found in the section on Turkey by Mark Stenhouse in *Jane's NATO Handbook, 1991–92.*

An authoritative statement by Turkish chief of staff General Dogan Güres on the new strategy and restructuring of the armed forces is contained in the June 1993 issue of the *Journal of the Royal United Services Institute for Defence Studies.* Graham E. Fuller and other authors address Turkey's changed geostrategic situation following the collapse of the Soviet Union in *Turkey's New Geopolitics: From the Balkans to Western China.* Turkish military leaders analyze the missions and capabilities of the individual service branches in a series of articles in a special 1993 issue of *NATO's Sixteen Nations* called "Defence of Turkey."

A book by a noted Turkish journalist, Mehmet Ali Birand, *Shirts of Steel: An Anatomy of the Turkish Armed Forces,* provides previously unfamiliar details on the military education system, military traditions and institutions, and the perspectives and aspirations of career officers.

Discussion of Turkey's human rights record can be found in publications by Amnesty International and in the annual *Country Reports on Human Rights Practices* published by the United States Department of State. (For further information and complete citations, see Bibliography.)

Appendix A

Table 1. Metric Conversion Coefficients and Factors

When you know	Multiply by	To find
Millimeters	0.04	inches
Centimeters......................	0.39	inches
Meters...........................	3.3	feet
Kilometers	0.62	miles
Hectares	2.47	acres
Square kilometers	0.39	square miles
Cubic meters	35.3	cubic feet
Liters	0.26	gallons
Kilograms	2.2	pounds
Metric tons	0.98	long tons
....	1.1	short tons
....	2,204.0	pounds
Degrees Celsius (Centigrade)	1.8 and add 32	degrees Fahrenheit

Table 2. *The House of Osman: Sultans of the Ottoman Empire,*
1281–1922

Name	Lineage	Reigned
Osman I	Son of the *gazi* Ertugrul	1281–1324[1]
Orhan	Son of Osman	1324–60
Murad I	Son of Orhan	1360–89
Bayezid I[2]	Son of Murad I	1389–1402
Süleyman[2]	Son of Bayezid I	1402–11
Musa[2]	Son of Bayezid I	1411–13
Mehmet I[2]	Son of Bayezid I	1413–21
Murad II	Son of Mehmet I	1421–44, 1446–51
Mehmet II	Son of Murad II	1444–46, 1451–81
Bayezid II	Son of Mehmet II	1481–1512
Selim I	Son of Bayezid II	1512–20
Süleyman I[3]	Son of Selim I	1520–66
Selim II	Son of Süleyman I	1566–74
Murad III	Son of Selim II	1574–95
Mehmet III	Son of Murad III	1595–1603
Ahmet I	Son of Mehmet III	1603–17
Mustafa I	Son of Ahmet I	1617–18
Osman II	Son of Ahmet I	1618–22
Mustafa I	Son of Ahmet I	1622–23
Murad IV	Nephew of Mustafa I	1623–40
Ibrahim	Brother of Murad IV	1640–48
Mehmet IV	Son of Ibrahim	1648–87
Süleyman II[4]	Son of Ibrahim	1687–91
Ahmet II	Son of Ibrahim	1691–95
Mustafa II	Son of Mehmet IV	1695–1703
Ahmet III	Son of Mehmet IV	1703–30
Mahmud I	Son of Mustafa II	1730–54
Osman III	Son of Mustafa II	1754–57
Mustafa III	Son of Ahmet III	1757–74
Abdül Hamid I	Brother of Mustafa III	1774–89
Selim III	Nephew of Abdül Hamid I	1789–1807
Mustafa IV	Cousin of Selim III	1807–08
Mahmud II	Brother of Mustafa IV	1808–39
Abdülmecid I	Son of Mahmud II	1839–61
Abdülaziz	Son of Mahmud II	1861–76
Murad V	Son of Abdülmecid I	1876
Abdül Hamid II	Son of Abdülmecid I	1876–1909
Mehmet V	Son of Abdülmecid I	1909–18

Table 2. The House of Osman: Sultans of the Ottoman Empire, 1281–1922

Name	Lineage	Reigned
Mehmet VI	Son of Abdülmecid I	1918–22[5]

[1] Date of beginning of reign is approximate.
[2] The period 1403–13, during which the sons of Bayezid I contested succession to the sultanate, is cited as an interregnum by many sources. Other sources date the beginning of the reign of Mehmet I from 1403.
[3] Süleyman II in some sources.
[4] Süleyman III in some sources.
[5] Sultanate abolished 1922; Abdülmecid II (brother of Mehmet VI) remained as caliph 1922–24.

Table 3. Presidents and Prime Ministers, 1920–95

President	Prime Minister	Period in Office
	Atatürk[1]	May 1920–January 1921
	Fevzi Çakmak[1]	January 1921–July 1922
	Rauf Orbay[1]	July 1922–August 1923
	Fethi Okyar[1]	August–October 1923
Atatürk (1923–38)	Ismet Inönü (CHP)[2]	November 1923–November 1924
	Fethi Okyar (Progressive Republican Party)	November 1924–March 1925
	Ismet Inönü (CHP)	March 1925–October 1937
Ismet Inönü (1938–50)	Celal Bayar (CHP)	October 1937–January 1939
	Refik Saydam (CHP)	January 1939–July 1942
	Sükrü Saraçoglu (CHP)	July 1942–August 1946
	Recep Peker (CHP)	August 1946–September 1947
	Hasan Saka (CHP)	September 1947–January 1949
	Semsettin Günaltay (CHP)	January 1949–May 1950
Celal Bayar (1950–60)	Adnan Menderes (DP)[3]	May 1950–May 1960
Cemal Gürsel (1960–66)	Cemal Gürsel[4]	May 1960–November 1961
	Ismet Inönü (CHP)	November 1961–February 1965
	Suat Hayri Ürgüplü (Independent)	February–October 1965
	Süleyman Demirel (AP)[5]	October 1965–March 1971
Cevdet Sunay (1966–73)	Nihat Erim (Independent)	March 1971–April 1972
	Ferit Melen[6] (NRP)[7]	April 1972
	Suat Hayri Ürgüplü (Independent)	April–May 1972
	Ferit Melen (NRP)	May 1972–April 1973
	Naim Talu (Independent)	April 1973–January 1974

Table 3. *Presidents and Prime Ministers, 1920–95*

President	Prime Minister	Period in Office
Fahri Korutürk (1973–80)	Bülent Ecevit (CHP)	January–November 1974
	Sadi Irmak (Independent)	November 1974–March 1975
	Süleyman Demirel (AP)	March 1975–January 1978
	Bülent Ecevit (CHP)	January 1978–October 1979
	Süleyman Demirel (AP)	October 1979–September 1980
Kenan Evren[8] (1980–89)	Bülent Ulusu (appointed)	September 1980–December 1983
	Turgut Özal (ANAP)[9]	December 1983–October 1989
	Ali Bozer[6] (ANAP)	October–November 1989
Turgut Özal (1989–93)	Yildirim Akbulut (ANAP)	November 1989–June 1991
	Mesut Yilmaz (ANAP)	June–November 1991
	Süleyman Demirel (DYP)[10]	November 1991–May 1993
	Erdal Inönü[11]	May–June 1993
Süleyman Demirel 1993–	Tansu Çiller (DYP)	June 1993–

[1] President of the Grand National Assembly.
[2] CHP—Cumhuriyet Halk Partisi (Republican People's Party).
[3] DP—Demokrat Partisi (Democrat Party).
[4] Interim government under Committee of National Unity.
[5] AP—Adalet Partisi (Justice Party).
[6] Acting prime minister.
[7] NRP—National Reliance Party.
[8] Evren functioned as head of the National Security Council, or de facto chief of state, from September 1980 to November 1982.
[9] ANAP—Anavatan Partisi (Motherland Party).
[10] DYP—Dogru Yol Partisi (True Path Party).
[11] Caretaker prime minister.

Table 4. Population by Age-Group, 1980, 1990, and 2000
(in percentages)

Age-Group	1980	1990	2000[1]
0–14	39.2	34.8	31.8
15–64	56.1	61.2	62.6
Over 65	4.7	4.2	5.6
TOTAL[2]	100.0	100.0	100.0

[1] Projected.
[2] Figures may not add to totals because of rounding.

Source: Based on information from *The Dorling Kindersley World Reference Atlas*, New York, 1994, 546

Table 5. Economically Active Population by Sector, Selected Years, 1970–93
(in thousands of workers over age fifteen)

Sector	1970	1980	1990	1993
Agriculture, fishing, and forestry	8,237	8,353	8,723	8,397
Construction	665	895	973	1,141
Manufacturing	1,343	2,057	2,553	2,693
Mining	156	188	202	131
Trade and hotels	886	1,429	2,093	2,338
Transportation and communications	417	612	808	898
Other, including services	1,330	2,168	3,012	3,104
Total civilian employment	13,034	15,702	18,364	18,702
Unemployment	871	1,376	1,590	1,530
Unemployment rate (in percentages)	6.3	8.1	8.0	7.6
CIVILIAN LABOR FORCE	13,905	17,078	19,954	20,232

Source: Based on information from Organisation for Economic Co-operation and Development, *OECD Economic Surveys: Turkey, 1995*, Paris, 1995, 9.

Table 6. *Summary of Consolidated Budget, 1988–93*
(in billions of Turkish lira) [1]

	1988	1989	1990	1991	1992	1993
Revenues						
Tax revenues	14,232	25,550	45,399	78,643	141,602	264,273
Non-tax revenues	3,355	5,819	11,174	18,104	32,622	87,119
Total revenues	17,587	31,369	56,573	96,747	174,224	351,392
Expenditures						
Current expenditures	7,460	16,660	33,452	60,403	114,221	204,829
Investments	3,564	5,818	10,055	17,146	29,239	53,161
Transfers to SEEs [2]	1,025	1,223	1,265	12,191	8,145	25,850
Interest payments	4,998	8,259	13,966	24,073	40,298	116,470
Other transfers	4,420	6,911	9,789	16,450	29,755	89,939
Total expenditures	21,447	38,871	68,527	130,263	221,658	485,249
Budget balance	–3,860	–7,502	–11,954	–33,516	–47,434	–133,857
Deferred minus advanced payments	–81	–639	–400	90	–12,005	7,754
Cash balance	–3,941	–8,141	–12,354	–33,426	–59,439	–126,103
Long-term borrowing (net)	2,609	5,578	7,983	4,200	19,446	51,197
Short-term borrowing (net)	1,064	1,452	2,263	23,509	41,372	75,251
Other (including errors and omissions)	268	1,111	2,108	5,717	–1,379	–345

[1] For value of the Turkish lira—see Glossary.
[2] SEEs—State Economic Enterprises.

Source: Based on information from Organisation for Economic Co-operation and Developmnent, *OECD Economic Surveys: Turkey, 1995*, Paris, 1995, 105.

Table 7. *Production of Major Agricultural Commodities, 1987–92*
(in thousands of tons)

Commodity	1987	1988	1989	1990	1991	1992
Cereals						
Wheat	18,932	20,500	16,200	20,000	20,400	19,318
Barley	6,900	7,500	4,500	7,300	7,800	6,900
Corn	2,600	2,000	2,000	2,100	2,100	2,100
Rye	385	280	191	240	250	225
Oats	325	276	216	270	255	250
Rice	165	158	181	230	200	215
Total cereals ...	29,307	30,714	23,288	30,140	31,005	29,008
Industrial crops						
Sugar beets	12,717	11,534	10,929	13,986	15,097	14,800
Cotton (lint) ...	537	657	565	655	539	605
Tobacco	177	212	270	288	243	320
Total industrial crops	13,431	12,403	11,764	14,929	15,879	15,725
Oilseeds						
Sunflower seed ..	1,100	1,150	1,250	860	800	950
Cottonseed	859	1,051	904	1,702	1,401	1,573
Sesame seed	43	45	37	39	43	34
Total oilseeds ..	2,002	2,246	2,191	2,601	2,244	2,557
Vegetables, fruits, and nuts						
Potatoes	4,300	4,350	4,080	4,300	4,600	4,500
Grapes	3,300	3,350	3,430	3,500	3,600	3,460
Oranges	700	740	740	739	835	824
Olives	600	1,100	500	1,100	640	750
Lemons	340	360	335	357	429	420
Hazelnuts (in shell)	280	353	456	375	315	520
Raisins	105	129	138	135	130	120
Dried figs	45	50	50	45	45	35
Olive oil	100	90	72	110	96	n.a.
Total vegetables, fruits, and nuts	9,770	10,522	9,801	10,661	10,690	10,629

n.a.—not available.

Source: Based on information from Economist Intelligence Unit, *Country Profile: Turkey, 1994–95*, London, 1994, 24.

Table 8. Energy Production, 1988–92
(in thousands of tons unless otherwise indicated)

	1988	1989	1990	1991	1992
Total coal (including lignite)	11,530	12,940	12,550	11,880	12,210
Crude petroleum	2,564	2,876	3,720	4,537	4,584
Main petroleum products	19,265	17,789	18,563	18,409	18,811
Electricity (in thousands of kilowatt hours)	48	52	58	58	67

Source: Based on information from Economist Intelligence Unit, *Country Profile: Turkey, 1994–1995*, London, 1994, 28; and Organisation for Economic Co-operation and Development, *Energy Balances of OECD Countries, 1991–1992*, Paris, 1994, 170.

Table 9. Exports by Commodity, 1987–92
(in millions of United States dollars)

	1987	1988	1989	1990	1991	1992
Agricultural products						
Cereals	266	441	315	342	287	419
Hazelnuts	391	359	266	456	366	291
Other fruits and vegetables	409	508	523	612	721	692
Cotton	20	141	160	191	193	46
Tobacco	314	266	480	419	564	309
Other industral crops and forestry products	97	289	53	57	284	268
Live animals and sea products	356	337	330	272	268	178
Total agricultural products	1,853	2,341	2,127	2,349	2,683	2,203
Mineral products	272	377	413	331	286	265
Processed and manufactured products						
Processed agricultural products	954	885	918	940	1,212	1,337
Textiles and clothing . . .	2,707	3,201	3,505	4,060	4,328	5,268

Table 9. *Exports by Commodity, 1987–92*
(in millions of United States dollars)

	1987	1988	1989	1990	1991	1992
Hides and leather	722	514	604	747	620	568
Chemicals	527	734	774	616	464	491
Petroleum products	232	331	254	287	277	231
Glass and ceramics	205	233	258	329	359	395
Iron and steel	852	1,458	1,349	1,612	1,452	1,558
Metal products and machinery	788	383	219	230	265	398
Electrical equipment and products	293	294	234	438	533	591
Other	785	911	972	1,020	1,119	1,410
Total processed and manufactured products..........	8,065	8,944	9,087	10,279	10,629	12,247
TOTAL	10,190	11,662	11,627	12,959	13,598	14,715

Source: Based on information from Organisation for Economic Co-operation and
Development, *OECD Economic Surveys: Turkey, 1995*, Paris, 1995, 96; and Economist Intelligence Unit, *Country Profile: Turkey, 1994–95*, London, 1994, 43.

Table 10. *Imports by Commodity, 1987–92*
(in millions of United States dollars)[1]

Commodity	1987	1988	1989	1990	1991	1992
Agricultural products and livestock	782	499	1,041	1,323	813	1,184
Mineral products						
Oil						
Crude oil	2,711	2,434	2,456	3,817	2,794	2,894
Oil products	245	343	522	805	962	865
Total oil	2,956	2,777	2,980	4,622	3,756	3,759
Other	444	427	448	172	198	161
Total mineral products	3,400	3,204	3,426	4,794	3,954	3,920
Processed and manufactured products						
Processed agricultural products	720	738	843	1,162	989	935
Manufactured products						
Chemicals	1,685	1,781	1,710	2,451	2,463	2,624
Rubber and plastics . .	488	525	485	807	848	986
Iron and steel	1,537	1,655	2,217	1,932	2,009	2,118
Non ferrous metals . .	418	412	421	537	452	426
Electrical appliances .	940	1,075	1,028	1,580	1,877	1,762
Motor vehicles	540	690	790	1,590	1,540	2,221
Other machinery	974	635	370	585	342	61
Other industrial products	2,799	3,121	3,461	5,541	5,760	6,635
Total manufactured products	9,381	9,894	10,482	15,023	15,291	16,833
Total processed and manufactured products	10,101	10,632	11,325	16,185	16,280	17,768
TOTAL	14,283	14,335	15,792	22,302	21,047	22,872

[1] C.I.F.—Cost, insurance, and freight.

Source: Based on information from Organisation for Economic Co-operation and Development, *OECD Economic Surveys: Turkey, 1995*, Paris, 1995, 97; and Economist Intelligence Unit, *Country Profile: Turkey, 1994–95*, London, 1994, 44.

Table 11. Major Trading Partners, 1988–95

Country	1988	1989	1990	1991	1992	1993
EXPORTS						
OECD countries[1]						
EU countries[2]						
Britain	576	616	744	676	796	835
France	499	595	737	689	809	771
Germany	2,178	2,196	3,076	3,413	3,660	3,654
Italy	955	978	1,106	972	943	750
Other	920	1,047	1,241	1,292	1,393	1,283
Total EU	5,128	5,432	6,904	7,042	7,601	7,293
Japan	209	233	239	226	162	158
Switzerland	265	174	293	246	223	216
United States	761	971	968	913	865	986
Other OECD	374	391	417	430	496	420
Total OECD	6,737	7,201	8,821	8,857	9,346	9,072
Central and East European countries	520	923	829	1,053	1,217	1,670
Middle East and North Africa						
Iran	546	561	495	487	455	290
Iraq	986	445	215	122	212	160
Other	1,924	1,798	1,742	2,085	2,096	2,293
Total Middle East and North Africa	3,456	2,804	2,452	2,694	2,763	2,743
Other	949	699	855	989	1,388	1,863
TOTAL EXPORTS	11,662	11,627	12,957	13,593	14,715	15,349
IMPORTS						
OECD countries						
EU countries						
Britain	739	728	1,014	1,166	1,187	1,546
France	829	745	1,340	1,227	1,351	1,952
Germany	2,067	2,225	3,523	3,232	3,754	4,533
Italy	1,006	1,071	1,727	1,845	1,919	2,558
Other	1,267	1,307	1,750	1,753	1,838	2,361
Total EU	5,908	6,076	9,354	9,223	10,049	12,950
Japan	555	530	1,120	1,092	1,113	1,621
Switzerland	344	412	537	489	688	651
United States	1,520	2,094	2,282	2,255	2,601	3,351
Other OECD	924	822	958	1,013	972	1,402
Total OECD	9,251	9,934	14,251	14,072	15,423	19,975
Central and East European coutnries	857	1,124	1,947	1,875	2,094	3,253

Table 11. Major Trading Partners, 1988–95

Country	1988	1989	1990	1991	1992	1993
Middle East and North Africa						
Iran	660	233	492	91	365	667
Iraq	1,441	1,650	1,047	0	1	0
Other	740	947	2,120	2,890	2,872	2,573
Total Middle East and North Africa	2,841	2,830	3,659	2,981	3,238	3,240
Other	1,391	1,902	2,445	2,119	2,116	2,961
TOTAL IMPORTS	14,340	15,790	22,302	21,047	22,871	29,429

[1] OECD—Organisation for Economic Co-operation and Development.
[2] EU—European Union.

Source: Based on information from Organisation for Economic Co-opearation and Development, *OECD Economic Surveys: Turkey, 1995*, Paris, 1995, 99.

Table 12. Summary of Balance of Payments, Selected Years, 1985–93
(in millions of United States dollars)

	1985	1987	1989	1991	1993
Exports (f.o.b.)[1]	8,255	10,322	11,780	13,667	15,610
Imports (f.o.b.)	−11,230	−13,551	15,999	21,007	29,772
Trade balance	−2,975	−3,229	−4,219	−7,340	−14,162
Services	22	33	1,622	2,499	4,014
Private transfers (net)	1,762	2,066	3,135	2,854	3,085
Official transfers (net)	222	324	423	2,245	73
Current account balance	−969	−806	961	258	−6,990
Private long-term capital (net)	856	1,388	2,456	1,562	6,839
Official long-term capital (net)	−594	453	−1,092	−939	−930
Capital account balance	262	1,841	1,364	623	5,909
Balance of payments	−707	1,035	2,325	881	1,081
Change in reserves	−361	137	2,471	−1,197	308

[1] f.o.b.—free on board.

Source: Based on information from Organisation for Economic Co-operation and Development, *OECD Economic Surveys: Turkey, 1995*, Paris, 1995, 100.

Table 13. Major Army Equipment, 1994

Type and Description	Country of Origin	In Inventory
Tanks		
Leopard	Germany	397
M–48	United States	3,004
M–60	-do-	932
Armored vehicles		
Infantry fighting vehicles	Turkey/United States	65
Armored personnel carriers		
M–113	United States	2,815
IAPC	United States/Turkey	125
BTR 60	Russia	300
AWC	Turkey	345
Self-propelled guns and howitzers		
105mm: M–52A1 and M–108	United States	389
155mm: M–44	-do-	168
175mm: M–107	-do-	36
203mm: M–55 and M–110	-do-	228
Towed artillery		
105mm: M–101A1 and others	-do-	640
150mm: Skoda	Czechoslovakia	161
155mm: M–114A1 and M–59	United States	613
203mm: M–115	-do-	162
Mortars		
107mm: M–30, some self-propelled	-do-	1,265
120mm: various	United States/Germany/ France	578
81mm: various, including self-propelled ..	-do-	3,175
Multiple rocket launchers		
227mm: MLRS	United States/Turkey	12
107mm	United States	23
Antitank guided weapons		
Milan	France	392
Cobra	Germany	186
TOW self-propelled	United States	365
Helicopters		
Cobra AH–1W/P	-do-	38
S–70A Sikorsky	United States	8
AB–204 Agusta Bell	Italy	14
AB–205 Agusta Bell	-do-	64
AB–212 Agusta Bell	-do-	2
UH–1H Iroquois	United States	96

Source: Based on information from *The Military Balance, 1994–1995*, London, 1994, 66–67

Table 14. Major Air Force Equipment, 1994

Type and Description	Country of Origin	In Inventory
Fighter-bombers and fighter-ground attack		
F–16C/D	United States/Turkey	138
F–5A/B	United States	195
F–4E	-do-	152
F–104G	Various NATO	24
Reconnaissance (armed)		
RF–5A	United States	20
RF–4E	-do-	26
Transports		
C–130E Hercules	-do-	13
C–160D Transall	Germany	19
CN–235	Spain/Turkey	52
Helicopters		
UH–1H Blackhawk utility	United States	21
Surface-to-air missile launchers		
Nike-Hercules	-do-	128
Rapier............................	Britain	24

Source: Based on information from *The Military Balance, 1994–1995*, London, 1994, 68.

Table 15. Major Naval Equipment, 1994

Type and Description	Country of Origin	In Inventory
Destroyers		
Gearing-class	United States	8
Carpenter-class	-do-	2
Sumner-class	-do-	1
Frigates		
MEKO–200 with Sub Harpoon SSM	Germany	4
MEKO–200	Turkey	4 (on order)
Berk-class	-do-	2
Koln-class	Germany	2
Knox-class with Sub Harpoon SSM	United States	8
Submarines		
Guppy-class	-do-	7
Type–209/1200	Germany/Turkey	6
Type–209/1400	Turkey	2
Tang-class	United States	2
Fast-attack craft		
Dogan-class (Lurssen 57) with Harpoon SSM	Germany/Turkey	8
Kartal-class (Jaguar) with Penguin SSM	Germany	8
Yildiz-class	Turkey	2 (on order)
Patrol craft		
Coastal and inshore	United States/Germany/ Turkey	29
Minelayers	United States/Denmark	3
Minesweepers	United States/France/ Canada	26
Amphibious		
Landing ships, tank	United States/Turkey	7
Landing craft, tank	Turkey	35
Landing craft, utility	-do-	2
Landing craft, mechanized	-do-	22
Naval Aviation		
Agusta-Bell AB–212 ASW shipborne helicopters	Italy	14
Grumman ST–2E Tracker ASW search	United States	14

Source: Based on information from *Jane's Fighting Ships, 1994–95*, London, 1994, 704–22.

Appendix B

Selected Political Parties and Labor Organizations

ANAP—Anavatan Partisi (Motherland Party). Founded in May 1983 under the leadership of Turgut Özal. The ruling party following the 1983 election, the center-right ANAP included mostly former members of the pre-1980 AP (Adalet Partisi) (*q.v.*) .

AP—Adalet Partisi (Justice Party). Established in 1961, one of the two major parties prior to the September 1980 coup, led by Süleyman Demirel. Following its dissolution by the National Security Council, many of its members subsequently joined the ANAP (*q.v.*) or the DYP (*q.v.*)

Birlik ve Baris (Unity and Peace). Splinter from RP (*q.v.*) in 1992.

BTP—Büyük Türkiye Partisi (Grand Turkey Party). Founded in May 1983 and banned the same month for having connections with the dissolved AP (*q.v.*). Its supporters then formed the center-right DYP (*q.v.*).

CHP—Cumhuriyet Halk Partisi (Republican People's Party). Founded in the 1920s and led by Atatürk until his death in 1938. Headed by Bülent Ecevit in the 1970s, it was one of the major parties prior to the 1980 coup. A majority of its deputies ultimately regrouped in the left-of-center SHP (*q.v.*); others joined the DSP (*q.v.*). Party reactivated by Deniz Baykal in 1992. In 1995 the SHP dissolved itself, and many members joined the CHP.

CNU—Committee of National Unity. Composed of thirty-eight officers who executed the May 1960 coup; the CNU governed the country until a constituent assembly was formed in January 1961.

Demokratik Partisi (Democratic Party)—Formed in 1971 by former AP (*q.v.*) members who disapproved of Süleyman Demirel's leadership; merged with the AP shortly before the 1980 coup. Not a successor to the DP (*q.v.*).

DEP—Demokrasi Partisi (Democracy Party). Pro-Kurd party formed in 1993 on demise of the HEP (*q.v.*), proscribed by Constitutional Court in June 1994.

Dev Sol—Devrimçi Sol (Revolutionary Left Party). A radical movement espousing Marxist ideology and advocating violent tactics against state institutions.

DISK—Türkiye Devrimçi Isçi Sendikaları Konfederasyonu (Confederation of Revolutionary Workers' Trade Unions of Turkey). Federation of trade unions second in importance only to Türk-Is (*q.v.*) before 1980. Banned after 1980, DISK was less influential in the mid-1990s than some of the other labor organizations.

DP—Demokrat Partisi (Democrat Party). Founded in 1946, the party secured power in the 1950 election. It was overthrown and declared illegal by the armed forces in 1960. Should not be confused with the Demokratik Partisi (*q.v.*). Party reactivated in 1992.

DSP—Demokratik Sol Partisi (Democratic Left Party). Founded in November 1985 by Rahsan Ecevit, wife of former CHP (*q.v.*) leader Bülent Ecevit, who had been banned from political activity. The party advocated a more radical variety of democratic socialism than the SHP (*q.v.*).

DYP—Dogru Yol Partisi (True Path Party). Founded in June 1983 after the dissolution of the BTP (*q.v.*). The center-right party was considered to be the successor to the banned AP (*q.v.*). Former AP leader Süleyman Demirel was its leader before becoming president. Head in 1995 was Prime Minister Tansu Çiller.

HADEP—Halkın Demokrasi Partisi (People's Democracy Party). Formed in June 1994 as pro-Kurd party.

Hak-Is—Türkiye Hak Isçi Sendikaları Konfederasyonu (Confederation of Turkish Just Workers' Unions). Pro-Islamist union.

HDP—Hür Demokrat Partisi (Free Democratic Party). A short-lived right-wing party founded in 1983 by former members of the MDP (*q.v.*) under the leadership of Mehmet Yazar. The HDP was disbanded the same year.

HEP—Halkın Emek Partisi (People's Labor Party). Formed in late 1991 to promote full equality of Kurds and Turks within Turkey. Outlawed in 1993.

HP—Halkçı Partisi (Populist Party). Founded in May 1983, it was one of the three parties allowed to compete in the 1983 general election. It merged with Sodep (*q.v.*) in November 1985 to form the SHP (*q.v.*).

MCP—Milliyetçı Çalisma Partisi (Nationalist Labor Party). Founded in July 1983 and originally named the Conservative Party, it changed its name in November 1985 to MÇP. The conservative nationalist party is considered to be the successor to the MHP (*q.v.*). In 1993 the party reassumed the name of the Nationalist Action Party (MHP).

MDP—Milliyetçi Demokrasi Partisi (Nationalist Democracy Party). Founded in May 1983 under the leadership of General Turgut Sunalp, the party never gained popular support and was dissolved in April 1986.

MHP—Milliyetçi Hareket Partisi (Nationalist Action Party). A militant, nationalist party led by Alparslan Türkes. It was associated with the pre-1980 violence and was banned following the coup. The MÇP (*q.v.*) was considered to be its successor prior to changing its name to MHP in 1993.

MISK—Türkiye Milliyetçi Isçi Sendikaları Konfederasyonu (Confederation of Turkish Nationalist Workers' Unions). Government-sponsored federation of labor unions.

MSP—Milli Sclamet Partisi (National Salvation Party). Founded in 1972 and dissolved in 1980, this conservative, religiously oriented party served in various government coalitions prior to the 1980 coup. Many of its members subsequently supported the RP (*q.v.*).

OZEP—Freedom and Labor Party. Splinter from SHP (*q.v.*) formed in 1992.

PKK—Partiya Karkere Kurdistan (Kurdistan Workers' Party). Founded in late 1960s. Initiated armed insurrection on behalf of an independent Kurdistan in 1984; fighting continued through 1995.

RP—Refah Partisi (Welfare Party; also seen as Prosperity Party). A religious party based on Islamic principles; successor to the MSP (*q.v.*).

SHP—Sosyal Demokrat Halkçı Parti (Social Democratic Populist Party). Formed in November 1985 by the merger of two left-of-center parties, Sodep (*q.v.*) and the HP (*q.v.*). Dissolved itself in mid-1995, and many members joined the CHP (*q.v.*).

Sodep—Sosyal Demokrat Parti (Social Democratic Party). Founded in July 1983, it had the support of the moderate left that had backed the pre-coup CHP (*q.v.*). Merged with the HP (*q.v.*) in 1985 to form the SHP (*q.v.*).

TISK—Türkiye Isveren Sendikaları Konfederasyonu (Turkish Confederation of Employers' Associations). A confederation of employers' associations, concerned primarily with labor-management relations.

TOB—Türkiye Odalar Birligi (Turkish Trade Association). Organization that has represented the interests of merchants and industrialists since the early 1950s. In later years, it has been identified primarily with small and medium-sized firms.

Türk-Is—Türkiye Isçi Sendikaları Konfederasyonu (Confederation of Turkish Trade Unions). The largest and most influential of the union federations.

Turkish Communist Party—Joined TWP (*q.v.*) in 1987 to form Turkish United Communist Party.

Türkiye Birlesik Komünist Partisi (Turkish United Communist Party). Created in 1987 by merger of TWP and Turkish Communist Party. Party was banned shortly thereafter, decriminalized in 1991, and then again proscribed.

TÜSIAD—Türk Sanayiçileri ve Is Adamları Dernegi (Turkish Industrialists' and Businessmen's Association). Organization that represents the interests of big business.

TWP—Turkish Workers' Party. Joined with Turkish Communist Party in 1987 to form the Türkiye Birlesik Komünist Partisi (*q.v.*).

VAP—Vatandas Partisi (Citizens' Party). Founded in March 1986 under the leadership of former ANAP (*q.v.*) member Vural Arıkan. A small center-right party, its two parliamentary deputies joined the DYP (*q.v.*) in December 1986.

Bibliography

Chapter 1

Ahmad, Feroz. *The Making of Modern Turkey.* New York: Routledge, 1993.

Ahmad, Feroz. *The Turkish Experiment in Democracy, 1950–1975.* Boulder, Colorado: Westview Press, 1977.

Ahmad, Feroz. *The Young Turks: The Committee of Union and Progress in Turkish Politics, 1908-1911.* London: Oxford University Press, 1972.

Alderson, Anthony D. *The Structure of the Ottoman Dynasty.* Westport, Connecticut: Greenwood Press, 1982.

Anderson, Perry. *Lineages of the Absolutist State.* London: New Left Books, 1974.

Arfa, Hassan. *The Kurds: An Historical and Political Study.* London: Oxford University Press, 1966.

Armstrong, Harold C. *Gray Wolf: The Life of Kemal Atatürk.* (Epilogue by Emil Lengyel.) New York: Capricorn, 1969.

Atıl, Esin. *The Age of Sultan Süleyman the Magnificent.* New York: Abrams, 1987.

Babinger, Franz. *Mehmed the Conqueror and His Time.* (Bollingen Series, No. 96.) Princeton: Princeton University Press, 1977.

Barchard, David. *Turkey and the West.* (Chatham House Papers, No. 27, published for the Royal Institute of International Affairs.) London: Routledge and Kegan Paul, 1985.

Batu, Hâmit, and Jean-Louis Bacqué-Grammont, eds. *L'Empire Ottoman, la république de Turquie et la France.* Istanbul: Isis, 1986.

Berberoglu, Berch. *Turkey in Crisis: From State Capitalism to Neo-Colonialism.* London: Zed Press, 1982.

Bianchi, Robert. *Interest Groups and Political Development in Turkey.* Princeton: Princeton University Press, 1984.

Bodurgil, Abraham. *Turkey: Politics and Government, A Bibliography, 1938–1975.* Washington: Library of Congress, 1978.

Bodurgil, Abraham, comp. *Kemal Atatürk: A Centennial Bibliography (1881–1981).* Washington: Library of Congress, 1984.

Bölükbasi, Süha. *The Superpowers and the Third World: Turkish-American Relations and Cyprus.* Lanham, Maryland: University Press of America, 1988.

Bournoutian, George A. *A History of the Armenian People,* 1. Costa Mesa, California: Mazda, 1993.

Braude, Benjamin, and Bernard Lewis, eds. *Christians and Jews in the Ottoman Empire: The Functioning of a Plural Society.* (2 vols.) New York: Holmes and Meier, 1982.

Bridge, Antony. *Süleiman the Magnificent: Scourge of Heaven.* London: Granada, 1983.

Brummett, Palmira. *Ottoman Seapower and Levantine Diplomacy in the Age of Discovery.* Albany: State University of New York Press, 1994.

Burton, J.A. "Relations Between the Khanate of Bukhara and Ottoman Turkey, 1558–1702," *International Journal of Turkish Studies,* 5, 1990–91, 83–103.

Cahen, Claude. *Pre-Ottoman Turkey.* New York: Taplinger, 1968.

Campany, Richard C., Jr. *Turkey and the United States: The Arms Embargo Period.* New York: Praeger, 1986.

Cemal, Pasa. *Memories of a Turkish Statesman, 1913–1919.* New York: Arno Press, 1973.

Cicek, Kemal. "Living Together: Muslim-Christian Relations in 18th-Century Cyprus as Reflected by the Shari'a Court Record," *Islam and Christian-Muslim Relations* [Birmingham, United Kingdom], 4, No. 1, 1993.

Cook, M.A., ed. *A History of the Ottoman Empire to 1730.* Cambridge: Cambridge University Press, 1980.

Davison, Roderic H. *Reform in the Ottoman Empire, 1856–1876.* Princeton: Princeton University Press, 1963.

Davison, Roderic H. *Turkey: A Short History.* (2d ed.) Huntingdon, United Kingdom: Eothen Press, 1988.

DeLuca, Anthony R. *The Great Power Rivalry at the Turkish Straits: The Montreux Conference and the Convention of 1936.* (East European Monographs.) Boulder, Colorado: Westview Press, 1981.

Devereux, Robert. *The First Ottoman Constitutional Period.* Baltimore: Johns Hopkins Press, 1963.

Dodd, Clement H., ed. *The Political, Social, and Economic Development of Northern Cyprus.* Huntingdon, United Kingdom: Eothen Press, 1993.

Dodd, Clement H., ed. *Turkish Foreign Policy: New Prospects.* Huntingdon, United Kingdom: Eothen Press, 1992.

Ertekün, Necati M. *The Cyprus Dispute and the Birth of the Turkish Republic of Northern Cyprus.* Nicosia, Northern Cyprus: Rustem, 1984.

Evin, Ahmet, ed. *Modern Turkey: Continuity and Change.* (Schriften des Deutschen Orient-Instituts.) Oplanden, West Germany: Leske and Budrich, 1984.

Farah, Caesar E., ed. *Decision Making and Change in the Ottoman Empire.* Kirksville, Missouri: Thomas Jefferson University Press, 1993.

Faroqhi, Suraiya. *Men of Modest Substance: House Owners and House Property in 17th-Century Ankara and Kayseri.* Cambridge: Cambridge University Press, 1987.

Findley, Carter V. *Bureaucratic Reform in the Ottoman Empire: The Sublime Porte, 1789–1922.* Princeton: Princeton University Press, 1980.

Findley, Carter V. *Ottoman Civil Officialdom: A Social History.* Princeton: Princeton University Press, 1989.

Finkel, Andrew, and Nükhet Sirman, eds. *Turkish State, Turkish Society.* New York: Routledge, 1990.

Frangakis-Syrett, Elena. *The Commerce of Smyrna in the Eighteenth Century, 1700–1820.* Athens: Center for Asia Minor Studies, 1992.

Frazee, Charles A. *Catholics and Sultans: The Church and the Ottoman Empire, 1453–1923.* New York: Cambridge University Press, 1983.

Frey, Frederick W. *The Turkish Political Elite.* Cambridge, Massachusetts: M.I.T. Press, 1965.

Geyikdagi, Mehmett Yasar. *Political Parties in Turkey: The Role of Islam.* New York: Praeger, 1984.

Göçek, Fatma Müge. *East Encounters West: France and the Ottoman Empire in the 18th Century.* New York: Oxford University Press, 1987.

Goffman, Daniel. *Izmir and the Levantine World, 1550–1650.* Seattle: University of Washington Press, 1990.

Gökalp, Ziya. *The Principles of Turkism.* Trans., Robert Devereux. Leiden, Netherlands: E.J. Brill, 1968.

Gunter, Michael M. *The Kurds in Turkey: A Political Dilemma.* Boulder, Colorado: Westview Press, 1990.

Gunter, Michael M. *"Pursuing the Just Cause of Their People"*: A *Study of Contemporary Armenian Terrorism.* New York: Greenwood Press, 1986.

Hale, William M. *The Political and Economic Development of Modern Turkey.* New York: St. Martin's Press, 1981.

Halley, Laurence. *Ancient Affections: Ethnic Groups and Foreign Policy.* New York: Praeger, 1985.

Harris, George S. *Turkey: Coping with Crisis.* Boulder, Colorado: Westview Press, 1985.

Hart, Parker T. *Two NATO Allies at the Threshold of War—Cyprus: A Firsthand Account of Crisis Management, 1965–1968.* Durham, North Carolina: Duke University Press, 1990.

Heper, Metin. "Islam, Polity, and Society in Turkey: A Middle Eastern Perspective," *Middle East Journal,* 35, No. 3, Summer 1981, 345–63.

Heper, Metin. *The State Tradition in Turkey.* Huntingdon, United Kingdom: Eothen Press, 1985.

Heper, Metin, and Ahmet Evin, eds. *State, Democracy, and the Military: Turkey in the 1980s.* New York: de Gruyter, 1988.

Heper, Metin, and Jacob M. Landau, eds. *Political Parties and Democracy in Turkey.* New York: Tauris, 1991.

Heyd, Uriel. *Foundations of Turkish Nationalism: The Life and Teachings of Ziya Gökalp.* London: Luzac, 1950.

Heyd, Uriel. "The Later Ottoman Empire in Rumelia and Anatolia." Pages 354–73 in P.M. Holt, Ann K.S. Lambton, and Bernard Lewis, eds., *The Cambridge History of Islam,* 1. Cambridge: Cambridge University Press, 1970.

Holt, P.M. "The Later Ottoman Empire in Egypt and the Fertile Crescent." Pages 274–92 in P.M. Holt, Ann K.S. Lambton, and Bernard Lewis, eds., *The Cambridge History of Islam,* 1. Cambridge: Cambridge University Press, 1970.

Howard, Harry N. *The Partition of Turkey: A Diplomatic History, 1913–1923.* New York: Ferig, 1966.

Inalcik, Halil. "The Emergence of the Ottomans." Pages 263–73 in P.M. Holt, Ann K.S. Lambton, and Bernard Lewis, eds., *The Cambridge History of Islam,* 1. Cambridge: Cambridge University Press, 1970.

Inalcik, Halil. "The Heyday and Decline of the Ottoman Empire." Pages 324–53 in P.M. Holt, Ann K.S. Lambton, and

Bernard Lewis, eds., *The Cambridge History of Islam*, 1. Cambridge: Cambridge University Press, 1970.

Inalcik, Halil. *The Ottoman Empire: The Classical Age, 1300–1600*. London: Weidenfeld and Nicolson, 1973.

Inalcik, Halil. *The Ottoman Empire: Conquest, Organization, and Economy*. London: Variorum, 1978.

Inalcik, Halil. "The Rise of the Ottoman Empire." Pages 293–323 in P.M. Holt, Ann K.S. Lambton, and Bernard Lewis, eds., *The Cambridge History of Islam*, 1. Cambridge: Cambridge University Press, 1970.

Islamoglu-Inan, Huri, ed. *The Ottoman Empire and the World Economy*. New York: Cambridge University Press, 1987.

Issawi, Charles. *The Economic History of Turkey, 1800–1914*. Chicago: University of Chicago Press, 1981.

Itzkowitz, Norman. *Ottoman Empire and Islamic Tradition*. Chicago: University of Chicago Press, 1980.

Jennings, Ronald C. *Christians and Muslims in Ottoman Cyprus and the Mediterranean World, 1571–1640*. New York: New York University Press, 1993.

Karpat, Kemal H. "The Memoirs of N. Batzaria: The Young Turks and Nationalism," *International Journal of Middle East Studies*, 6, No. 3, July 1975, 276–99.

Karpat, Kemal H. "The Military and Politics in Turkey, 1960–64: A Socio-Cultural Analysis of a Revolution," *American Historical Review*, 75, No. 6, October 1970, 1654–83.

Karpat, Kemal H. "Modern Turkey." Pages 527–65 in P.M. Holt, Ann K.S. Lambton, and Bernard Lewis, eds., *The Cambridge History of Islam*, 1. Cambridge: Cambridge University Press, 1970.

Karpat, Kemal H. "Political Developments in Turkey, 1950–70," *Middle Eastern Studies* [London], 8, No. 3, October 1972, 349–75.

Karpat, Kemal H. "The Transformation of the Ottoman State, 1789–1908," *International Journal of Middle East Studies*, 3, No. 3, July 1972, 243–81.

Karpat, Kemal H. *Turkey's Politics: The Transition to a Multi-Party System*. Princeton: Princeton University Press, 1959.

Karpat, Kemal H. "Turkish Democracy at Impasse: Ideology, Party Politics, and the Third Military Intervention," *Interna-*

tional Journal of Turkish Studies, 2, No. 1, Spring-Summer 1981, 1–43.

Karpat, Kemal H., ed. *Political and Social Thought in the Contemporary Middle East.* New York: Praeger, 1968.

Kasaba, Resat. "Izmir," *Review,* 16, No. 4, 1993, 387–410.

Kasaba, Resat. *The Ottoman Empire and the World Economy: The 19th Century.* Albany: State University of New York Press, 1988.

Kazancigil, Ali, and Ergün Özbudun, eds. *Atatürk: Founder of a Modern State.* London: Hurst, 1981.

Keyder, Çaglar. "Port Cities in the Ottoman Empire: Some Theoretical and Historical Perspectives," *Review,* 16, No. 4, 1993, 519–58.

Kinross, Patrick Balfour. *Atatürk: A Biography of Mustafa Kemal, Father of Modern Turkey.* New York: Morrow, 1965.

Kinross, Patrick Balfour. *The Ottoman Centuries: The Rise and Fall of the Turkish Empire.* New York: Morrow, 1977.

"Kurdistan in Turkey." Pages 38–94 in Gerard Chaliand, ed., *A People Without a Country: The Kurds and Kurdistan.* London: Zed Books, 1993.

Landau, Jacob M. "The Nationalist Action Party in Turkey," *Journal of Contemporary History* [London], 17, No. 4, October 1982, 587–606.

Landau, Jacob M. *Pan-Turkism in Turkey: A Study of Irredentism.* Hamden, Connecticut: Archon Books, 1981.

Landau, Jacob M., ed. *Atatürk and the Modernization of Turkey.* Boulder, Colorado: Westview Press, 1984.

Levy, Aviador. *The Sephardim in the Ottoman Empire.* Princeton: Darwin Press and Washington: Institute of Turkish Studies, 1992.

Lewis, Bernard. *The Emergence of Modern Turkey.* (2d ed.) New York: Oxford University Press, 1968.

Lewis, Bernard. *Studies in Classical and Ottoman Islam: 7th–16th Centuries.* London: Variorum, 1976.

Lewis, Geoffrey. *Modern Turkey.* New York: Praeger, 1974.

Lewis, Raphaela. *Everyday Life in Ottoman Turkey.* New York: Putnam, 1971.

Lindner, Rudi Paul. *Nomads and Ottomans in Medieval Anatolia.* (Research Institute for Inner Asian Studies.) Bloomington: Indiana University Press, 1983.

Lloyd, Seton. *Early Turkey: A Traveller's History of Anatolia.* Berkeley: University of California Press, 1989.

Macfie, A.L. "The Straits Question in the First World War, 1914–18," *Middle Eastern Studies* [London], 19, No. 1, January 1983, 43–74.

Mackenzie, Kenneth. *Turkey under the Generals.* (Conflict Studies, No. 126.) London: Institute for the Study of Conflict, 1981.

Mango, Andrew. *Turkey: The Challenge of a New Role.* Washington: Center for Strategic and International Studies, 1994.

Marcus, Aliza. "Turkey's Kurds after the Gulf War: A Report from the Southeast." Pages 238–47 in Gerard Chaliand, ed., *A People Without a Country: The Kurds and Kurdistan.* London: Zed Books, 1993.

Mardin, Serif A. *The Genesis of Young Ottoman Thought.* Princeton: Princeton University Press, 1962.

Mellaart, James. "Anatolia and the Indo-Europeans," *Journal of Indo-European Studies,* 9, Spring-Summer 1981, 135–49.

Mellaart, James. *Ancient Turkey.* Totowa, New Jersey: Rowman and Littlefield, 1978.

Nawawi, Mohammad A. "The Political-Economic Ideas and Achievements of the Kemalist Revolution: A Tentative Evaluation," *International Journal of Turkish Studies,* 2, No. 2, Winter 1981–82, 1–14.

Olson, Robert. *The Emergence of Kurdish Nationalism and the Sheikh Said Rebellion, 1880–1925.* Austin: University of Texas Press, 1989.

Ostrogorsky, George. *History of the Byzantine State.* (Rev. ed.) New Brunswick, New Jersey: Rutgers University Press, 1969.

Özay, Mehmet. "Turkey in Crisis: Some Contradictions in the Kemalist Development Strategy," *International Journal of Middle East Studies,* 15, No. 1, February 1983, 47–66.

Ozbudun, Ergun. *The Role of the Military in Recent Turkish Politics.* (Occasional Papers in International Affairs, No. 14.) Cambridge: Center for International Affairs, Harvard University, 1966.

Parla, Taha. *The Social and Political Thought of Ziya Gökalp, 1876–1924.* Leiden, Netherlands: E.J. Brill, 1985.

Pitcher, Donald E. *An Historical Geography of the Ottoman Empire.* Leiden, Netherlands: E.J. Brill, 1972.

Quataert, Donald. *Ottoman Manufacturing in the Age of the Industrial Revolution.* Cambridge: Cambridge University Press, 1993.

Ramazanoglu, Huseyin. *Turkey in the World Capitalist System: A Study of Industrialization, Power, and Class.* Brookfield, Vermont: Gower, 1985.

Robins, Philip. *Turkey and the Middle East.* New York: Council on Foreign Relations Press, 1991.

Runciman, Steven. *Byzantine Style and Civilization.* Baltimore: Penguin, 1975.

Runciman, Steven. *The Great Church in Captivity: A Study of the Patriarchate of Constantinople from the Eve of the Turkish Conquest to the Greek War of Independence.* Cambridge: Cambridge University Press, 1968.

Runciman, Steven. *A History of the Crusades.* (3 vols.) Cambridge: Cambridge University Press, 1951–54.

Rustow, Dankwart A. *Turkey: America's Forgotten Ally.* New York: Council on Foreign Relations Press, 1987.

Schick, Irvin Cemal, and Ertugrul Ahmed Tonak, eds. *Turkey in Transition: New Perspectives.* New York: Oxford University Press, 1987. ·

Shaw, Stanford J. *The Jews of the Ottoman Empire and Turkish Empire.* New York: New York University Press, 1991.

Shaw, Stanford J., and Ezel Kural Shaw. *History of the Ottoman Empire and Modern Turkey.* (2 vols.) Cambridge: Cambridge University Press, 1976.

Singer, Morris. "Atatürk's Economic Legacy," *Middle Eastern Studies* [London], 19, No. 3, July 1983, 301–11.

Sousa, Nasim. *The Capitulatory Regime of Turkey: Its History, Origin, and Nature.* Baltimore: Johns Hopkins Press, 1957.

Swanson, Glen W. "Enver Pasha: The Formative Years," *Middle Eastern Studies* [London], 16, No. 4, October 1980, 193–99.

Szyliowicz, Joseph S. "The Ottoman Empire." Pages 102–21 in C.A.O. van Nieuwenhuijze, ed., *Commoners, Climbers, and Notables: A Sampler of Studies on Social Ranking in the Middle East.* Leiden, Netherlands: E.J. Brill, 1977.

Tachau, Frank. *Turkey: The Politics of Authority, Democracy, and Development.* New York: Praeger, 1984.

Tachau, Frank, and Metin Heper. "The State, Politics, and the Military in Turkey," *Comparative Politics*, 16, No. 1, October 1983, 17–33.

Tapper, Richard, ed. *Islam in Modern Turkey: Religion, Politics, and Literature in a Secular State.* London: Tauris, 1991.

Turan, Osman. "Anatolia in the Period of the Seljuks and the Beyliks." Pages 231–62 in P.M. Holt, Ann K.S. Lambton, and Bernard Lewis, eds., *The Cambridge History of Islam*, 1. Cambridge: Cambridge University Press, 1970.

Van Bruinessen, Martin. *Agha, Shaikh, and State: The Social and Political Structures of Kurdistan.* Atlantic Highlands, New Jersey: Zed Books, 1992.

Volkan, Vamik D., and Norman Itzkowitz. *The Immortal Atatürk: A Psychobiography.* Chicago: University of Chicago Press, 1984.

Webster, Donald Everett. *The Turkey of Atatürk: Social Process in the Turkish Reformation.* Philadelphia: American Academy of Political and Social Science, 1939.

Weiker, Walter F. *The Modernization of Turkey: From Atatürk to the Present Day.* New York: Holmes and Meier, 1981.

Weiker, Walter F. *The Turkish Revolution, 1960–61: Aspects of Military Politics.* Westport, Connecticut: Greenwood Press, 1980.

Zürcher, Erik J. *Turkey: A Modern History.* New York: Tauris, 1994.

Chapter 2

Abadan-Unat, Nermin. *Women in the Developing World: Evidence from Turkey.* Denver: University of Denver Press, 1986.

Ahmad, Feroz. *The Making of Modern Turkey.* New York: Routledge, 1993.

Akin, Erkan, and Omer Karasapan. "Turkey's Tarikats," *Middle East Report*, No. 153, July–August 1988, 16–18.

Akin, Erkan, and Omer Karasapan. "The 'Turkish-Islamic Synthesis'," *Middle East Report*, No. 153, July–August 1988, 12–15, 50.

Aksit, Bahattin. "Islamic Education in Turkey: Medrese Reform in Late Ottoman Times and Imam-Hatip Schools in the Republic." Pages 145–70 in Richard Tapper, ed., *Islam in Modern Turkey: Religion, Politics, and Literature in a Secular State.* London: Tauris, 1991.

Arat, Yesim. "Islamic Fundamentalism and Women in Turkey," *Muslim World,* 80, No. 1, 1990, 17–23.

Arat, Yesim. *The Patriarchal Paradox: Women Politicians in Turkey.* Rutherford, New Jersey: Fairleigh Dickinson University Press, 1989.

Balim, Çigdem, Ersin Kalaycioglu, Cevat Karatas, Gareth Winrow, and Feroz Yasamee, eds. *Turkey: Political, Social, and Economic Challenges in the 1990s.* New York: E.J. Brill, 1995.

Berik, Gunseli. "State Policy in the 1980s and the Future of Women's Rights in Turkey," *New Perspectives on Turkey,* No. 4, 1990, 81–96.

Berik, Gunseli. *Women Carpet Weavers in Rural Turkey: Patterns of Employment, Earnings, and Status.* Geneva: International Labour Organisation, 1987.

Bozarslan, Hamit. "Political Aspects of the Kurdish Problem in Contemporary Turkey." Pages 98–113 in Philip G. Kreyenbroek and Stefan Sperl, eds., *The Kurds: A Contemporary Overview.* London: Routledge, 1992.

Cagli, U., and L. Durukan. "Sex Role Portrayals in Turkish TV Advertising: Some Preliminary Findings," *Middle East Technical University Studies in Development* [Ankara], 16, Nos. 1–2, 1989, 153–75.

Cragg, Kenneth. *The Call of the Minaret.* Oxford: Oxford University Press, 1964.

Delaney, Carol. *The Seed and the Soil: Gender and Cosmology in Turkish Village Society.* Berkeley: University of California Press, 1991.

The Dorling Kindersley World Reference Atlas. New York: Dorling Kindersley, 1994.

Eralp, Atila, Muharrem Tunay, and Birol Yesilda. *The Political and Socioeconomic Transformation of Turkey.* Westport, Connecticut: Praeger, 1993.

Gulalp, Haldun. "Islam and Postmodernism," *Contention,* 4, No. 2, Winter 1995, 59–70.

Gulalp, Haldun. "A Postmodern Reaction to Dependent Modernization: The Social and Historical Roots of Islamic Radicalism," *New Perspectives on Turkey,* No. 8, Fall 1992, 15–26.

Gursoy-Tezcan, Akile. "Mosque or Health Centre? A Dispute in a Gecekondu." Pages 84–101 in Richard Tapper, ed., *Islam in*

Modern Turkey: Religion, Politics, and Literature in a Secular State. London: Tauris, 1991.

Hassanpour, Amir. "The Kurdish Experience," *Middle East Report*, No. 189, July-August 1994, 2–7, 23.

Held, Colbert. *Middle East Patterns, Places, Peoples, and Politics.* Boulder, Colorado: Westview Press, 1989.

Kadioglu, Ayse. "Women's Subordination in Turkey: Is Islam Really the Villain?" *Middle East Journal*, 48, No. 4, 1994, 645–60.

Kagitcibasi, Cigdem, ed. *Sex Roles, Family, and Community in Turkey.* Bloomington: Indiana University Turkish Studies, 1982.

Kandiyoti, Deniz. "Sex Roles and Social Change: A Comparative Appraisal of Turkey's Women," *Signs: A Journal of Women in Culture and Society*, 3, No. 1, 1977, 57–73.

Kieser, Hans-Lukas. *Les Kurdes alevis face au nationalisme turc kemaliste: L'alevite du Dersim et son rôle dans le premier soulèvement kurde contre Mustafa Kemal, Kockiri, 1919–1921.* (Occasional Paper No. 18.) Amsterdam: Middle East Research Associates, 1993.

Kreyenbroek, Philip G. "On the Kurdish Language." Pages 68–83 in Philip G. Kreyenbroek and Stefan Sperl, eds., *The Kurds: A Contemporary Overview.* London: Routledge, 1992.

Kutschera, Chris. "Mad Dreams of Independence: The Kurds of Turkey and the PKK," *Middle East Report*, No. 189, July–August 1994, 12–15.

Marcus, Aliza. "City in the War Zone," *Middle East Report*, No. 189, July–August 1994, 16–19.

Mardin, Serif A. "Religion in Modern Turkey," *International Social Science Journal*, 29, No. 2, 1977, 279–97.

Meeker, Michael. "The New Muslim Intellectuals in the Republic of Turkey." Pages 189–222 in Richard Tapper, ed., *Islam in Modern Turkey: Religion, Politics, and Literature in a Secular State.* London: Tauris, 1991.

Migdalovitz, Carol. "Turkey: Ally in a Troubled Region." (Library of Congress, Congressional Research Service, 93–835F.) Washington: September 14, 1993.

Momen, Moojan. *An Introduction to Shi'i Islam: The History and Doctrines of Twelver Shi'ism.* New Haven: Yale University Press, 1985.

Pamuk, Sevket. "War, State Economic Policies, and Resistance by Agricultural Producers in Turkey, 1939–1945." Pages 125–42 in Farhad Kazemi and John Waterbury, eds., *Peasants and Politics in the Modern Middle East*. Miami: Florida International University Press, 1991.

Ramazanoglu, Huseyin. *Turkey in the World Capitalist System: A Study of Industrialization, Power, and Class*. Brookfield, Vermont: Gower, 1985.

Renda, Gunsel, and C. Max Kortepeter, eds., *The Transformation of Turkish Culture: The Ataturk Legacy*. Princeton: Kingston Press, 1986.

Stokes, Martin. "Music, Fate, and State: Turkey's Arabesque Debate," *Middle East Report*, No. 160, September–October 1989, 27–30.

Tapper, Richard, ed. *Islam in Modern Turkey: Religion, Politics, and Literature in a Secular State*. London: Tauris, 1991.

"Turkey." Pages 907–25 in *Middle East and North Africa, 1995*. London: Europa, 1994.

United States. Department of State. *Country Reports on Human Rights Practices for 1994*. (Report submitted to United States Congress, 104th, 1st Session, Senate, Committee on Foreign Relations, and House of Representatives, Committee on Foreign Affairs.) Washington: GPO, 1995.

Van Bruinessen, Martin. *Agha, Shaikh, and State: The Social and Political Structure of Kurdistan*. Atlantic Highlands, New Jersey: Zed Books, 1992.

Van Bruinessen, Martin. "Kurdish Society, Ethnicity, Nationalism, and Refugee Problems." Pages 35–65 in Philip Kreyenbroek and Stefan Sperl, eds., *The Kurds: A Contemporary Overview* London: Routledge, 1992.

Van Bruinessen, Martin. "The Kurds Between Iran and Iraq," *Middle East Report*, No. 141, July–August 1986.

Watt, W. Montgomery. *Islamic Political Thought: Basic Concepts*. Edinburgh: Edinburgh University Press, 1968.

Watt, W. Montgomery. *Muhammad: Prophet and Statesman*. Oxford: Oxford University Press, 1961.

White, Jenny B. "Linking the Urban Poor to the World Market: Women and Work in Istanbul," *Middle East Report*, No. 173, November–December 1991, 18–22.

White, Jenny B. *Money Makes Us Relatives: Women's Labor in Urban Turkey.* Austin: University of Texas Press, 1994.

Yalcin-Hekmann, Lale. "Ethnic Islam and Nationalism Among the Kurds in Turkey." Pages 102–20 in Richard Tapper, ed., *Islam in Modern Turkey: Religion, Politics, and Literature in a Secular State.* London: Tauris, 1991.

(Various issues of the following publications also were used in the preparation of this chapter: *Christian Science Monitor; Economist* [London]; Foreign Broadcast Information Service, *Daily Report: Europe; Middle East Economic Digest* [London]; *Middle East Insight; Middle East International* [London]; *The Middle East; New York Times;* and *Washington Post.*)

Chapter 3

Abac, Selcuk, et al. *Turkey's Banks and Banking System.* London: Euromoney, 1986.

Alireza, Bulent, and Nathaniel Kern. "Turkey: The New Player in the World of Oil," *Petroleum Politics,* 5, No. 2, 1994.

Aresvik, Oddvar. *The Agricultural Development of Turkey.* (Praeger Special Studies in International Economics and Development.) New York: Praeger, 1975.

Aricanli, Ali Tousun, and Dani Rodrik, eds. *The Political Economy of Turkey: Debt, Adjustment, and Sustainability.* New York: Macmillan, 1990.

Arslan, Ismail, and Sweder van Wijnbergen. "Export Incentives, Exchange Rate Policy, and Export Growth in Turkey," *Review of Economics and Statistics,* 75, No. 1, February 1993, 128–33.

Balassa, Bela. "Outward Orientation and Exchange Rate Policy in Developing Countries: The Turkish Experience." Pages 208–35 in Bela Balassa, ed., *Change and Challenge in the World Economy.* New York: St. Martin's Press, 1985.

Balim, Çigdem, Ersin Kalaycioglu, Cevat Karatas, Gareth Winrow, and Feroz Yasamee, eds. *Turkey: Political, Social, and Economic Challenges in the 1990s.* New York: E.J. Brill, 1995.

Barchard, David. *Turkey and the West.* (Chatham House Papers, No. 27, published for the Royal Institute of International Affairs.) London: Routledge and Kegan Paul, 1985.

Baysan, Tercan. "Some Economic Aspects of Turkey's Accession to the EC: Resource Shifts, Comparative Advantage, and

Static Gains," *Journal of Common Market Studies* [Oxford], 23, September 1984, 15–34.

Beeley, Brian W. "Progress in Turkish Agriculture." Pages 289–301 in Peter Beaumont and Keith McLachlan, eds., *Agricultural Development in the Middle East.* New York: Wiley, 1985.

Bilginsoy, Cihan. "Inflation, Growth, and Import Bottlenecks in the Turkish Manufacturing Industry," *Journal of Development Economics* [North Holland], 42, 1993, 111–31.

Celasun, M., and Dani Rodrik. "Debt, Adjustment, and Growth: Turkey." In J. Sachs, ed., *Developing Countries' Debt.* Chicago: University of Chicago Press, 1989.

Çiller, Tansu. "The Economics of Exporting Labour to the EEC: A Turkish Perspective." Pages 173–85 in Elie Kedourie, ed., *The Middle Eastern Economy.* London: Cass, 1976.

Connelly, A. Daniel. "Black Sea Economic Cooperation," *RFE/ RL Research Report* [Munich], 3, No. 26, July 1, 1994, 31–38.

Economist Intelligence Unit. *Country Profile: Turkey, 1994–95.* London: 1994.

Economist Intelligence Unit. *Quarterly Economic Review of Turkey.* (Annual Supplement, 1994.) London: 1994.

Eralp, Atila, Muharrem Tunay, and Birol Yesilada. *The Political and Socioeconomic Transformation of Turkey.* Westport, Connecticut: Praeger, 1993.

"Financial Times Survey—Turkey," *Financial Times* [London], May 21, 1992, 1–8.

"Financial Times Survey—Turkey," *Financial Times* [London], May 7, 1993, 1–8.

"Financial Times Survey—Turkey," *Financial Times* [London], April 15, 1994, 1–8.

Griffin, Keith B. *Land Concentration and Rural Poverty.* New York: Holmes and Meier, 1976.

Hale, William M. "The Traditional and the Modern in the Economy of Kemalist Turkey: The Experience of the 1920s." Pages 153–70 in Jacob M. Landau, ed., *Ataturk and the Modernization of Turkey.* Boulder, Colorado: Westview Press, 1984.

Herschlag, Zvi Yehuda. "Ataturk's Etatism." Pages 171–80 in Jacob M. Landau, ed., *Ataturk and the Modernization of Turkey.* Boulder, Colorado: Westview Press, 1984.

Karpat, Kemal H. *The Gecekondu: Rural Migration and Urbanization.* Cambridge: Cambridge University Press, 1976.

Kasnakoglu, Haluk. "Agricultural Price Support Policies in Turkey: An Empirical Investigation." Pages 131–57 in Alan Richards, ed., *Food, States, and Peasants: Analyses of the Agrarian Question in the Middle East.* (Westview Special Studies on the Middle East.) Boulder, Colorado: Westview Press, 1986.

Korars, John. "The Hydro-Imperative of Turkey's Search for Energy," *Middle East Journal,* 40, No. 1, Winter 1986, 53–67.

Krawczk, Lynn. "Turkey: Land of Potential and Problems," *Foreign Agriculture,* December 5, 1977, 10–12.

Krueger, Anne O. *Turkey.* (Foreign Trade Regimes and Economic Development Series.) New York: National Bureau of Economic Research, 1974.

Krueger, Anne O., and Okan H. Aktan. *Swimming Against the Tide: Turkish Trade Reform in the 1980s.* (International Center for Economic Growth.) San Francisco: ICS Press, 1992.

Mideast Newswire. "Europe, Turkey Set To Seal Customs Union Deal," March 3, 1995.

Nas, F.T., and Mehmet Odekon, eds. *Liberalization and the Turkish Economy.* New York: Greenwood Press, 1988.

Okyar, Osman. "Development Background of the Turkish Economy, 1923–1973," *International Journal of Middle East Studies,* 10, August 1979, 325–44.

Onis, Ziya, and James Riedel. *Economic Crises and Long-Term Growth in Turkey.* (Comparative Macroeconomic Studies.) Washington: World Bank, 1993.

Organisation of Economic Co-operation and Development. *Energy Balances of OECD Countries, 1991–92.* Paris: 1994.

Organisation of Economic Co-operation and Development. *OECD Economic Surveys: Turkey, 1994.* Paris: 1994.

Organisation of Economic Co-operation and Development. *OECD Economic Surveys: Turkey, 1995.* Paris: 1995.

Ozbudun, Ergun, and Aydin Ulusan, eds. *The Political Economy of Income Distribution in Turkey.* (The Political Economy of Income Distribution in Developing Countries, No. 1.) New York: Holmes and Meier, 1980.

Parvin, Manoucher, and Mukerrem Hic. "Land Reform Versus Agricultural Reform: Turkish Miracle or Catastrophe Delayed?" *International Journal of Middle East Studies,* 16, May 1984, 207–32.

Ramazanoglu, Huseyin. *Turkey in the World Capitalist System: A Study of Industrialization, Power, and Class.* Brookfield, Vermont: Gower, 1985.

Rodrik, Dani. "Some Policy Dilemmas in Turkish Macroeconomic Management." (Kennedy School of Government Discussion Paper No. 173D.) Cambridge: Harvard University, 1988.

Seddon, David. "Turkey: Economy." Pages 925–32 in *The Middle East and North Africa, 1995.* Europa: London, 1994.

Senses, Fikret, ed. *Recent Industrialization Experience of Turkey in a Global Context.* Westport, Connecticut: Greenwood Press, 1994.

"Survey of Turkey's South East Anatolian Project," *Financial Times* [London], July 24, 1992, 8, 10.

"Survey of Turkish Finance and Industry," *Financial Times* [London], November 25, 1993.

"Survey of Turkish Finance and Industry," *Financial Times* [London], November 3, 1994.

"Survey of Turkish Finance, Investment, and Industry," *Financial Times* [London], November 18, 1992.

Waldner, David. "Avoiding the Inevitable Pain: The Politics of Turkish Economic Reform," *Middle East Insight,* March–April 1995, 39–41.

(Various issues of the following publications also were used in the preparation of this chapter: *Briefing* [Istanbul]; *Financial Times,* [London]; International Monetary Fund, *Direction of Trade Statistics*; International Monetary Fund, *Government Finance Statistics*; International Monetary Fund, *International Financial Statistics*; *Middle East Economic Digest* [London]; *Middle East Journal*; *Middle East Report*; *Petroleum Intelligence Weekly*; World Bank, *World Debt Tables*; and World Bank, *World Tables.*)

Chapter 4

Abramowitz, Morton. "Dateline Ankara: Turkey after Ozal," *Foreign Policy,* No. 91, 1993, 164–81.

Ahmad, Feroz. "Islamic Reassertion in Turkey, *Third World Quarterly,* 10, No. 2, April 1988, 764–68.

Ahmad, Feroz. *The Making of Modern Turkey.* London: Routledge, 1993.

Ahmad, Feroz. "Military Intervention in Turkey," *MERIP Reports*, No. 93, January 1981, 5–24.

Ahmad, Feroz. "Politics and Islam in Modern Turkey," *Middle Eastern Studies* [London], 27, No. 1, January 1991, 3–21.

Ahmad, Feroz. "The Turkish Elections of 1983," *MERIP Reports*, No. 122, March–April 1984, 3–11.

Akin, Erkan, and Omer Karasapan. "Turkey's Tarikats," *Middle East Report*, No. 153, July–August 1988, 16–18.

Amnesty International. *Turkey: Torture, Extrajudicial Executives, and "Disappearances."* London: 1992.

Aricanli, Ali Tosun, and Dani Rodrik, eds. *The Political Economy of Turkey: Debt, Adjustment, and Sustainability.* New York: Macmillan, 1990.

Aybet, Gülnur. *Turkey's Foreign Policy and Its Implications for the West: A Turkish Perspective.* London: Royal United Services Institute for Defence Studies, 1994.

Bahcheli, Tozun. *Greek-Turkish Relations since 1955.* Boulder, Colorado: Westview Press, 1990.

Balim, Çigdem, Ersin Kalaycioglu, Cevat Karatas, Gareth Winrow, and Feroz Yasamee, eds. *Turkey: Political, Social, and Economic Challenges in the 1990s.* New York: E.J. Brill, 1995.

Barchard, David. *Turkey and the West.* (Chatham House Papers, No. 27, published for the Royal Institute of International Affairs.) London: Routledge and Kegan Paul, 1985.

Barkey, Henri J. "Turkish-American Relations in the Post-War Era: An Alliance of Convenience," *Orient* [Leverkusen, Germany], 33, No. 3, 1992, 447–64.

Bianchi, Robert. *Interest Groups and Political Development in Turkey.* Princeton: Princeton University Press, 1984.

Bilici, Faruk. "Sociabilité et expression politique islamistes en Turquie: Les nouveaux *vakifs*," *Revue française de science politique* [Paris], 43, No. 3, June 1993, 412–34.

Birand, Mehmet Ali. *The Generals' Coup in Turkey: An Inside Story of 12 September 1980.* London: Brassey's, 1987.

Birand, Mehmet Ali. *Shirts of Steel: An Anatomy of the Turkish Armed Forces.* London: Tauris, 1991.

Bodgener, Jim. "MEED Special Report: Turkey," *Middle East Economic Digest* [London], 38, No. 28, July 15, 1994, 7–12.

Bölükbasi, Süha. "Ankara, Damascus, Baghdad, and the Regionalization of Turkey's Kurdish Seccssionism," *Journal of*

South Asian and Middle Eastern Studies, 14, No. 4, June 1991, 15–36.

Bölükbasi, Süha. "Turkey, Syria, Iraq, and the Euphrates Dam," *Journal of South Asian and Middle Eastern Studies*, 16, No. 4, June 1993, 9–32.

Constitution of the Republic of Turkey, 1982. Ankara: Directorate General of Press and Information, 1982.

Couloumbis, Theodore A. *The United States, Greece, and Turkey: The Troubled Triangle*. New York: Praeger, 1983.

Cuny, Frederick C. *Northern Iraq: One Year Later.* (Carnegie Special Report.) Washington: Carnegie Endowment for International Peace, 1992.

Dahlberg, Robin, Christopher Keith Hall, Rhoda H. Karpatkin, and Jessica A. Neuwirth. *Torture in Turkey: The Legal System's Response*. New York: Committee on International Human Rights of the Bar of the City of New York, 1989.

Danielson, Michael N., and Rusen Keles. *The Politics of Rapid Urbanization: Government and Growth in Modern Turkey*. New York: Holmes and Meier, 1985.

Dodd, Clement H. *The Crisis of Turkish Democracy*. Beverley, United Kingdom: Eothen Press, 1983.

Dodd, Clement H., ed. *Turkish Foreign Policy: New Prospects*. Huntingdon, United Kingdom: Eothen Press, 1992.

Elahi, Maryam. "Clinton, Ankara, and Kurdish Human Rights," *Middle East Report*, No. 189, July–August 1994, 22–23.

Finkel, Andrew, and Nükhet Sirman, eds. *Turkish State, Turkish Society*. New York: Routledge, 1990.

Frelick, Bill. "The False Promise of Operation Provide Comfort: Protecting Refugees or Protecting State Power?" *Middle East Report*, No. 176, May–June 1992, 22–27.

Fuller, Graham E. "Turkey in the New International Security Environment," *Dis Politique*, 16, Nos. 3–4, 1992, 29–44.

Fuller, Graham E., Ian O. Lesser, Paul B. Henze, and J.F. Brown. *Turkey's New Geopolitics: From the Balkans to Western China.* (A Rand Study.) Boulder, Colorado: Westview Press, 1993.

Gunter, Michael M. *The Kurds in Turkey: A Political Dilemma*. Boulder, Colorado: Westview Press, 1990.

Harris, George S. *Turkey: Coping with Crisis*. Boulder, Colorado: Westview Press, 1985.

Helsinki Watch. *Paying the Price: Freedom of Expression in Turkey.* New York: 1989.

Heper, Metin. "The Recalcitrance of the Turkish Public Bureaucracy to 'Bourgeois Politics': Multi-Factor Political Stratification Analysis," *Middle East Journal,* 39, No. 4, Autumn 1976, 492–96.

Heper, Metin, ed. *Local Government in Turkey: Governing Greater Istanbul.* London: Routledge, 1989.

Heper, Metin, ed. *Strong State and Economic Interest Groups: The Post-1980 Turkish Experience.* New York: de Gruyter, 1991.

Heper, Metin, and Ahmet Evin, eds. *Politics in the Third Turkish Republic.* Boulder, Colorado: Westview Press, 1988.

Heper, Metin, and Ahmet Evin, eds. *State, Democracy, and the Military: Turkey in the 1980s.* New York: de Gruyter, 1988.

Heper, Metin, and Jacob M. Landau, eds. *Political Parties and Democracy in Turkey.* New York: Tauris, 1991.

Johnstone, Diana. "Turkey's Other NATO Link," *Middle East Report,* No. 160, September–October 1989, 17–18.

Karasapan, Omer. "Turkey and US Strategy in the Age of Glasnost," *Middle East Report,* No. 160, September–October 1989, 4–10, 22.

Kemal, Ahmet. "Military Rule and the Future of Democracy in Turkey," *MERIP Reports,* No. 122, March–April 1984, 12–15.

Keyder, Caglar. *State and Class in Turkey: A Study in Capitalist Development.* New York: Verso, 1987.

Kuniholm, Bruce R. "Turkey and the West," *Foreign Affairs,* 70, No. 2, Spring 1991, 34–48.

Kutschera, Chris. "Mad Dreams of Independence: The Kurds of Turkey and the PKK," *Middle East Report,* No. 189, July–August 1994, 12–15.

Laber, Jeri, and Lois Whitman. *Destroying Ethnic Identity: The Kurds of Turkey, An Update.* New York: Helsinki Watch Committee, March 1988.

Lorieux, Claude. "Turquie: Tansu Çiller face aux vieux démons," *Le Figaro* [Paris], July 7, 1993.

MacDonald, Scott B. "Turkey's 1991 Elections: Democracy Renewed or the Past Revisited?" *Middle East Insight,* 8, No. 3. January–February 1992, 25–30.

MacDonald, Scott B., and Amy Kaslow. "From Crisis to Cautious Recovery: Middle Eastern Economies after the Gulf War,

Part II," *Middle East Insight*, 8, No. 6, July–October 1992, 64–69.

Magnarella, Paul. "Desecularization, State Corporatism, and Development in Turkey," *Journal of Third World Studies*, 6, No. 2, 1989, 32–49.

Marcus, Aliza. "City in the War Zone," *Middle East Report*, No. 189, July–August 1994, 16–19.

Mardin, Serif A. *Religion and Social Change in Modern Turkey: The Case of Bediuzzaman Said Nursi.* Albany: State University of New York Press, 1989.

Margulies, Ronnie, and Ergin Yildizoglu. "The Political Uses of Islam in Turkey," *Middle East Report*, No. 153, July–August 1988, 12–17.

Margulies, Ronnie, and Ergin Yildizoglu. "Trade Unions and Turkey's Working Class," *MERIP Reports*, No. 121, February 1984, 15–20, 31.

Migdalovitz, Carol. "Turkey: Ally in a Troubled Region." (Library of Congress, Congressional Research Service, 93–835F.) Washington: September 14, 1993.

Onis, Ziya. "Privatization and the Logic of Coalition Building," *Comparative Political Studies*, 24, July 1991, 231–53.

Pevsner, Lucille, W. *Turkey's Political Crisis: Background, Perspectives, and Prospects.* New York: Praeger, 1984.

Pope, Hugh. "Turkey at the Crossroads," *Middle East International* [London], No. 454, July 9, 1993, 12–13.

Pope, Hugh. "Turkey: Radical New Message," *Middle East International* [London], No. 480, July 22, 1994, 13.

Robins, Philip. "Between Sentiment and Self-Interest: Turkey's Policy toward Azerbaijan and the Central Asian States," *Middle East Journal*, 47, No. 4, Autumn 1993, 593–610.

Robins, Philip. *Turkey and the Middle East.* London: Royal Institute of International Affairs and New York: Council on Foreign Relations Press, 1991.

Rouleau, Eric. "The Challenges to Turkey," *Foreign Affairs*, 72, No. 5, November–December 1993, 110–26.

Salamé, Ghassan. "Torn Between the Atlantic and the Mediterranean: Europe and the Middle East in the Post-Cold War Era," *Middle East Journal*, 48, No. 2, Spring 1994, 226–49.

Sayari, Sabri. "Turkey: The Changing European Security Environment and the Gulf Crisis," *Middle East Journal,* 46, No. 1, Winter 1992, 9–21.

Schick, Irvin Cemil, and Ahmet Ertugrul Tonak, eds. *Turkey in Transition: New Perspectives.* Oxford: Oxford University Press, 1987.

Sezer, Duygu Bazoglu. "State and Society in Turkey: Continuity and Change?" (Paper presented at Rand's 1992 Middle East Conference, Transformations of State and Society in the Middle East.) Santa Monica, California: 1993.

Stearns, Monteagle. *Entangled Allies: US Policy toward Greece, Turkey, and Cyprus.* New York: Council on Foreign Relations Press, 1992.

Steinbach, Udo. "Turkey-ECC Relations: Cultural Dimension." Pages 13–24 in Erol Manisali, ed., *Turkey's Place in Europe: Economic, Political, and Cultural Dimensions.* Istanbul: Uçer, 1990.

Tachau, Frank. *Turkey: The Politics of Authority, Democracy, and Development.* New York: Praeger, 1984.

Tapper, Richard, ed. *Islam in Modern Turkey: Religion, Politics, and Literature in a Secular State.* London: Tauris, 1991.

"Turkey." Pages 867–92 in *The Middle East and North Africa, 1994.* London: Europa, 1993.

Van Bruinessen, Martin. "Between Guerrilla War and Political Murder: The Workers' Party of Kurdistan," *Middle East Report,* No. 153, July–August 1988, 40–42, 44–46.

Yalcin-Heckmann, Lale. *Tribe and Kinship among the Kurds.* Frankfurt: Lang, 1991.

(Various issues of the following publications also were used in the preparation of this chapter: *Christian Science Monitor;* Foreign Broadcast Information Service, *Daily Report: Europe; Los Angeles Times; New York Times; Turkish Daily News* [Ankara]; and *Washington Post.*)

Chapter 5

Amnesty International. *Amnesty International Report, 1993.* New York: 1994.

Amnesty International. *Turkey: Dissident Voices Jailed Again.* New York: 1993.

Aris, Hakki. "A New Era in SSM Activities," *Military Technology* [Bonn], 17, No. 3, February 1994, 85–89.

Aybet, Gülnur. "Turkey in Its Geo-Strategic Environment." Pages 91–114 in Royal United Services Institute for Defence Studies, ed., *Defence Yearbook, 1992.* London: Brassey's, 1992.

Barkey, Henri J. "Turkish-American Relations in the Post-War Era: An Alliance of Convenience," *Orient* [Leverkusen, Germany], 33, No. 3, 1992, 447–64.

Barraclough, Colin. "The Kurds: A Fire in Turkey's Underbelly," *Insight*, 9, No. 43, October 25, 1993, 6–11.

Bayazit, Vural. "Black Sea and Mediterranean Challenges for the Turkish Navy," *NATO's Sixteen Nations* [Brussels], 39, January 1994, 67–69.

Bayazit, Vural. "The Turkish Naval Forces—Changing Tasks," *NATO's Sixteen Nations* [Brussels], 38, Special Issue, April 1993, 45–52.

Birand, Mehmet Ali. *Shirts of Steel: An Anatomy of the Turkish Armed Forces.* London: Tauris, 1991.

Bölükbasi, Süha. "Turkey Challenges Iraq and Syria: The Euphrates Dispute," *Journal of South Asian and Middle Eastern Studies*, 16, No. 4, Summer 1993, 9–32.

Brown, James. "Turkey in the Age of Glasnost," *Current History*, 89, No. 550, November 1990, 377–81.

Burhan, Halis. "The Turkish Air Force—Restructuring and Modernization in the New Era," *NATO's Sixteen Nations* [Brussels], 38, April 1993, 39–42.

Cowell, Alan. "Turks' War with Kurds Reaches a New Ferocity," *New York Times*, October 18, 1993, A3.

Davis, Brian L. *NATO Forces: An Illustrated Reference to Their Organization and Insignia.* London: Blandford, 1988.

"Defence of Turkey." *NATO's Sixteen Nations* [Brussels] (Special Issue), 1993.

Erdem, Vahit. "Constituting a Defence Industry Infrastructure," *NATO's Sixteen Nations* [Brussels], 38, April 1993, 89–95.

Farmen, William N., and Erwin F. Lessel III. "Forward Presence in Turkey: Case Study," *The DISAM Journal of International Security Assistance Management*, 15, No. 3, Spring 1993, 54–61.

Fuller, Graham E. "Turkey's New Eastern Orientation." Pages 37–98 in Graham E. Fuller and Ian O. Lesser, Paul B. Henze, and J.F. Brown. *Turkey's New Geopolitics: From the Balkans to Western China.* (A Rand Study.) Boulder, Colorado: Westview Press, 1993.

Gunter, Michael M. *The Changing Kurdish Problem in Turkey.* London: Research Institute for the Study of Conflict and Terrorism, 1994.

Güres, Dogan. "Turkey Defence Policy: The Role of the Armed Forces and Strategy, Concepts, and Capabilities," *Journal of the Royal United Services Institute for Defence Studies* [London], 138, No. 3, June 1993, 1–6.

Hale, William M. "Turkey, the Middle East, and the Gulf Crisis, *International Affairs* [London], 68, No. 2, Spring 1992, 679–92.

Henze, Paul B. "Turkey: Toward the Twenty-First Century." Pages 1–36 in Graham E. Fuller and Ian O. Lesser, Paul B. Henze, and J.F. Brown, *Turkey's New Geopolitics: From the Balkans to Western China.* Boulder, Colorado: Westview Press, 1993.

Ilter, Aydin. "The Turkish Gendarmerie—Facing the Future," *NATO's Sixteen Nations* [Brussels], 38, April 1993, 61–62.

Jane's Fighting Ships, 1993–94. Ed., Richard Sharpe. Alexandria, Virginia: Jane's Information Group, 1993.

Jane's Fighting Ships, 1994–95. Ed., Richard Sharpe. Alexandria, Virginia: Jane's Information Group, 1994.

Karadayi, Ismail Hakki. "The Turkish Land Forces—Duties, Responsibilities, and Organization," *NATO's Sixteen Nations* [Brussels], 38, April 1993, 29–34.

Kuniholm, Bruce R. "Turkey and the West," *Foreign Affairs,* 70, No. 2, Spring 1991, 34–48.

Lesser, Ian O. "Bridge or Barrier? Turkey and the West after the Cold War." Pages 99–140 in Graham E. Fuller and Ian O. Lesser, Paul B. Henze, and J.F. Brown, *Turkey's New Geopolitics: From the Balkans to Western China.* Boulder, Colorado: Westview Press, 1993.

Migdalovitz, Carol. "Turkey: Ally in a Troubled Region." (Library of Congress, Congressional Research Service, 93–835F.) Washington: September 14, 1993.

The Military Balance, 1993–1994. London: International Institute for Strategic Studies, 1993.

The Military Balance, 1994–1995. London: International Institute for Strategic Studies, 1994.

Robins, Philip. "Between Sentiment and Self-Interest: Turkey's Policy Toward Azerbaijan and the Central Asian States," *Middle East Journal,* 47, No. 4, Autumn 1993, 593–610.

Sezer, Duygu Bazoglu. "Europe's Eastern Bastion—New Vistas for Turkey," *NATO's Sixteen Nations* [Brussels], 38, February 1993, 10–15.

Stenhouse, Mark. "Turkey." Pages 313–19 in Bruce George, ed., *Jane's NATO Handbook, 1991–92.* Coulsdon, United Kingdom: Jane's Information Group, 1991.

Teimourian, Hazhir. "Turkey—The Challenge of the Kurdistan Workers' Party," *Jane's Intelligence Review* [Coulsdon, United Kingdom], 5, No. 1, January 1993, 29–32.

Turkey. Prime Ministry. State Institute of Statistics. *Statistical Yearbook of Turkey, 1993.* Ankara: 1993.

"Turkey." Pages 856–900 in *The Middle East and North Africa, 1994.* London: Europa, 1993.

United States. Arms Control and Disarmament Agency. *World Military Expenditures and Arms Transfers, 1991–1993.* Washington: GPO, 1994.

United States. Department of Defense. *Terrorist Group Profiles.* Washington: GPO, 1988.

United States. Department of State. *Country Reports on Human Rights Practices for 1992.* (Report submitted to United States Congress, 103d, 1st Session, Senate, Committee on Foreign Relations, and House of Representatives, Committee on Foreign Affairs.) Washington: GPO, 1993.

United States. Department of State. *Country Reports on Human Rights Practices for 1993.* (Report submitted to United States Congress, 103d, 2d Session, House of Representatives, Committee on Foreign Affairs, and Senate, Committee on Foreign Relations.) Washington: GPO, 1994.

United States. Department of State. *International Narcotics Control Strategy Report.* Washington: GPO, 1994.

United States. Department of State. *Patterns of Global Terrorism, 1992.* Washington: 1993.

United States. Department of State. *Patterns of Global Terrorism, 1993.* Washington: 1994.

United States. Department of State and the Defense Security Assistance Agency. *Congressional Presentation for Security Assistance, Fiscal Year 1994.* Washington: 1993.

Wyllie, James. "Turkey—Adapting to New Strategic Realities," *Jane's Intelligence Review* [Coulsdon, United Kingdom], 4, No. 10, October 1992, 450–51.

Wyllie, James. "Turkey's Eastern Crisis," *Jane's Intelligence Review* [Coulsdon, United Kingdom], 5, No. 11, November 1993, 506–507.

(Various issues of the following publications also were used in the preparation of this chapter: *Economist* [London]; Foreign Broadcast Information Service, *West Europe Report*; *Jane's Defence Weekly* [London]; *Keesing's Record of World Events* [London], *New York Times*; and *Washington Post.*)

Glossary

Alevi—(Alawi in Arabic), a heterodox Shia (*q.v.*) Islamic sect that has many followers in Turkey.

barrels per day—Production of crude oil and petroleum products is frequently measured in barrels per day, often abbreviated bpd or bd. A barrel is a volume measure of forty-two United States gallons. Conversion of barrels to tons depends on the density of the specific product. About 7.3 barrels of average crude oil weigh one ton. Heavy crude weighs about seven barrels per ton. Light products, such as gasoline and kerosene, average close to eight barrels per ton.

capitulations—Special agreements between the Ottoman Empire and various foreign governments giving those governments and their citizens and subjects specific exemptions from the laws of the empire.

Common Agricultural Policy—Agricultural support system of the EU (*q.v.*), under which farmers' incomes are maintained through a system of target prices for agricultural commodities.

etatism—Often considered as state socialism. In Turkish use, it involves state control of some industries and public services.

European Community (EC)—See European Union (EU).

European Currency Unit (ECU)—Instituted in 1979, the ECU is the unit of account of the EU (*q.v.*). The value of the ECU is determined by the value of a basket that includes the currencies of all EU member states. In establishing the value of the basket, each member's currency receives a share that reflects the relative strength and importance of the member's economy. In 1995 one ECU was equivalent to about one United States dollar.

European Union (EU)—Until November 1993, the EU was known as the European Community (EC). The EU comprises three communities: the European Coal and Steel Community (ECSC), the European Economic Community (EEC), and the European Atomic Energy Community (Euratom). Each community is a legally distinct body, but since 1967 they have shared common governing institutions. The EU forms more than a framework for free trade and economic cooperation: the signatories to the treaties governing the communities have agreed in principle to integrate their economies and ultimately to form a political union. Belgium, France, Italy, Luxembourg, the Netherlands, and the Federal Republic of Germany (West Germany) were charter members of the EU; Britain, Denmark, and Ireland joined on January 1, 1973; Greece became a member on January 1, 1981; Portugal and Spain entered on January 1, 1986; and Austria, Finland, and Sweden became members on January 1, 1995.

fiscal year—Calendar year since 1983.

gecekondus—Literally, "built overnight"; term used for shantyl-ike squatter housing erected on outskirts of large cities. Ottoman custom dictated that once a structure was built, it could not be destroyed.

gross domestic product (GDP)—A value measure of the flow of domestic goods and services produced by an economy over a period of time, such as a year. Only output values of goods for final consumption and intermediate production are assumed to be included in the final prices. GDP is sometimes aggregated and shown at market prices, meaning that indirect taxes and subsidies are included; when these indirect taxes and subsidies have been eliminated, the result is GDP at factor cost. The word *gross* indicates that deductions for depreciation of physical assets have not been made. *See also* gross national product.

gross national product (GNP)—The gross domestic product (*q.v.*) plus net income or loss stemming from transactions with foreign countries including income received from abroad by residents and subtracting payments remitted abroad to nonresidents. GNP is the broadest measurement of the output of goods and services by an economy. It can be calculated at market prices, which include indirect taxes and subsidies. Because indirect taxes and subsidies are only transfer payments, GNP is often calculated at factor cost by removing indirect taxes and subsidies.

imam—A word used in several senses. In general use and lower-cased, it means the leader of congregational prayers; as such it implies no ordination or special spiritual powers beyond sufficient education to carry out this function. Imam is also used figuratively by many Sunni (*q.v.*) Muslims to mean the leader of the Islamic community. Among Shia (*q.v.*) the word takes on many complex and controversial meanings; in general, however, it indicates that particular descendant of the House of Ali who is believed to have been God's designated repository of the spiritual authority inherent in that line. The identity of this individual and the means of ascertaining his identity have been major issues causing divisions among Shia.

International Monetary Fund (IMF)—Established along with the World Bank (*q.v.*) in 1945, the IMF is a specialized agency affiliated with the United Nations and is responsible for stabilizing international exchange rates and payments. The main business of the IMF is the provision of loans to its members (including industrialized and developing countries) when they experience balance of payments difficulties. These loans frequently carry conditions that require substantial internal economic adjustments by the recipients, most of which are developing countries.

lira—Turkish currency; 1 Turkish lira (TL) = 100 kurus. Value of the lira has fluctuated considerably. In 1989 US$1.00 = TL2,122; in 1991 US$1.00 = TL4,172; in 1993 US$1.00 = TL10,983; in January 1994 US$1.00 = TL 15,196; as of August 31, 1995, US$1.00 = TL47,963.

millet—A non-Muslim group or community in the Ottoman Empire organized under its own religious head, who also exercised important civil functions.

National Security Council (NSC—Mili Güvenlik Kurulu)— Under both the 1961 and the 1982 constitutions, the NSC comprised military and civilian personnel and was charged with reviewing national security policy. The generals who took control of Turkey's government in 1980 also constituted themselves as a National Security Council (Milli Güvenlik Konseyi); this body was abolished following the reestablishment of civilian government after the 1983 election. The former members of the 1980–83 NSC, except for President Evren, subsequently formed the Presidential Council, whose function was to advise the president. The Presidential Council was dissolved in 1989.

North Atlantic Treaty Organization (NATO)—In 1995 membership composed of Belgium, Britain, Canada, Denmark, Germany, Greece, Italy, Luxembourg, the Netherlands, Norway, Portugal, Spain, Turkey, and United States.

Shia (from Shiat Ali, the Party of Ali)—A member of the smaller of the two great divisions of Islam. The Shia originated in a dispute over who should be the legitimate successor to the Prophet; a majority of early Muslims accepted the tradition of community consensus to choose the leader, but a minority supported the claim of Ali, the Prophet's cousin, to inherit the mantle of leadership. Over time, theological differences emerged between the Shia and Sunni (*q.v.*). The Alevi (*q.v.*), Ismaili, Twelve Imam Shia, and Zayidi all are distinct Shia sects.

Sublime Porte (or Porte)—Ottoman Empire palace entrance that provided access to the chief minister, who represented the government and the sultan. Term came to mean the Ottoman government.

Sunni—(from Arabic *sunna*, tradition or precedent)—A follower of the larger of the two primary denominations of Islam.

tarikat (pl., *tarikatlar*)—A Sufi order or lodge, usually headed by a teacher or master known as a *seyh*, in which devotees undertake a path of instruction toward spiritual perfection.

Warsaw Treaty Organization—Formal name for Warsaw Pact. Political-military alliance founded by the Soviet Union in 1955 as a counterweight to the North Atlantic Treaty Organization (*q.v.*). Albania, an original member, stopped participating in Warsaw Pact activities in 1962 and withdrew in 1968. Members in 1991 included Bulgaria, Czechoslovakia, East Germany, Hungary, Poland, Romania, and the Soviet Union. Before it was formally dissolved in April 1991, the Warsaw Pact served as the Soviet Union's primary mechanism for keeping political and military control over Eastern Europe.

World Bank—Informal name used to designate a group of four affiliated international institutions: the International Bank for Reconstruction and Development (IBRD), the International Development Association (IDA), the International Finance Corporation (IFC), and the Multilateral Investment Guarantee Agency (MIGA). The IBRD, established in 1945, has as its primary purpose the provision of loans to developing countries for productive projects. The IDA, a legally separate loan fund but administered by the staff of the IBRD, was set up in 1960 to furnish credits to the poorest developing countries on much easier terms than those of conventional IBRD loans. The IFC, founded in 1956, supplements the activities of the IBRD through loans and assistance designed specifically to encourage the growth of productive private enterprises in the less developed countries. The MIGA, founded in 1988, insures private foreign investment in developing countries against various noncommercial risks. The president and certain senior officers of the IBRD hold the same positions in the IFC. The four institutions are owned by the governments of the countries that subscribe their capital. To participate in the World Bank group, member states must first belong to the International Monetary Fund (IMF—*q.v.*).

Index

Abbasid dynasty, 109
Abdül Hamld II, 26–27; forced to abdicate, 28, 32, 308
Abdülmecid, 35
Abkaz, 102
abortion, 91, 92
Abraham. *See* Ibrahim
Abu Hanifa, 109
acquired immune deficiency syndrome (AIDS), 144
Adalet Partisi. *See* Justice Party
administrative commission, 251
Adrianople, 17
adultery, 135
Aegean region, 78, 81; agriculture in, 81; climate of, 81, 84–86; immigrants in, 89; population density in, 87; rainfall in, 81; villages in, 131
Aegean Sea: conflict over, with Greece, 55–56, 66, 236, 297–98, 319, 337, 365
Afghanistan: relations with, 39; Soviet invasion of, 286
AFL-CIO. *See* American Federation of Labor-Congress of Industrial Organizations
agrarian reform, 176
Agricultural Bank of Turkey (Türkiye Cumhuriyeti Ziraat Bankası—TCZB), 180, 212, 213
agricultural production, 153, 178, 187–91; cropping patterns, 187–91; and rainfall, 180–81, 187
agricultural products (*see also under individual crops*): cash crops, 26, 176; citrus fruit, 81, 82, 176; cotton, 82, 83, 180, 182, 189, 206; exports of, 176, 178–79, 187, 220; fruit, 83, 176, 180, 190–91; grain, 82, 83, 97, 182, 187–89; nuts, 81, 190; oilseeds, 190; olives, 81, 176; opium poppies, 83, 190, 370; pulses, 182, 189; sugar beets, 189–90; tobacco, 81, 83, 176, 180, 189; vegetables, 82, 176, 190–91
Agricultural Supply Organization, 180
agriculture, 175–94; in Aegean region,

131; in Anatolian Plateau, 83; in Arabian Platform, 84; in Black Sea area, 81, 131; budget for, 251; commercial, 186; development of, 152, 176; employment in, 159, 161; export crops, 178; extension services, 180; government intervention in, 179; growth of, 176; income from, 176; investment in, 176; irrigation in, 82, 83, 180–82; land for, 182, 187; mechanization of, 129, 182; in Mediterranean region, 82, 131; modernization of, 150, 161, 182; as percentage of gross domestic product, 159, 176; research on, 180; self-sufficiency in, 175; subsidies for, 178, 179–80; subsistence, 149
Ağrı Dağı. *See* Mount Ararat
Agusta aircraft company, 353
Ahmet III, 22
AIDS. *See* acquired immune deficiency syndrome
air force, 339–41; insignia, 345, 348; ranks, 345, 348; reserves, 329; uniforms, 345
air force academy at Istanbul, 330, 340–41; selection for, 331–32
airports, 217; state control of, 171
Air Technical Schools Command, 341
Akbank TAS, 212, 213
Akbulut, Yildirim, 259, 266
Aktash, Timotheos Samuel, 122
Aktuel, 283
Albania: military relations with, 318; relations with, 66, 317
Alexander the Great, 9
Algeria: imports from, 202; seized by France, 25
Algiers: conquest of, 21
Ali ibn Abu Talib, 109, 114
Allied Land Forces Southeastern Europe, 48
Allies: guerrilla warfare against, 33; occupation of Turkey by, 32
Alp Arslan. *See* Mehmet ibn Daud

431

DYP. *See* True Path Party

earthquakes, 77
eastern highlands, 78, 84
Eastern Question, 23
EC. *See* European Community
Ecevit, Bülent, 55; arrested, 61; ban on
    political activities of, xxix, 258; politi-
    cal activities of, xxxiii, 5, 45, 49, 242,
    258, 269; as prime minister, 5; resigna-
    tion of, 52
Ecevit administration, 52
Ecevit, Rahşan, 63
economic austerity plans, xxix, 61, 150,
    153, 158, 226; unemployment under,
    161
Economic Cooperation Organization,
    288
economic crises: in 1970s, 153–54
economic depression, xxviii, 168
economic development, 152–54, 168
economic growth, 152; under develop-
    ment plans, 173
economic integration, 226–29; with
    Europe, 227
economic planning (*see also under indi-
    vidual plans*), 149, 150; under constitu-
    tion of 1961, 172; for development,
    150, 172–73; five-year plans, 172–73
economic policy: liberal, 149; under mil-
    itary rule, xxvii, xxix
economic problems: from Persian Gulf
    War, 149, 151, 152, 156–57, 315
economic protectionism, xxx
economic reform: advocated by Welfare
    Party, xxxii; under military rule, 43;
    under Özal, xxx, xxxiii, 150–51, 154–
    56, 224
economic stabilization program, 58, 68;
    under Demirel, 58–59; under Özal,
    61–62
economic ties: with Europe, 151–52
economy, 56–59; under Çiller, xxxviii–
    xxxix; informal, 150, 159; long-term
    prospects, 151; under Menderes, 4; of
    Ottoman Empire, 25–26, 27; under
    Özal, xxx; planning of, 38; role of gov-
    ernment in, 38, 167–75; structure of,
    159; in War of Independence, 152; in
    World War I, 152
Ecumenical Patriarchate of Constantino-

ple, 122–23
Edict of Milan (313), 11
education (*see also* schools), 139–43;
    access to, xxviii; adult, 142; under con-
    stitution of 1982, 239; equivalency
    program, 143; expansion of, 159; gov-
    ernment spending on, 325; middle-
    school, 140; of middle class, 126; post-
    secondary, 140–42; preschool, 139;
    primary, 139–40; religious, 74, 105,
    118, 139, 140, 278; secondary, 140; sec-
    ular, 74; and social advancement, 142;
    special, 142; stages of, 139; vocational,
    140, 143; of women, 139, 161
Egypt: invasion of Syria by, 23; occupied
    by Britain, 25; under Ottoman
    Empire, 21, 25; petroleum conces-
    sions in, 201; relations with, 294; trade
    with, 294–95, 353
Eisenhower Doctrine (1957), 299
elections: of 1946, 41; of 1950, xxvii, 4,
    41; of 1954, 41; of 1961, 43; of 1969,
    46; of 1973, 50; of 1977, 51; of 1979,
    52; of 1980, 28; of 1983, xxix, 5, 63,
    233, 255; of 1984, 257; of 1986, 63, 64;
    of 1987, xxxiii, 5, 258, 264, 267; of
    1989, 64, 259; of 1991, xxxiv, 66–67,
    242, 260, 266; of 1994, 261–62, 268
Electoral Law (1983), 241
electoral system, 240–41
electric power: demand for, 197, 203,
    204; distribution of, xxxi; generation,
    203; imports of, 203; privatization of,
    171; in rural areas, 203; sources of,
    203
elite, business, 124, 125–26; competition
    of, with political elite, 124; members
    of, 125; in villages, 131
elite, military, 254
elite, political, 254; acceptance into, 124;
    factions in, 125; competition of, with
    business class, 124; competition of,
    with Islamic activists, 235; social struc-
    ture of, 75, 124
elite, professional, 125
elite class, xxxviii; acceptance into, 20;
    under Atatürk, xxv; culture of, 74,
    133; education of, 74; social structure
    of, 124–25; in towns, 128; in urban
    areas, 125, 126; in villages, 131;
    women, 139
employers' associations, 276–77

foreign currency: reserves, 158
foreign economic relations, 220–29
foreign exchange, 220; shortages of, xxviii, 58, 223
foreign investment, 151, 225; encouraged, 68; growth of, 155; in mining, 205
foreign policy, xxxii, 235; under Atatürk, 39; and Kurdish problem, xxxvi–xxxvii
foreign relations, 285–301; with Afghanistan, 39; with Albania, 66, 317; with Armenia, 287, 314; under Atatürk, 39; with Azerbaijan, xxxv, 202, 236, 287–88, 314; with Bosnia and Herzegovina, 317; with Britain, 25; with Bulgaria, 66, 289, 318; with Central Asia, 66, 201, 236, 287, 288–89; with Egypt, 294; with Georgia, 287, 314; with Greece, xxxii, 55, 66, 298; with Hungary, 289; with Iran, xxxiii, 39, 201, 292–93, 306, 316–17; with Iraq, xxxiii, 39, 294, 306; with Israel, 294; with Kazakhstan, xxxv, 288; with Kyrgyzstan, xxxv, 288; with Macedonia, 66, 317; with Romania, 289; with Russia, 25, 286; with Soviet Union, 39; with Syria, 282, 292, 293–94, 306, 316; with Tajikistan, 288; with Turkmenistan, xxxv, 288; with Ukraine, 343; with the United States, 47, 235, 298–301; with Uzbekistan, xxxv, 288
forestry, 131, 176, 193; budget for, 251
Fourteen Points, 32
France: anti-immigrant stance of, 163; in Crimean War, 25; guest workers in, 162, 163; military training by, 339; occupation of Turkey by, 32, 308; Ottoman trade with, 21; territory acquired by, 25, 33; Turkish immigrants in, 90, 163; withdrawal of, 34; in World War I, 30
Freedom and Labor Party (OZEP), 269
fruit, 83, 180; citrus, 81
FYROM. *See* Macedonia, Former Yugoslav Republic of

Gallipoli, battle of, xxv, 30, 308
GAP. *See* Southeast Anatolia Project
gas, natural, 202; imports of, 202; pipelines, 202, 286; reserves, 198
GATT. *See* General Agreement on Tariffs

and Trade
Gaziantep: population of, 88
gazis: amirates of, 15; conquests of, 4, 14, 110; role of, 13, 17
GDP. *See* gross domestic product
gendarmerie, 360, 361, 362–65; deployed against Kurdish insurgents, 339; functions of, 360, 362, 364, 370
Gendarmerie Schools Command, 364
General Agreement on Tariffs and Trade (GATT), 223
General Directorate of Prisons and Houses of Detention, 373
General Directorate of State Hydraulic Works (Devlet Su Isleri—DSI), 181, 203
General Dynamics, 194, 340, 352
General Electric, 340, 352
General Management for Trade in Tobacco, Tobacco Products, and Alcoholic Spirits (Tütün Mamülleri, Tuz ve Alkol Isletmeleri Genel Müdürlügü— TEKEL): state control of, 171
General Motors, 209
General Staff, 142, 323; appointment to, 245; chief of, 311, 322, 323
geography, 75–86; of Anatolia, 75; location, 75
geology, 77–78; of Anatolian Plateau, 83
Georgia: borders with, 76; economic ties with, 229, 287; relations with, 287, 314
Georgians, 102, 282; distribution of, 102
geostrategic situation, 201–2
Germany: military training by, 27; Ottoman treaty with, 29; relations of, with Ottomans, 27, 28–29; in World War I, xxv
Germany, Federal Republic of (West Germany): emigration to, 101; financial aid from, 326; guest workers in, 90, 162, 163; joint ventures with, 306; Kurdish terrorism in, 355; matériel from, 343, 344, 353, 365; technical assistance from, 285; tourists from, 219; trade with, 222
GNP. *See* gross national product
Gökalp, Ziya, 27, 93
Gokchek, Melih, 268
Gordium, 7
Görtürk Empire, 13
gossip groups, 130
government, 241–53; corruption in, 64;

teau, 83, 180; in Arabian Platform, 84; budget for, 251; in Mediterranean region, 82, 180–81; in southeast Anatolia, xxxi, 68
Isbank, 212
Ishmael. *See* Ismail
Iskenderun: industry in, 207; port of, 217
Islam (*see also* secularism), 106–16, 277; birth control in, 92; conversion to, xxvi, 13, 15, 110; disestablishment of, xxvi, 74, 132; divorce under, 134; as foundation of Ottoman Empire, 111; inheritance under, 185; introduction of, 3; language of, 92; marriage under, 133; open expression of, 45; role of, xxv, xxvi; Turkification of, 117
Islam, Alevi, 116
Islam, Shia, 13
Islam, Sunni, 13; Istanbul as center of, 19; schools of, 109
Islamic calendar, 106, 117
Islamic Movement Organization, 359-60
Islamic political activism, xxv, xxxi, 5, 60, 235, 267, 278, 359
Islamist movement, 45, 105, 151, 235, 264, 279, 359–60; intellectuals in, 119–20; as security threat, 312, 359; terrorism by, 317
Ismet Pasha (*see also* Inönü, Ismet), 35; military actions of, 34
Israel: emigration to, 104; relations with, 294; trade with, 294–95
Istanbul, 75–76; established, 19; etymology of, 19, 111; Kurds in, 235; population of, 88; population density in, 87; port of, 217
Istanbul Stock Exchange, 213–14
Italy: Libya seized by, 28; occupation of Turkey by, 32, 308; war with, 32; withdrawal of, 34
Izmir (Smyrna): Kurds in, 235; port of, 217

janissary, 22, 111, 307
Jews, 104–5; emigration of, 104, 153; in Ottoman bureaucracy, 20; population of, 104, 120–21, 123
Jordan: British mandate in, 33
journalists: arrested, xxxvi, 234, 283, 354, 369

judges, 248, 250, 368
judiciary, 238, 248–50
Justice Commandos of the Armenian Genocide (JCAG), 358, 359
Justice Party (Adalet Partisi—AP) (see also Democrat Party, Democratic Party), xxxiv, 43, 49, 51, 62, 253, 256, 262, 263; in elections of 1961, 43; in elections of 1977, 51; founded, 5, 262; in power, 5

Kahramanmaras: political violence in, 59–60
Kahramanmaras Province: martial law in, 60
Kamal, Yashar, xxxvii
Karadag, Davut, 283
Karadayi, Ismail Hakki, 322
Karaites, 105
Karakaya Dam, 203
Karaman: population density in, 87
Karamanlis, Constantine, 55
Kastelli Bank: collapse of, 62
Kayseri: population of, 88
Kazakhstan: oil exploration in, 199–201; relations with, xxxv, 288
Kazandjian, Karekin Bedros, 122
Keban Dam, 203, 214
Kemal, Mustafa (see also Atatürk, Kemal), xxv, 4; military activities of, 305; and Young Turks, 27
Kemalism, xxvi, 4, 37; in armed forces, 309, 312; elements of, 4, 37, 74–75; maintenance of, 42, 45, 60, 62, 254
Keynes, John Maynard, 168
Knights of Saint John, 20
Kocaeli: population density in, 87; port of, 217
Kocbank, 213
Koç Holding Company, 213
Koksal, Sonmez, 365
Konya (Iconium), 14; population of, 88
Konya Air Base, 321
Konya Ovası (Konya Basin), 83; archaeological research at, 6; rainfall in, 86
Köprülü, Ahmet, 22
Köprülü era, 22–23
Köprülü family, 22
Köprülü, Mehmet, 22
Korean War: Turkish troops in, xxxii, 47, 299, 319

Contributors

Steven A. Glazer is Lecturer in the Department of History at George Mason University; he previously served as book review editor of the *Middle East Journal.*

Eric Hooglund is the Editor of *Critique: Journal for Critical Studies of the Middle East.* He has taught courses on the Middle East at several universities and formerly was editor of the *Middle East Journal.*

Helen Chapin Metz is Supervisor, Middle East/Africa/Latin America Unit, Federal Research Division, Library of Congress.

Fareed Mohamedi is Senior Economist, Petroleum Finance Company, and author of articles on the Middle East and international oil affairs.

Jean R. Tartter is a retired Foreign Service Officer who has written extensively on the Middle East and Africa for the Country Studies series.

Published Country Studies

(Area Handbook Series)

550–65	Afghanistan	550–36	Dominican Republic
550–98	Albania		and Haiti
550–44	Algeria	550–52	Ecuador
550–59	Angola	550–43	Egypt
550–73	Argentina	550–150	El Salvador
550–111	Armenia, Azerbaijan,	550–28	Ethiopia
	and Georgia	550–167	Finland
550–169	Australia	550–173	Germany, East
550–176	Austria	550–155	Germany, Fed. Rep. of
550–175	Bangladesh	550–153	Ghana
550–112	Belarus and Moldova	550–87	Greece
550–170	Belgium	550–78	Guatemala
550–66	Bolivia	550–174	Guinea
550–20	Brazil	550–82	Guyana and Belize
550–168	Bulgaria	550–151	Honduras
550–61	Burma	550–165	Hungary
550–50	Cambodia	550–21	India
550–166	Cameroon	550–154	Indian Ocean
550–159	Chad	550–39	Indonesia
550–77	Chile	550–68	Iran
550–60	China	550–31	Iraq
550–26	Colombia	550–25	Israel
550–33	Commonwealth Carib-	550–182	Italy
	bean, Islands of the	550–30	Japan
550–91	Congo	550–34	Jordan
550–90	Costa Rica	550–56	Kenya
550–69	Côte d'Ivoire (Ivory	550–81	Korea, North
	Coast)	550–41	Korea, South
550–152	Cuba	550–58	Laos
550–22	Cyprus	550–24	Lebanon
550–158	Czechoslovakia	550–38	Liberia

550–85	Libya	550–184	Singapore
550–172	Malawi	550–86	Somalia
550–45	Malaysia	550–93	South Africa
550–161	Mauritania	550–95	Soviet Union
550–79	Mexico	550–179	Spain
550–76	Mongolia	550–96	Sri Lanka
550–49	Morocco	550–27	Sudan
550–64	Mozambique	550–47	Syria
550–35	Nepal and Bhutan	550–62	Tanzania
550–88	Nicaragua	550–53	Thailand
550–157	Nigeria	550–89	Tunisia
550–94	Oceania	550–80	Turkey
550–48	Pakistan	550–74	Uganda
550–46	Panama	550–97	Uruguay
550–156	Paraguay	550–71	Venezuela
550–185	Persian Gulf States	550–32	Vietnam
550–42	Peru	550–183	Yemens, The
550–72	Philippines	550–99	Yugoslavia
550–162	Poland	550–67	Zaire
550–181	Portugal	550–75	Zambia
550–160	Romania	550–171	Zimbabwe
550–37	Rwanda and Burundi		
550–51	Saudi Arabia		
550–70	Senegal		
550–180	Sierra Leone